Social Welfare
Policy

Dedicated to Dr. W. Bernard Schiele,
who was committed to eliminating unjust social policies
and their consequences in his day.

Social Welfare
Policy

Regulation and Resistance Among People of Color

Jerome H. Schiele
University of Georgia
Editor

Los Angeles | London | New Delhi
Singapore | Washington DC

For information:

SAGE Publications, Inc.
2455 Teller Road
Thousand Oaks,
    California 91320
E-mail: order@sagepub.com

SAGE Publications India Pvt. Ltd.
B 1/I 1 Mohan Cooperative
    Industrial Area
Mathura Road, New Delhi 110 044
India

SAGE Publications Ltd.
1 Oliver's Yard
55 City Road
London EC1Y 1SP
United Kingdom

SAGE Publications Asia-Pacific
    Pte. Ltd.
33 Pekin Street #02-01
Far East Square
Singapore 048763

Printed in the United States of America.

Library of Congress Cataloging-in-Publication Data

Social welfare policy : regulation and resistance among people of color / editor Jerome H. Schiele.
    p. cm.
Includes bibliographical references and index.
ISBN 978-1-4129-7103-4 (pbk.)
    1. Social service—United States. 2. United States—Social policy. 3. Social service and race relations—United States. I. Schiele, Jerome H.

HV40.S61723 2011
362.8400973—dc22   2010032178

This book is printed on acid-free paper.

10   11   12   13   14   10   9   8   7   6   5   4   3   2   1

Acquisitions Editor:	Kassie Graves
Production Editor:	Karen Wiley
Copy Editor:	Amy Rosenstein
Typesetter:	C&M Digitals (P) Ltd.
Proofreader:	Jennifer Gritt
Indexer:	Holly Day
Cover Designer:	Candice Harman
Permissions Editor:	Adele Hutchinson

Contents

Acknowledgment

I want to express my deepest gratitude to Ms. Whitney Morreau, M.S.W., who was my research assistant at the University of Georgia and who reviewed several book chapter drafts. Thanks so much, Whitney.

Introduction

Jerome H. Schiele

RATIONALE FOR A RACISM-CENTERED PERSPECTIVE OF SOCIAL WELFARE POLICY ANALYSIS

This book offers a racism-centered framework to examine how American social welfare policies have regulated the lives of people of color and how people of color have resisted racist, social welfare policies. Although racism has received considerable attention in social work and the broader human services, some suggest that insufficient attention has been devoted to racism in the social welfare policy literature (Lieberman, 1998; Neubeck & Cazanave, 2001; Quadagno, 1994; Ward, 2005).[i] The problem, according

---

[i]Although the concept *social welfare policy* is used in this book's title, *social welfare policy* and *social policy* often are used interchangeably. An important distinction between the two, however, is that whereas the term *social policy* implies a broader understanding of a society's guidelines to regulate all of its social relationships, the term *social welfare policy* implies the more specific application of a society's guidelines to address, regulate, or solve social problems that produce material inequality. For many people, this inequality generates considerable difficulty in meeting their basic human needs, such as income, food, clothing, housing, and health care. Social workers and other human service professionals grapple with the outcomes, in the form of poverty and inequality, of these unmet human needs. For the purpose of this book, the additional human need of civil rights is added to this list. Although the problem of civil rights has traditionally been separated from social welfare policy concerns, the two are inextricable. Civil rights legislation essentially addresses the social problem of discrimination. Because people of color have historically been victimized by discrimination and because victims of discrimination often suffer poverty and material inequality, civil rights is included as a social welfare policy issue in this book. For more discussion on the distinction between the terms *social welfare policy* and *social policy*, see, for example, Karger and Stoesz (2005), Gil (1992), and Blau with Abramovitz (2004).

to Neubeck and Cazenave, is not that racism is omitted but that it does not receive primary attention. Neubeck and Cazenave contend that the primary attention on racism is precluded because social welfare policy is interpreted predominantly through three conceptual lenses: class-centered perspectives, gender-centered perspectives, and state-centered perspectives. Although these perspectives acknowledge the presence of racism in the formulation and implementation of social welfare policies, racism is viewed more as an epiphenomenon of social class, gender, or the state-polity structure (Neubeck & Cazenave, 2001).

Even when racism is discussed at length, it still is encapsulated within what are viewed as broader, more overarching and traditional social categories (Ward, 2005). For example, in their book *The Dynamics of Social Welfare Policy*, Blau with Abramovitz (2004) conceive racism and racial inequality as being subsumed under what they refer to as "three long-standing opposing political traditions—conservatism, liberalism, and radicalism" (p. 122), and a fourth tradition of feminism. Throughout their text, racism is explained within the context of these broader class-based and gender-based ideologies. Blau with Abramovitz give racism much attention, but racism is not presented as a stand alone ideology equal to the four political traditions they identify. Jansson's (2004) *The Reluctant Welfare State* also marginalizes the coverage of racism. Although Jansson integrates racism in most of his chapters by examining how what he calls *outgroups* were adversely affected by several social welfare policies throughout American history, his discussion of racism appears to be secondary to what might be referred to as his state-centered perspective. Additionally, Jansson's outgroups are not just people of color, but also include women, children, the aged, and gays and lesbians.

The marginalization of racism also can be discerned in Karger and Stoesz's (2005) *American Social Welfare Policy*. These authors' coverage of racism is primarily confined to 2 of their 18 chapters, a chapter on discrimination and one on poverty. Karger and Stoesz's approach to social policy is a pluralistic one in which an examination of the voluntary nonprofit, governmental, and corporate sectors of social welfare services is given prominent attention. However, little focus is aimed at applying this pluralistic approach to the problem of racism. The dominance of the state-centered and social class perspectives also can be gleaned in Popple and Leighninger's (2001) *The Policy-Based Profession*. In their book, Popple and Leighninger acknowledge racism as one of the social values that often influence how social problems are addressed, but they devote scant attention to the application of this value in social policy analysis for the lives of people of color. Finally, Day's (2006) *A New History of Social Welfare* also underscores the significance of a values analysis in understanding American social welfare policy. Although the value of white privilege is prominent in Day's value analysis, it competes with nine other values that she views as important in examining social welfare policy.

Whether consciously intended or not, racism has not been the exclusive or primary focus of major social welfare policy texts. This lack of adequate attention has led some to call for a *racism-centered* perspective of social welfare policy analysis (see, e.g., Davis & Bent-Goodley, 2004; Neubeck & Cazenave, 2001; Quadagno, 1994; Valocchi, 1994; Ward, 2005). Neubeck and Cazenave articulate this perspective most eloquently by maintaining that a racism-centered framework helps to illuminate what they refer to as "white racial hegemony" and its role in social welfare policy. They conceptualize white racial hegemony as "European Americans' systematic exercise of domination over racially subordinate groups" (p. 23). They further contend that from a racism-centered perspective, the state becomes a racialized state and "is the political arm of white racial hegemony" (p. 23). Here, the state is assumed to protect and promote the political, economic, and cultural interests of whites relative to people of color. Walters (2003) refers to this white bias in state affairs as "white nationalism" and argues that a major outcome of this form of nationalism is "policy racism" (p. 250). Policy racism, according to Walters, produces a racialized ideology that institutionalizes racism within all branches of government.

Quadagno (1994) suggests that the primary tension in the history of American social welfare policy is not class but rather racial conflict. Although she acknowledges the significance of class conflict and understands how class solidarity is hampered by racial tensions, Quadagno believes that racism has been the primary impediment to more progressive social welfare policies in the United States. She further contends that the racial tensions of the American welfare state represent a clash between using governmental intervention to secure and expand the positive freedom of African Americans and to protect the negative freedom of white or European Americans. Positive freedom is the ability to act on one's conscious purposes and to develop one's capabilities and potential, while negative freedom is autonomy from external constraints on one's speech, behavior, and associations (Quadagno, 1994). Positive freedom for African Americans is the ability to enjoy the full benefits of American citizenship and to be afforded equal opportunity. Negative freedom for European Americans is the right to free association and free speech with limited governmental interference. These divergent forms of freedom collide to generate opposing political and economic interests that become racialized, and this political collision has been at the core of debates and discussions over American social welfare policy (Quadagno, 1994).

Davis and Bent-Goodley (2004) offer a diversity perspective to justify the need to examine social policies and their impact on people of color. They contend that just as the lives of people of color have often been ignored in other areas of social work scholarship, they also have been marginalized in the arena of social policy. They further suggest that marginalizing the effects of social policy on people of color also is related to the devaluation of the ideas of scholars of color. Davis and Bent-Goodley state: "Rarely are complex social policy issues . . . as viewed by social work scholars of color . . . found in the literature" (p. ix). The unfortunate corollary of not relying heavily on the ideas of scholars of color is that the social work profession is weakened in its ability to challenge the injustices of many social policies (Davis & Bent-Goodley, 2004). A focus on race and its association with social welfare policy can help focus greater attention on the social problems that disproportionately affect people of color but that often affect Americans of any race.

This leads to an important theme of a racism-centered perspective of social welfare policy: its recognition that not all whites' interests are equally protected. A racism-centered perspective acknowledges the within-group political, economic, and cultural inequality among whites. However, it also maintains that this white, within-group stratification should not overshadow racially between-group differences in the way the state has treated people of color relative to whites. Racism has caused people of color collectively to have unique experiences with the state that whites collectively have not had (Neubeck & Cazenave, 2001; Quadagno, 1994; Walters, 2003). In short, a racism-centered perspective is needed to highlight the adverse experiences people of color have had with social welfare policies throughout America's history.

\\\ COMMON THEMEƒ OF RACIAL OPPREƒƒION AND THEIR ƒOCIAL WELFARE POLICY MANIFEƒTATIONƒ

Despite the particularities of their experiences with American social welfare policies, common themes of oppression and stigmatization have existed among the diverse groups of color throughout American history. Racism and the protection and advancement of the collective interests of whites were the glue that generated the shared experiences of oppression people of color had with white America. These shared experiences were guided by the following themes: 1) the notion that people of color were dominated by their emotions and that reasoning was beyond their ability; thus, people of color were thought to be intellectually inferior to whites; 2) because they were assumed to be dominated by their emotions, people of color were characterized as subhuman and immoral; and 3) character-izations of intellectual and moral inferiority also were extended to describe the culture of people of color as *uncivilized*.

These themes provided the political and intellectual justification for the mistreatment and discrimination of people of color by many of America's formative social welfare policies. In other words, these themes laid the foundation to justify the *social control* or regulation of people of color through social welfare policies. Socially controlling the behavior of people of color would help ensure that they would not threaten the polit-ical, economic, and cultural hegemony whites had over the American landscape (Feagin, 2000; Zinn, 2000). In this way, the social control fea-ture of social welfare policy can be understood as *racial regulation*.

Many examples of the racial regulatory feature of social welfare poli-cies abound. The Indian Removal Act of 1830 is a primary example. This Act forced the relocation of Native Americans who resided in the eastern part of the United States to designated areas west of the Mississippi river (Day, 2006). Native Americans, such as the Seminoles, Cherokees, and Choctaw, were stripped of the land that their ancestors had occupied well before the arrival of European colonists. A specific justification for this removal was the notion that the Native people's stewardship of the land was inferior and wasteful. As President Andrew Jackson (1830) queried:

> What good man would prefer a country covered with forests and ranged by a few thousand savages to our extensive Republic, studded with cities, towns, and prosperous farms, embellished with all the improvements which art can devise or industry execute ... and filled with all the blessings of liberty, civilization, and religion? (p. 2)

The tragedy of this Act was that not only were Native Americans removed from their land, but that also many died in the process of relo-cation and resistance (Day, 2006; Takaki, 1993; Zinn, 2000).

A similar example of the racial regulatory function of social policies among people of color was the white westward expansion into Texas, which was once a part of Mexico. This expansion demonstrated disregard for the Mexican people and their land laws. That the reason for this disregard was white superiority is unequivocal from the following remarks given by Stephen Austin, after which Austin, Texas, is named: "[My] sole and only desire," he proclaimed, was to "redeem [Texas] from the wilderness—to settle it with an intelligent, honorable and interprising [sic] people" (cited in Takaki, 1993, p. 174). Austin also invited whites to settle Texas "each man with his rifle," "passports or no passports" so that the "mongrel Spanish-Indian and Negro race" (cited in Takaki, 1993, p. 174) could be conquered. Once whites had conquered and taken Texas, several discriminatory laws were enacted against Mexicans (McWilliams & Meier, 1990; Takaki, 1993). Like African Americans, poll taxes were levied against Mexicans to squash their political participation; new land tax systems placed Mexicans at risk of losing their property, and a caste labor system that placed whites in management and foreman roles and Mexicans in perilous laborer positions was initiated (McWilliams & Meier, 1990; Takaki, 1993). Contemporary immigration debates that focus negatively on noncitizens crossing the U.S. border should be understood within this historical context of Anglo-American conquest and racism.

Asian Americans also have been racially controlled by American social welfare policies. For example, Chinese Americans who immigrated to the U.S. West Coast for higher paying jobs were met with discriminatory employment policies. One policy was the Foreign Miners Tax Act of 1850 (Wing, 2005). Because Chinese Americans had made significant inroads as miners in California, the Foreign Miners Act was aimed at suppressing the earnings of Chinese workers and eliminating any competition they may pose to white miners. The Act required that a payment of 3 dollars a month be made by these foreigners who did not desire citizenship (Takaki, 1993, 1998). Japanese immigrants suffered similarly from policies and practices of racial control, especially on the sugar plantations of Hawaii. In 1904, for example, the Hawaiian Sugar Planters Association banned Japanese and other Asian immigrants from holding skilled positions and reserved these positions for American citizens only (Takaki, 1993, 1998). Thus, as in many other cases among people of color, the Hawaiian workforce was racially stratified, with whites occupying skilled and supervisory positions while Japanese and other Asian immigrants were relegated to unskilled, low-paying work (Zia, 2000). The same should also be said for the Native Hawaiian population, who experienced labor exploitation, violence, and cultural defamation (Takaki, 1993, 1998).

African Americans also confronted the consequences of the regulatory domain of American social welfare policies, primarily through the social policy of slavery. American slavery controlled African Americans through the process of dehumanization (Akbar, 1996; Stampp, 1989). In slavery, African Americans' labor was exploited, and their culture and traditions were vilified. African Americans were deemed property, and the social policy of slavery reinforced this designation by attempting to strip African Americans of any memory or respect for their cultural past (Akbar, 1996; Kambon, 1992; Stampp, 1989). This overt exploitation and disparagement would last through the abolition of slavery and through the emergence of the system of legal racial segregation. As Morris (1984) notes, legal racial segregation promoted a tripartite system of domination in which African Americans were oppressed personally, politically, and economically. This system would not officially end until the 1960s.

◊◊◊ RACIAL CONTROL EPOCHS AND SOCIAL WELFARE POLICY

The method of social welfare policy regulation among people of color is consistent with and reinforced by the system of racial domination current at a specific time period. Social welfare policies emerged and are shaped by broad social, political, and economic factors that characterize a historical epoch (Gil, 1992). It can be argued that social welfare policies represent artifacts of a particular epoch and reflect that period's sociocultural ethos. At least three time periods have influenced the character of racial control in American social welfare policies: (1) the Era of Overt Racism (1607–1935), (2) the Era of Concealed Racism (1969–present), and (3) the Paradoxical Era (1935–1968).

Era of Overt Racism

In the era of overt racism, old-style racism was prevalent. Old-style racism was systematic racism expressed in highly explicit and conspicuous forms (Bobo, Kluegel, & Smith, 1997; Bonilla-Silva, 2001). In this racial system, racism was legal, and people of color were regulated through overt and often hostile means of racial control. People of color were blatantly barred from the rights and privileges of citizenship, and they frequently were victims of both mob and state-sponsored violence. In addition, justifications to explain racial inequality and oppression were grounded in explicit messages of white superiority. People of color were openly publicized to be biogenetically, intellectually, and morally inferior to whites. This presumed inferiority gave whites the right, indeed the obligation, to unequivocally regulate and subordinate people of color. Because the consequence of this old style racism was overt racial injustice, it may be characterized as the era of *oppression by terror.*

Some examples of social welfare policies applicable to this phase are the Indian Removal Act of 1830, the Immigration Restriction Act of 1924, the various slave codes of the 17th and 18th centuries, and the so-called *Jim* or *Jane Crow* segregation laws initiated and affirmed by the landmark, *Plessey v. Ferguson* U.S. Supreme Court ruling of 1896. Each of these policies was explicit in their intent to control and/or restrict the freedom of people of color, and they were unapologetic in protecting the sociocultural, political, and economic interests of whites. Their interpretation of race and racial distinctions was fixed and hierarchical. As whites were considered at the apex of this racial hierarchy, these policies fundamentally reinforced Thomas Jefferson's vision of the United States as an exceptional nation created for the advancement of a superior, white civilization (Jefferson, 1998/1782).

Era of Concealed Racism

Racism in the era since 1969 can be characterized as *new-style* racism. Bonilla-Silva (2001, 2003) contends that new-style racism is just as effective as old-style racism in maintaining racial injustice and inequality. He identifies several characteristics of new-style racism, some of which are as follows: (1) the increasing covert character of racism; (2) the denial by whites that racism continues to exits; (3) the practice of evading racial terminology and the increasing claim among whites that there is reverse racism; (4) the invisibility of the methods and apparati that reproduce racial disparities; and (5) the incorporation of nonthreatening people of color to portray the polity as race neutral.

New-style racism is covert in its expression because the explicit legal racism of the past was abolished by the various civil rights laws passed in the 1960s. No longer could the civil rights and liberties of people of color be denied, but this did not imply the end of racism. New racism relies less on legal restrictions and overt public pronouncements of people of color as inferior and more on the subtle mechanisms through which white racial superiority is preserved. The primary ideological mechanism upon which new racism relies is *color blindness*. Color blindness suggests that the old system of racial bias and particularism has given way to a new social system of race neutrality (Bonilla-Silva, 2001; Smith, 1995). In this new system, all citizens, regardless of race or color, are believed to have an equal opportunity to advance themselves and their families. Race or color no longer matters because the old racially prejudicial laws of the past are gone. Because people of color and whites can now legally engage in social integration, there is no longer the need to acknowledge and rely upon the old racial distinctions of the past. Obsolete is the need to identify and speak of people of color in racial or color terms; indeed, to do so is racist. Because of its reliance on color blindness, new style racism can be referred to as *oppression by denial*.

The Personal Responsibility and Work Opportunity Reconciliation Act of 1996 (PRA) is an example of a new style racism social welfare policy. Passed by Congress and signed into law by President Bill Clinton, the PRA eliminated Aid to Families with Dependent Children, made welfare benefits temporary and time limited, provided block grants to states to fund Temporary Assistance for Needy Family Programs (TANF), and required recipients to locate permanent employment (Personal Responsibility and Work Opportunity Reconciliation Act of 1996). The wording of the policy's findings (section 101) is largely race neutral. The findings conclude that the problem of poverty is caused by the high number of out-of-wedlock births. To reduce these births, the law promotes job training, employment, pregnancy prevention, and the formation of *healthy* (i.e., two-parent) families. Although the language of the law is largely race neutral, people of color, especially African and Hispanic Americans, may feel its effects the most. This is because of the higher rates of African and Hispanic American poverty, and these groups' overrepresentation on welfare rolls (DeNavas-Walt, Proctor, & Lee, 2006; U.S. Department of Health and Human Services, 2006).

Moreover, federal government intervention in the form of protection of civil rights and the distribution of income and resources has played a pivotal role in advancing people of color and correcting some of the historic practices of overt racism (Jansson, 2004). The notion of the federal government as *protector* of the material interests of people of color is contrary to the theme of federal devolution found in the PRA. By substantially limiting the federal government's role in helping the most vulnerable, who often and disproportionately are people of color, the PRA may not be racist in its intentions but has the potential to be racist in its effects. It has the potential to further racial inequality and exasperate the social problems already disproportionately faced by people of color (Davis & Bent-Goodley, 2004; Neubeck & Cazanave, 2001; Schiele, 1998). Indeed, recent evidence demonstrates that TANF recipients of color, especially Hispanic and African Americans, experience greater difficulty than white TANF recipients in securing stable employment once they leave the welfare rolls (Harknett, 2001; Parisi, McLaughlin, Grice, & Taquino, 2006).

The Paradoxical Era

In between the old era of overt oppression and the new one of concealed subjugation was a transitional period (1935–1968) that incorporated competing elements of the old and new systems of racial formation. This paradoxical era employed what might be referred to as a *mixed-methods* approach of racial oppression. In this epoch, social welfare policies were at times racially explicit (as with the Southern segregation laws), while at other times racially subtle and neutral in language but not in their execution. One book that describes this era from a social policy perspective is Katznelson's (2005) *When Affirmative Action Was White*. In it, Katznelson examines the policies of the New and Fair Deals under the Roosevelt and Truman administrations that stretched from 1933 to 1952. One of Katznelson's basic premises is that the policies of this era were characterized by race-neutral policy language but race-specific policy formation and implementation that ensured preferential treatment to whites. One example of this policy paradox was the Social Security Act (SSA) of 1935.

Katznelson (2005) contends that while the SSA of 1935 included language that was race neutral, its formation and implementation disadvantaged people of color, especially African Americans. In its formation, Katznelson describes how northern democrats collaborated with southern democrats in subverting and repressing civil rights issues in New Deal policies. Since southern democrats held many of the key congressional committee chairmanships, they could exercise considerable influence over whether or not a bill could make it through congress (Katznelson, 2005). As in the 1877 Hayes-Tillman compromise, white northern liberals formed an alliance with southern democrats to block policy provisions that could benefit people of color politically and economically. An example of this preclusion was the denial of welfare benefits to occupations in which African Americans were overly represented, such as domestic and agricultural workers (see Social Security Act of 1935).

Concerning the SSA's implementation patterns, Katznelson (2005) examines how these patterns frequently produced racial disparities that disadvantaged African Americans. For instance, Katznelson notes how white eligibility workers, especially in the South, would use more stringent criteria to determine black eligibility for Aid to Dependent Children (ADC). Southern states, in particular, used their states' rights discretion to impose stronger criteria to determine whether a potential black ADC household was *suitable*. This discrimination could be gleaned in data that demonstrate the underrepresentation of African American children on ADC. For example, while 48 percent of all of South Carolina's children were black, only 29 percent of them were recipients of ADC (Katznelson, 2005). African Americans also were excluded from all New Deal relief in some Georgia counties, and they were restricted to less than 1 percent of relief recipients in Mississippi (Katznelson, 2005).

〽️ THE SIGNIFICANCE OF RESISTANCE

Although the racial regulatory and discriminatory functions of social welfare policies are important to acknowledge and examine, it also is significant to recognize how people of color resisted and challenged these racially oppressive policies. A primary shortcoming of existing social welfare policy texts—even the ones that have placed racism at the center of their analyses—is that they do not examine in detail, as this book does, how people of color resisted the racist intentions and consequences of social welfare policies. These texts generally highlight the oppressive features of social welfare policies so that the victimization of people of color can be documented. However, they often do not include the resistance activities of people of color as a central theme in their texts. A possible corollary of excluding or marginalizing these activities is that people of color are subtly portrayed as idle in challenging oppressive social welfare policies. Examining the resistance activities of people of color offsets this portrayal by demonstrating their victorious attempts at empowerment.

People of color resisted the racially discriminatory policies of each of the three eras of racial policy control in numerous ways. This book will provide specific examples of how each group of color demonstrated this resistance. However, people of color share some common resistance strategies, three of which are as follows: (1) nonviolent direct action, (2) counterviolence, and (3) group self-help and mutual aid. At one time period or another, members of each group of color have considered these strategies legitimate methods of resistance.

Nonviolent Direct Action

Perhaps the most prevalent strategy employed by people of color to resist racially oppressive social welfare policies is nonviolent direct action. Civil rights activist, Dr. Martin Luther King Jr. (1963), viewed nonviolent direct action as a method to unearth the oppressive features of a community. For King, a primary goal of nonviolent direct action was to compel an oppressive regime to deal with its injustice:

> Nonviolent direct action seeks to create such a crisis and foster such a tension that a community which has constantly refused to negotiate is forced to confront the issue. It seeks so to dramatize the issue that it can no longer be ignored. (p. 81)

In this way, nonviolent direct action attempts to gain incremental concessions from the power elite in hopes that these cumulative concessions will ultimately destroy the entire system of injustice (King, 1963).

Throughout history, people of color have endeavored to dramatize the issue of racial injustice by using methods of nonviolent direct action. The most frequently used of these methods are strikes, boycotts, sit-ins, and protest marches. For example, in 1909, Hawaiian Japanese workers organized a strike to protest the unequal pay structure that advantaged white workers and disadvantaged Japanese plantation workers (Takaki, 1993, 1998). Seven thousand Japanese workers participated in the strike for a period of 4 months. Although the workers were forced to return to work after the 4 months, they won a victory. Shortly after the strike, the planters eliminated the racially unequal pay structure and increased the wages of Japanese laborers. This example demonstrates how Japanese laborers were able to draw attention to the issue of unequal pay and were able to gain concessions.

The protest strategies of nonviolent direct action among people of color have been based on the idea that although the United States has historically treated people of color with considerable disdain, this treatment should not preclude them from abandoning hope in America changing. Nonviolent direct action advocates were hopeful that racist social policies would change with persistent, courageous, and organized efforts of resistance. This hope was grounded in unrelenting optimism in the power and potential of positive social change and in the race-neutral, yet gender-specific, language of the U.S. Declaration of Independence. This language ensured "that all men are created equal, that they are endowed by their Creator with certain unalienable Rights, that among these are Life, Liberty, and the pursuit of Happiness" (United States National Archives and Records Administration, 2007).

Nonviolent direct action among people of color also was predicated on the idea that people of color deserved to be treated with dignity and justice. Whether coming to America as immigrants or slaves, or, in the case of Native Americans, already existing on the land, people of color worked assiduously to take care of their families and to build America into the major economic giant that it is today. It can be argued that contemporary American capitalism would not be as dominant and successful today had it not been for generations of forced free labor provided by Americans of African descent, the agricultural and physical survival lessons Native Americans gave to European settlers, the arduous and perilous labor of Chinese immigrants who help to construct America's early railroad system, and the slavelike labor of Mexican American tenet farmers and sharecroppers who cultivated the land and products of the American Southwest. This labor generated a vested interest among people of color in the survival and improvement of the United States. The American pie was not just for whites but also for people of color, because much of the pie had been made by them.

Counterviolence

Some people of color have felt that nonviolent direct action is insufficient to resist and prevent racial oppression. Instead, they have advocated for and engaged in counterviolence. Counterviolence can be defined as physical resistance or armed struggle in which oppressed groups engage to defend themselves against an unjust and repressive social order (Gil, 1998). As the concept implies, counterviolence is a response to violence and injustice initiated by dominant groups or what Gil calls *initial societal violence*. This initial violence is a significant component of the overall goal of human subjugation and represents the most conspicuous and coercive form of social control within the broader arsenal of domination (Gil, 1998; Oliver, 2001). Thus, counterviolence is interpreted by some subjugated groups as a legitimate response to a power structure that systematically and intentionally harms them.

Drawing on the African American experience of counterviolence, Worgs (2006) identifies four recurring themes of violent revolt. The first and most pervasive theme is that of justification. Violence is justified by the unrelenting harm and humiliation that racial oppression imposes on the oppressed. In other words, violence is logical when it is thought to be normal to strike someone who has struck the other first. The second theme is the need for people of color to garner "respect from their oppressors" (Worgs, 2006, p. 26). This theme assumes that because violence has been a primary historical means to subjugate groups, violence is often the only language that the oppressive power structure hears. Violence, then, demonstrates to the power structure that people of color will not tolerate abuse. The third theme is violence as an illustration of rage and a desire for vengeance. Here, counterviolence is a method through which people of color have "gotten back" at the perpetrators of oppression. In essence, this aspect of counterviolence represents the hatred among people of color that has been engendered by the hatred that propels racial oppression in the first place. The final theme examined by Worgs is the idea that counterviolence can have a humanizing effect for the oppressed. By resisting racial oppression physically, people of color can be liberated from not only their fears but also from their self-doubts. Here, counterviolence humanizes the oppressed by eliminating their internalized oppression (Fanon, 1963).

Many persons of color have rejected counterviolence as a method of resisting oppressive social welfare policies. They contend that the problem of oppression is exasperated when victims of oppression validate and promote hatred. For them, hatred is the source of oppression, and it must be eliminated all together. Nonetheless, it would be historically inaccurate to dismiss counterviolence as a method of resistance among people of color. First Nation people's attempts to challenge white western expansion, the slave insurrections of African Americans, and the challenges to police brutality and community exploitation posed by 1960s organizations such as the Young Lords, the Black Panthers, and the Red Guards are examples of how some people of color have concluded that counterviolence is an appropriate response to state-sponsored racial oppression.

Group Self-Help and Mutual Aid

People of color frequently have used self-help and mutual aid organizations as a strategy to respond to racist, American social welfare policies. Generally speaking, the purpose of self-help and mutual aid activities among people of color was twofold: (1) to provide social, economic, and emotional support and (2) to secure, protect, and advance the group's civil and human rights. The self-help and mutual aid activities of many groups of color were influenced substantially by a common cultural theme of cooperation, or what might be referred to as *group oneness*. Rather than employing what Trattner (1999) calls the *gospel of individualism* as their cultural shibboleth, several groups of color viewed individualism as an impediment to successful, effective, and long-lasting social welfare endeavors.

For example, in Japanese American social welfare philosophy, it was considered shameful when a community did not care for its indigent (Light, 1972). Extreme self-reliance and individualism were viewed as a primary cause of destitution because they demonstrated a person's lack of community and family integration. Similar to Japanese-American social welfare philosophy, Chinese Americans also reinforced the important and nonyielding obligation that community associations had to their members. A poignant example of this in Chinese American history is that employers were obligated to provide assistance to indigent relatives, and it also was customary for Chinese employers to hire additional employees in austere economic times rather than the capitalistic practice of laying off employees (Light, 1972).

The focus on collectivity also was reflected in the mutual aid organizations among people of color. For example, among Mexican Americans, mutual aid organizations were referred to as *mutualistas* (Aranda, 2001; Hernandez, 1983). A prototype of Chicano mutual aid organizations was the Alianza Hispano Americano. Founded in 1894, the organization provided a host of services, including civil rights protest and advocacy, burial and disability benefits, and direct relief assistance (Moore & Pachon, 1985), all aimed at collectively advancing Mexican Americans. Chinese-American mutual aid organizations were structured around a person's *Chinese district of origin, surname,* or *village/residential locale* (Light, 1972). An example of the collective orientation among these *associations* as they were called was the practice of keeping a barrel of rice in the foyer of a dwelling from which persons in need could take rice to feed their families. In return, the borrower was expected to either replace the rice or pay for it when her or his circumstances improved (Light, 1972).

Like the Chinese, the collective focus of African American mutual aid reflected the practice of the extended family concept. Black religious congregations were the locus and sponsorship of many mutual aid activities. Because of the racial vilification and subjugation caused by slavery, African American mutual aid was imbued with the ethic of race pride and racial uplift (Carlton-LaNey, 2001; Martin & Martin, 2002). Mutual aid activities among African Americans were often referred to as *race*

work, organized work aimed at counteracting African American stereotypes and at advancing the entire African American community
(Carlton-LaNey, 2001; Martin & Martin, 2002). Whether occurring
through nonsecular or secular methods, race work entailed a variety
of activities, from nonviolent direct protest to establishing a range of
human service organizations and businesses that met the daily needs of
African Americans.

░ PURPOJE AND BOOK OVERVIEW

The chapters in this book examine how American social welfare policies
have sought to regulate the lives of people of color historically or currently,
and they describe how people of color have organized to critique and resist
the racial control aspects of these policies. These chapters conceptually
link the focus on how American social welfare policies have racially controlled people of color with an analysis of how people of color have resisted
these policies. In this regard, a primary assumption of this book is that a
strengths perspective on people of color can be juxtaposed alongside a victimization framework to underscore both the struggles and victories of
people of color within the context of American social welfare policy.

The book is organized into four parts, each devoted to one of the four
major groups of color in the United States: (1) African Americans,
(2) Asian Pacific Americans, (3) Hispanic or Latino/Latina Americans, and
(4) Native Americans or First Nation peoples. Starting with Part I that
focuses on African Americans, Tricia Bent-Goodley's chapter examines
the problem of African American disproportionality in the foster care and
adoption systems and how this problem is a result of other social problems
in the African American community. She also discusses kinship care as a
form of resistance that can diminish the problem of black disproportionality and other problems that African Americans confront. Iris Carlton-
LaNey's chapter addresses the racial regulation of Jim Crow segregation
laws and their adverse consequences for the African American community
in the late 19th and early 20th centuries. To combat these oppressive laws,
Carlton-LaNey describes the resistance activities of the African American
women's club movement that showcased the leadership of black women
such as Ida B. Wells-Barnett. King Davis, Allen N. Lewis Jr., Ning Jackie
Zhang, and Albert Thompkins examine how the significant disparity in
involuntary psychiatric commitment policy and practice between African

American men and the general population can be viewed as a form of racial regulation. To resist this trend, the authors describe the advocacy activities of African American organizations, suggest that these activities should be enhanced, and present the need for more public policy to reduce and eliminate the high and disproportionate rates of involuntary commitments among African American men. Finally in this part, Schiele and Gadsden investigate how the Welfare Reform Act of 1996 can be conceived as a form of racial regulation for African Americans and how the relics of American slavery reinforce several of the regulatory themes found in the Act. The chapter also discusses the strategies that advocacy organizations have employed to resist the adverse consequences of the Act and identifies some of their pitfalls.

Part II presents how social welfare policy regulation and resistance have been manifested among Asian Pacific Americans. Hyunkag Cho provides a historical analysis of how immigration and other closely related policies have regulated the lives of Korean Americans and produced enormous hardships and challenges. Cho also discusses how Korean Americans have used multiple strategies to resist and offset the hardships of these policies such as self-help, protest, and policy advocacy activities that highlight their need to support themselves and to build coalitions with other oppressed groups. Rita Takahashi discusses how the unjust policies that supported the incarceration of Japanese Americans in the 1940s and their aftermath significantly regulated and restricted the lives of these persons. Takahashi also describes how contrary to many depictions of Japanese Americans as a passive group, many engaged in diverse forms of protest and resistance—from passive aggressive acts to open protests and physical violence—to resist the oppressive consequences of concentration camps. Anita Gundanna, Marianne R. Yoshioka, and Sujata Ghosh provide a multiple analysis of how Asian Americans have been racially regulated through policies and practices of exclusion, underscoring especially how the Welfare Reform Act of 1996 excludes this group in New York City. The authors also identify resistance efforts against this exclusion by presenting narratives of local community organizations and advocates and Asian American women survivors of domestic violence. Finally in this part, Qingwen Xu examines how immigration policies and deportation practices serve to regulate the lives of Chinese Americans and engender enormous psychosocial consequences. Xu also describes the resistance activities of the Chinese community against unjust immigration and deportation laws that focus on family strengths, advocacy of community-based organizations, and building broader coalitions with other groups.

Part III focuses on racial regulation of social welfare policies among Hispanic or Latino/Latina Americans and their policy resistance activities. Not unexpectedly, three of the four chapters in Part III underscore, in divergent ways, the racial regulation of immigration policies. Latino Americans are the fastest growing population in the United States (U.S. Census Bureau, 2009), and immigration policy issues are at the forefront of domestic social policy concerns and discussions. In this vein, Gregory Acevedo provides a comprehensive historical analysis of how immigration policies have oppressed, marginalized, and excluded Hispanics of various national backgrounds. He also discusses how various Hispanic groups have resisted these policies by focusing on efforts to expand their civil and political inclusion and participation. Ana L. León and Debora Ortega demonstrate how three relatively recent policies passed in 1996—the Illegal Immigration and Responsibility Act, the Antiterrorism and Effective Death Penalty Act, and the Welfare Reform Act—have created a combative and unwelcoming political, economic, and social milieu for Hispanic immigrants. The authors also describe resistance activities to these policies that focus on micro, mezzo, and macro levels of engagement that underscore mass protests, the actions of community and nonprofit organizations, and family support. Lisa Magaña's chapter addresses an issue that has received considerable attention recently: the Arizona immigration debate and law. Although her chapter was written before the stringent Arizona immigration law was passed, she presents the antecedents to the law and focuses on how it has produced considerable fear among Latinos to "call the police." She also presents how Latinos in Arizona have resisted the antecedents of the new law using various methods, with special focus on the engagement against a local county Sheriff and his allies. Catherine Medina focuses her analysis on the racial regulation of U.S. health care policies and how these policies frequently marginalize the poor health conditions of Latinos. She also describes how the Latino community, both within the public and private realms, has sought to resist these policies by changing the social fabric of health care disparities through alternative policy recommendations, research, and progressive political decision making by underscoring the work of a Connecticut community-based organization.

Part IV applies the themes of social welfare policy regulation and resistance to our Nation's first people, the Native or First Nation Peoples. Tessa Evans-Campbell and Christopher Campbell highlight the oppressive and racially regulatory policies associated with Indian Boarding Schools, which sought to assimilate Native children into an alien cultural worldview. The authors also describe how American Indian and Alaska Natives resisted these policies by employing micro-acts of aggression, overt collective resistance, and advocacy for alternative child welfare policies that are more culturally congruent and competent. Similar to the Campbell and Campbell chapter, Gordon Limb and Aaron Baxter also examine how the historic relationship between Native people and European Americans produced tensions around definitions of proper family socialization and child-rearing techniques. The authors also contend that the passing of Title IV-E and Title IV-B of the Social Security Act of 1935 is partially the result of Native American resistance to the hegemony of Eurocentric definitions of suitable family and child-rearing practices. Hilary N. Weaver demonstrates how Native American concepts and practices associated with spirituality and religion have been regulated by U.S. legal mandates. In other words, she examines how these laws have regulated and restricted the legal freedom of First Nation Peoples. Weaver also examines how these laws have been challenged and resisted and examines social movements that have sought to protect the religious freedom of Native Americans. Finally, the conclusion chapter summarizes some of the overarching themes of the book, offers two scenarios of how social welfare policy regulation and resistance among people of color might look in the future, and identifies and describes some important roles social work policy practitioners can assume to resist and eliminate racially regulatory social welfare policies.

It is my hope that the chapters in this book can offer social work students, professors, and policy practitioners some important knowledge, values, and skills that can be used to better understand the themes and activities of social welfare policy regulation and resistance among people of color. By underscoring these themes, more work can be targeted at diminishing the continuing significance and consequences of American racism within the context of social welfare policy analysis and practice.

〽 REFERENCEſ

Akbar, N. (1996). *Breaking the chains of psychological slavery*. Tallahassee, FL: Mind Productions and Associates.

Aranda, M. P. (2001). The development of the Latino social work profession in Los Angeles. *Research on Social Work Practice, 11,* 254–265.

Blau, J., with Abramovitz, M. (2004). *The dynamics of social welfare policy*. New York: Oxford University Press.

Bobo, L., Kluegel, J. R., & Smith, R. A. (1997). Laissez-faire racism: The crystallization of a kinder, gentler, antiblack ideology. In S. A. Tuch & J. K. Martin (Eds.), *Racial attitudes in the 1990s: Continuity and change* (pp.15–41). Westport, CT: Praeger.

Bonilla-Silva, E. (2001). *White supremacy and racism in the post-civil rights era.* Boulder, CO: Lynne Rienner.

Bonilla-Silva, E. (2003). *Racism without racists: Color-blind racism and the persistence of racial inequality in the United States.* Lanham, MD: Rowman and Littlefield.

Carlton-LaNey, I. (Ed.). (2001). *African American leadership: An empowerment tradition in social welfare history.* Washington, DC: NASW Press.

Davis, K. E., & Bent-Goodley, T. (2004). *The color of social policy.* Alexandria, VA: Council on Social Work Education.

Day, P. J. (2006). *A new history of social welfare* (5th ed.). Boston: Allyn & Bacon.

DeNavas-Walt, C., Proctor, B. D., & Lee, C. H. (2006). *Income, poverty, and health insurance coverage in the United States: 2005.* U.S. Census Bureau, Current Population Reports. Washington, DC: U.S. Government Printing Office.

Fanon, F. (1961). *Black skin, white masks.* New York: Grove Press.

Feagin, J. R. (2000). *Racist America: Roots, current realities, and future reparations.* New York: Routledge.

Gil, D. G. (1992). *Unraveling social policy* (5th ed.). Rochester, VT: Schenkman Books.

Gil, D. G. (1998). *Confronting injustice and oppression: Concepts and strategies for social workers.* New York: Columbia University Press.

Harknett, K. (2001). Working and leaving welfare: Does race or ethnicity matter? *Social Service Review, 75,* 359–385.

Hernandez, J. A. (1983). *Mutual aid for survival: The case of the Mexican American.* Malabar, FL: Robert E. Krieger.

Jackson, A. (1830, December 8th). *Case for the Indian removal act. First annual message to congress.* Retrieved June 4, 2010, from http://www.mtholyoke.edu/acad/intrel/andrew.htm

Jansson, B. (2004). *The reluctant welfare state: A history of American social welfare policies* (5th ed.). Pacific Grove, CA: Brooks/Cole.

Jefferson, T. (1998/1782). *Notes on the state of Virginia.* New York: Penguin Classics.

Kambon, K. K. (1992). *The African personality in America: An African-centered framework.* Tallahassee, FL: Nubian Nation Publications.

Karger, H. J., & Stoesz, D. (2005). *American social welfare policy: A pluralist approach* (4th ed.). Boston: Allyn & Bacon.

Katznelson, I. (2005). *When affirmative action was white: An untold history of racial inequality in twentieth-century America.* New York: W.W. Norton.

King, M. L. (1963). *Why we can't wait.* New York: Harper & Row.

Lieberman, R. C. (1998). *Shifting the color line: Race and the American welfare state.* Cambridge, MA: Harvard University Press.

Light, I. H. (1972). *Ethnic enterprise in America: Business and welfare among Chinese, Japanese, and Blacks.* Berkeley, CA: University of California Press.

Martin, E. P., & Martin, J. M. (2002). *Spirituality and the black helping tradition in social work.* Washington, DC: NASW Press.

McWilliams, C., & Meier, M. S. (1990). *North from Mexico: The Spanish-speaking people of the United States* (Updated ed.). New York: Praeger.

Moore, J., & Pachon, H. (1985). *Hispanics in the United States.* Englewood Cliffs, NJ: Prentice Hall.

Morris, A. D. (1984). *The origins of the civil rights movement: Black communities organizing for change.* New York: The Free Press.

Neubeck, K. J., & Cazenave, N.A. (2001). *Welfare racism: Playing the race card against America's poor.* New York: Routledge.

Oliver, W. (2001). Cultural racism and structural violence: Implications for African Americans. In L. See (Ed.), *Violence as seen through a prism of color* (pp. 1–26). Binghamton, NY: The Haworth Press.

Parisi, D., McLaughlin, D. K., Grice, S. M., & Taquino, M. (2006). Existing TANF: Individual and local factors and their differential influence across racial groups. *Social Science Quarterly, 87,* 76–90.

Personal Responsibility and Work Opportunity Reconciliation Act of 1996, Pub. L. No. 104-193. 22 August 1996. Washington, DC: U.S. Government Printing Office.

Popple, P. R., & Leighninger, L. (2001). *The policy-based profession: An introduction to social welfare policy analysis for social workers.* Boston: Allyn & Bacon.

Quadagno, J. (1994). *The color of welfare: How racism undermined the war on poverty.* New York: Oxford University Press.

Schiele, J. H. (1998). The personal responsibility act of 1996: The bitter and the sweet for African American families. *Families in Society, 79,* 424–432

Social Security Act of 1935, H.R. 7260. 14 August 1935. Washington, DC: U.S. Government Printing Office.

Smith, R. C. (1995). *Racism in the post-civil rights era: Now you see it, now you don't.* Albany, NY: State University of New York Press.

Stampp, K. M. (1989). *The peculiar institution: Slavery in the ante-bellum south.* New York: Vintage Books.

Takaki, R. (1993). *A different mirror: A history of multicultural America.* New York: Little, Brown.

Takaki, R. (1998). *Strangers from a different shore: A history of Asian Americans* (Updated and rev. ed.). New York: Little, Brown.

Trattner, W. I. (1999). *From poor law to welfare state: A history of social welfare in America* (6th ed.). New York: The Free Press.

U.S. Census Bureau. (2009). *Estimates find nation's population growing older, more diverse.* Retrieved June 4, 2010, from http://www.census.gov/newsroom/releases/archives/population/cb09-75.html

United States Department of Health and Human Services, Administration for Children and Families. (2006). *Characteristics and financial circumstances of TANF recipients.* Retrieved June 4, 2010, from http://www.acf.hhs.gov/programs/ofa/character/index.html

United States National Archives and Records Administration. (2007). *The Declaration of Independence of the thirteen colonies.* Retrieved June 4, 2010, from http://www.archives.gov

Valocchi, S. (1994). The racial basis of capitalism and the state, and the impact of the new-deal on African Americans. *Social Problems, 41,* 347–362.

Walters, R. W. (2003). *White nationalism, black interests: Conservative public policy and the black community.* Detroit, MI: Wayne State University Press.

Ward, D. E. (2005). *The white welfare state: The racialization of U.S. welfare policy.* Ann Arbor, MI: The University of Michigan Press.

Wing, B. (2005). Crossing race and nationality: The racial formation of Asian Americans, 1852–1965. *Monthly Review, 57,* 1–18.

Worgs, D. C. (2006). "Beware of the frustrated..." The fantasy and reality of African American violent revolt. *Journal of Black Studies, 37,* 20–45.

Zia, H. (2000). *Asian American dreams: The emergence of an American people.* New York: Farrar, Straus and Giroux.

Zinn, H. (2000). *A people's history of the United States: 1492–present.* New York: Harper Perennial.

Part I

Regulation and Resistance
Among African Americans

Regulating the Lives of Children

Kinship Care as a Cultural Resistance Strategy of the African American Community

Tricia B. Bent-Goodley

⧽⧽ INTRODUCTION

The disproportionate number of African American children in the child welfare system has grown to a point of grave concern (Hill, 2008; McRoy, 2004; Roberts, 2003). As of September 2007, there were 496,000 children in the foster care and adoption system in the United States (U.S. Department of Health and Human Services [USDHHS], 2008). One hundred thirty thousand (27 percent) were waiting to be adopted (USDHHS, 2008a). African American children, although only 15 percent of the U.S. child population (U.S. Census Bureau, 2003), represent 32 percent (162,722) of the children in out-of-home care (USDHHS, 2008b).

This chapter is dedicated to Nellie F. Bent and Lillian Carter "Big Momma," who have taught me the importance of using resistance as a tool for the preservation of our families and our children through their selfless example of quiet strength.

The disproportionality of African American children in the foster care system can be viewed as a form of racial regulation that devalues the strengths, resources, and culture of many African American families. The disproportionate removal of African American children from their homes serves to disempower African American families by severing the psychosocial and sociocultural ties between children and their familial traditions. This disconnection process is a major problem because it lessens the likelihood of African American children receiving the socialization necessary for helping to replicate traditions that protect and advance African American communities.

This chapter examines kinship care as a form of cultural resistance in the African American community, and it contends that this type of care helps offset and combat the problem of disproportionate removal of African American children from their homes. This chapter also conceives kinship care as a necessary strategy to reduce the social problems that African Americans disproportionately confront and that place African American children at risk of disproportionate removal.

Through a convergence of economic and job discrimination, public welfare, and the War on Drugs, African Americans have experienced significant vulnerability related to family structure and relationship building that has had residual effects on the number of children at-risk of removal from the home. Contemporary kinship care has evolved as a culturally based strategy that helps to preserve families, share traditions, and maintain connectedness despite multiple familial and societal challenges. The implications of this resistance effort are to find creative ways to help support this indigenous response, both within and outside of the community, while respecting and not diminishing it through formal social welfare policy regulation.

Formal kinship care has been defined as "care provided by relatives as foster care under auspices of the state," and informal foster care has been defined as "all other caregiving provided by relatives in the absence of a parent" (Harden, Clark, & Maguire, 1997). According to the U.S. Census Bureau (2000), more than 6 million children receive care from kin providers. Of these, more than 2 million children are known to the child welfare system (USDHHS, 2008a). Kinship care has often been viewed as a form of family preservation, resilience, and a conviction in the importance of keeping the family together (Scannapieco & Jackson, 1996). Although not viewed as a form of resistance, it does fit the conceptualization of passive resistance. Passive resistance has been articulated as a value-oriented form of resistance within the African American community and, as such, includes "a collective attempt to restore, protect, modify, or create values in the name of a generalized belief" (Smelser, 1962, p. 313). Unannounced and off the radar, caring for African American children, maintaining them in the home, and passing on family traditions and history are protective mechanisms that allow for family values and culture to be passed on to the next generation. This chapter examines the significance of this form of passive resistance as a strategy to combat the racial regulation of African American children.

\\\\ THE NATURE OF RESISTANCE IN THE AFRICAN AMERICAN COMMUNITY

> I can't believe I'm raising a three year old and a ten year old. I'm 58 years old you know. I would have never seen this for myself at this age in my life. I could have retired you know but not now. My husband died about 15 years ago with diabetes complications. Lord, I miss him. My daughter has a drug problem. She's been out there for years. I keep telling her that she's got to get herself together for these kids. I'm not always going to be around to take care of them you know but there [sic] not going into the system. I can tell you that. Not while I'm alive and still breathing. No. Those people just mess you up. No, for now, I can make it. It's hard though because everything is out of pocket. Things are so expensive. When they get sick, that costs money because they aren't under my health insurance. I would have to take my daughter to court and I'm not doing that. My oldest son helps me a lot with things. He comes by and talks to the 10 year old and gives me money when I need it. I've used almost all of my retirement money but I know that God will provide. This is what African American people do. We take care of our children and these are my babies. We'll work it out and get through just like our families have always done.

The above quote of a grandmother raising her grandchildren evidences a form of resistance. Resistance can take many forms. As described earlier, resistance can be active whereby there is an outward cry or act taken. However, resistance can also be unannounced, not as obvious but nonetheless present and powerful. Some definitions of resistance include "the power or capacity to resist"; "the inherent ability of an organism to resist harmful influences"; and "a psychological defense mechanism wherein a patient rejects, denies, or otherwise opposes the therapeutic efforts of a psychotherapist." Thus, resistance may take place without a conscious effort to oppose something but can be a defense mechanism activated when one feels a sense of eminent harm but also a sense of power and the ability to stand in opposition. It helps one to understand how African American families can build on strengths of communalism and the value of extended family through a sense of empowerment and capacity of rearing African American children.

Resistance in the African American community has an historical context that dates back to slavery when Africans Americans learned to read when literacy was a crime, formed lasting unions when it was illegal to marry, and those who maneuvered through the Underground Railroad when death was the result for escaping from slave masters (Franklin, 1997; Hill, 1997; Martin & Martin, 2005). The very nature of resistance, therefore, is a part of the experience of the African American community. Resistance is therefore linked to survival both individually and collectively. Frederick Douglass said, "Without struggle, there is no progress." The end of legalized slavery and the success of the Civil Rights Movement are evidence for many African Americans that success will come and that struggle is a natural part of achieving that success. Thus, resistance is not viewed as something abnormal or disabling. Resistance does not require outside recognition but instead action, sacrifice, and hope that things will be better.

One cannot talk about African American children and not be aware of the African American family, with its challenges and its strengths. African American children are inextricably linked to the family and the community (Hill, 1997). Despite major challenges in the African American family, African American children are still regarded as key to the survival of the community and at the heart of the African American family. The focus on family and prioritization of the success of African American children is critical to understand because despite contemporary challenges, the focus on the African American child remains and is still central to the life of the family. This idea feeds into the expectation that children are to be cared for despite the circumstances around their reason for being in care. Resistance also evidences how African American people make sense of social and economic challenges (Carlton-LaNey, 2001; Davis & Bent-Goodley, 2004). The response counters what people know about African American culture, its organization and bonding, even when it appears to be disorganized and fragmented. The response counters the misperception that African Americans are always seeking a handout and that there are more African Americans in the system then outside of the system. Resistance is then inextricably tied to the desire to maintain the connection within the African American family. The act of resistance speaks to a survival ethic that builds on strengths and defies stereotypes. It speaks to the ability to adapt and be fluid when confronted with challenges unseen.

\\\ DISPROPORTIONALITY OF AFRICAN AMERICAN CHILDREN IN THE CHILD WELFARE SYSTEM

At one time, formal systems did not provide services to African American children (Billingsley & Giovannoni, 1972; McRoy, 2004). African American children in need of care received services from African American providers through settlement houses, orphanages, and other structures developed to meet the needs of African American children (Hodges, 2001; Peebles-Wilkins, 1995). These responses often included a focus on life skills development, inclusion of the family and community, civic engagement, and building trust and connectedness with the family and community (Carlton-LaNey & Carlton Alexander, 2001; Hill, 1997; Peebles-Wilkins, 1995). These services were usually provided in the community, with providers deeply invested in the success of the child both while in and out of care. The sense of accomplishment was best met when the child was able to survive successfully beyond care and feel a sense of connection with others in the community. The large number of African American children in the mainstream child welfare system can be traced to the 1950s and 1960s, with overrepresentation of African American children being identified during the 1970s and 1980s as a point of concern (Jenkins et al., 1983). The rise in contemporary kinship care patterns were identified in the late 1980s and early 1990s (Geen, 2004). Currently, African American children are three times as likely as white children to be placed in out-of-home care (Hill, 2008). The reasons for this disproportionality have been largely attributed to the prevalence of substance abuse, HIV/AIDS, and poverty in the African American community (Chipungu & Bent-Goodley, 2003; McRoy, 2004; Roberts, 2003). Poor families are more likely than middle-income families to be identified for child abuse and neglect, and families with incomes under $15,000 are more likely to have substantiated cases of abuse and neglect compared with those making more than $30,000 (Chipungu & Bent-Goodley, 2004; Lindsey & Martin, 2003). Substance abuse has been identified in 50 to 78 percent of child welfare cases, yet, there continues to be limited substance abuse treatment facilities available in communities of color (Choi & Tittle, 2002; Semidei, Radel, & Nolan, 2001). The problem of children orphaned as a result of HIV/AIDS has received increased attention, as more than 125,000 children in the United States have been estimated to have lost their mother because of AIDS (Thaler, 2005). The full impact of AIDS has not yet been completely understood in the child welfare arena (Chipungu & Bent-Goodley, 2004). Unfortunately, African American people are disproportionately affected by poverty, substance abuse, parental incarceration, and HIV/AIDS (Bent-Goodley, 2003; Davis & Bent-Goodley, 2004). Consequently, these social factors have been identified as fueling the disproportionate numbers. Additional factors of limited cultural competence, functioning based on stereotypes and misconceptions of African American families, system bias, poor service provision, and insufficient training with how to engage and work with families of color have all been identified as fostering inequity within the child welfare system (Chipungu & Bent-Goodley, 2004; Cross, 2008; McRoy, 2004; Miller & Ward, 2008; Roberts, 2003; Rodenborg, 2004).

⧵⧵ CHALLENGEſ TO THE AFRICAN AMERICAN FAMILY AND ITſ IMPACT ON AFRICAN AMERICAN CHILDREN

It should be noted that nearly half of African American families continue to be led by both parents (Hill, 1997). Therefore, there is a continued effort to stay together and build lasting African American partnerships. However, it is the disproportionality of the number of African American children and families in crisis that is cause for concern and action. The role of contemporary kinship care is a response not only to the problems noted but also linked to historic inequity and discrimination that have intersected to make it more challenging for African American families to meet the needs of children. Consequently, the reasons for this disparity are not just rooted in child welfare policies but also at the intersection of antipoverty programs, employment practices, and drug-abuse policy.

Child Welfare Policies

Although there have been child welfare policies targeted to address the number of children in out-of-home care and child removal, they have proved to be insufficient with addressing disproportionality. The Child Abuse Prevention and Treatment Act of 1974 shifted from a focus on long-term foster care to promoting permanency, and the Adoption Assistance and Child Welfare Act of 1980 (P.L. 96–272) defined reasonable efforts to prevent children from being placed outside of the home. These acts were crucial in attempting to shift the thinking about how and why children should be placed outside of the home. However, the policy did not provide a clear interpretation of reasonable efforts, particularly as it relates to child poverty. As noted at the beginning of the chapter, poverty is one of the single most critical factors related to child removal, particularly within the African American community. African American children are often removed not because of abuse but because of issues of neglect, typically rooted in economic needs not being met. Therefore, although the policy importantly requires that reasonable efforts be made to keep children in the home, it does not address what constitutes reasonable efforts to maintain children in the home when the primary concern is child neglect resulting from economic need. As a result, this policy advances a racially regulatory feature for which it does not appear to be directed.

The Adoption and Safe Families Act (ASFA) of 1997 (P.L. 105–89) focuses on providing incentives to increase permanency and adoption among children in the foster care system and putting children on the fast track to adoption within 15 of the most recent 22 months. ASFA requires that adoption and permanency planning take place concurrently. Yet, ASFA provides financial incentives for adoption and no incentives, financial or otherwise, for permanency planning (U.S. General Accounting Office, 2002), which highlights the emphasis on expedited terminations of parental rights to allow for adoptions and not reunification. Termination of parental rights has been done such that women have learned about these proceedings after the fact or near the beginning of their child's adoption process (Roberts, 2003). Substance abuse programs have found it difficult to receive the large number of referrals for treatment, resulting in women being at risk of losing parental rights because of systemic inefficiencies. Although many states and judges have tried to address these issues innovatively, there is no requirement that they do so. Poor children and children of poor substance-abusing parents are at greater risk of child removal than middle-class parents and children of middle-class substance-abusing parents. Although ASFA was established to increase adoptions for children whose parents have not made changes, it also puts African American children in a system incentivized to have them adopted as opposed to reunified with their families. The fact that African American children will be disproportionately impacted by ASFA is not specified, but by being silent on the realities of how and why African American children enter into and stay in the child welfare system, ASFA contributes to and becomes a part of a racially regulatory system and does little to address the actual needs of disproportionality, inequity, and discrimination.

Discrimination in Employment

Unemployment and the disproportionate impact of joblessness created multiple challenges in the African American home (Franklin, 1997; Ricketts, 1989). African Americans were hard hit by the Great Depression. At the height of the Great Depression, 50 percent of African Americans were unemployed compared with 25 percent of Whites (Jewell, 2003). Unemployment rates soared for African American men in the 1950s and became even more established by the 1980s. As a result of discriminatory treatment, African American men were relegated to few employment opportunities and were challenged to find jobs that could support their families (Franklin & Moss, 2000). The high unemployment of African American men during this time contributed to rising separation within the family as men were challenged in societal expectations as provider and as women were forced to assume an even greater financial responsibility to sustain the family (Franklin, 2001). African American women were more likely to obtain jobs specifically confined to domestic work and, consequently, received lower wages because of their race and gender (Jewell, 2003; Tate, 1993). Thus, although African American women were working both within and outside of the home, their salaries were not sufficient enough to maintain the home. The once egalitarian mechanisms that supported the relationship were now strained (Franklin, 1997). Men could not provide the financial supports needed. Women were forced to serve as both financial provider and caregiver. This strain on the relationship coupled with the daily dosage of discriminatory treatment led to an increasing number of men leaving their families to seek new opportunities and return, or leave to avoid the shame and embarrassment of not being able to provide (Martin & Martin, 2005). Between the 1930s and 1950s, the rate of female-headed households was the same for African American and white females at 19 percent and 12 percent, respectively. It was after the 1950s that we saw a divergence. In 1950, white female-headed households were 8.5 percent of white families, and by 1980 the number rose to 11.2 percent. In 1950, African American female-headed households were 17.6 percent of African American families, and by 1980 the number rose to 37.8 percent, in part because of the high number of African American families that migrated from the South to Northern urban environments (Ricketts, 1989). Currently, 44 percent of African American families are headed by single women.

Impact of Aid to Dependent Children

Aid to Dependent Children (ADC) was created by the Social Security Act of 1935 as part of the New Deal and was structured as an antipoverty program to provide aid to mothers with children. Initially, African American families were not eligible to receive public assistance (Billingsley & Giovannoni, 1972). Only 15 percent of African American families were eligible to receive public welfare in 1935 (Jewell, 2003). It was in the 1960s that African Americans began to use public welfare services. There were two major issues associated with receiving ADC that prompted serious consequences for African American families. The "man-in-the-house" rule and the Flemming Rule both had racially regulated features that would prove to be highly problematic for African Americans. The "man-in-the-house" rule essentially stated that to receive income support, there could be no male in the home. Thus, this policy compounded the already complicated circumstances derived from rising unemployment among African American males (Stack, 1974). For women to retain income support, they could not have a male presence in the home, including the father. This stipulation complicated what was already a strained relationship by forcing African American men to hide, leave the home for periods of time, and keep their belongings out of sight so that the woman could maintain the benefits for the family. It also sent the message that black men were not needed in the home and could not make a contribution, discouraging marriage and making relationships more tenuous. ADC also limited the role of black men to solely being a financial resource as opposed to a vital part of the structural and emotional makeup of the family. This racially regulatory feature of ADC placed African American men out of the African American family by institutionally withholding income supports, conducting random checks in the home, and furthering a divide between black men and women, resulting in increasing numbers of black female-headed households and black children at-risk of out-of-home removal.

The second element of ADC with a racially regulatory feature was the Flemming Rule. The Flemming Rule was developed in the early 1960s with the intention of diminishing the state's role in dropping children from the welfare rolls based on unfair determinations of home suitability. The Flemming Rule was an administrative response to these inequities and was based on the idea that children should not suffer because of poor parental conduct. As a result, the child's economic needs were distinguished from the parent's economic needs. The children were distinguished and separated from the parental issues in order to maintain financial support for the children. Providing this federal home suitability plan allowed for more African American children to receive public welfare. Unfortunately, it also diminished the focus on supporting the family and separated the needs of children from their parents. Consequently, the idea that the child's needs are more important and supplant the parent's needs was established, and it also created the notion that the parent was not worthy of support as a result of poor parental conduct and choices.

The War on Drugs

The War on Drugs furthered these challenges. The 1973 New York Rockefeller Drug Laws made the penalty for the distribution and possession of drugs the same as second-degree murder. Other states began to mimic this legislation, creating a criminal justice system that incarcerated increasingly more people. Currently more than 46 percent of the prison population is African American (Beck & Harrison, 2001). Most (71 percent) are imprisoned for nonviolent crimes—one third of which are related to drugs. Despite being no more likely than whites to engage in crime (Blumstein, 1993), African Americans are seven times more likely to be incarcerated (Mauer, 1999). Families increasingly witnessed the use of substances to self-medicate and to escape issues of poor mental health, homelessness, joblessness, and poverty (Provine, 2007; Taifa, 2004). What further complicated this usage was the targeted criminal justice response in the African American community. Once the crack epidemic began in the 1990s, there was a full attack on low-level, nonviolent offenders who were largely drug users trying to get the funds and resources to feed their addiction (Bobo & Thompson, 2006; Taifa, 2004). This "war" has led to the mass incarceration of African Americans, particularly males, and increasingly females. Consequently, the growing numbers of African American children without biological parents able and willing to provide them with care increased. By 2000, 1.5 million children had an incarcerated parent, with African American children being nine times more likely to be in this position (Mumola, 2000). More than one half of these children were placed with a grandmother (Mumola, 2000). These policies in very many ways feed into a pipeline from the child welfare system to the criminal justice system that has had ubiquitous consequences for the African American family (Children's Defense Fund, 2007).

\\\\ KINSHIP CARE AS A FORM OF RESISTANCE: THE CASE FOR THE AFRICAN AMERICAN FAMILY

Kinship care did not just evolve as a reaction to the large numbers of children being removed from the home. It was also a response to the intersection of the negative impact of the policies and practices described above, and the persistent belief in the value of African American children staying within the family and community. Although grandmothers are often the primary caregivers, there are other family members that provide active care for children in extended family networks. Grandfathers, uncles, aunts, godparents, and nonblood or fictive kin often provide care to children without recognition or assistance from formal provider systems.

The Complicated Landscape of Kinship Care

Kinship care providers face many complicated challenges when trying to provide care for children. In addition to the challenges posed with explaining to a child why a parent is missing, absent, or incapable of providing for them, the kin provider also has to negotiate interactions with the parents and find the financial, emotional, and structural needs to support a child (Bent-Goodley & Brade, 2007; Berrick, 1998; Murphy, 2008; Ruiz, 2004). Kinship providers are often in declining or poor health, economically vulnerable, and with a limited *child-centered* support system (Geen, 2004). A child-centered support system is generally developed when one is engaged in regular childlike activities. For example, children who are connected with sports activities tend to have a support system that provides increased opportunities for socialization, respite care, and a sense of connectedness to the life of the child. Kin providers are often less familiar with the current child-centered support system and so they are disconnected from a number of supports within the community. In addition, some kin providers are embarrassed with the situation and feel a sense of guilt for their child or relative not succeeding in raising his or her children (Smith-Ruiz, 2008). This sense of shame or failure can complicate being able to parent and have the kin provider question his or her ability to be successful parenting the second time around. Finally, the children may have emotional and mental health issues that make it more challenging to parent them (Ruiz, 2004). The child may feel abandoned, angry, hurt and disappointed in the situation. Kinship caregivers have to balance all of these issues in addition to the child's desire to ultimately be with the parent despite the parent's inability or decision not to participate.

The Lack of Support From Formal Systems to Kinship Care Providers

Formal child welfare systems are increasing their involvement and regulation of kinship care arrangements (Berrick, 1998; Murphy, 2008). Until recently, many states provided no or limited financial supports to kinship care providers. The formal child welfare system also requires rules and regulations that are intended to improve child well-being and keep children safe. These processes can also be restrictive and punitive to kin providers (Murphy, Hunter, & Johnson, 2008; Simpson & Lawrence-Webb, 2009). For example, a grandparent may feel conflicted with terminating the parental rights of their child to receive financial benefits and they may be unwilling to deny the parent access to the child despite being required by child welfare officials to do so. For some kin providers, they are unfamiliar with and overwhelmed with the child welfare and social service systems. They may not only be resistant to seeking help from these systems, but they may not know where or how to access them (Murphy, 2008; Ruiz, 2004).

That's My Baby and I'll Take Care of Him: Parenting Against the Odds

Despite these challenges, kinship care providers continue to care for their children. They continue to make the necessary self- and familial sacrifices to parent. Parenting is often shared with other family members, such as aunts and uncles. The kin provider may have some other person in the family assisting with regular caregiving responsibilities and providing financial supports to meet the daily needs of the child. Because of the acceptance of a wide definition of family (Hill, 1997), there is an inherent support of these types of familial arrangements. Kinship care providers can obtain supports from additional informal networks, such as within faith-based communities. Tangible resources, such as food and clothing, can be accessed and available to providers. However, there are also intangible supports often available, such as mentorship and guidance from members of the community, that are generated from within the informal network. Although it has not eliminated the disproportionality of the number of African American children in out-of-home care, it has reduced the disproportionate number of African American children in formal care.

\\\\ IMPLICATIONS

Contemporary kinship care is a form of resistance to the challenges facing African American families. While focusing on preserving African American families, kinship care also is a means of combating the devastating effects of other social and economic ills that impact the African American community. Kinship care acknowledges the multiple challenges facing the family, but it also is a means of acknowledging the power within the community to provide for and sustain itself. As such, there are a number of implications to consider. First, kinship care disputes the incorrect perception that African Americans are not engaged in preserving the family and caring for African American children. There has been a sustained effort to ensure the preservation of the African American family and caring for African American children. Although formal systems have been organized to often separate the well-being of the family from the child, the African American community understands that the two are connected, and, therefore, the response cannot be separated. Amid growing demands, the African American community has been consistently challenged with being able to meet the multiple needs of families, and so the community must re-invest in examining how kinship care can be augmented internally to better meet the needs of vulnerable children and families.

Second, supporting kinship care constitutes more than the development of child welfare policies because the reason for contemporary kinship care is a result of a number of social, political, and economic policies and practices that have negatively impacted the African American community, along with poor critical support services not being available to the community. Although it is important to design child welfare policies that do not augment the vulnerability of African American children, it is also important to design policies that address continued discrimination in the employment and education arenas to support African American men and women in finding and creating jobs that will sustain their families. It is critical to provide African American families with the supports needed to build and sustain healthy relationships that allow them to move beyond the systemic inequity and challenges that have been uniquely experienced in the African American community. It is critical to develop substance abuse and HIV programs that are located within the community and able to meet the intersectional needs within the community from a cultural context as opposed to having services outside of the geographic area, services that are not culturally competent, or services that focus on one social problem when communities are actually facing the challenge of negotiating multiple problems. Finally, it is critical to address poverty and the economic needs facing African Americans. This type of response includes having child welfare policies that are cognizant of the larger issues of why many African American children are at greater risk of being placed outside of the home, rather than relying on micro-level factors only.

Finally, as policies and services are crafted to support this organized informal system of care, it is critical that the formal response does not disrupt or dismantle the informal systems that are already in place. There has to be a balance of being supportive and staying out of the way of this indigenous response to maintaining the preservation of the African American family. The regulation of the lives of African American children has already evidenced that formal systems are not better able to ensure the safety and well-being of children. A careful approach needs to be taken, with the indigenous community in the place of leadership, to decide how to best support this system of care without being disruptive, punitive, and harmful as formal providers attempt to be supportive.

Social workers are uniquely positioned to serve as advocates to advance kinship care policies that support families and create parity in compensation between kin and nonkin providers across jurisdictions. Because of social work's role in communities and the profession's emphasis on social justice and human rights, social workers must be at the forefront of reshaping child welfare legislation, antipoverty programs, employment practices and training, and equity in the criminal justice system with enhanced opportunities for treatment and improved service delivery. Although social workers are already engaged in these settings, it is important to become more strategically mobilized to advance legislation that truly responds to and supports indigenous responses to care. Social work scholars can engage in research that further examines the nature of kinship care as a resistance strategy and form of collective resilience. In addition, greater research is needed to examine intersectional issues associated with child welfare, employment, antipoverty, and criminal justice policies.

\\\\ CONCLUSION

Kinship care has played a critical and vibrant role in sustaining and preserving African American families and communities. Kinship care is a form of resistance not only to the removal of African American children from the home but also to the social ills negatively impacting African American communities. Despite increasing challenges within the community, African Americans continue to use kinship care as a means of sharing traditions, maintaining order, responding to needs, providing mutual aid, and transferring values from generation to generation. Although not utopic in its response, kinship care does provide a means of furthering African American families. It is evidence that there is an organized response to need that is still vibrant within the community and that African American children are valued and considered integral to the preservation of the community. As we honor this important tradition within the African American community, we must also respect its indigenous roots and allow the community to best define what it needs to thrive.

\\\\ REFERENCES

Beck, A., & Harrison, P. M. (2001). *Prison and jail inmates in 2000*. Washington, DC: United States Department of Justice.

Bent-Goodley, T. B. (Ed.). (2003). *African American social workers and social policy*. New York: The Haworth Press.

Bent-Goodley, T. B., & Brade, K. (2007). Domestic violence and kinship care: Connecting policy and practice. *Journal of Health and Social Policy, 22*, 65–83.

Bent-Goodley, T. B., & Carlton-LaNey, I. B. (Eds.). (2003). *NABSW 2003 policy statements.* Washington, DC: NABSW.

Berrick, J. (1998). When children cannot remain home: Foster family care and kinship care. *Future of Children, 8,* 72–87.

Billingsley, A., & Giovannoni, J. (1972). *Children of the storm: African American children and American child welfare.* New York: Harcourt Brace Jovanovich.

Blumstein, A. (2001). Race and criminal justice. In N. J. Smelser, W. Wilson, & F. Mitchell (Eds.), *America becoming: Racial trends and their consequences* (Vol. 1, pp. 21–31). Washington, DC: National Research Council.

Bobo, L., & Thompson, V. (2006). Unfair by design: The war on drugs, race and the legitimacy of the criminal justice system. *Social Research, 73,* 445–472.

Carlton-LaNey. I. B. (Ed.). (2001). *African American leadership: An empowerment tradition in social welfare.* Washington, DC: NASW Press.

Carlton-LaNey, I., & Carlton Alexander, S. (2001). Early African American social welfare pioneer women: Working to empower the race and the community. *Journal of Ethnic and Cultural Diversity in Social Work, 10,* 67–84.

Child Welfare League of America. (2008). *Kinship care: Fact sheet.* Retrieved June 4, 2010, from http://www.cwla.org/programs/kinship/factsheet.htm

Children's Defense Fund. (2007). *America's cradle to prison pipeline: A Children's Defense Fund Report.* Washington, DC: Author.

Chipungu, S., & Bent-Goodley, T. B. (2003). Race, poverty and child maltreatment. *APSAC Advisor, 15,* 9–10.

Chipungu, S., & Bent-Goodley, T. B. (2004). Meeting the challenges of contemporary foster care. *Future of Children, 14,* 75–94.

Choi, S., & Tittle, G. (2002). *Parental substance abuse and child maltreatment.* Chicago: Children and Family Research Center.

Cross, T. L. (2008). Disproportionality in child welfare. *Child Welfare, 87,* 11–20.

Davis, K. E., & Bent-Goodley, T. B. (Eds.). (2004). *The color of social policy.* Alexandria, VA: CSWE Press.

Franklin, D. L. (1997). *Ensuring inequality: The structural transformation of the African American family.* New York: Oxford University Press.

Franklin, D. L. (2001). *What's love got to do with it? Understanding and healing the rift between Black men and women.* New York: Simon & Schuster.

Franklin, J. H., & Moss, A. (2000). *From slavery to freedom* (8th ed.). New York: Knopf.

Geen, R. (2004). The evolution of kinship care policy and practice. *Future of Children, 14,* 131–150.

Harden, A., Clark, R., & Maguire, K. (1997). *Foster and informal kinship care.* Washington, DC: Retrieved June 4, 2010, from http://aspe.hhs.gov/HSP/cyp/xskincar.htm

Hill, R. (1997). *The strengths of African American families: Twenty-five years later.* Washington, DC: R & B Publishers.

Hill, R. (2008). Gaps in research and public policies. *Child Welfare, 87,* 359–367.

Hodges, V. (2001). Historic development of African American child welfare services. Carlton-LaNey, I. (Ed.), *African American leadership: An empowerment tradition in social welfare history* (pp. 203–214). Washington, DC: NASW Press.

Jewell, K. S. (2003). *Survival of the African American family: The institutional impact of U.S. social policy.* New York: Praeger.

Lawrence-Webb, C. (1997). African American children in the modern child welfare system: A legacy of The Flemming Rule. *Child Welfare, 76,* 9–30.

Martin, E., & Martin, J. (1995). *Social work and the African American experience.* Washington, DC: NASW Press.

Mauer, M. (1999). *Race to incarcerate: The sentencing project.* New York: The New Press.

McRoy, R. (2004). The color of child welfare. In K. E. Davis & T. B. Bent-Goodley (Eds.), *The color of social policy* (pp. 37–64). Alexandria, VA: CSWE Press.

Miller, O., & Ward, K. (2008). Emerging strategies for reducing racial disproportionality and disparate outcomes in child welfare: The results of a National Breakthrough Series Collaborative. *Child Welfare, 87,* 211–240.

Mumola, C. (2000). *Incarcerated parents and their children* [NCJ 182335]. Washington, DC: Bureau of Justice Statistics.

Murphy, S. Y. (2008). Voices of African American grandmothers raising grandchildren: Informing child welfare kinship care policy-practice. *Journal of Intergenerational Relationships, 6,* 25–39.

Murphy, S. Y., Hunter, A., & Johnson, D. (2008). Transforming caregiving: African American custodial grandmothers and the child welfare system. *Journal of Sociology and Social Welfare, 35,* 67–89.

National Association of Black Social Workers (NABSW). (April, 1972). *Position statement on transracial adoptions.* Presented at NABSW Conference, Nashville, TN.

Peebles-Wilkins, W. (1995). Janie Porter Barrett and the Virginia Industrial School for Colored Girls: Community response to the needs of African American children. *Child Welfare, 74,* 143–161.

Provine, D. (2007). *Unequal under law: Race in the war on drugs.* Chicago: University of Chicago Press.

Ricketts, E. (1989). The origin of African American female-headed households. *Focus, 12,* 32–36.

Roberts, D. (2003). *Shattered bonds: The color of child welfare.* New York: Basic Civitas Books.

Roberts, D. (2008). The racial geography of child welfare: Towards a new research paradigm. *Child Welfare, 87,* 125–150.

Rodenborg, N. (2004). Services to African American children in poverty: Institutional discrimination in child welfare? *Journal of Poverty, 8,* 109–130.

Ruiz, D. (2004). *Amazing grace: African American grandmothers as caregivers and conveyors of traditional values.* Westport, CT: Praeger.

Scannapieco, M., & Jackson, S. (1996). Kinship care: The African American response to family preservation. *Social Work, 41,* 190–196.

Simpson, G., & Lawrence-Webb, C. (2009). Responsibility without community resources: Informal kinship care among low-income, African American grandmother caregivers. *Journal of Black Studies, 39,* 825–847.

Smelser, N. J. (1962). *Theory of collective behavior.* New York: Free Press.

Smith-Ruiz, D. (2008). African American grandmothers providing extensive care to their grandchildren: Socio-demographic and health determinants of life satisfaction. *Journal of Sociology and Social Welfare, 35,* 29–52.

Stack, C. (1974). *All our kin: Strategies for survival in an African American community.* New York: Basic Books.

Taifa, N. (2004). Social policy implications of racial disparities in the criminal justice system. In K. E. Davis & T. B. Bent-Goodley (Eds.), *The color of social policy* (pp. 101–116). Alexandria, VA: CSWE Press.

Tate, G. T. (1993). Political consciousness and resistance among Black antebellum women. *Women & Politics, 13,* 67–89.

Thaler, J. (2005). *Parents with HIV/AIDS and their children in the child welfare system.* New York: National Resource Center for Family-Centered Practice and Permanency Planning at the Hunter College School of Social Work.

U.S. Census Bureau. (2003). *Child health USA 2003.* Washington, DC: Health Resources and Services Administration.

U.S. Census Bureau. (2004). The *African American population in the United States: March 2004 (PPL-186).* Washington, DC: Author.

U.S. Department of Health & Human Services (USDHHS). (2008a). *Trends in foster care and adoption—FY 2002 to FY 2007 AFCARS data.* Washington, DC: U.S. Children's Bureau.

U.S. Department of Health and Human Services (USDHHS). (2008b). *The AFCARS report: Preliminary FY 2006 estimates as of January 2008.* Washington, DC: Author.

U.S. General Accounting Office. (2002, June). *Foster care: Recent legislation helps states focus on finding permanent homes for children, but long-standing barriers remain* (GAO-02–585). Washington, DC: Author.

2

African American Club Women's Resistance to Oppressive Public Policy in the Early 20th Century

Iris B. Carlton-LaNey

⧷ INTRODUCTION

This chapter focuses on a set of laws and policies referred to as Jim Crow laws, which excluded African Americans from full participation in society. It also discusses how African American women resisted these laws through their community organization and advocacy activities. Jim Crow laws reflected a belief system that defined one person as less human and deserving than another. African Americans have long been disenfranchised in America, but they also fought against this injustice.

The Civil War and the subsequent Reconstruction momentarily shattered white supremacy, which returned with vengeance and with whites' flagrant determination to maintain control over the newly emancipated population. Disenfranchisement of Africans in American was largely completed by 1890. The 1896 Supreme Court decision in *Plessy v. Ferguson* crystallized the political process and provided a constitutional sanction for racial segregation (Franklin & Moss 1994; Walters, 2003). Even though these laws reigned supreme in American society, finding their way into the most mundane of life's circumstances, African American women via the women's club movement waged a constant war of resistance against their implementation. A manifestation of oppressive public policy, the Jim Crow Laws were unrelenting as were the African American women who, like Ida Bell Wells-Barnett, always "felt compelled to do something in the face of injustice or discrimination" (Bay, 2009, p. 10).

GENERAL OVERVIEW OF JIM CROW LAWS

So intense was the resolve to keep former slaves controlled and bound to the plantation that the distinction between chattel slave and wage laborer became an irrelevant notion. Where lynching failed to control African Americans and as hostility toward them increased, many states and cities passed laws and issued ordinances to further formalize and legalize African American disenfranchisement. These various laws, statues, and ordinances formed the "Jim Crow" legislation that governed attitudes, behaviors, and practices. Jim Crow laws varied widely as did their enforcement. State, county, and city Jim Crow laws were buttressed by additional related oppressive practices that impeded African Americans' economic and political involvement. These practices included sharecropping, debt peonage, convict leasing, school segregation, and voting restrictions (Barusch, 2009).

Jim Crow laws included various forms of exclusion and segregation. The plethora of Jim Crow laws separated African Americans in life and death. They were separated in courtrooms and cemeteries, in depots and on trains, in hospitals and on streetcars. They were banned from public and private establishments, including restaurants, parks, public pools, ocean beachfronts, libraries, and hotels. Georgia, for example, was the first state to pass Jim Crow streetcar laws in 1891. Like many of these laws, interpretation and implementation were left to the generally erratic discretion of the enforcer. By 1907, other states, including Florida, North Carolina, Oklahoma, Tennessee, Texas, and Virginia, followed with some version of state law, city ordinance, and/or company regulation, which segregated streetcars (Meier & Rudwick, 2002).

Jim Crow segregation affected nearly all aspects of African American life. Many courtrooms, for example, used specific Jim Crow bibles for African Americans and different ones for whites. Drinking fountains, public restrooms, and waiting rooms were segregated and differentiated with signs indicating "colored only" or "white only." There were also rules for racial etiquette that, for example, demanded that African American men remove their hats in the presence of whites, required that they step aside for white customers in retail stores, forbid them from trying on clothing and shoes before purchasing them, and demanded that African American men look at the ground when speaking to whites. In many cases, the consequences for violating the rules of etiquette and breaking Jim Crow laws were equally dire. In addition to these humiliating and dehumanizing practices, African Americans also faced economic hardships that tied them to the land and effectively prohibited their mobility. Sharecropping, debt peonage laws, and convict leasing were practices that ensured a ready pool of laborers to work for white plantations owners.

🕮 SHARECROPPING, DEBT PEONAGE, AND CONVICT LEASING

Sharecropping allowed landless farmers to use land that someone else owned, usually whites. The farmers were responsible for providing all of the labor associated with producing the crop (Perry & Davis-Maye, 2007). The profit was split at harvest time, with the landowner usually receiving more that his or her fair share and the cropper barely eking out a living while becoming more and more indebted to the landowner.

Debt peonage laws that legally bound formerly enslaved men and women to serve the creditor/landowner until a debt was paid existed in many states, including Alabama, Florida, Georgia, Mississippi, North Carolina, and South Carolina (Ruef & Fletcher, 2003). The U.S. Supreme Court upheld the peonage law on March 13, 1905, in the case of *Clyatt v. United States*, which was a White Georgia man convicted by the Circuit Court of Appeals of the Fifth Circuit of the State for holding two African American men in involuntary servitude (Ross, 1978).

The nefarious practice of convict leasing was also part of the Jim Crow era. This practice allowed landowners and other businesses to bid on contracts to have convicts released to them as laborers. The convicts were not paid for their labor and were housed and fed at the business's or landowner's expense. This practice also prevented race mixing among inmates, saved the state the expense of caring for the convict and provided lease holders access to cheap labor which was extremely attractive, but treacherous to the convicts. These workers had no protection and suffered atrocities at the hand of the property owners resulting in extremely high mortality rates (Rabinowitz, 1976).

ⵉⵉ THE JIM CROW CLIMATE OF VIOLENCE

The climate of Jim Crow created an atmosphere that encouraged whites to vent their anger and to engage in violent acts of aggression without fear of repercussions or retaliations. The violence of lynching, rape, and race riots robbed African Americans of any semblance of safety and protection. The practice of lynching was to intimidate and to punish via an atrocious and horrendous death often in a public venue. Lynching, often perpetuated by organizations such as the Ku Klux Klan, was justified by the purported ever-present menace of white women falling prey to African American men.

The usual response to lynching was to blame the victim for some imagined transgression and to ignore those who carried out the lynching. Prominent community citizens often actively or passively participated in lynching. Although lynching was allegedly associated with African American men victimizing white women, it tended to increase when interracial political and/or economic competition increased (Soule, 1992). The 1892 Memphis lynching of Tom Moss, Calvin McDowell, and Henry Stewart (Giddings, 1984) as well as the Wilmington Riots of 1898 are prime examples of the extent to which interracial political and economic competition were the obvious motives for the violence even though newspaper articles, in both cases, were said to have inflamed both groups' sensibilities via articles about white women's sexual abuse at the hands of African American men. So acceptable and justifiable was lynching that this form of homicide in polite company was differentiated as either a *good* or *bad* lynching. A good lynching was one that was orderly and methodical, without drunkenness and chaos. A good lynching, according to whites, was conducted by the best people of the community such as lawyers, farmers, merchants, and bankers (Allen, Als, Lewis, & Litwack, 2000).

Sexual violence was also used to control. Rape, by white men, indicated to African American women that they were always vulnerable and to

African American men that they were helpless to protect their wives, daughters, sisters, and so on. African American women were "sexual hostages" that, as historian Darlene Clark Hine (1989, p. 915) noted, "did not reduce their determination to acquire power to protect themselves and to become agents of social change." Obviously African American women were quick to realize that sexual violence was political. These sexual violations were usually not challenged, whereas white women's virtue was vehemently protected. African American women were even blamed for their victimization and labeled promiscuous and naturally immoral. On some occasions, African American girls were sent to training schools or institutions for wayward girls because of rape and/or resulting pregnancies, further victimizing and blaming them for being raped (Brice, 2005).

Violence against African Americans was further perpetuated through race riots. Whenever African Americans demanded fairer treatment, stood up for themselves, or audaciously pursued opportunities, whites responded with contempt and violence. The mass murders of African Americans at the hands of white mobs generally resulted from incidents that ignited the ire of whites in a particular community. Like many others, the Wilmington, North Carolina, riots of 1898 and the Atlanta Riots of 1906 resulted from claims that African American men sexually assaulted white women. Race riots were so widespread and deadly during the summer and fall of 1919 that the Renaissance poet James Weldon Johnson dubbed it the *Red Summer*. The most violent of these riots took place in Chicago, Washington, D.C., and Elaine, Arkansas.

The Elaine riot involved African American sharecroppers' efforts to unionize. A white sheriff's deputy tried to break up a union meeting at an African American church and was killed. The ensuing riot killed dozens of African Americans. Sixty-seven men were sentenced to prison for their alleged participation, and 12 others were convicted of the sheriff's murder. No whites were prosecuted for the murders of dozens of African American sharecroppers (Hine, Hine, & Harrold, 2008). Instead the violent atmosphere created by the Jim Crow culture festered and grew with continuous victimization of African American women, men, and children.

African Americans responses' to Jim Crow varied but usually involved establishing some mechanism for self-protection. Some migrated or fled to escape further victimization. Others directly protested the discriminatory practices, which generally resulted in further violence and death, while others resigned themselves to the patterns of segregation that ensured their second-class citizenship. The Jim Crow culture created a system of economy, polity, and ideology designed to control and oppress all African Americans. African American women felt especially challenged to confront this oppressive system of laws (Collins, 1990). As Giddings noted (1984, p. 81) these women "believed that their efforts were essential for reform and progress, and that their moral standing was a steady rock upon which the race could lean."

The discussion below examines ways that African American club women responded to the victimization caused by Jim Crow public policies during the early part of the 20th century. In addition to a constant stream of young African American women who migrated unaccompanied from the South to cities in the North, Midwest, and West, some African American women also dug in their heels, wherever they were, and fought the systemic tyrant of Jim Crow. Essentially, Jim Crow laws and practices negatively affected the African American community's ability to garner economic, political, social, and physical security. In an effort to combat the deleterious affects of Jim Crow, these women used multifaceted strategies of attack. The women engaged in what was called race work or racial uplift. Their activism was designed to make their segregation a little more tolerable or to transform the existing structures of oppression.

⫸ THE WOMEN'S CLUB MOVEMENT

Through the National Association of Colored Women's Clubs (NACW), which "quickly became the largest and most enduring protest organization in the history" of African Americans (Hine, 1989, p. 917), these women attacked the derogatory images and stereotypes that were projected onto them and moved on to establish strategies for change that endured well into the 20th century. According to Evans (2007), the African American club women's movement consisted of different types of organizations and groups, including secret orders such as the Eastern Star and the Daughters of Zion, sororities such as the Alpha Kappa Alpha Sorority, and an array of church groups such as the Ladies Auxiliary and the Women's Baptist Home Mission Society. Organized professional groups were also part of their movement and included groups such as the National Association of Colored Graduate Nurses and the Madam C. J. Walker Hair Culturists Union of America. Through these groups, women strengthened their skills and political force.

Founded in 1896, the NACW's existence was believed to be imperative to fight racial oppression and to promote upward mobility. There was sometimes friction and competition within and between these groups, but instead of inhibiting movement, this friction seemed to generate energy. More often than not, these women directed their indignation toward Jim Crow and not each other. In describing these club women's political maneuvers, Evans praised their political proficiency, indicating that they "carried out administrative coups, filibustered and stonewalled reminiscent of the most powerful board rooms and staterooms" (2007, p. 64). Club women understood the importance of standing together for effective planned change. They identified a number of strategies, including voting and education, as necessary for the transformation of structures of oppression. Their aim was to model appropriate behavior while resisting oppression and advocating for equity and fairness.

🎇 RESISTANCE TO JIM CROW

Prestage (1995, p.179) notes that African American women have been engaged in political activity throughout history. She describes their political involvement as (1) determined by the cultural and legal circumstances of the particular period in time, (2) involving tactics to change their disadvantaged status, and (3) escalating from nontraditional activities to a preponderance of traditional activities over time.

African women, who came to America in chains, mastered strategies of resistance during their enslavement and life on plantations. For them, everyday plantation life fostered a social and political environment worthy of retribution (Carlton-LaNey, 1999; Perry & Davis-Maye, 2007). They learned to feign cooperation. This practice, used by both men and women, was so well-known and widely used that it was named "puttin on ole massa" or "fooling massa." Always attuned to their vulnerability, the network of enslaved women in plantation communities provided an environment for training and testing political practices of resistance. This type of self-protection continued within the African American community and, in 1896, inspired Paul Laurence Dunbar to write what is arguably his finest poem, "We Wear the Mask." Dunbar's poem provides an insightful portrayal of African American life and captures what Hine called *dissemblance*. She describes dissemblance as behaviors and attitudes that African American women used to shield "the truth of their inner lives and selves from their oppressors" (1989, p. 912). Hine postulates that dissemblance continues today as a valuable protective factor among African American women.

African American women took both individual and collective initiatives of political activism to counter Jim Crow laws. They understood that they could not afford to be obvious in their protestation of indignities. They instead engaged in small, personal strategies to express their contempt and to fortify their resistance. Like the enslaved women's strategies of relaying covert messages hidden in songs, quilt patterns, and storytelling, Progressive Era reformers also used stealthy and disguised mechanisms. Although their political acts were sometimes veiled, they willingly took the risk sometimes feigning ignorance or using other evasive actions to avoid cooperation and to register their discontent. Charlotte Hawkins Brown, founder of North Carolina's Palmer Memorial Institute, masterfully ignored Jim Crow whenever possible. She, for example, turned a blind eye to racially separate waiting rooms, finding alternative seating in some neutral area. Described as a "political genius," Brown preferred to "overestimate possibility than to underestimate it" and "pushed the color line to the limits" at every turn (Gilmore, 1996, p. 185). Similarly African American schools steadily and quietly raised academic standards while publicly acknowledging their support for industrial education. Obtaining funding from whites was far easier to get for training domestic servants and farmers than for training scientists and philosophers (Fairclough, 2000).

African American race women of the Progressive Era inherited the skills that enslaved women used to survive antebellum plantation life, further honing them through their churches and women's clubs (Bent-Goodley, 2001; Giddings, 1984). For many African American women, race work or uplift work was ostensibly nonpolitical and innocuous enough so as to proceed with little skepticism from whites who saw it as harmless or nonthreatening (Fairclough, 2001). White women, via interracial cooperation committees, felt comfortable working with African American women and encouraged and supported their efforts albeit within the confines of strict Jim Crow laws (Carlton-LaNey, 2000).

African American women graciously accepted support, encouragement; financial contributions, and even reprimands from whites, yet they maintained clarity of purpose and unity of vision. They understood white women's predilections and conducted themselves with the utmost caution in their presence. Even Margaret Murray Washington, who tended to be conservative like her husband, Booker T. Washington, instructed the staff at Tuskegee Institute to contact her immediately when white women visited the campus because they could be so nasty and were not to be trusted (White, 1999). White women embraced interracial cooperation as a way to change African Americans' behaviors and to encourage their self-help activities, but they felt no compunction to fight for "structural changes in American laws and institutions" (Higginbotham, 1993, p. 197) and left African American women on their own where this was concerned.

African American women continued their political activities both individually and collectively far beyond the Progressive Era. Some of these women were part of the elite, while others were regular working-class women who took their destiny in their own hands. Pinky Pilcher, for example, of Greenwood, Mississippi, wrote to President Roosevelt on December 23, 1936, complaining about the white women who headed the local Public Works Administration (PWA). She said that the "poor white people is noting but Negro haters" who would not give work to blacks, but sent them to look for wash work when none existed. She further complained that the money paid out for poor white women to visit the colored people who were ill was being wasted and that African American women should be hired for that task since they visited their sick anyway (as cited in Lerner, 1972, p. 402). Pilcher's audacity in writing directly to president Roosevelt indicated courage and determination in advocating for individual and groups rights commonly ignored in favor of Jim Crow laws.

⚡ GROUP SURVIVAL AND INSTITUTION TRANSFORMATION

African American women utilized many available resources, and when resources did not exist, they created their own resulting in a parallel system of social welfare and education. They relied on their education, oratory skill, journalistic abilities, research and organizational skills, and business acumens to combat the structural institutions that Jim Crow laws supported. Collins (1990) noted that African American women engaged in two interdependent dimensions of activism: 1) the struggle for group survival and 2) the struggle for institutional transformation.

Their struggle for group survival involved actions to create spheres of influence within structures of oppression. Women's clubs, African American schools, and social settlements were some of the spheres of influence that these women created. Their struggle for institutional transformation included activities to change existing structures of oppression that were legalized by Jim Crow laws. Within this dimension of activism,

African American women fought against all legal and customary rules of suppression and subordination.

\\\\ VOTING

African American women advocated for the vote as critical to their ability to demand equal access to resources and to transform structures of oppression. Suffragists believed that women armed with the ballot could better improve conditions in the African American community while challenging Jim Crow practices. The fact that most African American women worked and were wage earners purported that their "labor needed the protection of the ballot" (Giddings, 1984, p. 121). Elizabeth Ross Haynes, Ida B. Wells-Barnett, and Nannie Helen Burroughs, among others, were vocal advocates for women's voting rights.

Ross Haynes said, "I have no fears in urging the women of the country, irrespective of race, to awake, register, vote, work and enlarge the fight for equality of opportunity in jobs, in office for women" (n.d.). Nannie Helen Burroughs, founder of the National Training School for Women and Girls in Washington, D.C., indicated that with the right to vote, African American women could influence the enactment of legislation for protection from rapists. In Burroughs' mind, voting would give women the ability to defend their virtue in court and would become a weapon of moral defense (Higginbotham, 1993; Hine, 1989, p. 918). Essentially, voting was viewed as a weapon that African American women could use to protect children and themselves from the vices of the streets such as gambling houses, saloons and political corruption.

Similarly, Ida B. Wells-Barnett was a zealot who vigorously attacked unjust policies while calling on African Americans to become more politically judicious. In January 1913, she organized the Alpha Suffrage Club of Chicago, which was the state's first African American women's suffrage group. These women's fight for suffrage was challenged by white suffragists' racism. To ensure inclusion in the 19th amendment, which granted women the vote, African American women had to lobby strenuously because white women were inclined to exclude them. African American women engaged in "speech making, in petitioning federal and state governments, and in campaigning for women's suffrage referendums . . . founded at least thirty groups, which were either women suffrage associations or women's clubs that had suffrage leaders" (Terborg-Penn, 2005, p. 207). Their struggles for both group survival an institutional transformation were obviously inter-dependent and overlapping.

African American women also ran for political office as a way to com-bat Jim Crow laws and to transform structures of oppression. Elizabeth Ross Haynes was elected coleader of the 21st Assembly District of New York in 1935. She was confronted with what she perceived to be gen-der prejudice primarily from her male coleader. She attempted an unsuc-cessful bid with another male coleader whom she respected as a fair and committed person. Although she failed to get reelected (Carlton-LaNey, 1997), she continued to adhere to the importance of women stepping "forward as aspirants, bargainers, and if necessary, contenders for the choices official plums" (Haynes, n.d.). Ida B. Wells-Barnett ran for Illinois State senate in 1930 but was defeated. She, like many other women's club leaders, held a political appointment as an adult probation officer for Chicago in 1913.

Maggie Lena Walker, president of the St. Luke Penny Savings Bank in Richmond, Virginia also ran for political office as Superintendent of the Public Instruction on Virginia's Lily Black Republican ticket (Schiele, Jackson, & Fairfax, 2005). She also held a political appointment as the governor' selectee to the Virginia Industrial School for Colored Girls' board of advisors after the institution came under state auspices (Marlowe, 1993). The Virginia Industrial School represented a sphere of influence within Virginia's segregated criminal justice system, and Walker's guber-natorial appointment to the board put her into a position to challenge existing rules that subordinated African American girls who were involved with this system. Many other African American clubwomen held political positions such as Mary McLeod Bethune, who was the Director of the Negro National Youth Administration during the Roosevelt administra-tion, and Mary Church Terrell, who was appointed superintendent of the Washington, D.C., schools.

〰 SCHOOLS, EDUCATION, AND AFRICAN AMERICAN HISTORY

Plessy v. Ferguson had enormous implications, turning back the clock in many spheres, including the educational arena. Even Oberlin College, which had modeled a 50-year history of admitting students irrespective of color, with no limitations on college campus life participation with the exception of interracial dating and marriage, embraced the segregation implicit in *Plessy v. Ferguson*. By 1882, the school had begun to separate students based on race in dining, housing, and in campus literary society participation (Waite, 2001). Prominent club woman Mary Church Terrell, a 1884 graduate of the school, found that 30 years later her daughter was denied housing in the campus dormitories because of the school's increased policy of racial discrimination. Terrell wrote to the university president expressing her anger and hopelessness at the school's backsliding. She also articulated her dismay with a "wicked and cruel country in which everything is done to crush the pride, wound the sensibilities, embitter the life and break the heart" of African Americans (cited in Waite, 2001). Even though Terrell was dispirited and disappointed, she seemed to be fortified in her resolve to challenge Jim Crow. Some years later she was instrumental, as a school board member, in getting the Washington, D.C., schools to incorporate African American history in their curriculum and to institute the celebration of Frederick Douglass Day (White, 1999) and, at age 72, she was picketing in protest against a segregated at a local restaurant in Washington, D.C.

The study of and appreciation for race history were seen as essential to race work and African American race pride. Race pride was political and antithetical to the mundane drudgery associated with a life of discrimination, isolation, and oppression. Although efforts to generate race pride may not appear to be political, these women knew full well that having a positive sense of self was essential to race empowerment, race preservation, and upward mobility.

Victoria Earle Matthews, via her White Rose Home (Waites, 2001), held an extensive collection of African American books in the home's library. Surrounding guest and residents of the home with books and newspapers that provided both information and positive images of themselves was a strategic mechanism for education, developing race pride, and encouraging activism. Ida B. Wells-Barnett's Negro Fellowship League and reading room similarly provided a place for residents and nonresidents alike to have access to newspapers and books, which were denied them through public libraries that were segregated. Libraries and reading rooms were a "common expression of racial pride" (Salem, 1990). These women also understood that ignorance doomed African Americans to powerlessness. Ergo education was empowering and represented a form of political activism (Collins, 1990).

Much like the club women of the era, Amy Jacques Garvey of the Universal Negro Improvement Association (UNIA) believed that women needed to accept their roles as "intellectuals and as political architects." To facilitate this development, she pleaded with them to cultivate a "taste for serious reading," to read widely, to give books as gifts, and to make reading a family event (as cited in Taylor, 2000, p. 115). She offered simple strategies to the UNIA women, encouraging them to save their old newspapers and to send them to others once they had read them (Taylor, 2000). Jacques Garvey's Women's Page in the Negro World effectively provided an arena for political activism and for teaching UNIA women.

\\\\ MECHANISMS FOR PROJECTING THE POLITICAL AGENDA

African American women were skillful organizers, attentive to political, economic, and social issues. They relied on each other to maintain motivation and to develop timely and appropriate strategies. In 1908, the National Association of Colored Graduate Nurses (NACGN) was organized. With 26 charter members, these professional women organized to address the "punitive power exerted over Black nurses by the state boards of examiners" (Mosley, 1996, p. 23). The NACGN campaigned against selected state boards of nursing and separate state boards of nursing examinations. They demanded to be evaluated based on the same standards as their white counterparts. In 1909, Ludie Andrews began legal proceedings against the Georgia State Board of Nurse Examiners for the opportunity to take the same licensure examination as whites. This continued for 10 years, after which time the Board of Examiners offered to license her. She refused unless other African American nurses were accorded the same opportunities. The Jim Crow racist attitudes of white nurses relegated African American nurses to the servant class, which limited opportunities for their full professional participation (Mosley, 1996).

In 1922, building on Wells-Barnett's legacy, African American women organized the Anti-Lynching Crusaders. This organization was founded by the NACW's sixth president Mary Talbert under the aegis of the National Association for the Advancement of Colored People (NAACP) ("How Did Black Women in the NAACP Promote the Dyer Anti-Lynching Bill, 1918–1923?" n.d.). The Anti-Lynching Crusaders' mission was to advocate for the passage of the Dyers Anti-Lynching Bill and to put an end to lynching.

Their strategy was to target 1 million women in an effort to raise 1 million dollars. Although they did not reach their financial mark, nor did they encourage legislators to enact an antilynching legislation, they made an impact by calling attention to lynching, and some suggest that they were instrumental in decreasing the number of lynchings that took place between 1924 and 1928 (Giddings, 1984).

As orators and public speakers, African American women fueled the discussions and engaged in activism that demonstrated the interwoven nature of politics, economic and social conditions, race history, and strategies for fighting Jim Crow. As a journalist, Wells-Barnett relied on accurate fact-finding. She believed in collecting evidence to inform her writing, pubic speaking, and activism. She was especially vigilant at using evidence to illustrate the heinous nature of lynching and to refute erroneous newspapers, which tried to justify various incidences of lynching. Confronting the culprit with indisputable evidence was part of her strategy. She often hired Pinkerton agents (from Allan Pinkerton's Agency) to assist her in investigating lynching incidents.

Wells-Barnett was particularly angered by the lynching of Sam Hose in Georgia. Hose was lynched after killing a white man in self-defense. Erroneous rumor had it that Hose raped the man's wife. With prominent whites involved, Hose was tortured and burned alive in a picnic-like atmosphere. His charred body parts were sold as souvenirs. Wells-Barnett immediately organized a committee in Chicago to raise funds needed to hire a detective to investigate the lynching. The investigator found that whites lied about the lynching. Wells-Barnett publicized the investigator's report at a mass meeting. She further circulated the report via articles written in African American and white newspapers, and finally issued the report via a publication titled *Lynch Law in Georgia* (McMurry, 1998).

The written word was an especially valuable tool for African American women's political work. Newspapers, newsletters, pamphlets, and even tracts provided the vehicle for club women to inform the community, spread their ideas, and gather support of those ideas. Wells-Barnett owned and edited four newspapers in her lifetime. The *Memphis Free Speech and Headlight* was the first and perhaps the most prominent. She used the pages of this rag to urge the people of Memphis to leave town after her friend Tom Moss was lynched.

Many African Americans heeded her words and left Memphis for presumably safer havens to the West. As the Memphis economy began to reflect the departure of droves of African Americans, two white representatives from the Memphis streetcar service approached Wells at her newspaper office asking her to encourage her readers to return to the streetcars and to reassure them that any discourtesy shown to them would be punished severely (Bay, 2009). Their appeal only reiterated to Wells-Barnett that her newspaper editorials were effective. Subsequently, she urged Africans Americans to continue the streetcar boycott and to save so that they could leave Memphis permanently. Wells-Barnett continued to avoid the streetcars and armed herself with a pistol and urged that others do the same, noting that in a lawless town a Winchester rifle ought to have an honored place in all African American homes.

Wells-Barnett also owned *The Chicago Conservator*, which she purchased from her husband. From 1878 to 1914, the *Conservator* provided coverage of racism and violence against African Americans with a focus on racial unity and militant responses as strategies for change. Between 1911 and 1914, she published the Negro Fellowship League newspaper, *The Fellowship Herald* (Bay, 2009; Giddings, 2008).

Others used newspapers similarly. Amy Jacques Garvey, as associate editor of the *Negro World*, wrote articles for the Women's Page. This section of the paper spoke specifically to women, urging their participation in the Pan-African movement and creating an open forum for them to share their opinions, ideas, and information (Taylor, 2000). Jacques Garvey was also a prolific writer. While she was the unofficial head of the UNIA, she wrote an editorial for the *Negro World* from 1924 to 1927. Simultaneously she produced the Women's Page nearly every week.

The Women's Era, the "first Black women's newspaper" (White, 1999) and the literary organ of the Boston Women's Era Club, was edited by the organization's founder Josephine St. Pierre Ruffin. *The Women's Era* kept members informed about "fashion, health, family life, and legislation" and served as a way for women to communicate and create a "viable national network" (Salem, 1990, p. 19). *The Women's Era* became the official publication of the NACW and served notice that they would "always have a defender as well as a national voice" (White, p. 54). *The Women's Era* was superseded by the *National Association Notes*.

In addition to newspapers, public speaking was also used to project their political voices. Maggie Lena Walker was known for her public speaking ability. She was said to have a powerful, low story-telling voice that sometimes moved listeners to tears about disenfranchisement while urging them to seek economic self-reliance (Marlowe, 1993). Mary Church Terrell was also an influential and highly sought after multilingual speaker. Mamie Garvin Fields, a South Carolina community activist and teacher, recalled Terrell's visit to Charleston, South Carolina. She described Terrell's voice as "wonderfully resonate" (1985, p. 191). Speaking at the Mt. Zion African Methodist Episcopal Church, the always elegant and picturesque Terrell wore a pink evening gown and long white gloves. She told the huge crowd of women that they had "more to do than other women [and that] they must go into [their] communities and improve them [and] go out into the nation and change it." She so enamored and inspired the women at the church with her message, poise, and regal affect that they "felt so stirred up, nobody wanted to wait till morning to pick up our burden again. Everywhere you might look, there was something to do" (1985, p. 191).

Madam C. J. Walker (Sarah Breedlove), a businesswoman and pioneer in African American women's hair and skin care products, also used the speakers' platform to urge women to seek economic self-reliance and political kudos. To ensure group survival, Walker organized a sales force of agents to use their economic self-reliance to combat racism and lynching. Her model of political activism helped to move African American women out of their roles as domestics and agricultural workers to empowered and self-efficacious independent business women.

In 1917, Madam C. J. Walker was part of a small group of Harlem leaders who attempted to persuade President Wilson to support antilynching legislation in the United States. The group traveled from New York to meet with President Wilson in Washington, D.C., but to no avail as he refused to see them. They left a 16-signatory petition for the President in lieu of their planned meeting. Madame Walker recalled this event later when she met with her agents at their annual Madam Walker Beauty Culturists Union Convention (Bundles, 2001). In her speech *Women's Duty to Women,* she urged the Walker Company women to become politically conscious. So motivated by Madam's speech, and conscious of the power that their number and money rendered, these women immediately sent a telegram to President Wilson requesting that he use his political and personal will to end race rioting and lynching.

Madam Walker, like most of the club women of the era, understood that the "purpose of her leadership was to build more leadership," and, as Nikki Giovanni later lamented, "The purpose of being a spokesperson [was] to speak until the people gained a voice" (Giovanni, 1988, p. 135). African American club women of the Progressive Era spoke until more and more women gained a voice. They petitioned, lobbied, marched, and pamphleteered. Despite extraordinary obstacles and numerous efforts that fell short of their target goal, they tacked Jim Crow from every angle and refused to give up their fight for equity and justice.

◯◯ IMPLICATIONS FOR SOCIAL WORK AND POLICY PRACTICE

The resistance activities in which these women engaged stand as a testament to their dogged determination, passion, and intellectual prowess. Contemporary policy practice could benefit from building on their legacy. The increasing numbers of women involved in the political arena today stand on these pioneer women's shoulders. Madeline Albright, Condoleezza Rice, and Hillary Clinton should recall Mary Church Terrell's 1904 multilingual speech (delivered in German, French, and English) at the International Congress of Women in Berlin, Germany, as an example of the initiation of women's policy practice on an international level. Maryland Senator Barbara Mikulski, MSW, whose social work practice evolved into community activism, stands on the shoulders of women like Ida Wells-Barnett, who failed in her bid for Illinois Senate in 1930 but whom, nonetheless, provided a model of determination, political independence. Others like Elizabeth Ross Haynes and Eartha Mary Magadine White successfully held public office in New York and Florida, respectively, and used their social work skills to become change agents for community empowerment. Moreover, social workers today must continue to lobby, both formally and informally, for intervention on behalf of outgroups and low power groups. We must use our voices as instruments for social change encouraging and politicizing social work students in the academy and new colleagues in the field.

Furthermore, it behooves our schools of social work and those engaged in policy practice to model race work via research, scholarship, and direct practice. As social work touts the imperatives of evidence-based practice, we must be certain to ensure that out-groups are included in the research. Anything short of that is unacceptable and renders the "evidence" invalid and faulty. Research implications are clear. It is unethical to apply practice interventions that have been tested on one group to another and expect the same results. History and culture have already negated this approach.

Future research could benefit from efforts to measure the contemporary effects of institutionalized discrimination and oppression and their effects on out-groups. Research should also include studying contemporary social work policy practice strategies to gauge their effectiveness and to improve and better target change activities. Our research should also involve analyzing evidence-based social work interventions to ensure that out-groups are appropriated represented and that application of the intervention is effective and does not further victimize vulnerable populations.

⦚ CONCLUƒION

African American female reformers were loathe to tolerate Jim Crow laws. They mobilized to fight these oppressive laws and policies on every front. They worked individually and via their webs of affiliation. Their efforts included nondramatic protest as well as aggressive and vehement resistance.

As with any intelligentsia, they did not always agree on strategy or tactic; nonetheless, they worked together with incredible adroitness and strategic subterfuge to ensure the sustainability of their families and communities. For them, issues of race were far more important that issues of gender, yet enmeshed in the politics of respectability, they especially targeted the uprightness of womanhood as essential to their work and engaged in their resistance movement with the *righteous discontent* of a people who knew that they deserved better.

⦚ REFERENCEƒ

Allen, J., Als, H., Lewis, J., & Litwack, L. (2000). *Without sanctuary: Lynching photography in America.* Santa Fe, NM: Twin Palms Publishers.

Barusch, A. (2009). *Foundations of social policy: social justice in human perspective.* Belmont, CA: Brooks/Cole.

Bay, M. (2009). *To tell the truth freely: The life of Ida B. Wells.* New York: Hill and Wang.

Bent-Goodley, T. (2001). Ida B. Wells-Barnett: An uncompromising style. In. I. Carlton-LaNey (Ed.), *African American leadership: An empowerment tradition in social welfare history* (pp. 87–98). Washington, DC: NASW Press.

Brice, T. (2005). "Disease and delinquency know no color line." Syphilis and African American female delinquency. *Affilia: Journal of Women and Social Work, 20,* 300–315.

Bundles, A. (2001). *On her own ground: The life and times of Madam C. J. Walker.* New York: Scribner.

Carlton-LaNey, I. (1997). Elizabeth Ross Haynes: An African American reformer of womanist consciousness. *Social Work, 42,* 573–583.

Carlton-LaNey, I. (1999). African American social work pioneers' response to need. *Social Work, 44,* 311–322.

Carlton-LaNey, I. (2000). Women and interracial cooperation in establishing the Good Samaritan Hospital. *Affilia: Journal of Women and Social Work, 15*(1), 65–81.

Collins, P. (1990). *Black feminist thought.* New York: Routledge.

Evans, S. (2007). *Black women in the Ivory Tower 1850–1954: An intellectual history.* Gainesville, FL: University of Florida Press.

Fairclough, A. (2000). "Being in the field of education and also being a Negro . . . seems . . . tragic": Black teachers in the Jim Crow South. *The Journal of American History, 87,* 65–91.

Fairclough, A. (2001). *Better day coming: Black and equality 1890–2000.* New York: Penguin Group.

Fields, M. G. (1985). *Lemon Swamp and other places: A Carolina memoir.* New York: The Free Press.

Franklin, J., & Moss, A. (1994). *From slavery to freedom: A history of African Americans.* NY: McGraw-Hill.

Giddings, P. (2008). *Ida: A sword among lions.* New York: Amistad.

Giddings, P. (1984). *When and where I enter: The impact of Black women on race and sex in America.* New York: Bantam Books.

Gilmore, G. (1996). *Gender & Jim Crow: Women and the politics of white supremacy in North Carolina, 1896–1920.* Chapel Hill: University of North Carolina Press.

Giovanni, N. (1988). *Scared cow . . . and other edibles.* New York: Quill/William Morrow.

Haynes, E. R. (n.d.). *Women aspire for political plums.* New Heaven, CT: Yale University, James Weldon Johnson Memorial Collection.

Higginbotham, E. (1993). *Righteous discontent: The women's movement in the Black Baptist Church, 1880–1920.* Cambridge, MA: Harvard University Press.

Hine, D. (1989). Rape and the inner lives of Black women in the Middle West. *Signs, 14,* 912–920.

Hine, D., Hine, W., & Harrold, S. (2008). *The African American odyssey.* Upper Saddle River, NJ: Pearson/Prentice Hall.

How Did Black Women in the NAACP Promote the Dyer Anti-Lynching Bill, 1918–1923? (n.d.). Retrieved January 23, 2009, from the Women and Social Movements, 1600–2000, website: http://womhist.alexanderstreet.com/lynch/intro.htm

Lerner, G. (Ed.) (1972). *Black women in white America: A documentary history.* New York: Vintage Books Edition.

Marlowe, G. (1993). Maggie Lena Walker. In D. Hine, E. Brown, & R. Terborg-Penn (Eds.), *Black Women in America: An historical encyclopedia* (pp. 1214–1219). Bloomington: Indiana University Press.

McMurry, L. (1998). *To keep the waters troubles: The Life of Ida B. Wells.* New York: Oxford University Press.

Meier, A., & Rudwick, E. (2002). *Along the color line: Explorations in the black experience.* Urbana: University of Illinois Press.

Mosley, M. (1996). A new beginning: The story of the National Association of Colored Graduate Nurses, 1908–1951. *Journal of the National Black Nurses Association, 8*(1), 20–32.

Perry, T., & Davis-Maye, D. (2007). Bein' womanish: Womanist efforts in child saving during the progressive era the founding of Mt. Meigs Reformatory. *Affilia: Journal of Women and Social Work, 22,* 209–219.

Prestage, J. (1995). In quest of African American political women. In T. Rueter (Ed.), *The politics of race: African Americans and the political system* (pp. 169–184). New York: M. E. Sharpe.

Rabinowitz, H. (1976). From exclusion to segregation: Southern race relations, 1865–1890. *The Journal of American History, 63,* 325–350.

Ross, E. (1978). *Black heritage in social welfare 1860–1930.* Lanham, MD: The Scarecrow Press.

Ruef, M., & Fletcher, B. (2003). Legacies of American slavery: Status attainment among southern blacks after emancipation. *Social Forces, 82,* 445–480.

Salem, D. (1990). *To better our world: Black women in organized reform, 1890–1920.* New York: Carlson Publishing.

Schiele, J., Jackson, S., & Fairfax, C. (2005). Maggie Lena Walker and African American Community Development. *Affilia, 20,* 21–38.

Soule, S. (1992). Populism and black lynching in Georgia, 1890–1900. *Social Forces, 71,* 431–449.

Taylor, U. (2000). "Negro Women are Great Thinkers as well as Doers": Amy Jacques-Garvey and community feminism in the United States, 1924–1927. *Journal of Women's History, 12,* 104–124.

Terborg-Penn, R. (2005). Suffrage. In D. Hine (Ed.), *Black women in America* (2nd ed., pp. 200–207). New York: Oxford University Press.

Waite, C. (2001). The segregation of black students at Oberlin College after Reconstruction. *History of Education Quarterly, 41,* 344–364.

Waites, C. (2001). Victoria Earle Matthews: Residence and reform. In I. Carlton-LaNey (Ed.), *African American leadership: An empowerment tradition in social welfare history* (pp. 1–16). Washington, DC: NASW Press.

Walters, D. (2003). *White nationalism black interest: Conservative public policy and the Black community.* Detroit, MI: Wayne State University Press.

White, D. (1999). *Too heavy a load: Black women in defense of themselves 1894–1994.* New York: W. W. Norton.

3

Involuntary Commitment Policy

Disparities in Admissions of African American Men to State Mental Hospitals

King Davis, Allen N. Lewis Jr., Ning Jackie Zhang, and Albert Thompkins

Harold, a frail black man close to 45 years of age, stood motionless before the judge as he declared him so severely mentally ill that he constituted a danger to himself and to others. Harold did not deny that he had taken food from a store without paying or that he frequently panhandled on the main street of the city. But, he gave no indication that he heard the judge when he commented that Harold was a menace, once again homeless, unemployed, using drugs, and wandering the streets. When asked by the judge whether he wanted to go to the state hospital, Harold did not respond. He stood eerily motionless throughout the abbreviated proceedings as though in a catatonic stupor. The psychiatrist reported that throughout the mental status exam, Harold remained completely silent, inattentive, inappropriate, and seemingly out of touch. However, he was certain that the diagnosis was paranoid schizophrenia and recommended immediate hospitalization. In less than 5 minutes, the judge agreed to involuntarily commit Harold to Central State Hospital 30 miles south of Richmond. This was Harold's 10th involuntary commitment in just over 2 years.

⧚ INTRODUCTION

Harold's story is indicative of a major social problem in American society: involuntary commitment to state mental hospitals, especially of African American men. Between 2000 and 2009, the federal government completed critical new reports on the linkages between race and mental illness (Department of Health and Human Services, 2001), issued the New Freedom Commission Report (NTAC; 2004), and passed an expanded version of mental health parity legislation (Wellstone & Domenici, 2008). The Center for Mental Health Services followed completion of the New Freedom Report with an effort to achieve twin nationwide goals of transformation of mental health systems and recovery by consumers. Following the shooting deaths of students and faculty at Virginia Tech University by an untreated mentally ill person, the Virginia legislature introduced an omnibus mental health policy bill to ease involuntary commitment criteria, clarify the responsibility of community treatment programs, and expand the state's right to exchange information between different segments of the mental health network (Cohen, Bonnie, & Monahan, 2008; Virginia General Assembly, 2008).

There were also updated research findings on the epidemiology of mental health problems and service usage in the population of the United States (Kessler et al., 2005; Wang et al., 2005; Wang et al., 2006). These studies reconfirmed that close to 25 percent of the U.S. population of adults will contract a mental health problem in their lives (American Psychiatric Association, 2000). There was also progress in development of the concepts of cultural competency and evidence-based practices and their relevancy across cultural, ethnic, and racial groups (Whaley & Davis, 2007). Frank and Glied (2006) chronicled the extent of these and related changes over the past 50 years. In their retrospective analysis, they identify major transformations in public policy, financing, shifts in power, alterations in the workforce, new pharmaceutical discoveries, and changes in the locus of care from inpatient to outpatient. Frank and

Glied, however, propose that some of the inveterate power and authority of the state has shifted to the federal government as a larger proportion of state mental health expenditures is offset by federal funds (Mark, Coffey, Vandivort-Warren, Harwood, & King, 2005). These authors conclude that overall mental health care in the United States has shown improvements in key areas over the past 50 years and in the first decade of the new century.

Manderscheid, Attay, and Rider (2009) recently examined specific trends in utilization of state mental hospitals and uncovered a significant reversal to the trends noted by Frank and Glied (2006). Manderscheid et al. distinguishes between persons admitted to state mental hospitals and persons who remain as residents for an extended period. The number of residents has declined steadily since 1958 starting in the Eisenhower administration and publication of Action for Mental Health (Joint Commission on Mental Illness and Health, 1961). Overall, admissions to public mental hospitals reflected a similar pattern of decline a decade later, and the slope of decline was equivalent to that of long-term residents. It appeared from data over the past 40 to 50 years that state hospitals would house significantly fewer individuals and might eventually close (Isaac & Armat, 1990).

The recent increase in admissions threatens these predictive policy assertions. Manderscheid et al. (2009) expresses concern that the pattern of declining psychiatric admissions, started in 1968, has been significantly reversed. Furthermore, Manderscheid et al. note that overall admissions to state mental hospitals increased by 21 percent since 2000. However, the trends toward increased voluntary and involuntary admissions are far from uniform and show continuation of long-term disparities by gender, race, and ethnicity (Manderscheid & Sonnenschein, 1987). The significance of these long-term disparities is easily lost in the angst over the reversal in the long-term decline of admissions to state mental facilities and the potential harm to more liberal commitment policies implemented since 1975 (Isaac & Armat, 1990). Consequently, there is an urgent need to identify, examine, contextualize historically, and discuss the continued disparities in voluntary and involuntary psychiatric admissions by gender, race, and ethnicity as potential factors in reversing long-term public mental health policy, increasing advocacy and voluntary participation, and planning new policy directions for the next decade of this century. By doing this, this chapter examines the racial, ethnic, and gender control features of these psychiatric admissions policies and offers some ideas to resist and change them.

\\\\ RACE AND PSYCHIATRIC ADMISSIONS

State psychiatric hospitalization in the United States began in the Commonwealth of Virginia in 1765 with the opening of Eastern Lunatic Asylum (Dain, 1968). This 18th-century Virginia asylum was an outgrowth of legislative and public fear about the potential for dangerousness, violence, and dependency of persons with severe mental illnesses (Dain, 1968). Virginia's legislative policies not only created the first state mental institution in America but also helped to link the concept of severe mental illness with dangerousness, violence, gender, social class, and race in the perception of the public (Phelan & Link, 1998). Initially, Virginia law assumed that only white men were vulnerable to problems of mental illness, and restricted access to state hospital services to others. However, by the middle of the 19th century, the perception of vulnerability to mental illness shifted and gave rise to state policies that would have a significant impact on increasing the social control of African American men well into the 21st century.

Affixing images of dangerousness, deviancy, and mental illness to newly released African American male slaves reinforced societal fear and rationalized the initiation of disproportionate usage of involuntary commitment (and institutionalization generally) as a solution, albeit more for control than treatment. The rapid growth in the number of prisons, local jails, orphanages, almshouses, tuberculosis sanatoria, and state mental institutions appeared to offer political solace to a fearful public as well as jobs and revenue in predominately rural local economies (Rothman, 1970).

Up to 1800, most admissions to state mental institutions were voluntary, sought either by the individual with a mental illness or pursued by a family member. As the public fear of mental illness increased, the Virginia legislature passed the first statutes in the United States in 1806 that allowed the state to involuntarily commit persons considered as severely mentally ill for an indeterminate period (Bell, 1980; Deutsch, 1949; *Wyatt v. Stickney*, 2010). However, passage of the involuntary commitment statute and its application to newly freed African men at the end of slavery in 1865 seemed to shift the preponderance of public fear and psychiatric admissions in the United States disproportionately toward race just at the time this population was extended the right to vote and equal protection.

The Virginia Legislature acted on pseudo-scientific predictions that former male slaves were particularly vulnerable to psychiatric imbalance and could constitute a danger and risk (Aptheker, 1943; Hampton

Institute, 1940; Jordan, 1968). Thus, former male slaves had to be controlled by a series of public policies that provided structure, a modicum of health/psychiatric care, and safety for the general public. The Central Lunatic Asylum for Colored Insane fulfilled part of the policy mandate of the Virginia Legislature as well as the concerns of the Freedman's Bureau (Drewry, 1916).

From 1865 to 1965, the rates of admissions to psychiatric facilities by race increased substantially, greatly exceeding the proportion of blacks (men and women) in the population of the United States. This disparity has remained a major feature of mental health care, as revealed in the most recent data on admissions (Manderscheid, Atay, & Rider, 2009; Schacht & Higgins, 2002). A variety of studies at the state level documented the exceptionally high rates of admissions of African Americans, particularly males in urban areas, throughout the majority of the 20th century. Lindsey and Paul (1989) and Rosenfield (1984) conducted studies that showed African American males at almost double the risk of involuntary commitment compared with European Americans when social class and diagnosis were controlled. These authors proposed that findings from earlier studies should not be the basis for public policy, because the primary contributive factors reflect what the authors called racial labeling in the pathway to care.

\\\\ CHANGE/ AND TREND/ IN OVERALL ADMI//ION/ TO /TATE MENTAL HO/PITAL/

The number of state mental institutions and the number of admissions of African Americans climbed steadily in the 20th century (Deutsch, 1948; Grob, 1973; Manderscheid et al., 2009). Admissions of African Americans maintained their disproportionately high rates throughout the first half of the 20th century, reflecting the predictions made by Cartwright (1851) and Jarvis (1844) in the 19th century. By the mid-1950s, the number of residents of state mental institutions in the United States approached 600,000 persons (Joint Commission on Mental Illness and Health, 1961), and the number of state mental hospitals across the nation reached more than 350 (Manderscheid et al., 2009). The costs of these increased admissions and longer lengths of stay were close to $6,000 per person per year midway through the 20th century, with all funds derived from state general fund budgets without federal financial participation until the passage of Medicare and Medicaid legislation in 1965. The financial impact of state hospitalization influenced states to accept desegregation and deinstitutionalization. However, few studies of the differential impact of these two policy decisions have been made on the disproportionately large population of African Americans formerly housed in state mental institutions. Deinstitutionalization appeared unplanned and uncoordinated, potentially contributing to the problem of displacement and homelessness of low-income African American populations in urban areas.

A cursory review of the data on admissions (Table 3.1) to inpatient psychiatric facilities (Manderscheid & Sonnenschein, 1987; Scheffler, 1991; Snowden & Cheung, 1990) shows the disproportionately high rates of admissions by race to all types of facilities in the 1980s. These data (Snowden & Cheung, 1990; Snowden & Holschuh, 1992) show that between 1980 and 1992, the rate of admissions for all persons to state hospitals in the United

Table 3.1	Admission Rates per 100,000 to State Hospitals in 1980 by Gender, Race, and Ethnicity

Population	Rates per 100,000
African Americans	364.2
Male	512.7
Female	233.5
Native Americans	306.4
Male	381.1
Female	234.1
Hispanic Americans	146.0
Male	206.3
Female	88.8
European Americans	136.8
Male	182.2
Female	94.1
Asian Americans	75.4
Male	104.2
Female	48.8
All Populations	163.6
Male	219.8
Female	111.1

States was approximately 163.6 per 100,000. However, the admissions rate to state hospitals for consumers of African descent for those same years was 364.2 per 100,000 (Manderscheid & Sonnenschein, 1987).

When age is considered, the long-term relationship between admissions to psychiatric hospitals and race and gender is more pronounced. For example, the rate of admissions to state psychiatric hospitals for African American males between the ages of 18 to 24 was 598 per 100,000, while the national mean rate was 163.6 (Manderscheid & Sonnenschein, 1987). The most excessive rate found was for male consumers of African descent between the ages of 25 to 44, where 753 per 100,000 were admitted to state psychiatric hospitals (Manderscheid & Sonnenschein, 1987). Although admissions are not indicative of actual prevalence rates of mental illness in the population, the data demonstrate a clear pattern of inpatient utilization differentiated by race, gender, and class.

Manderscheid et al. (2009) reported on recent trends in admissions and residents of state mental hospitals at the start of the 21st century. These authors note that for the past 38 to 40 years, the annual number of admissions has declined steadily, along with the number of long-term residents and the number of institutions. However, their research found that between 2002 and 2005, annual admissions actually increased by 21 percent. Although the authors identify this reversal in admissions as noteworthy, there are significant variations and patterns in race, ethnicity, and admissions shown in Table 3.2. These are important markers that should be considered in determining the direction for future public mental health policies.

It is this recent overall increase that has raised concerns about the need to revisit policy. However, the underlying concern could be the potential increases in costs. In the period from 2002 to 2005, the average cost per admission was $191,000, based on the number of admissions (47,000) and the gross national mental health budget of 9 billion dollars. As admissions rise, states and the federal government become concerned that their obligations to meet these costs versus further investments in community alternatives may be compromised. Changes in admissions offer insight into this policy dilemma. The number of admissions of Asian Americans declined by 65 percent during the years 2002 to 2005, while the number of admissions for African Americans increased by only 10 percent. These are significant reversals in earlier patterns for these two groups. It is unclear what factors are influencing these changes in rates in the three highest ranking groups or in the major decline in the Asian American population or the modest decline in African Americans.

| Table 3.2 | Admissions to State Mental Institutions by Race, 2002–2005 |

Groups	Admits in 2002	Admits in 2005	% Change	% of All Admits in 2002	% of All Admits in 2005	Change in All Admits	% Change in All Admits
African Americans	46,639	51,261	9.9%	29.94%	27.17%	4,622	-9.25% (-2.77)
American Indians	2,284	3,069	34.4%	1.46%	1.62%	785	10.96% (0.16)
Asian Americans	6, 310	2,184	-65.4%	4.05%	1.15%	-4,126	-71.6% (-2.90)
Hispanic Americans	10,534	14,433	37.0%	6.76%	7.65%	3,899	13.1% (0.89)
European Americans	89,973	117,702	30.8%	57.77%	62.03%	27,729	7.3% (4.26)
Totals	155,740	188,649	21.13%			32,909	21.13%

Could the increase in admissions be a reflection of major changes in the American economy, a substantial increase in stress for Hispanic American groups, or are the increases in admission for Native Americans a reflection of dual diagnoses? Table 3.3 shows the admissions numbers by year and for five racial/ethnic groups.

It is unclear from these studies what factors affect the number or rank order of admissions by ethnicity, race, or language spoken. The consistency of the data over many decades raises numerous questions about the structure of mental health systems and their ability to provide services to populations of color without prejudice or clinical unfairness. Increasingly, the role of involuntary commitment policies seems important.

Table 3.4 presents admissions percentages by race for 2002 and compares these percentages with the group's proportion in the U.S. population. In 2002, 29.94 percent of all admissions to state mental institutions were African Americans. However at the time, this group represented only 12 percent of the population of the United States, and African American males less than 6 percent of the total population. This is the clearest and most sustained disparity pattern in the data. By 2005, 27.17 percent of all admissions were African Americans, approximately a 2.8

Table 3.3	Number of Admissions by Year, Race, and Ethnicity, 2002–2005		

Population	Admissions in 2002	Admissions in 2005	% Increased 2002–05
European Americans	89,973	117,702	30%
African Americans	46,639	51,261	9.9%
Hispanic Americans	10,534	14,433	37%
Asian Americans	6,310	2,134	−63%
Native Americans	2,284	3,068	34%
Total	155,740	188,649	21.13%

Table 3.4	Admissions by Year, Race, and Percentage of U.S. Population, 2002	

Population	% of Admissions in 2002	% of U.S. Population in 2002
European Americans	57.77%	75%
African Americans	29.94%	12.3%
Hispanic Americans	6.76%	12.6%
Asian Americans	4.05%	3.6%
Native Americans	1.46%	0.9%

percent reduction from 2002 but a 10 percent increase in the actual number of total admissions of all groups combined. During this period, the increase in the number of African American admissions was significantly lower than the expected frequency, although the rate remained disparate. A study by Schacht and Higgins (2002) found that the percentage of African Americans admitted to state mental institutions was three times their proportion in the general population of the United States.

In the most comprehensive study of race and admissions (Table 3.5), Lewis, Davis, and Zhang (2010) found that the percentage of African Americans admitted to the state's psychiatric hospitals was two times their number in the state's population over the period 1970 to 1990. The

Table 3.5	Admission Rates in Virginia by Race and Population, 1990			
1990	Virginia Population	Group's Percentage of Total Population of Virginia	Hospital Admissions	Percentage of Total Admissions in Virginia*
European Americans	4,791,739	76.19	68,653	63.54*
American Indians	15,282	0.24	135	0.12*
Asian Americans	159,053	2.53	579	0.54*
African Americans	1,162,994	18.49	37,872	35.05*
Hispanic Americans	160,288	2.55	811	0.75*
Total	6,289,356	100	108,050	100

*Note: The differences between these percentages are statistically significant.

differences were statistically significant. These findings parallel earlier studies that showed a disproportionate, but unexplained, rate of admissions to state psychiatric hospitals by African Americans (Malzberg, 1953; Malzberg, 1959; Manderscheid & Sonnenschein, 1987; Pasamanick, 1959). One can assume that the pattern of admissions by race and gender, however, are linked to the utilization of involuntary commitments and the perpetuation of stereotypes of African American men generally as dangerous to others. The presence of severe mental illness increases the sense of danger.

\\\\ CHANGEſ AND TRENDſ IN LEGAL ſTATUſ

States have historically relied on four related statutory policies for managing admissions to its publicly funded mental hospitals. The long-term presence of these policies, and their ability to withstand most early 20th-century court challenges, reflects the continued control of public mental health policy and services by the state (*Olmstead v. L.C.*, 1999; Stewart, 1975; *Wyatt v. Stickney*, 2010).

Virginia was the first state to pass legislation (1806) allowing individuals to be committed to a mental institution against their will. The development of this coercive approach was viewed as necessary to protect the Commonwealth from an increasingly larger number of persons who were so mentally ill as to be unable to manage their own affairs. There was also a perception of a risk to the general public from violence by persons with lunacy who lacked the judgment to seek or accept voluntary status. The Virginia legislation prompted a number of actions nationally over the next century:

1. Every state developed an involuntary commitment statute based to some extent on the Virginia law;

2. Court challenges to coercive commitments have increased throughout the United States, resulting in numerous changes to the earlier laws and a shift towards outpatient commitments and a liberalization of the policy;

3. The commitment statutes have been applied unevenly, with disproportionately higher rates for African American men than for other populations;

4. Involuntary commitments have become the predominant method of admitting individuals, regardless of race, to state mental hospitals.

Two overlapping forms of voluntary admissions to state mental hospitals exist: Individuals can voluntarily request admission, or a relative, policy officer, or public official can request that a person be voluntarily admitted. There are also two forms of involuntary admission: a court can order that a person be civilly committed; and, a court can involuntarily commit a person accused of a criminal act. This latter type of admission is seen as the most severe and usually results in the person being confined to a secure forensic unit within a state mental hospital. To be civilly committed, an individual must be considered a danger to self or others or must be too gravely disabled to care for themselves as in the California commitment statutes (Gottstein, 2009). The new Virginia commitment statutes have discarded the concept of "imminent danger" to likelihood of future harm (Cohen et al., 2008).

Rosenfield's 1984 study of involuntary admissions in New York City was one of the earliest efforts to investigate the relationship between gender, race, and involuntary commitments. Rosenfield sought to test a number of hypotheses as well as determine the extent to which labeling theory helped to explain the disproportionate admissions by gender and race. Her study found that gender was an important predictive factor in involuntary admissions. African American men were two to three times more likely to be admitted involuntarily than other populations. In addition, Rosenfield found that the risk of involuntary commitment for African American men increased when their path to evaluation and treatment involved the police and when they were examined by European male physicians.

Ramm (1989) indicated that the risk of involuntary commitments of African Americans increased depending on the region and state in which the commitment took place. He proposed that involuntary commitments of African Americans were most likely in the deep southern states, with almost twice the number of involuntary commitments among African Americans as European Americans. The pattern identified by Ramm reflects the initial southern post–Civil War racial fears, the southern origins of the involuntary commitment statute, and the origins of mental hospitalization segregated by race. Although initiated in the 19th century, these idiosyncratic polices bode poorly for African American men. However, Davies, Thornicroft, Lessem, Higginbotham, and Phelan (1996b) found that in European countries, particularly Britain, the use of involuntary commitments was highest among African Caribbean immigrants than for other populations.

Schacht and Higgins (2002) gathered and analyzed data from the national database of state mental health programs to explore the overall usage of involuntary admissions (Table 3.6).

These authors found that the United States continues to use involuntary admissions far more frequently than other nations. For example, whereas involuntary admissions account for only 10 percent of admissions in Europe, Schacht and Higgins (2002) found that 83 percent of all admissions in the United States were involuntary. Schacht and Higgins also found that there were some distinct differences in the use of involuntary criminal versus involuntary civil statues with regard to race, ethnicity, and admissions (see Table 3.7). The authors were uncertain what factors explain the variation in use of involuntary commitments (Schacht & Higgins, 2002).

Table 3.6	Distribution of State Hospital Admissions by Type

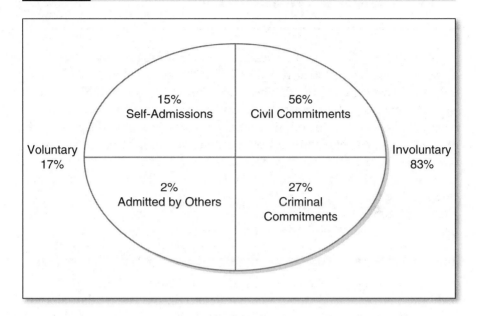

Table 3.7	Legal Status by Race and Admission, 2002

Group	Voluntary Self	Voluntary by Other	Involuntary Civil	Involuntary Criminal	Total Involuntary
African American	14%	2%	52%	33%	85%
American Indian	16%	6%	57%	22%	79%
Asian/Pacific Islander	12%	1%	41%	47%	88%
Hispanic	17%	1%	46%	36%	82%
White	15%	3%	59%	23%	82%
Other	13%	2%	55%	31%	86%
Total	15%	2%	56%	27%	83%

☒ CHANGEƒ AND TRENDƒ IN DIAGNOƒEƒ ON ADMIƒƒION

Schacht and Higgins (2002) looked at data on admissions from 215 mental health facilities in 2002. In that year, the 215 facilities admitted 57,600 individuals over the age of 18. The most significant finding in their study was the frequency of schizophrenia as a diagnosis at admission of individuals regardless of race or ethnic background. For example, 68 percent of Asian Americans were admitted with a diagnosis of schizophrenia, while 65 percent of African Americans were similarly diagnosed (see Table 3.8).

Data drawn from the National Institute of Mental Health (Manderscheid & Sonnenschein, 1987) showed that African Americans were more frequently diagnosed on admission with severe mental illness than other ethnic or racial populations. Admissions of blacks to state mental hospitals showed that 56 percent of these individuals received a primary diagnosis of schizophrenia, while only 38 percent of all individuals admitted received a similar diagnosis. Hispanic Americans too received a disproportionately high rate (44 percent) of severe mental illness diagnoses on admission to state mental institutions. Flaskerud and Hu (1992), Garretson (1993), Jones and Gray (1986), and Lawson, Heplar, Holladay, and Cuffel (1994) concluded that the primary reason for the disproportionate rate of severe mental illness diagnoses are errors made by diagnosticians who are unfamiliar with mental illness as it is manifested in populations of color.

Findings from the nation's largest mental health database in Virginia also identified a disproportionate frequency of severe mental illness by race. In Table 3.9, the authors (Lewis et al., 2009) found

Table 3.8 Diagnosis of Schizophrenia at Admission, 2002 and 1985

	Diagnosis of Schizophrenia	
Population	2002	1985
Asian/Pacific Islanders	68%	32%
African Americans	65%	56%
Hispanic Americans	58%	44%
Euro-Americans	48%	31%
Native Americans	37%	32%
All Populations	38%	

Table 3.9 Diagnosis to Virginia State Hospitals by Race

	Paranoid Schizophrenia (295.30)	Paranoid Schizophrenia Severe With Psychotic Features (295.34)	Schizo-Affective Disorder (295.70)	Schizophrenia Undifferentiated (295.90)	Psychotic Disorder Not Otherwise Specified (298.90)	Group's Percentage of Total Population of Virginia
European Americans	N = 7,473	2,448	8,828	6,928	3,892	
	% = 51.40*	37.20*	53.62*	52.06*	49.76*	80.00
African Americans	N = 6,979	4,124	7,540	6,316	3,872	
	% = 48.00*	62.67*	45.63*	47.46*	49.50*	19.00
Totals	14,539	6,581	16,525	13,309	7,822	

Note: The numbers for the "Other" category that include Hispanic Americans, Asian Americans, and Native Americans are not reflected in this table, though they are included in the totals.

Chi-square statistics: DF = 18, P-value < .0001.

*The differences between these percentages are statistically significant.

statistically significant differences by race in the diagnosis of severe mental illness.

⟨⟨ REJIJTING DIJPARITIEJ IN INVOLUNTARY COMMITMENT POLICY

Involuntary commitment to psychiatric hospitals has a significant impact on individuals regardless of gender, race, or ethnicity. However, the long history of disproportionately higher rates of voluntary and involuntary commitments of African American men raises multiple questions about racial bias, impact, and strategies for change. Involuntary institutionalization is an extreme form of social and physical control that relies on predictions of dangerousness to remove and displace individuals from their communities and life patterns. The use of dangerousness criteria and involvement with the police and courts helps to perpetuate the negative societal imagery of African American men and helps to rationalize the removal of their human and civil rights through the use of the involuntary statute. In doing so, African American men spend longer than average lengths of stay in state mental institutions and suffer a loss of personal control of their lives, loss of the right to vote, and may be forced to use psychotropic medications. Rosenfield (1987) documents the extent to which race plays such an instrumental role in removing the rights of African American men suspected of being a danger to self or others as viewed through the eyes of the judicial system. This pattern of disproportionate admissions has been operative since 1870.

Numerous challenges have been made to force changes in the content, implementation, and outcomes of involuntary commitment policies in the United States over the period from 1970 to 2008. (See Table 3.10 for 2002 and 2005 data.) Few of these challenges have been based on racial disparities. Legal challenges in the state and federal courts, advocacy by family and consumer organizations, and university research outcomes have forced individual states to abandon some long-standing policies and practices that were considered unconstitutional (*Olmstead v. L.C.*, 1999; Stewart, 1975; *Wyatt v. Stickney*, 2010). After U.S. Supreme Court rulings in 1975, states gradually discontinued the practice of long-term confinement without treatment or discharge plans. In addition, states were forced through the Donaldson ruling (Stewart, 1975) to replace the concept of "inability to care for one's self" as the primary standard for involuntary commitment. An inability to care for self suggested that the individual lacked the capacity because of their mental illness to meet their needs in such a way to ensure their survival. Long-term questions about mental capacity have been projected onto African American men and used to rationalize various forms of inequity (Scott, 1997). In its stead, the court ruled that the concept of an "imminent danger to oneself or others" was a constitutionally valid basis for involuntary commitment that had the effect of reducing the right to freedom but not the right to treatment. Regrettably, the insertion of concepts of danger and violence as the acceptable clinical standards that constitute a legal basis for involuntary commitment policies may have helped to solidify the perception of mental illness as a criminal act and as a threat to the safety of the general public (Phelan, 1998). The U.S. Supreme Court's emphasis on concepts of imminent danger and violence was based on the belief that clinicians could assess and predict the risk of violence with some reasonable accuracy (Stewart, 1975). However, where gender and race are concerned, the ability of clinicians to reach accurate diagnoses has been shown to be extremely limited (Jones & Gray, 1986; Lawson et al., 1994; Whaley, 2004).

State governments also introduced outpatient commitments as alternatives to inpatient hospitalization in response to court challenges to highly publicized crimes by persons with mental illness (Cooper, 2005; Steadman, Gounis, & Dennis, 2001; Telson, 2000). Although used in 38 states as an alternative to hospitalization, outpatient commitment and its clinical outcomes remain highly controversial because some versions permit forced pharmaceutical treatment and some have a disproportionate impact by gender and race (Rohland, Roher, & Richards, 2000).

Table 3.10	Number of Admissions by Year, Race, and Ethnicity, 2002 and 2005		
Population	Admissions in 2002	Admissions in 2005	% Increased 2002–2005
European Americans	89,973	117,702	30%
African Americans	46,639	51,261	9.9%
Hispanic Americans	10,534	14,433	37%
Asian Americans	6,310	2,134	−63%
Native Americans	2,284	3,068	34%
Total	155,740	188,649	21.13%

Recent changes in involuntary commitment policy rely on the concept of "future harm." As with the concept of imminent danger, the statute change assumes that mental health professionals can predict with some accuracy that an individual will act in a way that offers substantial future harm to himself or to others in the community. The concept of future harm seems to contradict the court ruling in 1975, which appeared to question whether rights could be restricted based on unscientific predictions of future behavior. The likelihood of a future violent perpetrated act by a mentally ill person gives the court and the community mental health organizations considerably greater latitude in assessing whether an individual should be committed. However, the absence of clear science also introduces the potential for bias in assessing future potential for harm. The disproportionate application of such a concept forms the basis of resistance and concern in both New York, in response to Kendra's Law (Cooper, 2005) and in California in response to the Assembly Bill 1421 that mandates Assisted Outpatient Treatment (AOT) (Beckley, 2008).

Despite the multiple changes in involuntary commitment policies throughout the United States over the last 30 years, several of the questionable racial outcomes of these policies have remained relatively unchanged. Although there has been considerable legal and scholarly opposition to involuntary inpatient and outpatient commitment, close to 85 percent of all admissions in the first decade of this century have been involuntary—civil or criminal (Schacht & Higgins, 2002). This compares with 10 percent for European nations. The recent changes in the Virginia statute suggest an even greater ease of applying involuntary commitment. In addition, the percentage of African Americans admitted to state mental hospitals remains two to three times their numbers in the general population, a disturbing trend that was initiated decades ago. Findings from the Commonwealth of Virginia's long-term database show these patterns as early as 1900 (Central State Hospital, 1917) through the 1990s (Lewis et al., 2009). Although state government eschews comparing the rate of admissions with population size, it is a reasonable statistic because several recent studies reconfirm that there is no statistical difference in rates of illness by race (Kessler et al., 2005) unless there is a major traumatic event (Kessler, Galea, Jones, & Parker, 2006). An important reason for the continued disproportionate number of African American admissions is the use of involuntary commitment statutes, findings of bias in clinical evaluations, and involvement of police officers in varying phases of the path of treatment (Chun-Chung Chow, Jaffee, & Snowden, 2003; Davies, Thornicroft, Lessem, Higginbotham, & Phelan, 1996a; Jones & Gray, 1986; Lawson et al., 1994; Lindsey &

Paul, 1989; Phelan & Link, 1998; Whaley, 2004). The sudden increase in involuntary criminal commitments of both Asian American and Hispanic American consumers raises new questions of legal fairness in the utilization of these laws.

After decades of successful lawsuits challenging involuntary commitments, there is no national public policy governing involuntary commitments or challenges to the continued racial bias that has been so overt. Commitment policy remains under the aegis of state governments but subject to periodic external court rulings that bring about incremental changes in their content, practice, implementation, and effects. Rulings by the courts have been applied to constitutional rights and guarantees that affect all mental health consumers and their families. However, mental health advocacy in African American and other communities of color seems to be a low priority. Challenges and resistance have tended to derive from organizations outside of these communities and without leadership from their professional mental health organizations (social work, rehabilitation counseling, psychology, and psychiatry). No sustained movement has been launched in the African American community that seeks to narrow the disproportionate application of involuntary commitment laws. In 2005, efforts by African American groups to stop Assembly Bill 1421 in California or prevent the long-term extension of Kendra's Law in New York were unsuccessful and had limited support within the community. In both states, community groups cited the disproportionate impact on African Americans with mental illness but were unable to sustain an advocacy drive.

⁑ PARTICIPATION IN POLICY CHANGE EFFORTS BY AFRICAN AMERICAN ORGANIZATIONS

The risk of involuntary commitment is significant for African American men like Harold who have been frequent residents of state hospitals and involved in numerous court hearings to determine their mental status. Involuntary commitment is but one of numerous policies developed by states that have major risks for African American men with serious mental illness. Is mental health care a civil right? Is access to accurate diagnoses a constitutionally guaranteed provision? Are there protections for persons who are brought before the courts to be evaluated for involuntary commitment that can change their lives? In response to these questions generally, there have been major legal challenges that have modified the public mental health policies in every state. However, the involvement of African American organizations in the process of resistance and change in this and related mental health policies is fragmented, underdeveloped, inconsistent, and given a low priority.

African Americans have two related approaches to advocate for changes in public mental health policy at the local, state, or federal level. The first type is internal in which change strategies are developed, implemented, supported, and evaluated separately by African American organizations. Internal strategies can be developed and guided by professional guild organizations or by groups of consumers or family members or through collaboration. Internal strategies are often dependent on corresponding funding strategies that rely on resource generation within this community and its members. In some instances, the financial resources are obtained through memberships, donations, fund-raising events, conferences, or external grants. A number of African American guild organizations were developed during the mid-1960s and continue to make sporadic efforts to influence public mental health policy: Black Psychiatrists of America, Association of Black Psychologists, Association of Black Social Workers, and the Black Nurses Associations. An evaluation of most of the guild organizations shows that each suffers from being undercapitalized. The organizations have been unable to maintain a paid staff and have limited mechanisms for obtaining funding on an ongoing basis. As a result their ability to maintain a regular presence in either the state capitals or in Washington is severely limited. The research centers have fared considerably better. Each has been able to obtain federal, state, and foundations funding to allow development of clear research agendas that examine clinical services and public policy issues, particularly around Medicaid.

In addition, to the guild organizations a small number of policy and research groups have developed and play a major role in providing data that has the potential to influence public policy in mental health. These include the University of Michigan Center for Research on Ethnicity, Culture, and the Center for Mental Health Services Research at Berkeley, the University of Pittsburgh's Center for the Study of Race and Social Problems, and the Department of Psychiatry and Behavioral Science at Howard University. Each of these research centers builds on the policy orientation and interests of the lead researchers who helped to develop their focus and agenda and their principal external funding sources. There have been several family and consumer groups who have sought to influence public mental health policy, but almost all of these groups have had considerable difficulty identifying financial resources and evaporated between 1999 and 2005.

One of the more innovative internal efforts to influence public mental health policy stems from the National Leadership Council (NLC) that formed in 2001. This national group was created to build a national policy development process by bringing many of the other national African American organizations together under a single policy umbrella. The NLC is the only African American mental health organization that seeks to build such a broad-based coalition that cuts across the range of African American organizations. Once it was incorporated, the organization grew rapidly but has recently been unable to generate financial support to maintain its staff and nationally focused mission. Few of the national civil rights organizations have placed importance on mental health policy issues that appear incompatible with their civil rights orientation and focus. Overall, the influence of internal organization efforts on public policy has been minimal, with little enthusiasm that these groups will have a decided influence in the near future.

The major impact on public mental health policy in the United States has come through organizations external to the African American community. The Bazelon Center, the National Alliance for the Mentally Ill, Mental Health America, the National Association of State Mental Health Program Directors, the National Association of Community Behavioral Health, the Carter Center, Institute of Medicine, and several mental health policy centers have been the major sources of policy change. The actions, involvement, and budgets of these organizations contribute to their ability to hire the staff to provide a consistent presence at both the state and federal governmental levels. African American mental health issues profit directly from the activities of these groups.

Mental health policy has not been an issue of major importance of discussion in African American communities or within the civil rights organizations that led these communities for decades. The stigma that accompanies mental illness may be the key factor that explains the absence of attention to mental illness. However, the long-term struggle for basic civil rights that were denied to African Americans is a logical explanation for the priority given to these issues vis-à-vis mental health. In the current climate, it may be prudent for the various African American mental health organizations to merge their interests and resources in an effort to build a single viable organization that can take the leadership in collaboration with external organizations in the non-governmental sector where the most substantive involvement in public mental health policy continues to be crafted.

⟋ INFORMING SOCIAL WORK PRACTICE AND RESEARCH

Severe and persistent mental illness has presented a formidable set of challenges to the United States since the 18th century. In response to increasing numbers of mentally ill, the southern states and eventually the nation developed a variety of working assumptions to both explain the frequency and distribution of such illnesses in the population as well as guide treatment, prevention, and ensure public safety.

Africans in America were one of the no-status groups seen as immune from the vagaries of mental illness because they were not legally allowed to own property or participate in commerce for close to 100 years. However, as the Civil War came to closure, new hypotheses about the distribution of mental illness in the population were proposed but with fewer connections to involvement in commerce. These newer perspectives offered dire predictions of exaggerated rates of illness within Africans in American owing to a weaker mental capacity and a loss of structure (Scott, 1997). Beliefs about the vulnerability and risk of Africans in America were subsequently reflected in excessive rates of mental hospitalization, followed by high rates of sterilization, long lengths of stay, high rates of death, and involuntary commitments (Central State Hospital, 1917). The terse predictions of Cartwright (1851) and Babcock (1895) were indirectly reinforced through the rate of inpatient admissions and the deleterious impact on newly reformed families and communities. From 1865 to 1965, their hypotheses covertly formed the basis of state mental health policy (U.S. Congress, 1963).

After these false hypotheses were invalidated (Fischer, 1969; Kessler & Neighbors, 1986; Kessler, Abelson, & Zhao, 1998; Kramer, Von Korff, & Kessler, 1980), there were minimal changes in the rates of admission by gender, race, and ethnicity (Manderscheid & Sonnenschein, 1987). Midway through the 20th century, however, public policy turned toward deinstitutionalization. Because African Americans were disproportionately residents of state mental institutions, unplanned deinstitutionalization resulted in homelessness, jailing, idleness, and recidivism. At the close of the 20th century, mentally ill African American populations remained disproportionately residents of state mental institutions and disproportionately homeless (Folson et al., 2005). Their own civil rights organizations have not made disparities in involuntary commitments a high priority, nor does it appear that mental health generally has reached the level of priority as health disparities. Despite the Surgeon General's Report on Culture, Race, and Ethnicity, change in policy has been slow to occur.

What can social work do about these historically entrenched policy problems? First, social work offers a conceptualization for framing the multiple problems of disparities by gender, race, and ethnicity. Social justice is defined here as

> a basic value and desired goal in democratic societies and includes equitable and fair access to societal institutions, laws, resources, opportunities, rights, goods, services, and responsibilities for all groups and individuals without arbitrary limitations based on observed or interpretations of differences in age, color, culture, physical or mental disability, education, gender, income, language, national origin, race, religion or sexual orientation. (Davis, 2004, p. 236)

Social work can be instrumental in helping to increase the visibility of mental health disparities generally and involuntary commitments specifically within the nation. Social work can assist in raising the priority given to mental health causes within communities of color. Field placements in African American organizations and churches can be helpful in increasing the level of mental health literacy in these forums.

Social work's long-term investment in cultural competency and the parallel linkages to evidence-based practice is a valuable addition to the historical debate about disparities (Whaley & Davis, 2007). However, social work must broaden the research base of evidence-based practices to ensure that the populations that are included in samples of the models include populations of color. In addition, social work research must include practice-based evidence as a comparison with evidence based practice models.

Much of the early history of mental health care in the United States is parallel to the foci of social work. This includes the societal interest in work, productivity, community involvement, financial assistance, human rights, and recovery. Social work must continue to support various policies that both guarantee parity between health and mental health benefits, universal health coverage, and broadened support for reentry of persons with mental illness into their communities.

CONCLUSION

As Harold's commitment hearing neared its conclusion, the new medical director of the department of mental health stood and asked the court whether he could ask Harold a question. At the sound of his voice, Harold's demeanor changed. He recognized the physician by name, smiled, and indicated that he had missed seeing him in the community clinic, recalled the date of their last meeting well over a year before, and apologized for his appearance. He seemed clear, aware of the date, year, and time. His affect was no longer flat and he did not seem delusional or paranoid. The involuntary commitment to the state hospital was dismissed by the judge, and Harold was referred to the community mental health center for follow-up and his misdemeanor charges dropped. No advocacy organization from within Harold's community came forward to petition for an alternative resolution.

Several things emerged from the outcome of Harold's commitment hearing that has currency for this chapter. First, mental health advocacy is in exceptional short supply in African American communities. During the court hearing, Harold did not have advocates from the community who petitioned the court to consider other alternatives and options. The traditional civil rights and religious organizations were noticeably absent from this and all other hearings. Representatives of the Urban League were not there nor were the black mental health guilds. Nor were there advocates present prior to the hearing who questioned the repeated involuntary commitments that fall so disproportionately by race. The silence of the advocates on these issues in key forums reflects the low priority given mental health but also the elasticity of the community's boundaries and its ability to accept and manage behavior found unacceptable outside.

The court depended on the findings of the consulting psychiatrist and the police officers who were involved; each testified that Harold was a menace and potentially harmful to himself and the community at large. Could advocates have placed these assertions in another context? Could advocates have identified a viable alternative that would have protected Harold's rights but also brought him culturally appropriate care? Could there have been a system that did not rely on the police, whose involvement almost always assures commitment and heightens the risk of danger and harm? The court and its officers generally accepted the precedents that have been established for many years in processing individuals off the streets of the city, through the court system, and into the state hospital, even when there are numerous appearances by the same person in an abbreviated period. What is the cost of this repetitive circular process in human and financial resources? Ultimately who pays? What changed Harold's commitment hearing was the presence of administrative advocates who saw fragmentation in their own system, deplored the duplication of effort, questioned the limited time to make accurate assessment, abhorred the sheer waste of human life, and the rejection of the mental health turnstile for low-income African American men. These advocates recognized that meaningful change in the turnstile requires more than resistance. Substantive change requires a level of active and informed involvement in all phases of the court, police, and the treatment community based on a broad understanding, acceptance, and demand for social justice from within communities where disparities have a long and debilitating history.

⚞ REFERENCES

American Psychiatric Association. (2000). *Diagnostic and statistical manual of mental disorders* (4th ed., Text rev.). Washington, DC: Author.

Aptheker, H. (1943). *American negro slave revolts.* New York: International.

Babcock, J. W. (1895). The colored insane. In National Conference of Charities and Corrections (Ed.), *Proceedings* (pp. 184–186). Boston: National Conference of Charities and Corrections.

Beckley, N. (2008). *Threat to African Americans.* Los Angeles: The Church of Scientology International.

Bell, L. V. (1980). *Treating the mentally ill from colonial times to the present.* New York: Praeger.

Cartwright, S. (1851). Report on the diseases and physical peculiarities of the Negro Race. *New Orleans Medical Surgical Journal, 7,* 692–705.

Central State Hospital. (1917). *Forty-seventh annual report* (Rep. No. 47). Richmond, VA: Superintendent of Public Documents.

Chun-Chung Chow, J., Jaffee, K., & Snowden, L. (2003). Racial/ethnic dispariites in the use of mental health services in poverty areas. *American Journal of Public Health, 93,* 792–797.

Cohen, B. J., Bonnie, R. J., & Monahan, J. (2008). *Understanding and applying Virginia's new statutory civil commitment criteria.* Unpublished manuscript.

Cooper, M. (2005, April 7). Racial disproportion seen in applying Kendra's Law. *The New York Times,* p. B-4.

Dain, N. (1968). *History of Eastern State Hospital.* Williamsburg, VA: Colonial Williamsburg Foundation.

Davies, S., Thornicroft, G., Lessem M., Higginbotham, A., & Phelan, M. (1996a). Ethnic differences in risk of compulsory psychiatric admission among representative cases of psychosis in London. *British Medical Journal, 312*(2), 533–536.

Davies, S., Thornicroft, G., Lessem M., Higginbotham, A., & Phelan, M. (1996b). Ethnic differences in risk of compulsory psychiatric admission among representative cases of psychosis in London. *British Medical Journal, 312*(2), 533–536.

Davis, K. (2004). Social work's commitment to social justice. In K. Davis & T. Bent-Goodley (Eds.), *The color of social policy* (pp. 229–244). Alexandria, VA: Council on Social Work Education.

Department of Health and Human Services, Substance Abuse and Mental Health Services Administration, Center for Mental Health Services. (2001). *Mental health: Culture, race, and ethnicity: A supplement to mental health: A report of the Surgeon General.* Rockville, MD: Author.

Deutsch, A. (1948). *The shame of the states.* New York: Harcourt Brace.

Deutsch, A. (1949). *The mentally ill in America: A history of their care and treatment from Colonial times* (2nd ed.). New York: Columbia University.

Drewry, W. F. (1916). *Central State Hospital* (Vol. III). Baltimore: Johns Hopkins University Press.

Fischer, J. (1969). Negroes, whites and rates of mental illness: Reconsideration of a myth. *Psychiatry, 32,* 438–446.

Flaskerud, J. H. & Hu, L. T. (1992). Relationship of ethnicity to psychiatric diagnosis. *Journal of Nervous and Mental Disease, 180,* 296–303.

Folson, D. P., Hawthorne, W., Lindamer, L., Gilmer, T., Bailey, A., Golshan, S., et al. (2005). Homelessness among patients in a public mental health system: prevalence, risk factors, and utilization of mental healthcare services among 10,340 patients. *American Journal of Psychiatry, 162,* 370–376.

Frank, R. G., & Glied, S. (2006). *Better but not well.* Baltimore: Johns Hopkins University Press.

Garretson, D. J. (1993). Psychological misdiagnosis of African Americans. *Journal of Multicultural Counseling and Development, 21,* 119–126.

Gottstein, J. B. (2009). *Psychiatry: Force of law.* Retrieved January 5, 2009, from http://psychrights.org/force_of_law.htm

Grob, G. (1973). *Mental institutions in America: Social policy to 1875.* New York: The Free Press.

Hampton Institute. (1940). *The negro in Virginia.* New York: Hastings House.

Isaac, R. J., & Armat, V. C. (1990). *Madness in the streets: How psychiatry and thelaw abandoned the mentally ill.* New York: The Free Press.

Jarvis, E. (1844). Insanity among the colored population of the free states. *American Journal of the Medical Sciences, 7,* 71–83.

Joint Commission on Mental Illness and Health. (1961). *Action for mental health.* New York: Science Editons.

Jones, B. E., & Gray, B. A. (1986). Problems in diagnosing schizophrenia and affective disorders among blacks. *Hospital and Community Psychiatry, 37,* 61–65.

Jordan, W. D. (1968). *White over black: American attitudes toward the negro, 1550–1812.* Chapel Hill: University of North Carolina Press.

Kessler, R. C., Abelson, J., & Zhao, S. (1998). The epidemiology of mental disorders. In J.Williams & K. Ell (Eds.), *Advances in mental health research: Implications for practice* (chap. 1). Washington, DC: NASW Press.

Kessler, R. C., Berglund, P., Demler, O., Jin, R., Merikangas, L. R., & Walters, E. E. (2005). Lifetime prevalence and age-of-onset distributions of DSM IV disorders in the National Comorbidity Survey replication. *Archives of General Psychiatry, 62,* 593–602.

Kessler, R. C., Galea, S., Jones, R. T., & Parker, H. A. (2006). Mental illness and suicidality after hurricane Katrina. *Bulletin of the World Health Organization, 84,* 930–939.

Kessler, R. C., & Neighbors, H. W. (1986). A new perspective on the relationships among race, social class and psychological distress. *Journal of Health and Social Behavior, 27,* 107–115.

Kramer, M., Von Korff, M., & Kessler, L. (1980). The lifetime prevalence of mental disorders: Estimation, uses and limitations. *Psychological Medicine, 10,* 429–436.

Lawson, W. B., Heplar, H., Holladay, J., & Cuffel, B. (1994). Race as a factor in inpatient and outpatient admissions and diagnosis. *Hospital and Community Psychiatry, 45,* 72–74.

Lewis, A., Davis, K., & Zhang, N. (in press). Admissions of African American men to psychiatric hospitals: Historical and current statistical trends. *International Journal of Public Policy.*

Lindsey, K. P., & Paul, G. L. (1989). Involuntary commitments to public mental institutions: Issues involving the overrepresentation of blacks and assessment of relevant functioning. *Psychological Bulletin, 106,* 171–183.

Malzberg, B. (1953). Mental diseases among Negroes in New York State, 1939–41. *Mental Hygiene, 37,* 450–476.

Malzberg, B. (1959). Mental disease among Negroes: An analysis of first admissions in New York State, 1949–1951. *Mental Hygiene, 43,* 422–459.

Manderscheid, R. W., Atay, J. E., & Rider, R. A. (2009). Changing trends in state psychiatric hospital use from 2002 to 2005. *Psychiatric Services, 60,* 29–34.

Manderscheid, R. W., & Sonnenschein, M. A. (1987). *Mental Health, United States, 1987.* Rockville, MD: U.S. Department of Health and Human Services.

Mark, T. L., Coffey, R. M., Vandivort-Warren, R., Harwood, H. J., & King, E. C. (2005). U.S. Spending for mental health and substance abuse treatment, 1991–2001. *Health Affairs,* pp. 133–142.

NTAC. (2004). Answering the challenge: Responses to the President's new Freedom Commission Final Report. *Network, 8.*

Olmstead v. L. C. (1999). 527 U.S. 58.

Pasamanick, B. A. (1959). A survey of mental disease in an urban population II: Prevalence by race and income. In B. A. Pasamanick (Ed.), *Epidemiology of mental disorder.* Washington, DC: American Association for the Advancement of Science.

Phelan, J. C., & Link, B. G. (1998). The growing belief that people with mental illnesses are violent: the role of the dangerousness criterion for civil commitment. *Social Psychiatry Psychiatric Epidemiology, 33,* S7–S12.

Ramm, D. (1989, Fall). Overcommitted. *Southern Exposure,* pp. 14–17.

Rohland, B. M., Roher, J. E., & Richards, C. C. (2000). The long-term effect of outpatient commitment on service use. *Administration and Policy in Mental Health, 27,* 283–294.

Rosenfield, S. (1984). Race differences in involuntary Hospitalization: Psychiatric vs. labeling perspectives. *Journal of Health and Social Behavior, 25,* 14–23.

Rothman, D. (1970). *The discovery of the asylum.* Boston: Little, Brown.

Schacht, L. M., & Higgins, K. M. (2002). *Race/ethnicity of clients served in state hospitals.* Alexandria, VA: NASHMPD Research Institute.

Scheffler, R. M. (1991). Differences in mental health service utilization among ethnic subpopulations. *International Journal of Law and Psychiatry, 14,* 363–376.

Scott, D. M. (1997). *Social policy and the image of the damaged black psyche 1880–1996.* Chapel Hill: University of North Carolina Press.

Snowden, L., & Cheung, F. (1990). Use of inpatient mental health services by members of minority groups. *American Psychologist, 45,* 291–298.

Snowden, L., & Holschuh, J. (1992). Ethnic differences in emergency psychiatric care and hosptialization in a program for the severely mentally ill. *Community Mental Health Journal, 28,* 281–291.

Steadman, H. J., Gounis, K., & Dennis, D. (2001). Assessing the New York City involuntary outpatient commitment pilot program. *Psychiatric Services, 52,* 330–336.

Stewart, W. F. (1975). *O'Connor v. Donaldson.* 563[422 U.S.], 575–576.

Telson, H. (2000). Outpatient Commitment in New York: From pilot program to state law. *George Mason University Civil Rights Law Journal, 11,* 41–82.

U.S. Congress. (1963). Mental Retardation Facilities and Community Mental Health Centers Construction Act of 1963. Public Law 88–164.

Virginia General Assembly. (2008). The Omnibus Mental Health Act. H 499, Chapter 1– Chapter 850. Code of Virginia (H 499).

Wang, P. S., Demler, O., Olfson, M., Pincus, H. A., Wells, K. B., & Kessler, R. C. (2006). Changing profiles of service sectors used for mental health care in the United States. *American Journal of Psychiatry, 163,* 1187–1198.

Wang, P. S., Lane, M., Olfson, M., Pincus, H. A., Wells, K. B., & Kessler, R. C. (2005). Twelve-month use of mental health services in the United States. *Archives of General Psychiatry, 62,* 629–640.

Wellstone, P., & Domenici, P. (2008). Wellstone and Domenici Mental Health Parity and Addiction Equity Act of 2008. 29 U.S.C. 1185a, 712. U.S.C.

Whaley, A. L. (2004). Paranoia in African-American men receiving inpatient psychiatric treatment. *American Academy of Psychiatry and the Law, 32,* 282–290.

Whaley, A. L., & Davis, K. (2007). Cultural competence and evidence based practice in mental health services: A complementary perspective. *American Psychologist, 62,* 563–574.

Wyatt v. Stickney. (2010). 344 F. Supp. 373 (AL. 1974).

4

Racial Control and Resistance Among African Americans in the Aftermath of the Welfare Reform Act of 1996

Jerome H. Schiele and Ellarwee Gadsden

░░ INTRODUCTION

Racial control and resistance have been recurring themes in American society, and African Americans often have been at the center of these events. Since their importation as slaves, African Americans have been regulated by many types of social welfare policies, slavery being the primary example. However, the themes of racial regulation found in slavery have persisted and continue to shape contemporary social welfare policy debates and development. The Personal Responsibility Act of 1996 is one example of how this form of racial regulation continues, but its regulatory features have also provided opportunities for resistance among advocacy organizations that primarily serve low-income African American individuals, families, and communities. The Personal Responsibility and Work Opportunity Reconciliation Act of 1996, better known as the Welfare Reform Act of 1996, ended the long-time Federal Aid to Families with Dependent Children (AFDC) Program established by the 1935 Social Security Act and replaced it with the new Temporary Assistance to Needy Families (TANF) program. A major departure from AFDC, TANF is a block grant system provided to the states by the federal government that limits welfare entitlements to no more than 5 years.

This chapter examines the historical themes of racial regulation as they pertain to African Americans and describes how these themes have been replicated in the Personal Responsibility Act of 1996. This Act has particular relevance for African Americans because they are overrepresented in the total number of recipients of the TANF program. In 2006, almost two fifths (38 percent) of TANF recipients were African American (U.S. Health and Human Services, 2006), although African Americans represented about 13 percent of the total U.S. population that year (U.S. Census Bureau, 2006). The chapter also examines some of the ways organizations have intervened to thwart some of the perilous consequences of the Act and it underscores some of the pitfalls of these organizations' activities. The chapter ends with some recommendations for social welfare policy practice and research.

⑊ HISTORICAL THEMES OF AFRICAN AMERICAN REGULATION

A comprehensive analysis of African Americans should simultaneously acknowledge their victim-hood and their victories. Understandably so, much has been written about black victim-hood because African Americans have been one of the most subjugated and vilified groups in America (Anderson, 1994; Asante, 2003; Dubois, 1961; Hacker, 1992; Marable, 2002; Turner, Singleton, & Musick, 1984; E. Williams, 1944; C. Williams, 1987). However, this persistent subjugation should be balanced against the many brave individual and organized efforts African Americans have undertaken to resist their oppression. If these efforts had not occurred, African Americans would not have survived the albatross of racial terrorism and would be a faded memory of American history. Nonetheless, African Americans' involuntary entry into the United States as slaves and their prolonged intergenerational captivity placed them at significant risk of systematic victimization. Even after slavery was officially abolished in 1865 by the 13th Amendment to the U.S. Constitution, African Americans endured another 100 years of legal injustice until the landmark civil rights legislation of the 1960s. Although legal racial discrimination is over, African Americans continue to experience subjugation under new forms of oppression that are more symbolic, subtle, and seductive (Bobo, Kluegel, & Smith, 1997; Collins, 1998; Kambon, 1998; Marable, 2002; Schiele, 2002).

All American institutions have played a role in the subjugation of African Americans. African Americans have been victimized politically, economically, socially, physically, mentally, and culturally. This organic exposure to oppression even reaches into the realm of institutions whose official aim is to promote benevolence and to eliminate social problems. These institutions are said to serve a social welfare function and are usually sanctioned by social welfare policies. Social welfare policies can be defined as "principles, guidelines, or procedures that serve the purpose of maximizing uniformity in decision making regarding the problem of dependence in our society" (Popple & Leighninger, 2001, p. 26). This definition implies that social welfare policies are benevolent attempts at lifting persons out of poverty and improving their socioeconomic status. This view contends that social welfare policies serve a social *treatment* function that buffers vulnerable people from stressful life events. Several others, however, conceive social welfare policies as instruments of social control and repression (Abramovitz, 1996; Neubeck & Cazenave, 2001; Piven & Cloward, 1971; Quadagno, 1994; Trattner, 1983). As tools of social control, social welfare policies attempt to regulate and monitor societal groups who are considered *deviants* and threats to the cultural, economic, and political order. These deviant groups are believed to threaten the social order in five important ways: (1) by not successfully adopting what are considered essential American cultural values and norms; (2) by being an economic drain on society by their excessive dependence on the public dole; (3) by engaging disproportionately in criminal acts, especially violent street crimes; (4) by their anger and resentment toward the broader society, which could proliferate into organized resistance efforts; and (5) by their reproductive behavior and birth rates, which could generate undesirable demographic shifts and political dislocations.

As a poignant example of a group designated as deviant, African Americans have been portrayed as threats to the social order in all of the above five ways. The origin of this portrayal is U.S. slavery. U.S. slavery lasted from roughly 1660 to 1865, a total of 205 years. (The year 1660 is the date used because it was around this time that Virginia introduced the first slave codes into the newly formed English colonies. These codes committed Africans into servitude for life. For a discussion, see Bennett, 1966.) This means that African Americans were enslaved longer than they have been free. When including the additional 100 years of legal racism that only ended as late as the mid-1960s, African Americans have been politically free only for about 40 years. Because the African American experience emerges significantly from intergenerational captivity, slavery can be viewed as the context through which the social construction of people of African descent as deviants was formed. For African Americans, American social welfare policies, such as the Personal Responsibility Act, seek to reinforce and reproduce the legacy of American slavery that has as its core theme the ethic of white supremacy (Jewell, 1989; Neubeck & Cazanave, 2001; Schiele, 2000). This ethic essentially proposes that people of European descent are inherently superior to other racial groups in the important realms of intellect, morality, and culture. The Personal Responsibility Act contributes to this belief by regulating the potential threat African Americans pose to the social order generated by the white supremacy ethic (Jewell, 1989; Neubeck & Cazanave, 2001; Schiele, 2000). The degree to which African Americans are perceived to deviate from this ethic corresponds well with the manner and method in which social welfare policies have been justified and implemented historically. American social welfare policies, including the Personal Responsibility Act, endeavor to regulate and reinforce the white supremacy ethic among African Americans in three critical ways: 1) by compelling African Americans to adopt and adhere to dominant, European American (i.e., Eurocentric) cultural values and norms; 2) by promoting the idea that African Americans are an economic drain on society because they are indolent; and 3) by portraying African Americans as inherently criminal and sexually licentious. Although the character of these social control techniques have varied with and corresponded to the demands of specific epochs, this chapter assumes that American slavery represents their genesis.

Regulating Cultural Values and Norms

Social welfare policies, such as the Personal Responsibility Act, can be seen as inculcators and protectors of the cultural values and norms of those in power (Blau with Abramovitz, 2003; Day, 2003; Trattner, 1999). They serve to validate the cultural values and norms of dominant societal groups and to invalidate the cultural values and norms of vilified and stigmatized people. The role that social welfare policies play in cultural validation and invalidation reinforces a form of domination known as *cultural oppression.* Cultural oppression can be understood as the regulation of cultural values for the purpose of universalizing a dominant group's experiences and interpretations by establishing them as the norm (Schiele, 2005; Young, 1990). Within cultural oppression, the values and interpretations of divergent cultural groups who share a common geopolitical space are unequally endorsed. The experiences and interpretations of those who control societal institutions are validated and imposed onto all who rely on these institutions, while the experiences and interpretations of groups who exert less or no control are devalued and deemed subordinate. Relative to other racial groups in the United States, people of European ancestry have had more power and privilege. This power advantage has elevated the experiences and interpretations of European Americans as the human benchmark of the American sociocultural landscape (Ani, 1994; Schiele, 2005). These experiences and interpretations are by no means monolithic, but they are distinctive. However, the power advantage and institutional ubiquity of this cultural distinctiveness allow the experiences and interpretations of European Americans to significantly shape what frequently is referred to as the American experience.

The cultural oppression framework suggests that American social welfare policies, such as the Personal Responsibility Act, serve a cultural imposition and univeralization function by excluding values and interpretations that reflect the cultural experiences of many African Americans. By denying the cultural experiences of African Americans, social welfare policies penalize and stigmatize African Americans when they fail to internalize dominant, Eurocentric cultural values and norms. For example, a major cultural value that permeates the Personal Responsibility Act is the primacy of marriage and the nuclear family (Personal Responsibility and Work Opportunity Reconciliation Act of 1996). Other family forms, such as single-mother families, are considered deviant. One family form that has characterized many African American families for years is that of the extended family type (Billingsley, 1992; Hill, 1999; Martin & Martin, 1978; McAdoo, 1997; Nobles, 1978). The black extended family type not only accentuates the significance of blood relatives other than those in the nuclear family, but also considers persons not related by blood as family members, too. Billingsley (1968) called the latter family form "augmented" families, and, by including nonkin persons as family members, this family form demonstrates what Kambon (1998) refers to as the "self-extension" orientation of African Americans. In this orientation, African Americans are said to have a cultural tradition and proclivity that promote human inclusion. This inclusive character is based on a spiritual worldview that underscores the commonality and interconnectedness of all human beings. Others suggest that the practice and validation of the extended family among African Americans represent creative family adaptations to the disruption of black family life engendered by slavery (Billingsley, 1968).

Because African American families have relied on extended family networks more so than European American families (Billingsley, 1968, 1992), and have demonstrated higher rates of marital disruption and out-of-wedlock births (Sweeney & Phillips, 2004), they often have been vilified as abnormal and unstable. Both Frazier (1939) and Moynihan (1965) promoted this view of black families, which Dodson (2007) refers to as the *cultural ethnocentric* paradigm of black family studies. The cultural ethnocentric perspective reinforces cultural oppression by suggesting that all families in the United States should conform to the European American, middle to upper class standards of family life that place considerable importance on the nuclear family with its corresponding rigid, gender roles. The cultural ethnocentric perspective has had a major influence over American social welfare policy development. This can be seen by the heavy attention these policies give to the importance of marriage and to the condemnation of out-of-wedlock births. These themes were central to the Personal Responsibility Act of 1996 that *ended welfare as we know it,* that is, by eliminating the United States' primary income maintenance program, Aid to Families with Dependent Children. By suggesting that families are normal and stable only when they are nuclear, African American families that rely on other family forms such as the extended family are believed to imperil America's moral and cultural fiber.

Regulating Indolence

Because of their dependence on the public dole, those for whom social welfare policies are targeted often are viewed as an economic drain on society. The Personal Responsibility Act, for example, protects and regulates this concern mostly by embracing a punitive character. This punitive character is based on the fundamental assumption that the poor are indolent, that many of them are *undeserving* of economic assistance and, instead, are in need of cultural indoctrination. The punitive character of American social welfare policy extends to its English and puritanical roots that bifurcated the poor into *deserving* (i.e., children, the disabled, and the elderly) and *undeserving* (i.e., able-bodied adults) (Day, 2003). This bifurcation is based heavily on the convergence of the cultural values of individualism and the protestant (Calvinistic) work ethic (Day, 2003). Individualism is the belief that all personal success and failure are attributed to the individual alone. The protestant work ethic suggests that one's economic status is evidence of the degree of God's grace and blessings. In other words, God blesses those who are prosperous and successful because of their willingness to work diligently and persistently. Likewise, the wretched conditions of the poor are punishments from God for their failure to work, and work hard (Day, 2003).

African Americans have been particularly victimized by American social welfare policy's punitive character and its use of religious ideas to support domination. Much of American slavery's justification emanated from distorted interpretations of biblical texts. Martin and Martin (2002) refer to these distortions as "religious mythomania," and its purpose was to use biblical texts to demonstrate that persons of African descent were predestined for servitude and suffering. One of the most popular forms of religious mythomania was the Hamitic myth. According to this myth, "Ham, Noah's son, had looked upon his father's nakedness and he and his descendents were cursed with black skin color" (Martin & Martin, 2002). Because being black was a curse from God, people of African descent were deemed inherently inferior and suitable for subordination.

Although African Americans were considered disposed for servitude, this did not imply that they would be willing to work, and work hard. Instead, enslaved Africans were thought to be indolent, and this indolence required elaborate and harsh interventions to force enslaved Africans to work. Some of these interventions were public beatings and maiming, denial of special privileges, and threats of selling one to a more brutal slave owner and of breaking up one's family (Stampp, 1956). The control and manipulation of the enslaved African's social context to force her or him to labor would serve as a model for later social welfare policies aimed at correcting the assumed, inherent indolence of African Americans. For example, the Personal Responsibility Act requires that recipients work, and if they do not, their time to receive welfare payments is reduced by the time that they do not work.

Regulating Criminality and Sexual Licentiousness

American social welfare policies, including the Personal Responsibility Act, also have been used to stigmatize African Americans as criminals and as sexually unrestrained. Although both African American men and women have been equally portrayed as both, African American men usually have been portrayed as violent criminals and African American women as sexually promiscuous (Lemelle, 1995). Akbar (1996) explains that this pejorative portrayal of black men and women stems from the legacy of slavery. In slavery, black men's worth was associated with their degree of physical strength and prowess. Regulating this assumed prowess was a primary concern of slave owners because, if left unchecked, it could be employed to overcome and subdue slave masters and their families. Slave masters also were concerned about the potential confluence of this prowess with an emancipative consciousness. The combination of a liberation consciousness juxtaposed against the perceived corporal strength among enslaved black men posed a significant threat to the social order of white patriarchy. Some of the best examples of this threat were the insurrections enslaved black men led. Persons such as Nat Turner demonstrated how potent organized black male resistance could be. Because of the potential posed by the convergence of black male physical strength and a liberation consciousness, any activity in which enslaved black men engaged without the sanction of slave owners was considered criminal. In essence, slavery produced the notion that independent black male action was a crime: it violated the law of white male hegemony (Akbar, 1996).

Because enslaved black women were perceived as physically weaker than enslaved black men, slave owners were less concerned about any physical threat or harm black women could pose. Instead, black women were vilified and exploited for their supposedly, extraordinarily sexual promiscuity. Since they were considered property, white males who owned them could take advantage of them sexually at anytime, which generated and reinforced the image of the hypersexual black woman (Akbar, 1996).

Black women were also deemed sexually licentious because of the randomness with which enslaved black men and black women often had sexual encounters. The institution of American slavery only allowed minimal opportunity for enslaved black men and women to come together as a formal union of husband and wife. Gutmann (1997) presents some of these examples and demonstrates how well many enslaved Africans were able to form viable and stable male/female relationships. However, other scholars underscore how slavery prevented many enslaved Africans from establishing stable intergender relationships (Frazier, 1939; Moynihan, 1965). These writers note how enslaved women were used as breeders and as sources of concubinage, and how their roles as mothers were significantly compromised and attenuated. The years of intergenerational objectification of enslaved black women for their sexual and reproductive function promoted the view that black women's worth lied primarily in their sexual abilities. As with enslaved black men, the *problem* of enslaved black women's sexual licentiousness was believed to lie in them, not in the environmental conditions of slavery. This logic continues today in the Personal Responsibility Act. African American women, especially low-income, single mothers, continue to be stigmatized as sexually irresponsible, and social welfare policies such as the Personal Responsibility Act attempt to regulate this behavior by vilifying and decontextualizing black single motherhood (Brewer, 1988; Thomas, 1998).

◊◊ RACIAL REJIJTANCE AND THE PERJONAL REJPONJIBILITY ACT OF 1996

The Personal Responsibility Act has regulated the lives of African Americans, and the legacy of American slavery has been a primary factor in this control. However, the history of slave revolts and uprisings serve as indicators that African Americans are willing to resist oppressive social welfare policies. More specifically, this section of the chapter discusses how organizations that primarily serve low-income African Americans have organized to resist the policy's oppressive features or consequences.

Themes and Activities of Welfare Resistance

Since 1935, public assistance was an entitlement, as long as a white family possessed the eligibility requirements, conceivably they could continue to receive benefits. The fact that African Americans were largely excluded from receiving welfare, though they were eligible, is not widely known. It was not until the major upheaval of the civil rights movement in the 1960s that discrimination barriers to welfare entitlement programs were lifted. Subsequently, these programs became more punitive and stigmatized than they had already been. Eventually, welfare came to be perceived as a national social problem involving Cadillac driving welfare queens and drive-by urban thug youth from single-parent homes. All were cast as an irresponsible underclass that needed to be required to work, to be self-sufficient, in order to gain respect for themselves from society.

Rabble is a word used to pejoratively describe the disorganized poor, and the term rabble rouser is used to describe their disdained leadership. If the poor are disorganized, they cannot effectively address their plight and are criticized accordingly (Wilson, 1997). But, if the poor organize and use the power of their numbers to call attention to the injustice of their circumstances, they are feared and told they are wearing the mantle of victimhood. For African Americans, specifically, the forces arrayed against their organizing around their poverty have been enormous, rendering their successes fleeting. They have more eagerly organized to protest racism than poverty with interesting results. The short-lived welfare rights movement, led by African American women, was a rare exception. It was replaced by the bureaucratic National Welfare Rights Organization, which was supposed to help them help themselves and each other, but it was run by white middle-class men who professed to be empathetic to the cause. The image of welfare mothers battling the system for more for their children morphed into the Reganesque welfare queen stereotype, with Clinton ending "welfare as we had come to know it" by signing the Personal Responsibility Act in 1996 that created TANF.

TANF has four goals as defined by law: (1) to assist needy families so children can be cared for in their own homes or the homes of relatives, (2) to end dependence by promoting work and marriage, (3) to prevent and reduce out-of-wedlock pregnancies, and (4) to encourage two-parent family formation and maintenance (Coven, 2005). What has been the response to TANF? Neither the National Welfare Rights organization nor any other organization responded with nationwide efforts to resist this law. Resistance appears called for but seems limited by an all-encompassing bureaucratic oppressiveness. Schram (2002) might call the resistance that occurs now "radical incrementalism." That is, making small changes here and now in ways that build in the possibility for bigger changes later. Resistance such as this has occurred, often in unlikely places and sometimes by a coalition of diverse groups. These coalitions advocate helping primarily African Americans to achieve some measure of success despite TANF's seemingly opposite purpose.

For example, BUILD (Baltimoreans United in Leadership Development), a powerful player in Baltimore for 15 years, became concerned that many of its members, predominantly African American, were employed but could not live on their wages. They joined in a campaign with a labor union to advocate for a living-wage initiative. This initiative was supported the efforts of ACORN (the Association of Community Organizations for Reform Now) and other unions. By 2001, at least 155 living-wage initiatives had been put forward in 43 states. By 2007, national organizations such as the National Association for the Advancement of Colored People (NAACP) supported *The Fair Minimum Wage Act of 2007*, which would increase the minimum wage, $5.15 an hour, by $2.10 an hour over a 2-year period. It has been more than 9 years since the last increase in the minimum wage—the longest period in the history of the law (NAACP, 2007).

Another incremental approach in resistance to TANF has been successful but not yet as far reaching as the increase in the minimum wage. This involves attending college. "Welfare reform was not designed with the goal of poverty alleviation, but rather as a way to reduce the size of the welfare caseload. It emphasizes rapid entry into the workforce, and does not allow clients to receive benefits if they are pursing higher education" (Boyer, 2006, p. 24). A form of organized resistance to this would be for community organizations to take on the *shared* responsibility to secure opportunities and provide resources for single mothers by finding ways for them to attend or continue college to get a better paying job. This cause does not focus specifically on African Americans. Neither did that of increasing the minimum wage. For many this has been intentional. For example, Delgado suggested that welfare rights, or resisting welfare wrongs, involve a collaborative of *traditional civil rights groups* with allies from immigrant and women's advocacy organizations to effectively plan and execute welfare reforms that focus on race and gender equity (Delgado, 2000). The NAACP pointed out that raising the federal minimum wage would positively impact African Americans disproportionately. BUILD and ACORN are both largely African American in membership and focus on issues central to them and have impacted a variety of ethnic groups around Baltimore and the United States where African Americans are disproportionately poor. Thus, improving poverty conditions, in general, are bound to improve the conditions of large numbers of African Americans.

Jones-DeWeever and Gault (2006) posit that the lasting economic benefits associated with postsecondary education are especially key to the economic well-being of women and particularly crucial for women of color. They point out that just some exposure to higher education decreases the poverty rate for African American women a great deal—from 41 percent among those without a high school degree down to 17 percent for those with some postsecondary education.

According to Jones-DeWeever and Gault (2006), before TANF, most states permitted welfare recipients to attend postsecondary institutions under the Job Opportunities and Basic Skills Training program (JOBS). Although some states limited access to higher education, they assert, most allowed clients enough time to complete a 4-year degree. TANF reformed that. The new policies favored immediate employment over education. Only those clients who were the most well-equipped experienced some little improvement in their standard of living. The poorest families became significantly worse off under this reform, with most states narrowly interpreting the TANF legislation as allowing college attendance for less than 12 months. In Baltimore, small advocacy groups worked with a local community college to "redefine" education, work, and training such that it included enough hours for clients, most of whom were African American, to obtain an AA degree (Anonymous, personal communication, October 2008). Because they believed themselves to be operating in a gray zone, they did not push for a replication of their definitions across the state of Maryland. Their *sub rosa* behavior is reminiscent of a past era when, in many states, it was a punishable offense to teach African Americans to read. Another nonprofit group based in Oakland, California, LIFETIME, provides support to welfare participants seeking to enroll in and successfully complete postsecondary education. Although the clarion call is yet to be heard nationwide, LIFETIME's work was rewarded in its home state. By 2008, California had passed legislation allowing welfare participants to attend higher education institutions any time throughout their entire 5-year TANF eligibility period (Jones-DeWeever & Gault, 2006).

Slavery in the United States was an oppressive policy that affected only African Americans. Initially, it was thought that the Civil Rights movement also only pertained to African Americans, although people of other races had been actively involved. But, that movement articulated and demonstrated to others that racial oppression was not the only type of oppression experienced by Americans, even African Americans in the 1950s and 1960s. Although African Americans now are disproportionately found on the country's welfare rolls, it is questionable whether focusing on them alone would re-reform that system, particularly with the cost of maintaining the system having decreased by about 50 percent. The country's incarceration rates have only recently come under scrutiny, not because more than half of those imprisoned are African Americans, but because the cost of keeping them there is increasing as the American economy declines. If African Americans, particularly African American single mothers, are to successfully throw off the mantle of welfare's oppression, they should attempt to achieve this collaboratively, Delgado suggests. Ernst (2009), however, cautions that there needs to be a continued focus on race no matter the degree of collaborative efforts "in states with both higher income inequality and where welfare parents may be associated with racially stigmatized groups" (p. 185). In addition, advocacy groups serving multiple constituencies have been found to be the most vulnerable, financially (Reid, Boris, & Ho, 2004). The local Baltimore organization BUILD appears to follow Delgado's (2000) suggestion. ACORN, conversely, having grown out of the 1970s welfare rights movement and thought of by many as an African American organization, continues to proffer a racial frame or designation, its current difference only being that Latinos are included in its racial/ethnic frame.

Organization Vulnerability and Sustainability

Taking on a racially nonidentifiable community organization label will not necessarily keep these organizations out of the crosshairs of the opposition to achieving their goals. The reality is that many public charity nonprofits have developed a rear-guard action in response to their advocacy-based fears, now known to be legitimate. They have worried that what has recently happened to organizations such as ACORN will, happen to them. This is fear on a major scale. In 2008 public charities accounted for almost 60 percent of all reporting nonprofit organizations (Blackwood, Wing, & Pollak, 2008). In 2005, the latest year for which data are available, 29 percent of nonprofit revenues came from governments grants, reimbursements, and contracts (Bass, Guinane, & Turner, 2003). The loss of government funding, even its threat, could be a debilitating blow for an African American community organization heavily government dependent, either as individual members or as an organization as a whole.

As community organizing of poor African Americans begins its reascendance and broadens beyond welfare rights reform to focus on increased political power, ACORN's current tribulations are a legitimate concern for other African American serving nonprofits with a social welfare policy focus. The more success it achieves, the more likely it is to be attacked by oppressive forces (Fitrakis, 2009). ACORN's fate highlights the importance of the need for oppressed African American people to maintain perpetual vigilance as they seek to organize and politically free themselves. More is required of Afro-centered grassroots organizations than the arduous work of responding to the vagaries of an oppressive welfare system and organizing to resist them. As these community organizations become institutionalized, both their leaders and followers need more than Saul Alinsky's "curiosity, irreverence, imagination, sense of humor, . . . blurred vision for a better world . . . , free and open mind, and political relativity" (The Philanthropic Initiative, 2006, pp. 1–2). As said in a *Nonprofit Quarterly* column, "There is no tabulation of 'good works' or 'good politics' . . . that can and should be used to excuse failures of ethics and good management practice" (Cohen, 2009). As African American welfare rights and similar activist service organizations that conduct advocacy as a secondary activity reorganize themselves and grow to become large institutions such as ACORN, or the Urban League, they must look beyond their mission and even collaborative goals. Growth needs to occur if they are to survive. With few exceptions, smaller organizations are much more vulnerable than larger ones to environmental vicissitudes. Overall, large organizations tend to be somewhat stronger financially and fare better during economic hard times (Reid, Boris, & Ho, 2004). Because there are powerful oppressive forces that continue to be able to successfully advocate for repressive social welfare policies that are not supported by public consensus (Guildford, 2007), the decline in the size of the welfare rolls has created more sympathetic attitudes toward welfare recipients (Reisch & Sommerfeld, 2002). If they are to succeed over the long-term, unlike ACORN, they must not just *do* good, they must *be* good. Also, their donors, contractors, and clients all have a stake in their financial well-being (Reid, Boris, & Ho, 2004). Thus, their survival will require they focus on what some consider the mundane: a good, firm organizational structure.

Welfare rights organizations that represent oppressed African Americans, which play important roles that provide voice and influence for disadvantaged and disenfranchised communities, should have commensurate power (*Nonprofit Quarterly*, 2009). An organization with that level of influence and power must be above reproach, ethically and structurally. ACORN has been discussed because it, like the Urban League, is one of the few existing service and advocacy organizations serving primarily African Americans nationwide. Much can be learned from this organization's difficulties that can be of help to fledgling and growing welfare rights organizations as they valiantly seek to stem the suffering of and advocate for African Americans who have been disproportionately impacted by the severe 2008–2010 recession (U.S. Bureau of Labor Statistics, 2009). And, as their representation among welfare recipients becomes increasingly pronounced (Reisch & Sommerfeld, 2002), what these organizations should take away from ACORN's recent experiences are presented in great detail in Harshbarger and Crafts's (2009) program evaluation report, *An Independent Governance Assessment of ACORN: The Path to Meaningful Reform*.

The report stated that the organization had lost public trust primarily (though not solely) as a result of management deficiencies. This should be of concern to all such organizations, because weak and ineffective management leaves grassroots community organizations vulnerable to oppressors who seek to cripple them and abandon the marginalized clients they are trying to help. Their findings were that there was a need for the use of basic principles of organizational governance, accountability, and compliance, and for written procedures, training, and regular on-site supervision (Cohen, 2008). These deficiencies point to how easily a grassroots organization and its leadership can lose their way and become vulnerable as they fight the fight to protect and advocate for marginalized African Americans. Grassroots advocacy organizations such as welfare rights groups must stay focused and true to their mission and refuse to take on any and all new projects and services without thought or concern about management and implementation (Cohen, 2008). Growth should be planned, making sure that an adequate infrastructure is in place in the process. Also, they must strive to keep their organization simple; the more complicated the governance structure, the less likely the organization will be governed by its stakeholders and constituents, and the more vulnerable it will be to criticism from outsiders (Cohen, 2008). Of note is that much of ACORN's publicized difficulties had to do with how feigned problems were inconsistently (mis)handled by direct service workers. This is not surprising given that grassroots organizations, frequently understaffed and underfunded, can tend to overly focus on provision of their core services, with those who do it best becoming the supervisors of those providing direct services to clients. These supervisors often receive little or no supervision or management training.

ACORN's problems of lack of adequate "written procedures, training, and regular on-site supervision" are squarely supervision issues. Although these phenomena are not limited to nonprofits, poor and inadequate supervision can have cataclysmic consequences for them, ultimately contributing to their demise. In their eager heartfelt desire to help their clients, hiring, promoting, and training good supervisors are easily overlooked. However, it is just such a weakness that renders these types of organizations vulnerable to those who do not support their advocacy efforts. Good and adequately trained managerial supervisors possess desirable characteristics such as loyalty, initiative, decisiveness, fairness, self-confidence, and integrity. Permutter, Bailey, and Netting (2001) add that they should be professionals with oversight, evaluation, and responsibility for the work performance and accountability of those they supervise. In addition, the authors point out that, as such, good supervisors can play a key role in advocacy organizations, interacting both with upper level management and with direct service workers and organizers. Welfare advocates have chosen this field largely because of their social awareness and concern for the marginalized. Permutter, Bailey, and Netting go on to say that they need to be confident as to the valuable contributions their grassroots organizations make. They also need to feel professionally competent and demonstrate that via competent performance.

\\\\ CONCLUSION AND IMPLICATIONS

This chapter has examined and presented the historical themes of racial control among African Americans and has described some ways in which these themes, as manifested in the Personal Responsibility Act of 1996, have been resisted, primarily by social welfare organizations that primarily serve low-income African Americans. These organizations limitations and vulnerabilities in advocating for this population were also discussed. This discussion highlighted, in part, that social welfare policy advocates and their activities exist within an overall context of oppression that often hinders their activities. In addition, the same system of oppression also unfortunately sustains the need for these advocacy organizations in the first place. Thus, social welfare policy advocates working on behalf of the African American poor need to pay more attention to developing strategic ways of fighting against racial, and other forms of, oppression organically. Fighting against oppressive social welfare policies like the Personal Responsibility Act are noble, but these organizations need to engage in a more holistic critique and opposition to the political-economic and sociocultural values that sustain oppression in the United States. Cultural values, fostered in large part by the mass media, such as individualism, self-reliance, materialism, and spiritual alienation, have created an American society at high risk of creating and sustaining oppressive activities. A more detailed and thorough critique of America's philosophical foundation is needed by these organizations and we believe will strengthen their ability to more effectively prevent the advent of oppressive social welfare policies.

Finally, more research is needed to examine the effectiveness of social welfare advocacy organizations. This research should, among other things, seek to examine the factors that hinder and facilitate advocacy efforts and the conditions that help to maintain them. Additionally, this research should focus on identifying more strategies to enhance the political participation of African American mothers who are most likely to be the recipients of TANF. The question of how can more African American low-income mothers become involved in advocacy and resistance efforts needs to be examined with greater attention and focus. This research should draw heavily on the social movement and community development literature and should focus on highlighting the strengths and resources of low-income African American families and communities, no matter how devastating they may appear to be. Mary Church Terrell, prominent African American social reformer of the late 19th and early 20th centuries, used to end many of her speeches by stating that "the darkest part of the night is just before the dawn." Perhaps more resistance to oppressive social welfare policies like the Personal Responsibility Act are just around the corner if we truly believe in human transformation and are willing to make the personal sacrifices necessary to elicit its power.

⸗ REFERENCES

Abramovitz, M. (1996). *Regulating the lives of women* (2nd ed.). Boston: South End Press.

Akbar, N. (1996). *Breaking the chains of psychological slavery.* Tallahassee, FL: Mind Productions.

Anderson, C. (1994). *Black labor, white wealth: The search for power and economic justice.* Edgewood, MD: Duncan & Duncan.

Ani, M. (1994). *Yurugu: An African-centered critique of European cultural thought and behavior.* Lawrenceville, NJ: Africa World Press.

Asante, M. (2003). *Erasing racism: The survival of the American nation.* New York: Prometheus Books.

Bass, G. D., Guinane, K., & Turner, R. (2003, July). *An attack on nonprofit speech: Death by a thousand cuts.* Retrieved October 3, 2009, from http://www.ombwatch.org/files/npadv/PDF/ANSjul03es.pdf

Bennett, L. (1966). *Before the Mayflower: A history of the negro in America, 1619–1964.* Chicago: Johnson Publishing.

Billingsley, A. (1968). *Black families in white America.* Upper Saddle River, NJ: Prentice Hall.

Billingsley, A. (1992). *Climbing Jacob's ladder: The enduring legacy of African-American families.* New York: Simon & Schuster.

Blackwood, A., Wing, K. T., & Pollak, T. H. (2008). *The non-profit almanac in brief.* Washington, DC: Urban Institute. Retrieved December 21, 2009, from http://www.urban.org/UploadedPDF/411664_facts_and_figures.pdf

Blau, J., with Abramovitz, M. (2003). *The dynamics of social welfare policy.* New York: Oxford University Press.

Bobo, L., Kluegel, J. R., & Smith, R. A. (1997). Laissez-faire racism: The crystallization of a kinder, gentler, antiblack ideology. In S. A. Tuch & J. K. Martin (Eds.), *Racial attitudes in the 1990s: Continuity and change* (pp. 15–41).Westport, CT: Praeger.

Boyer, K. (2006). Reform and resistance: A consideration of space, scale and strategy in legal challenges to welfare reform. *Antipode, 38*(1), 22–44.

Brewer, R. M. (1988). Black women in poverty: Some comments on female-headed families. *Signs, 13,* 331–339.

Cohen, R. (2008, July). An independent governance assessment of ACORN: The path to meaningful reform. *The Nonprofit Quarterly.* Retrieved January 1, 2010, from http://www.nonprofitquarterly.org/index.php?option=com_content&view=article&id=1650:an-independent-governance-assessment-of-acorn-the-path-to-meaningful-reform&catid=149:rick-cohen&Itemid=117

Collins, P. H. (1998). *Fighting words: Black women and the search for justice.* Minneapolis: University of Minnesota Press.

Coven, M. (2005). *An introduction to TANF.* Washington, DC: Center for Budget and Policy Priorities.

Day, P. J. (2003). *A new history of social welfare* (4th ed.). Boston: Allyn & Bacon.

Delgado, G. (2000, November 2). Racing the welfare debate. *COLORLINES.* Retrieved May 2, 2009, from: http://www.colorlines.com/printerfriendly.php?ID=71

Doane, A. W. (2003). Rethinking whiteness studies. In A. W. Doane & E. Bonilla-Silva (Eds.), *White out: The continuing significance of racism* (pp. 3–18). New York: Routledge.

Dodson, J. E. (2007). Conceptualizations of African American families. In H. McAdoo (Ed.), *Black families* (pp. 67–82). Thousand Oaks, CA: Sage.

Dubois, William, E. B. (1961). *The souls of black folk.* New York: Fawcett Publications.

Ernst, R. (2009). Working expectations: Frame diagnosis and the welfare rights movement. *Social Movement Studies, 8*(3), 185–201.

Fitrakis, B. (2009, September). Why the right wing hates and wants to smash ACORN. *The Columbus Free Press.* Retrieved January 1, 2010, from http://freepress.org/columns/display/3/2009/1773

Frazier, E. F. (1939). *The negro family in the United States.* Chicago: University of Chicago Press.

Guildford, J. (2007, Spring). Ellen Reese, Backlash against welfare mothers: Past and present. *Reviews/Comptes Rendus: Labour/Le Travail, 59,* 284–285. Retrieved January 1, 2010, from http://www.historycooperative.org/journals/llt/59/br_14.html

Gutmann, H. G. (1997). *The black family in slavery and freedom, 1750–1925.* Chicago: University of Chicago Press.

Hacker, A. (1992). *Two nations: Black and white, separate, hostile, unequal.* New York: Charles Scribner's Sons.

Hamilton, B. E., Martin, J. A., & Ventura, S. J. (2009). Births: Preliminary data for 2007. *National Vital Statistics Reports, 57*(12), 1–23.

Harshbarger, S., & Crafts, A. (2009). *An independent governance assessment of ACORN: The path to meaningful reform.* Boston: Proskauer.

Hill, R. (1999). *The strengths of African American families: Twenty-five years later* (2nd ed.). Lanham, MD: University Press of America.

Jewell, S. K. (1989). *Survival of the black family: The institutional impact of American social policy.* New York: Praeger.

Jones-DeWeever, A. A., & Gault, B. (2006). *Resilient and reaching for more: Challenges and benefits of higher education for welfare participants and their children.* Washington, DC: Institute for Women's Policy Research.

Kambon, K. (1998). *African/black psychology in the American context: An African-centered approach.* Tallahassee, FL: Nubian Nation Publications.

Lemelle, A. J. Jr., (1995). *Black male deviance.* Westport, CT: Praeger.

Marable, M. (2002). *The great wells of democracy: The meaning of race in American life.* New York: Basic Civitas Books.

Martin, E. P., & Martin, J. M. (1978). *The black extended family.* Chicago: University of Chicago Press.

Martin E., & Martin, J. (2002). *Spirituality and the black helping tradition in social work.* Washington, DC: NASW Press.

McAdoo, H. (2007). *Black families* (4th ed.). Thousand Oaks, CA: Sage.

Moynihan, D. P. (1965). *The negro family: The case for national action.* Washington, DC: U.S. Department of Labor, Office of Policy Planning and Research.

National Association for the Advancement of Colored People. (2007). *Senate to vote on minimum wage today!* Retrieved May 3, 2009, from http://www.naacp.org/get-involved/activism/alerts/110uaa-2007-1-31

Neubeck, K. J., & Cazenave, N. A. (2001). *Welfare racism: Playing the race card against America's poor.* New York: Routledge.

Nobles, W. (1978). Toward an empirical and theoretical framework for defining black families. *Journal of Marriage and the Family, 40*(4), 679–688.

Orlowski, R. (2005). *Grassroots feminism at its most personal.* New York: Routledge.

Perlmutter, F. D., Bailey, D., & Netting, F. E. (2001). *Managing human resources in the human services: Supervisory challenges.* New York: Oxford University Press.

Personal Responsibility and Work Opportunity Reconciliation Act of 1996 (PRWORA, Pub.L. 104-193, 110 Stat. 2105, enacted August 22, 1996). Washington, DC: U.S. Government Printing Office.

The Philanthropic Initiative. (2006). *Alinsky Redux—Organizing principles.* Boston: Author. Retrieved December 21, 2009, from: http://www.tpi.org/downloads/docs/Karoff-imagined/Alinsky_Redux.pdf

Piven, F. F., & Cloward, R. A. (1971). *Regulating the poor: The functions of public welfare.* New York: Vintage Books.

Popple, P. R., & Leighninger, L. (2001). *The policy-based profession: An introduction to social welfare policy analysis for social workers.* Boston: Allyn & Bacon.

Quadagno, J. (1994). *The color of welfare: How racism undermined the war on poverty.* New York: Oxford University Press.

Reid, E., Boris, E., & Ho, A. (2004). *The scope and dimensions of U.S. civil rights and civil liberties organizations at the beginning of the 21st century.* Washington, DC: The Urban Institute. Paper presented at the International Society for Third Sector Research Conference July 11–13, 2004, Toronto, Canada.

Reisch, M., & Sommerfeld, D. (2002, March). Race, welfare reform, and nonprofit organizations. *Journal of Sociology & Social Welfare, 29*(1), 155–177.

Schiele, J. H. (2000). *Human services and the afrocentric paradigm.* Binghamton, NY: The Haworth Press.

Schiele, J. H. (2002). Mutations of Eurocentric domination and their implications for African American resistance. *Journal of Black Studies, 32*(4), 439–463.

Schiele, J. H. (2005). Cultural oppression and the high risk status of African Americans. *Journal of Black Studies, 35*(6), 802–826.

Schram, S. F. (2002). *The praxis of poor people's movements: The politics of survival, the lonely struggle of everyday resistance, and the radical incrementalism of welfare rights.* Paper presented at the annual meeting of the American Political Science Association, Boston, MA.

Schram, S. F. (2006). [Serendip posting 18066]. Message posted to http://serendip.brynmawr.edu/forum/viewforum.php?forum_id=356#18066

Stampp, K. M. (1956). *The peculiar institution: Slavery in the Ante-Bellum South.* New York: Vintage Books.

Sweeney, M. M., & Phillips, J. A. (2004). Understanding racial differences in marital disruption: Recent trends and explanations. *Journal of Marriage and Family, 66*(3), 639–650.

Thomas, S. L. (1998). Race, gender, and welfare reform: The antinatalist response. *Journal of Black Studies, 28,* 419–446.

Trattner, W. (1983). *Social welfare or social control: Some historical reflections on regulating the poor.* Nashville: University of Tennessee Press.

Trattner, W. I. (1999). *From poor law to welfare state: A history of social welfare in America* (6th ed.). New York: The Free Press.

Turner, J. H., Singleton, R., & Musick, D. (1984). *Oppression: A socio-history of black white relations in America.* Chicago: Nelson-Hall.

U.S. Bureau of Labor Statistics. (2009). *Labor Force Statistics from the current population survey: Labor force characteristics by race and ethnicity, 2008.* Washington, DC: Author. Retrieved January 1, 2010, from http://www.bls.gov/cps/race_ethnicity_2008_unemployment.htm

U.S. Census Bureau. (2003). *Table A-3. Mean earnings of workers 18 years and over, by educational attainment, race, Hispanic origin, and sex: 1975 to 2002.* Retrieved December 28, 2005, from http://www.census.gov/population/socdemo/education/tabA-3.pdf

U.S. Census Bureau. (2004). *Table POV29. Years of school completed by poverty status, sex, age, nativity and citizenship: 2003.* Retrieved December 30, 2005, from http://ferret.bls.census.gov/macro/032004/pov/new29_100_01.htm?catid=58:npq-in-the-news&Itemid=54

U.S. Census Bureau. (2006). *Population estimates. Statistical abstract of the United States, 2006.* Washington, DC: Author.

U.S. Health and Human Services, Administration for Children and Families. (2006). *TANF seventh annual report to Congress.* Washington, DC: Author.

Williams, C. (1987). *The destruction of black civilization: Great issues of a race from 4500B.C. to 2000 A.D.* Chicago: Third World Press.

Williams, E. (1944). *Capitalism and slavery.* Chapel Hill: University of North Carolina Press.

Wilson, W. J. (1997). *When work disappears: The world of the new urban poor.* New York: Vintage.

Young, I. (1990). *Justice and the politics of difference.* Princeton, NJ: Princeton University Press.

Part II

Regulation and Resistance Among Asian Pacific Americans

5

A Historical Understanding of Korean Americans' Immigration and Resistance Against All Odds

From Hawaii to New York

Hyunkag Cho

 INTRODUCTION

The African American leaders in South Los Angeles (L.A.) shared their frustration at a community meeting in 2007 over deteriorating conditions in their poverty and violence-filled community. The 1992 L.A. riot has been referred to as one of the worst incidents of civil unrest in U.S. history; 3 days of violence in L.A. were sparked by the acquittal of L.A. police officers who stopped and brutally beat an African American driver, Rodney King. The African American community was furious at the acquittal of the officers, but their anger did not develop against the "racist" judicial and social systems. Instead, they expressed their anger against Korean Americans who suffered the most economic damage from the riot (Chang & Diaz-Veizades, 1999, p. 26). Why, and how, did this riot happen? Did African American rioters perceive Korean Americans as "one of them" who took advantage of African Americans for their own social and economic gains? How have the "nonfriendly" relationships between Korean and African Americans developed? What systematic mechanisms in the U.S. social policies impose and reinforce tensions between Korean and African Americans?

The United States is a nation of immigrant groups; groups arriving at different times, encountering different opportunities and challenges, interacting, and often competing, with other immigrant groups. Immigration policies are regulatory and have critical impacts on the lives of nonimmigrants as well as immigrants. Socioeconomic demands and needs shape U.S. immigration policies (Park & Park, 2005). When the United States has high demand for labor, immigrants are recruited from all over the world. When immigrants begin to compete with American workers or are perceived by policymakers to take more from the United States than give to it, various restrictions are imposed on immigrants. Consequently, immigration policies consist not only of the terms and conditions for entry into the United States but also of social and economic policies that include social welfare systems (e.g., the provision of housing, education, health care, welfare benefits), labor market, and social integration of immigrants (National Conference of State Legislatures, 2009). This chapter addresses the hardships and challenges faced by Korean Americans in the broad context of those immigration and social welfare policies.

\\\\ HIJTORY OF KOREAN IMMIGRATION TO THE UNITED JTATEJ

In 1903, the first Korean immigrants left their homeland to work on Hawaii plantations that had high demand for cheap labor (Meinig, 2004). They were mostly unskilled laborers in Korea (Hurh & Kim, 1984) and sought better economic opportunities by escaping Korea, whose political and economic conditions were increasingly worsened by Japanese colonization. This first Korean immigration responded to the U.S. demand for cheap labor, which is the first defining characteristic of Korean Americans. They would have to remain "cheap" not only in their direct labor cost, but also in their indirect costs, such as social services and benefits. Although Korean immigrants on Hawaiian plantations made lives through hard work, the living conditions on the plantations were extremely severe: hard work under the hot sun, low wages, and isolated living facilities (Hurh & Kim, 1984). Thus, most Koreans left the plantations to move to the cities or the mainland. They eventually engaged in various economic activities such as manufacturing jobs, small businesses, and professional jobs, forming the archetype of Korean American (Choy, 1979).

The size of Korean American population remained small as a result of the National Origins Act of 1924, which banned immigration from Asia until the Immigration and Naturalization Act of 1965 lifted the ban and the population increased dramatically. Thousands of Koreans arrived every year after 1965 and settled in the United States, currently accounting for 0.5 percent of the U.S. population, or 1,555,293 in 2007 (U.S. Census Bureau, 2008). Post-1965 Korean immigrants differ from their predecessors; they are "educated, professionals, and middle class" (Chang & Diaz-Veizades, 1999, p. 18). In 2007, 52 percent of Korean Americans held a bachelor's degree or higher, almost double the 27.5 percent of the total U.S. population; 44 percent of Korean Americans' employment was related to management and professional occupations; and 11.8 percent of Korean Americans were self-employed, which was also almost twice the national rate (6.7 percent). The median family income was $64,406 and poverty rates were 10.7 percent (U.S. Census Bureau, 2008). The majority of Korean Americans are no longer unskilled laborers who work on the plantations but new urban settlers who are either self-employed through small businesses, or managerial, service, or professional workers. Like their predecessors who moved to Hawaii for better economic opportunity, Korean immigrants tend to concentrate in highly populated states or metropolitan areas that are more likely to offer "economic opportunities for entrepreneurs and laborers as well as social networks and cultural resources" (Chung, 2007, p. 29). In 2007, one third of Korean Americans, or 463,958, lived in California, making L.A. the biggest Korean community, with 295,673 Korean Americans. New York City (NYC) is the second biggest, with 202,030 (U.S. Census Bureau, 2008).

Some Koreans bring with them investment capital to start small businesses, which tend to concentrate in labor-intensive retail businesses, such as grocery and liquor, restaurant, apparel and accessory, and dry cleaning and laundry. For instance, in 2004, 60 percent of NYC independent produce stores and 80 percent of nail salons were Korean owned, while 66 percent of Chicago dry cleaning and laundry businesses in 1991, and 24 percent of Southern California liquor retailers in 1990 were owned by Korean Americans (Lee & Kang, 2004; Min, 1998; Yoon, 1997). Running small businesses in minority communities is another defining characteristic of Korean Americans, and those businesses locate in those areas partly because of Korean Americans' limited capital and lack of business experience (Park, 2005). In 1994, customers of Korean-American businesses in L.A. were 53 percent Latino Americans, 26 percent whites, and 17 percent African Americans, while in NYC in the same year, Korean American businesses had a clientele base of 39 percent African Americans, 37 percent Latino Americans, and 19 percent whites (Chang & Diaz-Veizades, 1999). Post-1965, Korean immigrants moved to the United States with small capital, enough to help them settle in the new, strange land, but not enough to establish their residences and businesses in mostly white neighborhoods. They had no choice but to establish small businesses in neighborhoods of other minorities, such as African and Latino American, and compete for social and economic resources. The strategy of Korean immigrants to find niche business opportunities among whites and the other minorities might contribute to complicated, even hostile, relationships between Korean Americans and other minorities.

\\\ CONFLICTS WITH OTHER MINORITIES

Many Korean American small business owners have achieved high degrees of success and are recognized as the model minority (Takaki, 1998). However, that success came at the expense of intensified conflicts between Korean American businesses and other minorities, especially African Americans. Although conflicts have occurred elsewhere, L.A. experienced the worst. Two murder incidents in 1991 sparked intense hostilities between African and Korean Americans after a few small-scale boycotts by the former against the latter (Chang & Yu, 1994). During a dispute over payment, a 15-year-old African American girl, Latasha Harlins, was shot to death by a Korean grocer in March. The Korean grocer, convicted of manslaughter, was sentenced to 10 years in prison and released on 5-year probation the following October. Harlins's parents were eventually paid $300,000 as compensation by the Korean grocer's insurance (Min, 1996). Three months after Harlins's death, a 42-year-old African American man, Lee Arthur Mitchell, was killed by a Korean grocer during an alleged robbery attempt. The Korean grocer was not convicted of the killing because the police determined he acted in self-defense. African Americans denounced the finding as too lenient and the police decision too unreliable (Martin, 1993). Protests by African Americans initially took place in front of the two stores but quickly spread to other Korean American businesses as the protesters were outraged at the responses of the criminal justice system. Although the protests gradually waned, African Americans' deep-rooted mistrust of criminal justice systems and frustration over long-lasting hardships for their communities remained unchanged, waiting for another incident to reveal them.

On April 29, 1992, the white police officers who were convicted for beating an African American motorist, Rodney King, were acquitted by the jury. Rioting broke out in the evening after the verdict and lasted for 3 days, in which at least 53 were dead, 2,300 injured, and almost a billion dollars in property lost (Schoch & Lin, 2007). What began as protests against the verdict rapidly evolved into violent riots, looting and burning business properties, and assaulting vehicles and people. Korean merchants suffered the most economic damages: they incurred about 30 percent of the property losses compared with 12 percent of Hispanics and 9 percent of other Asians (Tierney, 1994). Korean Americans were only one target of rioting. Included in 53 deaths were 25 African Americans, 16 Latino Americans, 8 whites, and 1 Korean, most of whom were shot, stabbed, strangled, or burned (Crogan, 2002). Of 12,127 who were arrested related to the riot, 43 percent were Latino Americans, 34 percent African Americans, and 14 percent whites (Ong & Hee, 1993). The L.A. riots are often defined not as Korean–African American conflicts, but as multiethnic conflicts involving Latino Americans and whites as well as Korean and African Americans (Chang, 1995). L.A. Koreatown, the center of the riots, suffered the worst socioeconomic effects of the riot.

⧵⧵ THEORETICAL EXPLANATIONS OF INTERETHNIC CONFLICTS

Numerous theories have been proposed regarding racial and ethnic conflicts. Although many are applicable to any racial and ethnic relations, some are mores relevant to relations and conflicts between racial and ethnic minorities. Human ecology theory explains inter-minority conflicts as the result from the process of competition for scarce resources (Gans, 1973). This theory explains the nature of competition between groups with different interests but fails to explain various levels of social environment factors, such as racial discrimination and socioeconomic inequality, which affect the process of competition and succession (Chang, 1995). Realistic group conflict theory has much in common with human ecology theory in its perception of inter-minority conflicts as the process of competition for scarce resources (Jackson, 1993); however, differing from human ecology theory, it emphasizes deterministic effects of inequality in socioeconomic and materialistic resources on intergroup conflicts, Further, it explains social and psychological aspects of group conflicts by integrating competition, socioeconomic inequality, prejudices, and associated behaviors in a unified framework. Unfortunately, this theory provides little information on how and why the competitive environment is established.

Middleman minority theory addresses those ethnic minorities that take an intermediate rather than low-status role of middleman between the dominant majority group and other minority groups that occupy lower social status (Bonacich, 1973). Jewish and Indian entrepreneurs in the early- to mid-20th century in the United States are good examples of middleman minorities. The theory proposes that middleman minorities experience racial and ethnic conflicts that stem from their social positioning as middleman minorities. It would explain the L.A. riot as follows: Newly arriving immigrants with some level of economic means (e.g., Koreans) select such intermediate occupations as trade and commerce that do not need strong ties to the host society and become middleman minorities (e.g., Korean American small businesses) between the high-end, big entrepreneur (e.g., whites) and the low-end entrepreneur or low-waged workers (e.g., African and Latino Americans). Middleman minorities provide goods and services to other minorities that are neglected and abandoned by the white large businesses (Light & Bonacich, 1988). They face antagonism from both the dominant majority group and lower status minorities. White businesses try to win the competition with middleman minorities by introducing discriminatory government measures and policies to limit expansion of middleman minority entrepreneur. African and Latino Americans, who are low-wage workers and customers of middleman minorities, ask for higher wages and more respect, often violently (e.g., L.A. riots). White large businesses are no different from Korean small businesses in profiting by exploiting African and Latino Americans through low wages and discriminatory practices. However, because of the nature of day-to-day interactions between customers and small-scale merchants, middleman minorities often serve as scapegoats by absorbing the anger toward a dominant group as well as the crime, and the complaints of cheap labor costs (Chung, 2007). Asian Americans, as a middleman minority, are often praised as the model minority. Once stereotyped as hard working, fiscally responsible, and cooperative, they are "forced to conform to the 'model minority' mold" (Takaki, 1998, p. 477). They are depicted as too self-sufficient to need social welfare services. Other minorities, impoverished African and Latino Americans, are blamed for their poverty because there is the model minority that achieves more successes under the similar minority conditions. Thus, social inequality becomes an individual problem, not a social problem. Interethnic tensions and conflicts become problems between them and not ones with which the larger society should be concerned.

Middleman minority theory excels other theories in explaining racial and ethnic conflicts within the broad context of social environments: the formation of the competitive arena in which groups with different interests compete for scarce resources, the buildup of tension between groups, and interconnected relations among groups in which a tension between two groups can easily spill over to the third group. Many racial and ethnic conflicts in major cities can be explained by the theory: violent clashes between Jewish and African Americans in the 1960s (Gans, 1973; Katz, 1967); tensions and conflicts between Cuban and African Americans in Miami in 1980 (Park, 2002); Latino–African American confrontations in L.A. in 1992 and thereafter (Chang, 1994; Hernandez, 2007); hardships for African Americans who continue to be forced into the lower status of social stratification as other minorities "invade" their territory as middleman minorities (Lee & Bean, 2007); and biases and prejudices built up between migrating and native groups (Hall, 2008; Yu, 1994). Although middleman minority theory is useful for understanding complex relations and conflicts between racial and ethnic groups, it should be applied with caution. It is a theoretical and abstract ideal that is simplified to specifically address relations and conflicts between groups that consist of the dominant majority group, migrating groups as middleman minorities, and native minorities with the lower social status. As a result, some elements of the theory are not supported by the research that examined specific racial and ethnic conflicts involving complicated group conditions and dynamics (e.g., Boyd & Xu, 2003; Lee, 2006).

\\\ REGULATING KOREAN AMERICANS

Korean Americans have two defining characteristics—a cheap labor force and a middleman minority—that have been maintained and reinforced by immigration and social welfare policies. Immigration policies have consequences on labor market because most immigrants have to work to support themselves and their families (Briggs, 2008). Immigration policies aim to control the number, characteristics, qualities, and nature of immigrants in accordance with needs and conditions of labor market. Most industries seek cheap labor to maximize their profits. Keeping labor cost low is accomplished not only by lowering such direct labor costs as wages but also by minimizing such indirect labor costs as social welfare to help labor meet basic ends so that they can stay in labor market. In this context, social welfare policies are not separable from immigration policies. Many social welfare policies are to "stop feeding mouths that are already here," while immigration policies are to "eliminate additional mouths to feed" (Leong, 2002, p. 233). Since being first introduced to the United States as the cheap labor force, Korean Americans have worked hard to meet their ends. Some have succeeded as middlemen and been celebrated as the model minority. However, they have to suffer a double whammy—being identified as one of minorities by the dominant majority group and being a target of other minorities that perceive the middleman as "one of them" who takes advantage of other minorities in order to maintain the interests of the dominant group (Chang, 1994). Immigration and social welfare policies have had dynamic impacts on the already complicated status of the middleman.

Regulatory Immigration Policies

Korean Americans are not homogenous. They include entrepreneurs, workers, and the undocumented. Immigration policies have differential impacts on those groups. The Immigration Act of 1965 allowed a wide range of groups to immigrate to the United States without discrimination based on race and ethnicity. It has been revised several times, and particularly significant changes were made in 1990 and 1996. The Immigration Act of 1990 aggressively strengthened employment-based immigration by only accepting those with high skills and qualifications and restricting those who are poor or low skilled. The preference for high-skilled immigrants over the poor, low-skilled immigrant was further strengthened through subsequent legislation in 1996, 1998, and 2000 (Park & Park, 2005). The effect of this change in the immigration policy is especially strong for Asians, as 60 percent of employment-based immigration in 2001 was Asians (Office of Immigration Statistics, 2002). This trend will help strengthen the status of Asians, including Korean Americans, as the model minority. As a result, the middleman status of Korean Americans is more likely to be enhanced, which may contribute to more intensified relations between Korean and African Americans.

Not all Korean Americans settle in the United States as the middleman. Many of them struggle to meet their basic ends. Immigration policies also affect them. The Illegal Immigration Reform and Immigrant Responsibility Act of 1996 makes it difficult for poor, working-class immigrants to bring their family members to the United States by imposing a high income requirement (125 percent above the federal poverty line) on sponsorship for family members. It also allows employers to demand immigration documents from job applicants who look foreign, making it easy to discriminate against immigrants (Leong, 2002). Many working-class Korean Americans have to live separate from family members because of the requirement of high income for sponsorship, so high that one third of Korean immigrants who entered before 1996 could not have met this income requirement. Indeed, the number of Korean immigrants entering the United States through family sponsorship decreased by 20 percent from 1995 to 2002 (Park & Park, 2005).

A stricter process for legal immigration results in a larger number of undocumented immigrants. The number of undocumented residents increased from 8.4 million in 2000 to 11 million in 2005 (Passle, 2005). The number of undocumented immigrants deported from the United States has increased dramatically, from 30,039 in 1990, to 188,467 in 2000, and finally to 319,282 in 2007. The number of deported Koreans also increased, from 191 in 1998 to 417 in 2007 (Office of Immigration Statistics, 2008). Undocumented Korean immigrants are estimated to account for at least 18 percent of Korean immigrants (Lee, 2005). One third of Korean workers employed in low-wage industries in NYC in 2006 were undocumented (Korean Workers Project, 2007). Undocumented immigrants are much more vulnerable to exploitation by employers because of their unstable immigration status and are more likely to work for low wages without job security. In NYC, 47 percent of Korean workers employed in low-wage industries in 2006 had to work more than 60 hours a week, and 73 percent worked without overtime payment (Korean Workers Project, 2007).

Since 1990, immigration policies have produced a huge number of undocumented Korean immigrants, making it difficult for immigrant workers to join family members and leaving many of them vulnerable to labor exploitation. At the same time, employment-based immigration has enhanced the middleman status of Korean Americans with economic means. As a result, the process of social stratification among Korean Americans accelerates, making relations between Korean Americans and other minorities more complicated than ever. For instance, working-class Korean Americans live in the conditions that are less similar to their compatriots who are middlemen than to working-class African and Latino Americans, with whom they have to compete for limited employment opportunities. The socioeconomic commonality among working-class minorities may suggest multiethnic cooperation for improving living and working conditions of impoverished minorities. However, cooperation across racial and ethnic divide is often hard to achieve. It may be not because blood is thicker than class interest, but because race and class are strongly interwoven into the lives of minorities just as they are in the majority population. Furthermore, individual differences in Korean Americans are often ignored and lumped together into the single collective image of the model minority, which makes it difficult to initiate and maintain multiethnic cooperation.

Regulatory Social Welfare Policies

The Personal Responsibility and Work Opportunity Reconciliation Act of 1996 (welfare reform) ended welfare and has had multiple negative impact on immigrant communities. Legal immigrants entering after welfare reform are not eligible for federal means-tested benefits (e.g., Medicaid) for 5 years. All undocumented immigrants are not eligible for most federal public assistance. Welfare reform made all noncitizen immigrants, including legal permanent residents, ineligible for Supplemental Security Income (SSI) and food stamp benefits, with exemptions for veterans, military personnel, refugees, and asylees. SSI and food stamp benefits were restored in 1997 but mostly for immigrants who entered before welfare reform.

Providing social welfare benefits differently based on recipients' citizenship, rather than on legal immigration status, has had devastating impact on immigrants. Before welfare reform, 30 percent of Asian immigrants and 42 percent of Korean immigrants 65 and over received

SSI and food stamp benefits (Shinagawa, 1996). After welfare reform, the percentage of noncitizens in California receiving welfare benefits decreased by half, from 28 percent in 1994 to 14 percent in 1998 (Borjas, 2002). The percentage of cases newly approved for welfare benefits decreased by 71 percent between 1996 and 1998 (Zimmermann & Fix, 1998). Given that 22 percent of Korean Americans over 65 lived in poverty in 2007 (U.S. Census Bureau, 2008) and 37 percent of all immigrant children lived with families with food insecurity in 1999 (Capps, 2001), the devastating impact of welfare reform on noncitizen immigrants may be much worse than the numbers show. The impact, however, is different according to immigration status. On the one hand, noncitizen immigrants entering after 1996 have no way to receive welfare benefits other than becoming a citizen through naturalization. Applications for citizenship have rapidly increased since the late 1990s, forming a huge backlog (Singer, 2004). Besides long waiting times in the application process, the number of petitions denied by the Immigration and Naturalization Service also skyrocketed, from 9 percent in 1995 to 26 percent in 2001 (Park & Park, 2005). On the other hand, undocumented immigrants have never been eligible for federal welfare benefits, making their living conditions dire. Contrary to the misconception that undocumented immigrants exploit the welfare system without contributing to the country, they indeed contribute more to the United States than they receive in assistance (Fujiwara, 1998). Immigrants are reported to take only $5 billion in social services compared with contributing $90 billion in taxes (Hernandes-Truyol, 1997). Given that as of 2004, 30 percent of all foreign-born workers in the United States were undocumented, representing 4.3 percent of the total U.S. labor force (Hing, 2007), it is clear that embracing foreign-born workers as a legitimate labor force and giving them the same welfare benefits as citizens is much more beneficial to the country than illegalizing and criminalizing them.

\\\\ RESISTANCE OF KOREAN AMERICANS

Until the 1990s, Korean Americans were almost invisible and were excluded from both central and local politics because of their relatively recent arrival and small population size compared with other minorities, such as African and Latino Americans. Instead of politicizing themselves,

Korean Americans relied heavily on their ethnic enclaves for survival and easy settlement, and for isolation from affairs outside the enclaves. The L.A. riots and subsequent waves of anti-immigrant legislation shook the entire Korean community, challenging their perceptions of themselves and the outside world. Complaints and sporadic violent protests of African Americans against Korean Americans vividly brought the realization that it was irresponsible and even dangerous not to make efforts to build and maintain healthy and sustainable relationships with other minorities. Korean Americans eventually came to feel the strong need for civic participation. Moreover, Korean Americans immediately responded to the harsh backlashes to anti-immigrant reforms by seeking out cross-racial-ethnic cooperation.

Self-Help and Protest

Self-help is often the only way for immigrants to obtain necessary resources and respond to challenges, particularly when they are not visible nor heard in the social and political arena. When Korean businesses faced boycotts by African Americans in NYC and L.A., other Koreans across the country, both business owners and residents, helped them withstand the boycott by donating thousands of dollars, sending letters, and forming self-help organizations (Yoon, 1997). Although self-help strategies give immediate relief to affected community members, the root of the problems, the multifaceted causes of conflicts between Korean and African Americans, are overlooked or ignored.

On May 1, 1992, the third day of the L.A. riots, thousands of Korean Americans staged the largest Asian American rally in U.S. history, a peace march through Koreatown, the center of the riot. Participants called for peace and justice for Rodney King, and some African and Latino Americans joined in solidarity (Yu, 1994), showing a high level of awareness of the causes of interethnic conflicts and creating a milestone in building multiethnic coalitions. Demonstrations and protests are sometimes effective in educating the public and influencing public policy. In response to the anti-immigrant reforms in 1996, Korean Americans joined other immigrants in protests at almost every major metropolitan city (Park & Park, 2005). Demonstrations and protests were sometimes not shown as effective by themselves, however, when organized and done well, they imposed huge pressure on a legislature to make changes to disputed policies.

Campaign and Lobbying

Numerous campaign activities have influenced the legislative process. In 1997, on inauguration day, the National Telegram Campaign to Restore Immigrant Benefits sent 2,600 telegrams to President Clinton. This organized effort is recognized as contributing significantly to the restoration of SSI for immigrant seniors (Lee, 2005). In 1998, Korean Americans also participated in a national campaign to restore food stamps for immigrant families, sending thousands of paper plates to members of Congress. Food stamps were eventually restored in the same year. In 1999, when a variety of immigrant advocacy groups launched the Fix 96 campaign to urge Congress to amend anti-immigrant provisions in immigration and welfare reform bills, more than 130 low-income Korean immigrant seniors visited members of Congress and left a strong impression on policymakers. An advertising campaign against anti-immigrant reforms has also been frequently utilized by Korean Americans. A Justice for Immigrants ad appeared in the *Washington Post* in 1995 and a Dollar-A-Person ad in the *Washington Post* in 2005. In 2000, the ambitious Full Participation of Immigrants Campaign to legalize undocumented immigrants was launched. Korean Americans sent tens of thousands of letters to both Republican and Democratic parties and held meetings with representatives of each, urging them to incorporate pro-immigrant provisions in their party platforms. In 2006, tens of thousands of postcards, which showed images of Asian American families, were delivered to members of Congress, urging humane immigration reform (Lee, 2005).

The restoration of SSI, food stamps, and other benefits for immigrants is the product of these protests and campaigns as well as a variety of other immigrant-sponsored activities, some initiated by local community-based organizations and others by larger national-level organizations and coalitions.

Community-Based Organizations and Coalitions

Immigrants groups are largely various, and each group also includes numerous subgroups. The Korean American community is no exception, and various community-based organizations have been established to address specific interests of subgroups. They have provided social services and programs to Korean Americans, such as mutual support, senior programs, and youth development programs. Prior to 1992, these programs were primarily based on ethnic solidarity (Chang & Diaz-Veizades, 1999). Organizers, workers, and clients were mostly Korean Americans, excluding members of other minorities, either implicitly or explicitly, and were ill-equipped for the challenges and tasks that emerged after the L.A. riots and anti-immigrant reforms in the 1990s. The changes since 1990s required broad cooperation with other minorities. As a result, new community organizations that are more open to other minorities than traditional community organizations have evolved. Organizations based on ethnic solidarity are still useful in providing immediate support and relief (the Korean American Victims Association after the L.A. riot; the Korean Youth and Community Center as the largest social service agency in L.A. Koreatown; and the Korean American Race Relations Emergency to support Korean grocers facing boycotts in NYC), but increasing number of organizations began to embrace other minorities; the Korean American Resource & Cultural center in Chicago and the Korean Immigrant Workers Alliance in L.A. (Chung, 2007).

In 1983, the Black-Korean Alliance (BKA) was the first coalition in which Korean and African Americans worked together to address sporadic disputes between Korean merchants and African American customers in L.A. Consisting of individuals from churches, community organizations, charities, and business associations, the BKA tried to build healthy relations between the groups by disseminating positive information about each other, sponsoring cultural awareness and crime prevention meetings, and developing consensus between two groups about respectful behaviors. Unfortunately, it dissolved right after the L.A. riots and before it might been influential enough to resolve intensive conflicts such as the riot (Chang & Diaz-Veizades, 1999).

Korean Americans also participated, in 1992, in other multiethnic coalitions, such as the Asian Pacific Americans for a New Los Angeles and the Multicultural Collaborative; the New York Immigration Coalition is another example of Korean Americans' active participation in multiethnic coalition building. Founded in 1987 in response to anti-immigrant legislation in New York, it has since evolved into one of the largest multiethnic advocates for immigrants in New York, promoting and protecting the rights of immigrants and their family members, and mobilizing member groups to respond to emerging issues that affect immigrants ("The New York Immigration Coalition," 2008). The national wave of anti-immigrant reforms in the 1990s encouraged Korean Americans to form a larger organization to address national issues that were well beyond the scope and capacity of individual community-based organizations. The National

American Service & Education Consortium (NAKASEC) was founded in 1994 with community-based organizations across the country as member groups. Many of the activities for pro-immigrant reforms described in the previous section were initiated or organized by NAKASEC. Its activities include advocacy for civil and immigrant rights, and the promotion of the full participation of Korean Americans in American society (NAKASEC, personal communication, August 14, 2008).

Responses of Korean Americans to interethnic conflicts and anti-immigrants reforms have mostly resulted in positive impacts on their community as well as state and federal-level policy changes. Their socio-economic hardships have been somewhat relieved by self-help effort and services and support from community-based organizations. Protests, campaigns, and lobbying have led to changes in several critical provisions of anti-immigrant legislation. Interethnic conflicts have been better recognized, understood, and addressed by activities of multiethnic coalitions. Although there is still much more work to do toward healthy and fair integration of immigrants into mainstream society, the dedication, commitment, and achievements of immigrants are promising.

〰 IMPLICATIONƒ

The experiences of Korean Americans provide implications for social work policy, practice, and research. Since anti-immigrant policies have sweeping impacts on all immigrant groups, the importance of building multiethnic coalitions and coordinating the activities of each immigrant group is essential. Multiethnic coalition and coordination can be effective in maximizing influences on policymakers, educating members of each group about the need and importance of going beyond ethnic divides, and educating the others about the contributions of immigrants. Multiethnic coalition building often takes a long time. A coalition means differences among members. Getting together beyond differences requires some degree of sacrifice from member groups, which is not possible without trust among the members. Trust cannot be formed if one's gain is perceived as the other's loss. For instance, community-based organizations that serve their own ethnic community tend to perceive other organizations that serve other minorities as potential competitors. Therefore, pro-immigrants policy coalitions needed new ethnic organizations that were more open to other minorities than traditional community-based organizations. Although roles and contributions

of multiethnic coalitions are different from those of community-based organizations, they support each other. If the latter were water, the former
would be fish. Building respectful and mutually productive interorganiza-
tion relationships helps not only establish strong communities with ethnic
solidarity but also achieves political and socioeconomic advancement for all
immigrants. Obtaining support from each community before trying to
bring the communities together would be one example of such endeavor
(Chang & Diaz-Veizades, 1999). Previous research contributed to the basic
understanding of multiethnic relations (Bobo, 1999; Bonacich, 1973).
However, much remains to be explored concerning the connection between
ethnic solidarity and multiethnic collaboration. Questions for future
research include the following: Under what conditions does ethnic solidarity promote multiethnic collaboration? What are the processes of such promotion? How do differences across the ethnic groups affect the processes
and outcomes of multiethnic collaboration?

Another implication of the Korean American experience relates to the
heterogeneity within an immigrant group. The Korean American population is diverse: business-owners, workers, and the undocumented; those
who arrived decades ago and those who arrived after 1996; those whose
primary language is Korean and those who are fluent in English. African
and Latino Americans populations are also diverse. There is no such thing
as issues or conflicts between all Koreans and all African Americans.
Conflicts between Korean and African Americans in major cities may be
conflicts between Korean merchants and low-income African American
customers. The immigration and welfare reform in 1996 had a devastating impact on immigrants who entered after 1996 and on undocumented
immigrants but not necessarily on those who entered before 1996. Low-
wage, undocumented Korean workers may be closer to the low-wage
African American and Latino American workers than to Korean business
owners. Nevertheless, some issues are easier than others to draw unified
support from most immigrant communities. For instance, expanding the
eligibility of seniors and children for welfare benefits is an issue to unify
all immigrant and minority groups. However, protecting undocumented
workers by raising their wage would rarely be supported by business owners who have benefited from the vulnerability of undocumented workers.
Therefore, to be successful and effective, community organizers and
coalition builders should have a comprehensive understanding of the different nature, characteristics, and interests of diverse subgroups of the
larger ethnic community. Utilizing this understanding, they can identify
specific goals for specific groups and decide the best organizing strategies

to achieve those goals. Future research is needed because we do not yet know much about relations between within-group heterogeneity and multiethnic collaboration. Questions for future research may include the following: Whether, and under what condition, can the social class- or gender-based multiethnic collaboration be realized beyond ethnic divide? What are the processes of such collaboration? How do the collaboration processes affect ethnic communities before, during, and after the collaboration?

One of issues in the intersection of race and social class is the relationship between immigrants and organized labor. "Immigration is, in its fundamental aspects, a labor problem" (Gompers, 1925, p. 125). One of the functions of social welfare is to help workers stay in labor markets. Thus, it would be desirable if the resistance of Korean Americans to regulatory immigration and social welfare policies were joined by labor unions. Over the past several years, Korean immigrant workers in various metropolitan areas have worked with local labor unions to improve working conditions of low-wage workers (Eyck, 2007). Most recently in 2009, the nation's two major labor federations, the American Federation of Labor-Congress of Industrial Organizations (AFL-CIO) and Change to Win, have joined forces to support legalizing the status of illegal immigrants already in the United States, declaring:

> Immigration reform must . . . reduce the exploitation of immigrant workers. . . . The most effective way to do that is for all workers—immigrant and native-born—to have full and complete access to the protection of labor, health and safety and other laws. (AFL-CIO & Win, 2009)

Because most alliances between immigrants and labor unions are still at the initial stages of development, it is too early to discuss their success and effectiveness. However, it is promising that immigrants and organized labor unions to have begun to work together to achieve synergy.

〰 CONCLUSION

This chapter began with the frustrating remark by an African American civil rights attorney and showed in the subsequent discussion that her frustration was related, at least partially, to conflicts between Korean and

African Americans. Middleman minority theory was proposed as the guiding framework to understand the unique position of Korean Americans as middlemen between the white majority group and African American minority who occupy the lower social status. Since 1990, immigration and social welfare legislation were regulatory policies that unfairly control the lives of immigrants by limiting the number and type of work available, and eligibility for welfare benefits. These policies also forced unnecessary competition between minorities. Finally, a variety of resistance efforts of Korean Americans, either by themselves or in cooperation with other minorities, were discussed, some of which were shown to be effective.

Nobody wants to experience the next riot against any minority in the United States. To prevent the next riot, it is essential for immigrant groups to clearly understand that African Americans' hardship is not an exclusive issue, but an issue for all minorities. Hardship is a problem for Korean and Latino Americans, and for minorities, immigrants, and organized workers. Harmony and solidarity within a minority group, among minorities, and among workers with a variety of racial, ethnic, and cultural differences are not impossible to achieve. It only takes time and effort.

░ REFERENCEſ

AFL-CIO, & Win, C. T. (2009). *The labor movement's framework for comprehensive immigration reform.* Retrieved May 10, 2009, from http://www.aflcio.org/issues/civilrights/immigration/upload/immigrationreform041409.pdf

Bobo, L. D. (1999). Prejudice as group position: Microfoundations of a sociological approach to racism and race relations. *Journal of Social Issues, 55*(3), 445–472.

Bonacich, E. (1973). A theory of middle man minorities. *American Sociological Review, 38,* 583–594.

Borjas, G. J. (2002). Welfare reform and immigrant participation in welfare programs. *International Migration Review, 36*(4), 1093–1123.

Boyd, R. L., & Xu, X. (2003). Did retail enterprise among White immigrants benefit from the residential segregation of Blacks? A study of large northern cities in the early 20th century. *Social Science Quarterly, 84*(4), 934–945.

Briggs, V. M., Jr. (2008). Immigration policy: The nation's most fundamental labor law. *Perspectives in Business, 5*(1), 5–9.

Capps, R. (2001). *Hardship among children of immigrants: Findings from the 1999 National Survey of America's Families.* Washington, DC: Urban Institute.

Chang, E. T. (1994). Los Angeles "riots" and the Korean-American community. In H. Kwon (Ed.), *Korean Americans: Conflict and harmony* (pp. 159–176). Chicago: Center for Korean Studies, North Park College and Theological Seminary.

Chang, E. T. (1995). The impact of the civil unrest on community-based organizational coalitions. In E. Yu & E. T. Chang (Eds.), *Multiethnic coalition building in Los Angeles* (pp. 117–133). Los Angeles: Institute for Asian American and Pacific Asian Studies, California State University, Los Angeles.

Chang, E. T., & Diaz-Veizades, J. (1999). *Ethnic peace in the American city: Building community in Los Angeles and beyond.* New York: New York University Press.

Chang, E. T., & Yu, E. (1994). Chronology. In E. Yu (Ed.), *Black-Korean encounter: Toward understanding and alliance* (pp. xiii–xvi). Los Angeles: Institute for Asian American and Pacific Asian Studies.

Choy, B. (1979). *Koreans in America.* Chicago: Nelson Hall.

Chung, A. Y. (2007). *Legacies of struggle: Conflict and cooperation in Korean American politics.* Stanford, CA: Stanford University Press.

Crogan, J. (2002, May 02). The L.A. 53. *LA Weekly.* Retrieved from http://www.laweekly.com

Eyck, T. T. (2007, May 1). Worker centers increasingly are forging alliances with unions. *Monthly Review.*

Fujiwara, L. H. (1998). The impact of welfare reform on Asian immigrant communities. *Social Justice, 25*(1), 82–104.

Gans, H. (1973). Negro-Jewish conflict in New York City. In D. E. Gelfand & R. D. Lee (Eds.), *Ethnic conflicts and power: A cross-national perspective* (pp. 218–230). New York: Wiley.

Gompers, S. (1925). *Seventy years of life and labor* (Vol. 2). New York: E. P. Dutton.

Hall, R. E. (2008). Manifestations of racism in the 21st century. In R. E. Hall (Ed.), *Racism in the 21st century: An empirical analysis of skin color* (pp. 25–44). New York: Springer.

Hernandes-Truyol, B. E. (1997). Reconciling rights in collision: An international human rights strategy. In J. F. Perea (Ed.), *Immigrants out: The new nativism and the anti-immigrant impulse in the United States* (pp. 254–276). New York: New York University Press.

Hernandez, T. K. (2007, January 7). Roots of Latino/black anger: Longtime prejudices, not economic rivalry, fuel tensions. *Los Angeles Times.* Retrieved June 15, 2010, from http://www.latimes.com/news/opinion/la-op-hernandez7jan07,0,2489.story?coll=la-opinion-rightrail

Hing, B. O. (2007, May 8). *Promoting family values and immigration.* Paper presented at the House Judiciary Subcommittee on Immigration, Washington, DC.

Hurh, W. M., & Kim, K. C. (1984). *Korean immigrants in America: A structural analysis of ethnic confinement and adhesive adaptation.* Madison, NJ: Fairleigh Dickinson University Press.

Jackson, J. W. (1993). Realistic group conflict theory: A review and evaluation of the theoretical and empirical literature. *Psychological Record, 43,* 395–413.

Katz, S. (Ed.). (1967). *Negro and Jew: An encounter in America.* London: Macmillan Company.

Korean Workers Project. (2007). *"Forgotten workers": A study of low-wage Korean immigrant workers in the metropolitan New York area.* Retrieved August 11, 2008, from http://www.aaldef.org/docs/KWP_2006WorkerSurvey_analysis.pdf

Lee, E. S. (2005). The political awakening of Korean Americans. In H. Chun, K. C. Kim, & S. Kim (Eds.), *Koreans in the windy city: 100 years of Korean Americans in the Chicago area* (pp. 337–350). New Haven, CT: Centennial Publication Committee of Chicago, East Rock Institute.

Lee, E., & Kang, M. (2004). *Gender and ethnic niche formation: Korean immigrant women in the nail salon industry.* Paper presented at the annual meeting of the American Sociological Association, San Francisco, CA.

Lee, J. (2006). Constructing race and civility in urban America. *Urban Studies, 43*(5–6), 903–917.

Lee, J., & Bean, F. D. (2007). Reinventing the color line: Immigration and America's new racial/ethnic divide. *Social Forces, 86*(2), 561–586.

Leong, A. (2002). How public-policy reforms shape, and reveal the shape of, Asian America. In L. T. Vo & R. Bonus (Eds.), *Contemporary Asian American communities: Intersections and divergences* (pp. 229–248). Philadelphia: Temple University Press.

Light, I., & Bonacich, E. (1988). *Immigrant entrepreneurs: Koreans in Los Angeles, 1965–1982.* Berkeley: University of California Press.

Martin, T. (1993). From slavery to Rodney King: Continuity and change. In H. R. Madhubuty (Ed.), *Why L.A. happened: Implications of the '92 Los Angeles rebellion* (pp. 27–40). Chicago: Third World Press.

Meinig, D. W. (2004). *The shaping of America: A geographical perspective on 500 years of history.* New Haven, CT: Yale University Press.

Min, P. G. (1996). *Caught in the middle: Korean communities in New York and Los Angeles.* Berkeley: University of California Press.

Min, P. G. (1998). *Changes and conflicts: Korean immigrant families in New York.* Boston: Allyn & Bacon.

National Conference of State Legislatures. (2009). *Immigrant policy issues overview.* Retrieved May 5, 2009, from http://www.ncsl.org/programs/immig/immigpolicy overview.htm

The New York Immigration Coalition. (2008). Retrieved November 13, 2008, from http://www.thenyic.org

Office of Immigration Statistics, U.S. Department of Homeland Security. (2002). *2001 statistical yearbook of the immigration and naturalization service.* Retrieved May 12, 2009, from http://www.dhs.gov/xlibrary/assets/statistics/yearbook/2001/IMM2001.pdf

Office of Immigration Statistics, U.S. Department of Homeland Security. (2008). *2007 yearbook of immigration statistics.* Retrieved December 9, 2008, from http://www.dhs.gov/xlibrary/assets/statistics/yearbook/2007/ois_2007_yearbook.pdf

Ong, P., & Hee, S. (1993). *Losses in the Los Angeles civil unrest April 29-May 1, 1992.* Los Angeles: UCLA Center for Pacific Rim Studies.

Park, E. J. W. (2002). Asian Pacific Americans and urban politics. In L. T. Vo & R. Bunus (Eds.), *Contemporary Asian American communities: Intersections and divergences* (pp. 202–215). Philadelphia: Temple University Press.

Park, E. J. W., & Park, J. S. W. (2005). *Probationary Americans: Contemporary immigration policies and the shaping of Asian American Communities.* New York: Routledge.

Park, K. (2005). Koreans in the United States. In M. Ember, C. R. Ember & I. Skoggard (Eds.), *Encyclopedia of diasporas: Immigrant and refugee cultures around the world* (pp. 993–1003). New York: Springer.

Passle, J. S. (2005). *Estimates of the size and characteristics of the undocumented population.* Washington, DC: Pew Hispanic Center.

Schoch, D., & Lin, R. (2007, April 29). 15 years after L.A. riots, tension still high. *Los Angeles Times.* Retrieved June 15, 2010, from http://www.latimes.com/news/local/la-me-riots29apr29,1,1344245,full.story?ctrack=1&cset=true

Shinagawa, L. H. (1996). The impact of immigration on the demography of Asian Pacific Americans. In B. O. Hing & R. Lee (Eds.), *The state of Asian Pacific America: Reframing the immigration debate.* Los Angeles: LEAP Asian Pacific American Public Policy Institute and UCLA Asian American Studies Center.

Singer, A. (2004). Welfare reform and immigrants: A policy review. In P. Kretsedemas & A. Aparicio (Eds.), *Immigrants, welfare reform, and the poverty of policy* (pp. 21–34). Westport, CT: Praeger.

Takaki, R. (1998). *Strangers from a different shore: A history of Asian Americans.* Boston: Back Bay Books.

Tierney, K. J. (1994). Property damage and violence: A collective behavior analysis. In M. Baldassare (Ed.), *The Los Angeles riots: lessons for the urban future* (pp. 149–173). Boulder, CO: Westview Press.

U.S. Census Bureau. (2008). *American community survey.* Retrieved November 28, 2008, from http://factfinder.census.gov

Yoon, I. (1997). *On my own: Korean businesses and race relations in America.* Chicago: University of Chicago Press.

Yu, E. (1994). Community-based disaster management: The case of Los Angeles Koreatown during the April 29 riots. In H. Kwon (Ed.), *Korean Americans: Conflict and harmony* (pp. 135–157). Chicago: Center for Korean Studies, North Park College and Theological Seminary.

Zimmermann, W., & Fix, M. E. (1998). *Declining immigrant applications for Medi-Cal and welfare benefits in Los Angeles County.* Retrieved October 29, 2008, from http://www.urban.org/url.cfm?ID=407536

6

Japanese American Resistance to World War II

Executive, Legislative, and Judicial Policies

Rita Takahashi

 **INTRODUCTION**

Between 1942 and 1946, more than 125,000 persons were incarcerated in United States concentration camps or restricted in their actions and movements, based solely on their Japanese ancestry. After the United States declared war on Japan in December 1941, the U.S. government also singled out all persons of Japanese ancestry in the United States and imposed a series of policies, procedures, and laws that applied only to them and only because they happened to be of the same heritage as the "enemy" (Fugita & Fernandez, 2004; Herman, 1974; Murray, 2008; Takahashi, 1978, 1980). The vast majority of all Japanese Americans residing in the United States were banished from the West Coast and held in U.S. concentration camps built for their exclusive incarceration. Almost all were initially housed in the U.S. Army–operated Wartime Civil Control Administration *assembly centers* and then transferred to more *permanent* camps run by a civilian federal agency, the War Relocation Authority (WRA). Both camp administrations were established specifically to establish, operate, and maintain the U.S. concentration camps for persons of Japanese ancestry (Daniels, 1971; Girdner & Loftis, 1969; Grodzins, 1949).

The establishment and maintenance of the exclusion, restriction, and incarceration policies and programs were initiated by President Franklin Delano Roosevelt and sanctioned by the legislative and judicial branches of government (Herman, 1974). By Executive Order 9066, the green light was given to the military to take whatever action it decided to exclude and remove all persons from areas the military designated. It was always understood, however, that the target population was Japanese Americans (Daniels, 1971, 1975; Girdner & Loftis, 1969; Grodzins, 1949). The Legislative Branch followed suit by passing Public Law 503, which made it a crime to disobey exclusion orders. The Judicial Branch upheld the constitutionality of executive and legislative branch policies and actions (Grodzins, 1949; Odo, 2002; Takahashi, 1978, 1980). The Judicial Branch even upheld the suspension of basic citizen rights, including the right to receive specific charges justifying incarceration, the right to confront the accuser, and the right to individual hearing and trial (Daniels, 1971; Grodzins, 1949; Irons, 1989; Odo, 2002; Takahashi, 1978, 1980).

More than 46 years after the United States instituted Japanese American exclusion and incarceration policies and programs, the U.S. government and President acknowledged the wrongs and apologized to each surviving individual. On August 10, 1988, President Ronald Reagan signed the Civil Liberties Act into law. This Act called for individual monetary payments ($20,000) to persons of Japanese ancestry who were oppressed, repressed, and banished from 1941–1946, based solely on their ancestral heritage (Daniels, Taylor, & Kitano, 1991; Hatamiya, 1993; Hohri, 1988; Maki, Kitano, & Berthold, 1999; Odo, 2002).

The vast majority of the 125,000 persons affected by Executive Order 9066 were incarcerated in U.S. concentration camps, and all were restricted in their movement. When the 1988 Act was passed into law, researchers and analysts estimated that only about half of the eligible excluded persons would actually receive redress because many were deceased (Commission on Wartime Relocation and Internment of Civilians [CWRIC], 1983). In 1988, over 46 years had already passed since all persons of Japanese ancestry were excluded from the entire states of California and Alaska, western halves of Oregon and Washington, and southern portion of Arizona.

This chapter identifies specific U.S. government policies (executive, legislative, and judicial) that were formulated and implemented with explicit purposes of restricting, controlling and regulating the lives of a specific group of persons—Asian Americans generally and Japanese Americans specifically. The purposes of this chapter are to identify, discuss, and analyze reactions and responses to these discriminatory policies, particularly the multiple forms of resistance that carried over for decades after initial policy implementation. Focus and attention are given to Executive Order 9066 and related regulatory and restrictive policies that led to the U.S. government's 4-year operation of U.S. concentration camps for persons of Japanese ancestry. The chapter closes with attention to the impact and implications for resistance to restrictive and regulatory policies designed for a whole class of persons, such as all persons of Japanese ancestry. This section identifies areas for future research and social action, and it pinpoints roles for and responsibilities of social workers in monitoring discriminatory policies having adverse implications for equity and social justice.

※ HIJTORICAL GOVERNMENT POLICIEJ TO REJTRICT, REGULATE, AND CONTROL

Executive Order 9066 was one among many policies that was designed to restrict, regulate, and control the lives of Japanese Americans. From the 1800s, a series of national, state, and local discriminatory policies were instituted to stifle the freedom and movement of persons of Japanese and Asian ancestry in the United States (Chang & Azuma, 2006; Ichioka, 1988; Takahashi, 1978, 1980). When persons of Asian ancestry began to compete in the marketplace and gained strength in their areas of work, some in the historically privileged or advantaged position began to feel threatened. As a result, continuous policies were passed to keep persons of Asian ancestry in check and in a disadvantaged position (Chang & Azuma, 2006; Ichioka, 1988; Okihiro, 2001; Takahashi, 1978, 1980). Further, there were efforts to "Americanize" Japanese and Asian Americans through actions that precluded or discouraged Asian languages and cultural practices (Bosworth, 1967, p. 151). Policies directed at one Asian group spilled over and had impact on other Asian American groups. Many viewed all persons of Asian ancestry as similar or almost one and the same. To follow are examples of anti-Asian policies that had impact on persons of Japanese ancestry:

1790: U.S. Naturalization Act stipulated that only "free white persons" were eligible to become naturalized citizens. As a result of this law, many immigrants of Japanese ancestry never became citizens, despite their will and decades-long residency in the United States (Ichioka, 1988; Knoll, 1986; Odo, 2002; Takahashi, 1978).

1870: U.S. Naturalization Act prohibited wives of Chinese laborers from entering the United States (Baron & Gall, 1996). The 1870 legislation extended naturalization rights to former slaves of African descent, but denied naturalization to immigrants of Asian ancestry because they were "aliens ineligible for citizenship" (Ichioka, 1988, p. 1).

1882: U.S. Chinese Exclusion Act prohibited Chinese laborers from entering the United States and prohibited courts from issuing citizenship to Chinese already in the United States. Although this law was intended to last 10 years, it was extended two times: first, in 1892 to renew the law for another 10 years and second, in 1902 to renew again and keep the law in force indefinitely (Tung, 1974). In 1943, this exclusion act was finally repealed after 61 years (Knoll, 1986; Odo, 2002; Tung, 1974).

1906: San Francisco School Board ordered Japanese, Chinese, and Korean children to be segregated in Oriental Public School (Baron & Gall, 1996; Grodzins, 1949; Miyamoto, 1986). Officials were afraid that the students of Asian ancestry were "crowding whites" when there were only 93 students of Asian ancestry in 72 San Francisco schools at all grade levels (Takahashi, 1978). Twenty-five were U.S. citizens (Baron & Gall, 1996, p. 36).

1913: California Alien Land Law made persons who were ineligible for citizenship unable to purchase agricultural land and prohibited from agricultural land leases for more than 3 years (Girdner & Loftis, 1969, pp. 59–60; Takahashi, 1978). Similar alien land laws were passed in other states, including Arizona, Idaho, Kansas, Louisiana, Minnesota, Missouri, Montana, New Mexico, Nebraska, Oregon, Texas, and Washington (Baron & Gall, 1996, p. 44; Girdner & Loftis, 1969, p. 62; Okihiro, 2001, p. 183).

1920: California Alien Land Law was amended to prohibit Asian immigrants from serving as guardians of land purchased in the name of minor children. It also prohibited land leasing to "aliens" or minors represented by ineligible "aliens" (Baron & Gall, 1996, pp. 48–49; Girdner & Loftis, 1969, pp. 60–61). Clearly, the amended law was designed to "drive the Japanese out of farming" (Ichioka, 1988, p. 227).

1922: U.S. Cable Act revoked U.S. citizenship to women who married an alien who was ineligible for citizenship (Girdner & Loftis, 1969, p. 70; Ichioka, 1988, p. 253; Okihiro, 2001, p. 184). After divorce or death, the woman could regain citizenship through naturalization processes. The Cable Act was amended in 1931, allowing women to retain U.S. citizenship after marrying an alien ineligible for citizenship (Baron & Gall, 1996, p. 57; Okihiro, 2001, p. 184).

1924: U.S. Immigration Act (Quota Immigration or National Origins Act) stopped immigration from Asian countries, except the Philippines (which was a U.S. protectorate). Persons of Asian ancestry were to be excluded from entry into the United States, although some did manage to get through (Barde, 2008). This law not only stifled immigration from Japan, but it also insulted Japanese immigrants. According to Ichioka (1988), the "Japanese immigrant leaders felt doubly affronted by the 1924 Immigration act because it ranked the Japanese, not as the equal of Europeans" (p. 250).

1938: President Franklin D. Roosevelt issued a proclamation setting quotas for immigration, in compliance with the Immigration Act of 1924. Under this Presidential Proclamation, "The immigration quotas ranged from 100 for China, India, and Japan, to 65,721 for Great Britain, 17,853 for Ireland, and 27,370 for Germany" (Baron & Gall, 1996, pp. 61–62).

1942 (February 19): President Franklin D. Roosevelt issued Executive Order 9066, which paved the way for en masse exclusion of Japanese Americans from the entire West Coast of the United States and Alaska. Persons of Japanese ancestry were restricted in their movement and ultimately banished from the West Coast during World War II. The vast majority were forcefully removed from their homes and incarcerated in camps (Bosworth, 1967; CWRIC, 1982, 1983; Daniels, 1971, 1975; Drinnon, 1987; Fugita & Fernandez, 2004; Gordon &

Okihiro, 2006; Odo, 2002; Okihiro, 2001; Takahashi 1978, 1980; Weglyn, 1976).

1942 (March 2): The commanding general of the U.S. Amy's Western Defense Command, Lt. General John L. DeWitt, issued Proclamation Number 1, establishing military areas in which all persons of Japanese ancestry would be removed and excluded. This included the western halves of California, Oregon, and Washington, and southern third of Arizona (Takahashi, 1980, p. 618).

1942 (March 18): Executive Order 9102 established the War Relocation Authority, which gave power and authority of its director to "formulate and effectuate a program for the removal . . . of the persons or classes of persons . . . for their relocation, maintenance, and supervision" (Takahashi, 1980, p. 623).

1942 (March 21). Passed by the 77th U.S. Congress, Public Law 503 sanctioned the exclusion and incarceration of Japanese Americans. Violations of the Federal Government's "restriction" orders were declared against the law, punishable with a fine or imprisonment, or both (Takahashi, 1980, p. 626).

1942 (March 22): The first large group of West Coast excluded Japanese Americans arrived at the Manzanar, California, concentration camp. This group was banished and moved from Los Angeles (Takahashi, 1980, p. 618). Subsequently, large groups were forcefully and quickly removed from Alaska, Arizona, California, Oregon, and Washington. On a case-by-case basis, persons of Japanese ancestry were removed and incarcerated from other states, the largest of which was Hawaii.

1940s: Through its decisions in three major cases, the U.S. Supreme Court validated Executive Order 9066 and the ensuing policies that restricted, excluded, controlled, banished, and/or incarcerated all persons of Japanese ancestry living in the United States. They affirmed the lawfulness of government actions, and sanctioned en masse exclusion and incarceration based solely on ancestral heritage. The Court also allowed suspension of basic constitutional rights during time of war (Irons, 1989; Takahashi, 1980).

The 1940s U.S. policies to exclude and incarcerate persons of Japanese ancestry were among many discriminatory policies that were instituted over the previous 150 years. Policies passed at national, state, and local levels were used to prevent persons of Asian ancestry from garnering economic resources and gaining power and influence. Instead, the policies and programs were designed to keep them in more subservient, subordinate, and unequal places and positions (Chang & Azuma, 2006; Daniels, Taylor & Kitano, 1991; Girdner & Loftis, 1969; Ichioka, 1988).

When the United States declared war with Japan, many used this as an opportune time to rid the country of a group they were clamoring to remove or fragment for decades. This chapter focuses on the domestic U.S. policies and programs that were instituted during World War II, which were specifically designed to reduce the presence and influence of Japanese Americans from West Coast areas, where they were gaining economic power and dominance in some key areas, such as agricultural and fishing industries (Takahashi, 1978, 1980). As outlined above, officials at local, state, and national levels worked for years to stunt growth and development in communities of Asian backgrounds. For some, the many legislative successes mentioned above were not enough. To rid the country of the Asian "menace," some demanded complete exclusion or removal (Odo, 2002; Okihiro, 2001).

During World War II, policymakers justified en masse exclusion, incarceration, and other discriminatory policies on grounds of *national security* and *military necessity* since the United States was at war with Japan. They claimed that, to secure the nation, Japanese Americans needed to be banished from the West Coast and held in concentration camps (Kurashige & Murray, 2003; Okihiro, 2001; Takahashi, 1978, 1980). Only persons of Japanese ancestry were singled out for this en masse policy, not any other group whose ancestors were from other countries at war with the United States, including Germany and Italy. This exclusion and incarceration policy ran counter to multiple U.S. intelligence sources (Federal Bureau of Investigation, State Department, U.S. Office of Naval Intelligence, and more), which consistently submitted the lack of need for such mass removal of Japanese Americans from the West Coast (Takahashi, 1980).

Government officials hoped to eradicate the "Japanese problem" on the West Coast by dispersing them in small numbers throughout the country (Takahashi, 1980, p. 2). They used international sparks (the bombing of Pearl Harbor and subsequent declaration of war with Japan) and crises to justify discriminatory domestic policies that many pushed for years—to weaken Japanese American presence and influence in many economic areas.

In addition to ridding key areas from economic competition, the plan was also to use the captive Japanese Americans for cheap or free labor. Knowing about the agricultural experience and expertise of many Japanese Americans, some government officials hoped to use their labor to develop federal land for little to no federal dollars. There was considerable behind-the-scenes communications about using Japanese Americans to develop agricultural lands, irrigation systems, and canals operated by the U.S. Interior Department. Government officials talked of using expert Japanese American agriculturalists to develop American Indian reservations run by the Interior Department's "Indian Services" (Takahashi, 1980, p. 101) or the Bureau of Indian Affairs. Among the federal lands identified for development were the following: Colorado River Reservation, Yuma Reservation, Pima Reservation, and Gila River Reservation (Takahashi, 1980).

A counselor from Agriculture and Conservation wrote to the Secretary of Interior even before Executive Order 9066 was signed, saying that interning Japanese Americans on Indian reservation land "would enable the Indian Department to put the ground in shape for agricultural occupation by the Indian on removal of the Japanese, possibly without any expense for that preparation. Give that a thought" (Takahashi, 1980, p. 101).

Another government official, a Chief Engineer and General Manager, wrote to the Secretary of Interior 2 weeks after Executive Order 9066 was signed, suggesting that, "If the Japanese run out of work on the Colorado River Reservation, part of them could be employed on the Yuma Reservation for enlarging and improving the drainage system and another part could be employed on the Pima Reservation in planting 5,000 to 8,000 acres in guayule" (Takahashi, 1980, p. 101).

\\\\ POLICY, PROTEST, AND RESISTANCE

This chapter addresses Executive Order 9066 and its ongoing impact for the past 68 years. It reveals how many persons resisted and protested various facets of the discriminatory policy over a period of decades, including growths and spin-offs from the original 1942 discriminatory and exclusionary policy. Contrary to many depictions of "the quiet Americans" (Hosokawa, 1969) who remained silent in the face of oppression, repression, and governmental controls, many engaged in diverse forms of protest and resistance—from passive aggressive acts to open protests and physical violence. Resistance and protest were prevalent and ongoing in the concentration camps (Chin, 2002; Okihiro, 1973, 2001; Takahashi, 1980). Because this chapter cannot possibly cover all protests, it will present only a few examples of reactions to oppression, repression, and control, drawn from three time periods: before, during, and after the restriction and exclusion period.

This chapter includes intra-group resistance and protests, where persons of Japanese ancestry reacted to and resisted the actions of other Japanese Americans who appeared to carry out the discriminatory policies of governments or oppressors. It was difficult to reach and react to the oppressors when one has little power, authority, or contact with oppressors—in this case, government officials—so many resorted to protesting against the agents in their midst who appeared to be the mouthpiece or supporters of the policy-making oppressors.

Protest and Resistance Before Exclusion and Incarceration

In the weeks right after the United States entered World War II, persons of Japanese ancestry went about their business and carried on with school, work, and community life. Very few knew that the U.S. government was hatching a plan to exclude them from their homes, banish them from entire West Coast areas, and incarcerate them in concentration camps. Most could not even imagine this because the vast majority of Japanese in America were U.S.-born citizens. Also, most non-U.S. citizens resided in the United States for more than 20 years, and many would have become citizens if naturalization opportunities were open to them. They were ineligible for citizenship because of their ancestry. Almost all were in the United States for many years because of prior alien land and exclusion laws that banned land ownership and further immigration to persons from Japan.

Although most Japanese Americans knew nothing about the planned exclusion, a few in Japanese American organizations heard about plans and attempted to provide input. One, the Japanese American Citizens League (JACL), met with government authorities (both military and civilian) and testified at congressional hearings (Kurashige & Murray, 2003; Odo, 2002; Okihiro, 2001; Takahashi, 1980). Their positions became the source of many protests by Japanese Americans throughout the exclusion period and long after (Okihiro, 2001). In fact, the remnants of distaste, disillusionment, and disappointment are still alive today, now 68 years later (Chin, 2002). This will be addressed in the last major section of this chapter.

The predominant position of the JACL in the pre-exclusion period (and after) was one of full cooperation with any government action and accommodation with and implementation of their edicts. Various aspects of JACL's collaboration and cooperation with government officials' agency authority are addressed in many books and publications, including Bangarth (2008), Chin (2002), Daniels (1989), Drinnon (1987), Fiset (2009), Hansen (1995), Hata and Hata (2006), Hayashi (2004), Hohri et al. (2001), Howard (2008), Kashima (2003), Kurashige (2008), Kurashige and Murray (2003), Mackey (1998, 2000, 2001, 2002), Muller (2001, 2007), Murray (2008), Okihiro (1973, 2001), Robinson (2001, 2009), Takahashi (1978, 1980), and Thomas and Nishimoto (1946). Critics submit that JACL collaborated and cooperated with government officials in submissive ways in an effort to *prove* their patriotism and to win accolades from the authorities.

One who took early exception with JACL's patriotism and accommodation stand was James M. Omura, a journalist (Chin, 2002; Hansen, 2005; Kurashige & Murray, 2003; Odo, 2002). Because he continuously and consistently spoke out, he became "Public Enemy Number One" to JACL (Omura quoted in Hansen, 1995, p. 262) because, according to Omura, "I was the one who was going up there all the time and speaking against the JACL-accepted policy of cooperating. I was opposed to our cooperating." (p. 262). For this, Omura said that Mike Masaoka, a JACL leader and Field Secretary, said, "We'll get you" (p. 263).

In February 1942, Omura testified at the San Francisco hearings held by the U.S. House of Representatives John R. Tolan Committee (Select Committee Investigating National Defense Migration). In addition to San Francisco, the Tolan Hearings were held in Portland, Seattle, and Los Angeles to receive testimonies about the upcoming "evacuation" of Japanese Americans from the West Coast. Omura said he "took a stand against the evacuation policy, and I took a stand against the JACL" (quoted in Hansen, 1995, p. 263). In his testimony, Omura questioned whether the "Gestapo has come to America." In an interview, Omura explained his protest position:

Basically, I didn't think we should take it [exclusion and incarceration] lying down. Certainly we should protest. And we should also resist it as far as we could. If at some point we couldn't, why, at least we would have left behind a record that we had gone unwillingly.

This other way, where you're collaborating and everybody says they're going to do what the government says because they said it, goes against the grain. The way I had been brought up and educated, I had a great admiration for those individuals and people who had stood up against tyranny and fought injustice in a crisis. I felt this was a crisis of tremendous import, and I wanted to at least leave a mark of dignity. Even if we had to go eventually, we would fight it until that point. (quoted in Hansen, 1995, p. 264)

What made Omura and many other Japanese Americans very angry was that the JACL represented itself as if they were the voice for all Japanese Americans, as if selected or elected to convey a collective position (Takahashi, 1980). On the contrary, many opposed the accommodation stand, and protested more against JACL than even the U.S. government. In many ways, the JACL became the mouthpiece for the U.S. government, and they were the buffer between and ultimately target for the masses and government. The government latched onto the organization willing to "go along" with their policies and sell them to the people. According to researcher Alice Yang Murray, "The organization's history of accommodation and assimilation helped JACL leaders persuade the government, once the war broke out, that the league represented all Japanese Americans" (Murray, 2008, p. 106).

JACL collaborated with various government officials before and during the exclusion period, including the military, intelligence agencies, and civil administrations. One top military officer, for example, met with JACL leaders and established friendships. According to Muller (2001), John J. McCloy, a military officer responsible for many concentration camp policies,

had gotten to know Mike Masaoka and several other JACL leaders early in 1942, at the time when the government was removing the Nikkei from the West Coast. McCloy had been pleased by the JACL's stance of cooperation and had struck up a strong friendship with Masaoka. (Muller, 2001, p. 44)

A March 9, 1942, article in the *Oakland Tribune* (California) newspaper quoted National JACL President, Saburo Kido, affirming the JACL's cooperative stance before exclusion:

[W]e are going into exile as our duty to our country because the President and the military commander of this area have deemed it a necessity. We are gladly cooperating because this is one way of showing that our protestations of loyalty are sincere. (quoted in Thomas & Nishimoto, 1946, p. 21)

Years after the camps closed, during hearings before the Evacuation Claims Commission in 1954, Mike Masaoka also explained JACL's position:

[A]lthough we steadfastly refused to concede to its legality or need, the JACL decided that it was our patriotic duty as Americans to abide by this wartime decision and to urge the Japanese, aliens and citizens alike, in the areas concerned to cooperate in their own removal to the best of their respective abilities. We appreciated the great economic losses, the sacrifices, and the suffering that such a mass movement entailed, but we felt we had no alternative. We were in no position, even if we had wanted to do so, to challenge the Army in this matter. . . .

Nevertheless, once JACL's policy was agreed upon, we did everything possible to cooperate with the various military and government agencies concerned. (U.S. House of Representatives, Subcommittee #5 of the Committee on the Judiciary, 1954)

In addition to Omura, others protested JACL's pre-exclusion stand, including Joseph Yoshisuke Kurihara, who was born in Hawaii. As an older Nisei (U.S.-born, second-generation person of Japanese ancestry), Kurihara was a U.S. Army veteran of World War I. He deeply and strongly opposed the exclusion and incarceration, and felt especially betrayed that, he and other Japanese American veterans, were cast into concentration camps, as if an enemy alien. In his words, he "felt sick" upon hearing that Mike Masaoka and JACL leaders took a position of compliance with government orders when they met with General John DeWitt, the military person charged with carrying out Executive Order 9066. About the JACL meeting with DeWitt, he further stated:

Truly it was my intention to fight this evacuation. . . . They accomplished not a thing. All they did was to meet General DeWitt and be told what to do. These boys claiming to be the leaders of the Nisei were a bunch of spineless Americans. Here I decided to fight them and crush them in whatever camp I happened to find them. I vowed that they would never again be permitted to disgrace the name of the Nisei as long as I was about. (Thomas & Nishimoto, 1946, p. 368)

After being forced into concentration camps, Kurihara expressed his ultimate form of protest by renouncing his U.S. citizenship. Although he had never been to Japan prior to his renunciation, he did so because of his disillusionment with the U.S. government. In his words:

> My American friends . . . no doubt must have wondered why I renounced my citizenship. This decision was not that of today or yesterday. It dates back to the day when General DeWitt ordered evacuation. It was confirmed when he flatly refused to listen even to the voices of the former World War Veterans and it was doubly confirmed when I entered Manzanar. We who already had proven our loyalty by serving in the last World War should have been spared. The veterans asked for special consideration but their requests were denied. . . .
>
> To DeWitt, we were all alike. "A Jap's a Jap. Once a Jap, always a Jap." . . . I swore to become a Jap 100 percent, and never do another day's work to help this country fight this war. My decision to renounce my citizenship there and then was absolute. (Kurihara, manuscript in Thomas & Nishimoto, 1946, p. 369)

To address impending exclusion and incarceration, other organizations came together in an attempt to stave off what was to come. One U.S.-born, second-generation Japanese American (Nisei) leader, Togo Tanaka, was instrumental in establishing the United Citizens Federation (UCF), a group of 12 major Nisei groups. According to Kurashige (2008), on February 19, 1942,

> Tanaka had spurred the creation of the UCF in order to challenge the narrow and misguided leadership he attributed to Slocum's wing of the AAC and JACL. . . . Tanaka believed that mass mobilization and diplomatic protest stood a remote chance of staving off the internment. . . . The UCF meeting thus became an occasion for alternative Nisei voices to be heard. (p. 127)

Other protests came in the form of refusing to abide by government orders and discriminatory laws that singled out an entire group based on Japanese ancestry alone. Individuals who refused to cooperate and failed to comply with government orders that they deemed unfair, unjust, and unconstitutional brought their individual cases of resistance all the way to the U.S. Supreme Court (Irons, 1989). Their original court cases were being heard while other Japanese Americans were being forcefully removed from their homes and confined in concentration camps. It was not until years later that these three court cases reached the Supreme Court, which upheld their convictions. Through their decisions, rendered during World War II, the U.S. Supreme Court ruled on the constitutionality of the curfew laws, exclusion orders, and continued detention and incarceration.

Forty years later, the three cases were brought back for litigation, and the convictions for curfew and exclusion order violations emanating from Executive Order 9066 were vacated (Irons, 1989; Odo, 2002). Separate petitions for writ of error coram nobis were filed by Gordon Hirabayashi, Fred Korematsu, and Minoru Yasui after "newly uncovered documents from government files, some of which disclosed that the Justice Department lawyers who handled the internment cases before the Supreme Court had charged their superiors with suppressing evidence and lying to the justices" (Irons, 1989, p. 125; Odo, 2002).

The three petitioners had their cases heard in the 1980s in three separate federal district courts in Portland, Oregon (Yasui case), Seattle, Washington (Hirabayashi case), and San Francisco, California (Korematsu case). After 5 years of ongoing court action, convictions for all three were vacated because of suppression of evidence and wrong-doing on the part of government officials (Irons, 1989; Odo, 2002).

Within days of the U.S. government's announcement of the exclusion and incarceration policies, the wartime domestic policies went into effect. Some (e.g., those residing on Terminal Island in Southern California) were given just 48 hours to leave their homes, while others had weeks or months. All in all, there was little time to organize efforts to effectively protest and resist government policies and actions.

People did not even have sufficient time to take care of personal matters and businesses before vacating their homes and closing businesses, and time to organize was impossible for most. Even civil liberties and rights organizations were caught off guard by the extreme policies, as few imagined such would ever occur on U.S. soil. Many were unaware until it was too late. The exclusion orders were issued quickly, and the U.S. Army rapidly assembled camps to hold the thousands who were forcefully removed on short order (Takahashi, 1978, 2007).

Protest and Resistance During Exclusion and Incarceration

After Japanese Americans were forced from their homes and incarcerated in camps, protests and resistance rose to great heights within all the camps (Takahashi, 1980). The forms of resistance varied from the under-the-surface variety to the overt expressions of anger, riots, and outright violence (Murray, 2008; Odo, 2002; Okihiro, 1973, 2001). Some renounced their citizenship while a few committed suicide (Takahashi, 1980). Although it was more difficult for some to protest overtly against administration and the U.S. government's policies, it was much easier to direct wrath against Japanese Americans who were seen as aligned with the oppressor (Howard, 2008; Murray, 2008; Robinson, 2009; Takahashi, 1980, 1998). As previously mentioned, the central organization pinpointed as collaborators with government, and essentially government agents, was the JACL. As a result, they were the recipients of overt actions of protest and physical violence. In camp, JACL leaders were severely criticized and ultimately ostracized by other camp residents. In some camps, they were threatened with or recipients of violence, and some had to be removed from camps for their own safety (Murray, 2008; Takahashi, 1980).

JACL leaders were labeled *stool pigeons*, *lap dogs*, and *inus* (Japanese word for *dogs*) (Takahashi, 1978, 1980). Many resented not only JACL's compliance with government, but their overt assistance to them. It was well-known that some JACL leaders turned in names to the government intelligence agencies, including the Federal Bureau of Investigation (FBI), Office of Naval Intelligence (ONI), and military police. In the December 11–13, 1941, reports by the JACL's Anti-Axis Committee in Los Angeles, the following entry appears under "Committee on Intelligence":

> Lyle Korimako is the chairman of the Committee on Intelligence, whose duty is to investigate all cases where loyalty to America is questioned and to report to the office of Mr. R. H. Hood of the Federal Bureau of Investigation. (reprinted in Daniels, 1989, "Reports of the Anti-Axis Committee")

Protests and violence within the camps were substantial in many camps, leading the WRA director to call in help to control the *trouble-makers*. According to Hayashi, the FBI was called in to prevent the Army from coming in and taking over the administration of camps. The WRA Director, Dillon Myer, "allowed FBI Special Agent Myron Gurnea to visit all ten camps in January 1943 to make recommendations for the prevention of 'outbreaks, riots, or other disturbances' . . ." (Hayashi, 2004, p. 149). Further, Myers "secretly" gave directors of each concentration camp "discretionary power to remove troublemakers" (p. 149).

Adding to the discussion of JACL's connection to intelligence agencies, Frank Chin (2002) has repeatedly stated his disappointment in a so-called civil rights organization that let its members and community down. In his words,

> The Japanese American Citizens League was organized with the name, and illusion, of being a civil rights organization. The JACL believed the Nisei should shed their Japanese characteristics and be assimilated by the dominant whites. Publicly, they went through the motions of representing Japanese America and claimed to be the only nationally organized group capable of representing Japanese America. Covertly, they worked against Japanese American civil rights as "confidential informants to the FBI." They were also covert informants to Army intelligence and the Office of Naval Intelligence. . . . It was the JACL's self-appointed mission to prevent or discredit all test cases seeking to prove that the selective military orders and concentration camps violated Japanese American civil rights. Their aim was the absorption and assimilation of Japanese America into the white population, thereby rendering civil rights irrelevant. (p. xvii)

Much of the physical unrest in the early camp period was directed toward the JACL. This was the community's response to JACL's claim that they represented the voices of the masses. In this regard, Murray (2008) pinpointed the disconnection:

> Even as the league represented itself as the voice of Japanese Americans outside the camps, JACL leaders such as Tokie Slocum and Fred Tayama were being attacked as *inu*, or "informers," within the camps. Protesters condemned the JACL for "collaborating" with government authorities and betraying the ethnic community. (pp. 116–117)

In addition to the wide-ranging protests against agents viewed as aligned with government oppressors, other protests and resistance were directed at the government's WRA policies, programs, and administrators.

Many demonstrated their disagreements and refusals to comply by subverting, ignoring, or outwardly protesting or rioting. For example, when the government mandated responses to a *loyalty questionnaire,* many deliberately affirmed negative responses, despite their true loyalty to the United States. Others protested and pressured others to respond negatively. Many recognized the dangers lurking behind such loyalty questionnaires and objected to the messages and disparities such a questionnaire sent to them despite their citizenship. Eric Muller published a book in 2007 focusing on such loyalty inquiries and addressed the case of Japanese Americans in terms of "legalized racial oppression" (Muller, 2007, p. 2). Describing the "loyalty bureaucracy" involved, he said:

> The federal government's enterprise of evaluating the loyalty of Japanese Americans in World War II began with racist presumptions and ended with distortions and misrepresentations under oath. And the path from beginning to end, from agency to agency, was for the most part charted not by reference to anything real or true about the allegiances of Japanese Americans but by reference to the preconceptions, needs, and desires of the agencies themselves. . . . this was an enterprise that can teach us a number of valuable lessons. But it is not an enterprise to emulate. (p. 7)

Another example of widespread protest within the camps was the refusal to sign up for the military service, despite an all-out effort to recruit volunteers. Many were very angry that they were denied the right to enlist right after the war began, and now, while incarcerated, they were initially asked and later forced to serve. Excludees wondered how they could be asked to serve when they were treated like *enemy aliens* locked in camps, and while their families remained detained under watchful eyes of armed military police and barbed wire. Many not only refused, but they pressured others to do the same. Some who did initially volunteer had to do so quietly and secretly, lest they could be severely criticized or even physically harmed (Takahashi, 1980).

Protests continued throughout the incarceration, leading camp officials to separate the "troublemakers" from the others. The U.S. government operated two isolation camps—one in Moab, Utah, and the other at Leupp, Arizona (Drinnon, 1987; Kashima, 2003)—before converting Tule Lake camp (in Northern California) into a larger, more permanent "segregation" center. Clearly, the isolation and segregation camps were created to isolate and control dissent and to keep it from expanding.

Further, it was used as a mechanism of control, where protesters were labeled disloyal or suggested to be disloyal (Takahashi, 1980).

The protests and unrest in the camps were effective in that they drew attention to the existence of such camps and the injustices involved. The media covered stories about the protests, and this did not make camp administration and government look good. In turn, this put pressure on administration to be more fair and just in all its activities, including the delivery of food and other essentials.

Excluded and detained Japanese Americans decided that they could not, in good conscience, go along with yet another government order that contradicted their treatment and that of their family. They resisted the call to serve and brought their protest to the courts. They challenged the constitutionality of the exclusion and incarceration orders through their refusal to comply with draft orders from the government while their freedom was denied. Many were severely punished with imprisonment for protesting and refusing draft orders (Hohri, 2001; Mackey, 2002).

Other protests were also effective in the courts. A fourth major court case, Ex parte Mitsuye Endo, was rendered on December 18, 1944, contributing to the termination of the en masse exclusion orders (Odo, 2002). Just hours before the Supreme Court's ruling in Endo, the War Department announced on December 17, 1944, that the exclusion order would be revoked effective January 2, 1945. Dillon Myer, former Director of the War Relocation Authority, said there was "no doubt in my mind that the prospect of a ruling against the validity of detention in the Endo case was one of the major factors which finally persuaded the War Department to revoke the exclusion orders" (Myer, 1971, p. 267).

The Supreme Court ruled that the government could not continue to hold loyal citizens: "Loyalty is a matter of the heart and mind, not of race, creed, or color. . . . When the power to detain is derived from the power to protect the war effort against espionage and sabotage, detention which has no relationship to the objective is unauthorized" (quoted in Myer, 1971, p. 269).

Protest and Resistance After Exclusion and Incarceration

Almost 60 years after the incarceration, wounds were opened yet again when the Japanese American National Memorial was to be constructed in Washington, D.C., near the U.S. Supreme Court. Once again, the issue of JACL's collaborative and cooperative stand with the U.S. government over exclusion and incarceration arose. Many protested when the National Japanese American Memorial Foundation (NJAMF) Board proposed to include Mike Masaoka's words—what was part of the JACL Creed—on the memorial (JAVoice.com, 2000; Odo, 2002; Takahashi, 2000). Masaoka represented compliance and cooperation with government, despite obvious oppression, repression, and discrimination in the exclusion and incarceration orders. For many, Masaoka and his words contradicted civil rights and social justice foundations. Clearly, despite the passage of time, the issues over which there was considerable protest remained alive and strong today.

The protest over the words had everything to do with the writer and what the words represented in the minds of many. Many questioned how Japanese Americans can wrap themselves around words that did not ring true, in light of the discriminatory policies directed at persons based on ancestral heritage. The edited message (and proposed memorial inscription), originally written by Masaoka in 1940, said: "I am proud that I am an American of Japanese ancestry. I believe in this nation's institutions, ideals and traditions; I glory in her heritage; I boast of her history; I trust in her future" (Odo, 2002).

About these words and the JACL Creed, author and former excludee/detainee, William Hohri (2001), said:

> The creed, even in its brief excerpt, reveals the flourish of empty rhetoric, designed to seduce not inform. (p. 160)
>
> This praise is a crude, patronizing joke—on Japanese America. . . .
>
> It is also a joke that many, if not most, of us Japanese Americans do not "get." (p. 160)

Offering an alternative viewpoint, Hohri said:

> Deeds do speak louder, more insistently, more persistently than words. Deeds make us who we are. Deeds educate us and inform our decisions now and in the future. Many deeds cause pain or embarrassment and teach us what to avoid. Failure can be a good teacher. And there are rare deeds that give us hope and faith, that make life worth living and give us direction. (pp. 167–168)

I was one of three NJAMF board members who protested the inclusion of Mike Masaoka's words on the memorial. Community members learned of the three board member's opposition, and many encouraged the three to bring the fight to the broader community, nationally. As a result, I was one of the founders of JAVoice.com: Committee for a Fair and Accurate Memorial, which was established in 1999 as a community-based grassroots movement to put pressure on the NJAMF Board and U.S. Department of Interior to strike the words and Masaoka name from the memorial (JAVoice.com, 2000b; Takahashi, 2000). This protest movement was substantial in that, it garnered the support from a broad-based foundation of persons who not only experienced the exclusion and incarceration, but who also carefully studied and researched the subject. Many scholars joined forces with JAVoice.com and helped to generate a groundswell of protest and opposition. As a result, a petition was written and electronically signed by more than 707 persons nationwide, protesting the inclusion of the JACL Creed and Masaoka attribution. This petition, written to the Secretary of U.S. Department of Interior, Bruce Babbitt, and personally delivered to John G. Parsons, Associate Regional Director, Lands, Resources and Planning, National Capital Region, U.S. National Park Service of the U.S. Department of Interior. The full resolution said:

RESOLUTION

To the U.S. Department of Interior

WHEREAS, Construction of a national Japanese American memorial will be completed and dedicated on U.S. Department of Interior, National Park Service (NPS) land in Washington, D.C. on 9 November 2000;

WHEREAS, Thousands of individuals and organizations donated more than $11 million in time and money to the National Japanese American Memorial Foundation (NJAMF), expecting this permanent memorial to educate the public about the Japanese American experience and to reflect, inclusively and accurately, the community's values of equality, justice, tolerance, respect, and human dignity;

WHEREAS, These values and ideals prevailed among Japanese Americans during the darkest days of World War II, despite prejudice and discrimination, as displayed in many different forms, ranging from military service to legal struggles by resisters of conscience who fought against constitutional infringements, U.S. Government exclusion orders and concentration camp edicts;

WHEREAS, The U.S. Department of Interior, National Park Service (NPS) has the authority and duty to ensure that memorials on NPS land are accurate, correct, and appropriate;

WHEREAS, The NPS and NJAMF have failed in their responsibility to the public by approving memorial inscriptions containing problematic and controversial inscriptions, despite due notice and knowledge of these problems;

WHEREAS, The NPS and the NJAMF acted insensitively and disrespectfully by including the misquotation of a "creed," which was written by a private (not elected) individual they know reflects an organizational perspective of only a limited segment of the Japanese American community, and which they know causes widespread pain and objections; and

WHEREAS, The NJAMF, supported by the NPS, imposed their will on the public without proper notice to the community and ample opportunities for public response, using similar processes to the ones enacted by certain Japanese American "leaders" during World War II, but this time without the excuse that this similar and intolerant position was being forced upon them by "emergency" circumstances;

RESOLVED, That the undersigned individuals, organizations, and institutions, go on record objecting to the NPS's failure to fulfill its mandate to ensure accuracy and integrity of the memorial, and protesting the NJAMF's lack of respect for and sensitivity to the rich diversity of the Japanese American community;

RESOLVED, That the undersigned submit it is imperative that the NPS carry out its responsibilities by reconsidering, reviewing, and analyzing its approval of the memorial inscriptions, making necessary revisions, and deleting the misquoted controversial "creed"; and

(Continued)

(Continued)

RESOLVED, That the Secretary of the U.S. Department of Interior over-
see the integrity of this Japanese American national memorial and
fully investigate the NPS to ensure that it has fulfilled its duties, oblig-
ations, and mandates.

(JAVoice.com, 2000a)

In an article published by the *San Francisco Examiner,* Annie Nakao
reported that JAvoice.com submitted 707 signatures to the U.S.
Department of interior opposing the "problematic and controversial"
memorial inscriptions. Further, she reported:

> Rita Takahashi, one of three dissident NJAM board members, called
> the decision to include Masaoka "mind-boggling," because his name
> and words were "a total contradiction of what the memorial is
> about" (quoted in Murray, 2008, p. 424).
>
> Nakao further explained that Masaoka's words "do not reflect
> divergent wartime experiences of Japanese Americans—anger, resis-
> tance, and protest—which many feel have long been muzzled in the
> name of patriotism" (quoted in Murray, 2008, p. 425). Quoting
> Dale Minami, the memorial controversy was a clash between "those
> who wanted to cooperate and those who wanted to resist." Further,
> Nakao's article quotes Minami saying that the memorial "omits
> that diversity of responses from Japanese Americans and to that
> extent, it does not reflect a true history" (quoted in Murray, 2008,
> p. 425). In agreement, Steve Yoda referred to the monument as "a
> whitewashing of the community's history" (quoted in Murray,
> 2008, p. 426).

Despite the prolonged protest, the Masaoka name and words were
inscribed on the National Japanese American Memorial. It was difficult
to change the Board's position when most members of the Board were
long-time JACLers. In fact, the most vociferous proponents of including
these words and Masaoka's name were his close friend and long-time
JACLer, Bill Hosokawa, and his brother-in-law, former U.S. Congressman
and Secretary of Transportation, Norman Mineta. The grassroots organizers and activists fought strong and hard to resist a repeat injustice, just

as many Japanese Americans did before them. Given the composition of the Board and the power (real and perceived) of some members, it was difficult to overcome the drive to memorialize Masaoka. In his book *Resistance*, William Hohri (2001) described what happened:

> Though there was a vigorous battle waged by a small minority within the board of the National Japanese American Memorial Foundation, they were repeatedly overwhelmed—and outvoted— with the argument that the majority rules, even on matters of historical accuracy. (p. 161)

The memorial was built and dedicated in 2000. It includes a stone slab attributing Mike Masaoka to the brief words edited from the JACL Creed.

∭ IMPACT OF AND IMPLICATIONS FOR OF SOCIAL WORK RESISTANCE

Resistance and protest actions during all time periods—before, during, and after the discriminatory policy implementation—yielded important results that continue today. Although the protests may not have yielded all the desired results at the time (concentration camps continued to be built and maintained), it had significant impact through the years to follow. Officials and representatives were forced to account for their actions, and they knew their activities were monitored, as attention was called to the wrongs.

The greatest impact stemming from the resistance and protest actions were felt later, during the next 60 years (and now going on 70 years) after the policies were implemented. From the resistance actions, policymakers, scholars, writers, and the general public have become mindful of what transpired, resulting in efforts to redress past wrongs and to implement measures to prevent repeat discriminatory policies.

The impact of the resistance and protests are felt on many levels—from policy authorization and resource allocation to publications in multiple sources and public presentations to educate and mandate. Forty-six years after Executive Order 9066 was signed, the U.S. government issued an official apology and granted $20,000 redress to each eligible persons affected by the exclusion orders. Further, dollars for community and public education were provided by the U.S. government and multiple states.

Additional changes that occurred decades after the resistance actions include the following: Court convictions for violating U.S. government orders were vacated, and a U.S. National memorial to Japanese American experiences and patriotism was erected on prime federal land (controlled by the National Park Service) near the nation's capitol and U.S. Supreme Court buildings.

All these activities and educational sources have been a deterrent for potential repeat discriminatory policies. When subsequent U.S. crises arose at various times (e.g., Iranian conflicts, 9/11, and wars in Afghanistan and Iraq), many were reminded of and diverted from disastrous policies designed for entire reference groups rather than individuals.

The fact that impacts of resistance and protests are felt over long periods of time should propel social workers to always advocate for what is right, even if immediate results may not be apparent at the time. Social workers should consistently take strong stands and demand equity and fairness. The legacies of such action will be permanently etched for influence in future actions. There must be permanent records that social workers spoke out against wrongs, persisted through time, and worked every angle to achieve justice.

The implications involving this Japanese American group have relevance and applications to all other population groups who have been historically oppressed, underserved, and underrepresented. It reveals the centrality of diverse inter- and intra-group cooperation and collaboration to be effective and to achieve collective results. It presents many ripe areas for further research and action, as presented in the following 10 sample questions.

1. How can/should social work values and principles be applied as foundations to spur efforts for social action and social justice?

2. What can the social work profession do to encourage more research by social workers that leads to policy and program changes and social action agendas?

3. What strategies, tactics, and individual and group drives are effective in the short- and long-run change? How do cultural, social, historical, economic, political, legal, experiential, people, and time contexts impinge on the selection of strategies, tactics, and drives?

4. What are the essential factors that lead to short-term versus long-term results stemming from resistance?

5. What dynamic and changing forces lead to change in policies, programs, and practices?

6. What are points of resistance to policy change? How can social workers lead efforts in resistance movements—both change agent addressing resistance and as a group engaging in resistance?

7. What analyses and reflections do change agents and resisters have to offer? What can we learn from them?

8. How do educational factors stemming from resistance and protest get converted into future policy actions? How can we educate and inform others to have long-term deterrent and proactive impact?

9. What can change agents do to keep the resistance agenda alive and on the front burner in group collaborative and cooperative efforts? How can the collective be expanded to incorporate a broader range of diverse groups in the collaborative?

10. Resistance and protest take time, energy, and perseverance. What motivates and drives one to continue over time, despite many hardships? How can one predict follow-ups?

〰 SUMMARY AND CONCLUSION

Being successful in policy change efforts is not just about achieving immediate results, but it is also about taking a stand, setting realistic expectations (that substantial results may take a long time), and staying the course over the long run, despite difficulties and adversities. It means standing up for what one believes is right and being firm about what is just, despite constraints and limitations with regard to power and control. It also means being patient and confident that the impact of one's actions may not be felt immediately but may be realized by many generations to come.

One must make decisions on how to react in situations that are unjust, unfair, and plain wrong. Whether one decides to cooperate, collaborate, and support, or whether one decides to refuse to *go along*, resist, or protest, one must draw upon one's values, beliefs, will, resources, interests, goals, and more. Fighting for justice is time-consuming and often heart-wrenching, but the payoff can be very significant.

This chapter addresses the positions and decisions made by Japanese Americans, in response to federal policies that were designed to repress, restrict, exclude, and oppress. Many chose to engage in various forms of resistance and protest. Various forms of protest are outlined in this chapter, covering three major periods: Before exclusion and incarceration, during exclusion and incarceration, and after exclusion and incarceration. Examples of protests and resistance during each period are discussed in separate sections.

Persistence, resiliency, and drive powered many to protest and resist injustices. Although they may not have prevented wrongs from occurring, they certainly influenced actions that may have been more destructive without their protests. Further, their resistance and protest revealed that, principled people who stand on foundations of justice will do so because it is right, and because it serves a greater collective good. Consequences to individual self may be harsh and severe, but results for the larger collective are often great, and usually reaped over the long term.

⦚ REFERENCES

Bangarth, S. (2008). *Voices raised in protest: Defending North American citizens of Japanese ancestry, 1942–49*. Vancouver: University of British Columbia Press.

Barde, R. E. (2008). *Immigration at the Golden Gate: Passenger ships, exclusion, and Angel Island*. Westport, CT: Praeger.

Baron, D. G., & Gall, S. B. (Eds.). (1996). *Asian American chronology*. New York: U.X.L./I.T.P.

Bosworth, A. R. B. (1967). *America's concentration camps*. New York: W. W. Norton.

Chang, G. H., & Azuma, E. (Eds.). (2006). *Before internment: Essays in prewar Japanese American history. Yuji Ichioka*. Stanford, CA: Stanford University Press.

Chin, F. (2002). *Born in the USA: A story of Japanese America, 1899–1947*. Lanham, MD: Rowman and Littlefield.

Commission on Wartime Relocation and Internment of Civilians. (1982). *Personal justice denied*. Washington, DC: U.S. Government Printing Office.

Commission on Wartime Relocation and Internment of Civilians. (1983). *Personal justice denied: Part 2, recommendations*. Washington, DC: U.S. Government Printing Office.

Daniels, R. (Ed.). (1971). *Concentration camps USA: Japanese Americans and World War II*. Hinsdale, IL: The Dryden Press.

Daniels, R. (Ed.). (1975). *The decision to relocate the Japanese Americans*. Philadelphia: J. B. Lippincott.

Daniels, R. (Ed.). (1989). *American concentration camps: A documentary history of the relocation and incarceration of Japanese Americans, 1942–1945*. (Vol. 2). New York: Garland Publishing.

Daniels, R., Taylor, S. C., & Kitano, H. H. L. (Eds.). (1991). *Japanese Americans: From relocation to redress* (Rev. ed.). Seattle: University of Washington Press.

Drinnon, R. (1987). *Keeper of concentration camps: Dillon S. Myer and American racism.* Berkeley: University of California Press.

Fiset, L. (2009). *Camp Harmony: Seattle's Japanese Americans and the Puyallup Assembly Center.* Urbana: University of Illinois Press.

Fugita, S. S., & Fernandez, M. (2004). *Altered lives, enduring community: Japanese Americans remember their World War II incarceration.* Seattle: University of Washington Press.

Girdner, G., & Loftis, A. (1969). *The great betrayal: The evacuation of Japanese-Americans during World War II.* New York: Macmillan.

Gordon, L. & Okihiro, G. Y. (Eds.). 2006. *Impounded: Dorthea Lange and the censored images of Japanese American internment.* New York: W.W. Norton.

Grodzins, M. (1949). *Americans betrayed: Politics and the Japanese evacuation.* Chicago: University of Chicago Press.

Hansen, A. A. (1995). *Japanese American World War II evacuation oral history project: Part IV: Resisters.* Munich, Germany: K.G. Saur.

Hansen, A. A. (2005). Peculiar odyssey: Newsman Jimmie Omura's removal from and regeneration within Nikkei society, history, and memory. In L. Fiset & G. M. Nomura (Eds.), *Nikkei in the Pacific Northwest: Japanese Americans and Japanese Canadians in the twentieth century* (pp. 278–307). Seattle: University of Washington Press.

Hata, D. T., &. Hata, N. I. (2006). *Japanese Americans and World War II: Mass removal, imprisonment, and redress* (3rd ed.). Wheeling, IL: Harlan Davidson.

Hatamiya, L. T. (1993). *Righting a wrong: Japanese Americans and the passage of the Civil Liberties Act of 1988.* Stanford, CA: Stanford University Press.

Hayashi, B. M. (2004). *Democratizing the enemy: The Japanese American internment.* Princeton, NJ: Princeton University Press.

Herman, M. (Compiler & Ed.). (1974). *The Japanese in America, 1843–1973: A chronology and fact book.* Dobbs Ferry, NY: Oceana Publications.

Hohri, W. M. (1988). *Repairing America: An account of the movement for Japanese-American redress.* Pullman: Washington State University Press.

Hohri, W. M. with Koshiyama, M., Kuromiya, Y., Hoshizaki, T., & Emi, F. S. (2001). *Resistance: Challenging America's wartime internment of Japanese-Americans.* Lomita, CA: The Epistolarian.

Hosokawa, B. (1969). *Nisei: The quiet Americans.* New York: William Morrow.

Howard, J. (2008). *Concentration camps on the home front: Japanese Americans in the House of Jim Crow.* Chicago: University of Chicago Press.

Ichioka, Y. (1988). *The Issei: The world of the first generation Japanese immigrants, 1885–1924.* New York: Free Press.

Irons, P. (Ed.). (1989). *Justice delayed: The records of the Japanese American internment cases.* Middletown, CT: Wesleyan University Press.

JAVoice.com. (2000a). *Petition and resolution to the U.S. Department of Interior.* Retrieved June 16, 2010, from http://www.javoice.com/resolution.html

JAVoice.com. (2000b). [Website]. Retrieved June 16, 2010, from http://www.javoice.com/index.html

Kashima, T. (2003). *Judgment without trial: Japanese American imprisonment during World War II.* Seattle: University of Washington Press.

Knoll, T. (1986). Asian Americans and American immigration law. In H.-C. Kim (Ed.), *Dictionary of Asian American history* (pp. 51–54). New York: Greenwood Press.

Kurashige, S. (2008). *The shifting grounds of race: Black and Japanese Americans in the making of multiethnic Los Angeles.* Princeton, NJ: Princeton University Press.

Kurashige, L., & Murray, A.Y. (Eds.). (2003). *Major problems in Asian American history.* Boston: Houghton Mifflin.

Mackey, M. (Ed.). (1998). *Remembering Heart Mountain: Essays on Japanese American internment in Wyoming.* Powell, WY: Western History Publications.

Mackey, M. (Ed.). (2000). *Heart Mountain: Life in Wyoming's concentration camp.* Powell, WY: Western History Publications.

Mackey, M. (Ed.). (2001). *Guilt by association: Essays on Japanese settlement, internment, and relocation in the Rocky Mountain West.* Powell, WY: Western History Publications.

Mackey, M. (Ed.). (2002). *A matter of conscience: Essays on the World War II Heart Mountain draft resistance movement.* Powell, WY: Western History Publications.

Maki, M. T., Kitano, H. H. L., & Berthold, S. M. (1999). *Achieving the impossible dream: How Japanese Americans obtained redress.* Urbana: University of Illinois Press.

Miyamoto, S. F. (1986). *Japanese in the United States.* In H.-C. Kim, *Dictionary of Asian American history* (pp. 7–12). New York: Greenwood Press.

Muller, E. L. (2001). *Free to die for their country: The story of the Japanese American draft resisters in World War II.* Chicago: University of Chicago Press.

Muller, E. L. (2005, Spring). Law and contemporary problems: Judgments judged and wrongs remembered: Examining the Japanese American civil liberties cases on their sixtieth anniversary. *Duke University School of Law, 68*(2).

Muller, E. L. (2007). *American inquisition: The hunt for Japanese American disloyalty in World War II.* Chapel Hill: University of North Carolina Press.

Murray, A. Y. (2000). *What did the internment of Japanese Americans mean? Readings selected and introduced by Alice Yang Murray.* Boston: Bedford/St. Martin's Press.

Murray, A. Y. (2008). *Historical memories of the Japanese American internment and the struggle for redress.* Stanford, CA: Stanford University Press.

Myer, D. S. (1971). *Uprooted Americans: The Japanese Americans and the War Relocation Authority during World War II.* Tucson: University of Arizona Press.

Odo, F. (Ed.). (2002). *The Columbia documentary history of the Asian American experience.* New York: Columbia University Press.

Okihiro, G. (1973, Fall). Japanese resistance in America's concentration camps: A re-evaluation. *Amerasia Journal, 2*(1), 20–34.

Okihiro, G. Y. (2001). *The Columbia guide to Asian American history.* New York: Columbia University Press.

Robinson, G. (2001). *By order of the President: FDR and the internment of Japanese Americans.* Cambridge, MA: Harvard University Press.

Robinson, G. (2009). *A tragedy of democracy: Japanese confinement in North America.* New York: Columbia University Press.

Takahashi, R. (1978). *"Military necessity": An effective rhetorical tool for policy implementation and social change.* Unpublished competency paper, Pittsburgh, PA: University of Pittsburgh.

Takahashi, R. (1980). *Comparative administration and management of five War Relocation Authority camps: America's incarceration of persons of Japanese descent during World War II.* Doctoral dissertation. Pittsburgh, PA: University of Pittsburgh.

Takahashi, R. (1998). *Japanese American activists speak: What the insiders know about redress* (Videotape). San Francisco: Author and San Francisco State University's Edison Uno Institute.

Takahashi, R. (2000, July 11). *Rita Takahashi open letter to National Japanese American Memorial Foundation.* Retrieved June 16, 2010, from http://www.javoice.com/takahashi1.html

Takahashi, R. (2007). U.S. concentration camps and exclusion policies: Impact on Japanese American women. In G. Kirk &. M. Okazawa-Rey (Eds.), *Women's lives: Multicultural perspectives* (4th ed.). Mountain View, CA: Mayfield Publishing.

Thomas, D. S., & Nishimoto, R. (1946). *The spoilage: Japanese American evacuation and resettlement.* Berkeley: University of California Press.

Tung, W. L. (1974). *The Chinese in America 1820–1973.* Dobbs Ferry, NY: Oceana Publications.

U.S. Commission on Wartime Relocation and Internment of Civilians. (1982, December). *Personal justice denied: Report of the Commission on Wartime Relocation and Internment of Civilians.* Washington, DC: U.S. Government Printing Office.

U.S. Commission on Wartime Relocation and Internment of Civilians. (1983, June). *Personal justice denied, Part 2: Recommendations: Report of the Commission on Wartime Relocation and Internment of Civilians.* Washington, DC: U.S. Government Printing Office.

U.S. House of Representatives, Subcommittee No. 5 of the Committee on Judiciary, 83rd Congress. (1954). *"Appended Section" On H.R. 7435, August-September, 1954,* Serial No. 23, Washington, DC: U.S. Government Printing Office.

Weglyn, M. (1976). *Years of infamy: The untold story of America's concentration camps.* New York: William Morrow.

7

Social Exclusion as a Form of Regulation

Experiences and Lessons Learned in the New York Asian American Community

Anita Gundanna, Marianne R. Yoshioka, and Sujata Ghosh

﹌ INTRODUCTION

The story of Asians in America is multifaceted with roots dating back hundreds of years to America's colonial days. As integral as Asian American individuals, families, and communities have been to shaping today's American society as we know it, their story has primarily been one of exclusion—of being distanced and isolated from mainstream American society and norms. Almost 200 years ago, broad sweeping immigration and domestic policies were created to ban Asians from coming to America and to specifically discriminate against those who had already come to call it home. Although these exclusionary practices are no longer so blatant in policy today, their legacy of oppression and implicit regulation remains. We see this in the creation and implementation of recent social welfare policies, where significant barriers continue to function to block members of the Asian American communities from receiving the services that they need and that are available to them.

We will begin this chapter with a brief description of the phenomenon of Asian American regulation and exclusion, starting with U.S. immigration policies; weaving in the creation and perpetuation of the model minority myth; and highlighting recent social policy, such as the 1996 Welfare Reform Act, where the exclusion of Asian Americans can be seen in the implementation of the policy. We will discuss how the Asian American community, specifically in New York City, experiences this exclusion; and efforts to resist the implicit regulation of the community on the macro, micro, and mezzo levels. This is best illustrated through stories of local community organizations and advocates in their fight for inclusion in policy and access to services; and through stories of Asian American women survivors of domestic violence, a vulnerable population facing barriers to accessing much needed services and supports.

It is important to note that the Asian American population is extremely diverse and complex, representing different nationalities, ethnicities, religions, cultures, classes, languages, education levels, and migration experiences in the least. In this chapter, Asian American or Asian Pacific American refers to people of South Asian, Southeast Asian, East Asian, and/or Pacific Island origin, representing more than 30 countries. This diversity creates difficulties in representing the community as a whole. Still, there are common threads that weave the community together, some of which are the communities' experiences of exclusion and their perpetual struggle to find a voice.

\\\ THE JOCIAL EXCLUJION OF AJIAN AMERICANJ: FROM IMMIGRATION TO JOCIAL WELFARE POLICY

Social exclusion refers to dynamic processes by which social protections available to members of a society are deprived to a group of individuals who then have little recourse to alter their situation (Raveaud & Salais, 2001; Vleminckx & Berghman, 2001). Social exclusion can pertain to the social, economic, and/or political factors that function to exclude individuals within a society from civic participation. This includes access to civic and political rights and available services (Berman & Phillips, 2000; Byrne, 1999).

Although individuals may move themselves into an excluded state through their own actions, exclusion may result from the act of an external entity, such as a government in its implementation of policies (Myers, 2004). In this way, social exclusion constitutes a form of social control or regulation.

The history of America's immigration policy aimed at people of Asian descent has been overtly socially exclusive, based solely on race and ethnicity. The earliest significant influx of people from Asia to America was in the early to mid-1800s, when people from China were brought to the Americas as indentured servants (Bared & Bobonis, 2006; Gyory, 1998). As the Chinese began to work increasingly in the mining and railroad industries, and also decided to come on their own accord from China to join in the search for the "American Dream," waves of anti-Chinese sentiment permeated the country (Rhoads, 2002).

At first, the Chinese immigrants were summarily excluded from many opportunities, such as receiving schooling and owning property. The exclusion from opportunity eventually turned to fear and hatred of the Chinese by the latter half of the 1800s, with negative propaganda and violent attacks against Chinese businesses, communities, and individuals (Zia, 2000). Finally, in 1882 the Congress passed the Chinese Exclusion Act, barring anyone Chinese from immigrating and denying American citizenship to Chinese in America (Fisher & Fisher, 2001; Rhoads, 2002).

In the late 1800s, after Chinese immigration was curtailed, people from other Asian countries such as India, Korea, Japan, and the Philippines began to come to America as laborers (Lee, 2002). But as they began to work and establish their lives, they often faced a similar plight to the Chinese with negative propaganda promoting fear, hatred, and race-based exclusion. Wang (2008) discusses the nativist sentiment toward Chinese and Japanese immigrants through the late 1880s that was reflective of anti-immigrant sentiments and fueled conflict between these two communities. Zia (2000) notes that regardless of their country of origin and that they did not yet identify as a common group, all Asians in America "were subject to the same anti-Asian laws barring citizenship, landownership, and equal access to education and housing" (p. 33).

A review of U.S. immigration history shows that labor unions have exerted much influence on definitions of who is considered a desirable immigrant (Martin, 1991). This was the case in 1905 when the Asiatic Exclusion League formed by labor unions to prevent East Asians from immigrating to America and getting jobs (Zia, 2000). By 1908, immigration from Japan was temporarily halted (Wang, 2008) and the Immigration

Act of 1917 created an "Asiatic Barred Zone" to shut out all Asians, especially those from Japan and China. Eventually, the Johnson-Reed Immigration Act of 1924, based solely on the presumed desirability of races and nationalities, was passed by the federal government and stopped *all* immigration from Asian countries (Wang, 2008). In 1942, America officially turned its discriminatory practices inward as witnessed by the horrifying evacuation and internment of Japanese Americans, which lasted until well after World War II and affected more than 100,000 people (Renteln, 1995).

Although laws banning all immigration and naturalization of Asians were repealed in the 1950s, the United States continued to implement a national quota system with regard to immigration (Forney, 1970). The quotas set allowed for relatively low immigration from Asian countries. It was not until 1965 when Asians were finally allowed to enter the United States in significant numbers, when the United States ended the system of quotas based on race and national origin (Kennedy, 1966; Luibheid, 1997).

Although eventually the overtly exclusionist, regulatory, and racially targeted immigration and domestic policies and events came to an end, their legacy remains. Underlying fears and misrepresentations of Asians in America, and the idea that they are outsiders and not "American"—in fact that they may even pose a threat to American security or jobs—continues.

\\\\ THE PERSONAL RESPONSIBILITY AND WORK OPPORTUNITY RECONCILIATION ACT AND THE EXCLUSION OF ASIAN AMERICANS

New forms of exclusion of Asian Americans currently exist within the implementation of the 1996 reform of U.S. welfare policy. The Personal Responsibility and Work Opportunity Reconciliation Act (PRWORA) was conceived of largely during a period of growing anti-immigrant sentiment, and the belief that immigrants were creating too much "burden" on the American taxpayer by receiving benefits (Fix & Passel, 2002). In fact, the law aimed to end the availability of comprehensive benefits that were considered to be a draw for "less desirable" new immigrants with lower education levels and job skills. PRWORA ended federally funded welfare programs, including food stamps and Supplemental Security Income (SSI) to large groups of immigrants, and devolved decisions about cash assistance and Medicaid to the state level, leaving many legal immigrants vulnerable to possible state-level discrimination in benefits provision (Stoesz, 1999).

What welfare reform has meant for Asian Americans is not well understood, as the population and its subgroups have not been specifically studied in detail either before or after reform (Ong & Ishikawa, 2006). The invisibility of Asian Americans around PRWORA-related research is in itself a form of exclusion and implicit regulation, as it prevents understanding and the ability to respond to the Asian American community needs.

It is possible that the lack of interest in researching the impact of PRWORA on Asian American community is related to the model minority myth. *Model minority* is a term that attributes success, wealth and all successful indicators of a particular group to their racial/ethnic background, thereby setting higher standards for one minority against other minorities (Wong & Halgin, 2006). The myth is a sociopolitical construct that has served to skew mainstream society's perception of the Asian American community. It also removes the community from the dialogue and analysis around welfare and welfare reform. The model minority myth has not only divided and pitted minority against minority, but has also functioned to silence Asian American claims of struggle.

Imposing a stereotype of the "good" and "quiet" minority onto the Asian American community suppresses community voice and creates a structure of self-regulation. The internalization of this stereotype by community members has furthered silenced the community (Takaki, 1989), weakening Asian Americans' overall political voice and denying the need for Asian Americans to be involved in the larger social welfare dialogue.

Some researchers speculate that certain Asian subgroups, such as the elderly, the limited English proficient, those requiring SSI, or the Southeast Asian population consisting heavily of political refugees, have been impacted by welfare reform significantly more than others (Ong & Ishikawa, 2006). But this speculation is largely not supported by research and making the impact of welfare reform on the Asian American community hard to determine.

☰ AJIAN AMERICANJ IN NEW YORK CITY: IGNORED REALITIEJ

Today, Asian Americans are among the fastest growing groups in the country (Barnes & Bennett, 2002). According to the 2000 Census, New York City has the largest number of Asian Americans in the United States at more than 800,000 (9.8 percent of the U.S. Asian American population) (U.S. Census

Bureau, 2002). Asian Americans live across all five boroughs of New York City, with numerous ethnic-specific enclaves such as Chinatown and Koreatown. Despite beliefs otherwise, perpetuated by the model minority myth, Asian Americans in New York City have multiple needs and struggle with poverty, lack of education, cultural divides, challenges related to immigrating and attaining immigration status, and limited English proficiency.

New York City Center for Economic Opportunity (CEO) recently revised federal poverty measures and in 2008 released data showing that Asians in New York City have the second highest poverty rate at roughly 25 percent (New York City Center for Economic Opportunity, 2008). All prior data using federal poverty measures showed Asians in New York City at an 18 percent poverty rate, second lowest to the non-Hispanic white population (10 percent). Using the new CEO measures as opposed to Federal measures, Asian New Yorkers show the largest increase in poverty rate among all race/ethnic groups. Along with revising the general thresholds of poverty to appropriately reflect current individuals' and families' needs, a main difference between the federal and CEO measures is that the CEO counts the effect of benefits and public programs such as food stamps in the lives of low-income families. The striking difference in the Asian poverty rate between the two calculations could be interpreted to mean that Asians in New York City have not benefited from public programs as much as other race/ethnic groups.

CEO data also show that almost 90 percent of Asian New Yorkers are foreign born themselves or are children living with foreign-born parents. Among other race/ethnic groups in New York City, Asian Pacific Americans have the highest rate of household linguistic isolation (28 percent), defined by the U.S. Census as a household where no one over the age of 14 speaks English "very well." Additionally, 20 percent of all Asian American high school students still fail to graduate from high school, far less that one would expect of any "model" population (Greene & Forster, 2003).

The current landscape of New York City's Asian American communities has been shaped by the many experiences of its different ethnic groups. Large influxes of Asian Americans came to New York City once U.S. immigration laws were relaxed in the 1960s. Since then, each Asian ethnic community has had a unique experience with the mainstream American society. For example, Korean New Yorkers faced challenges in the 1980s and early 1990s through years of tension with the African American community (Diaz-Veizades, 1999). In the early 1990s, the Korean American and African American communities joined together to in an attempt to bridge their cultural differences (Chang, 1992).

By the early 1970s, New York's Chinese American community had established a bustling Chinatown—a hub for culture and business that drew many Chinese immigrants to work and settle within the area. Seeing the growing needs of their community, a group of concerned members formed the Chinese Community Social Service and Health Council in 1978 and began advocating for increased language access to public social and health service programs. In 2001–2002, various efforts within New York's South Asian community were begun to organize against the backlash the community felt in New York post-9/11. The community was shook with increasing amounts of random bias crimes, and multiple South Asian men, most often the sole financial supports to their families, were unlawfully detained and deported (Mathur, 2006). There have been numerous other efforts to address specific issues that have risen up over the years in these and other Asian ethnic communities, including the Vietnamese, Indian, Pakistani, Filipino communities—far too varied and rich to be covered here. All of these efforts have impacted not only specific Asian American ethnic communities, but also other immigrant and minority non-Asian communities in New York City similarly fighting for social justice. They have helped shape much of New York as we know it today.

☒ MAKING OURSELVES KNOWN: STRENGTHS AND CHALLENGES AS A PAN-ASIAN COALITION RESISTS

Despite the significance and contributions of the Asian American population in New York City, and the challenges the community has faced and responded to, the Asian American voice is barely represented at the larger city, state, and federal policy-making tables. And the voice has been all but silenced in the city's social welfare dialogue. Although they are serving the fastest growing population in New York City, Asian American community organizations currently receive only 0.24 percent of the City's government social service contract dollars (Simm, 2002).

In 1986, recognizing the inadequacies of New York City's public service infrastructure, including education, social, and health service institutions, in meeting the needs of all Asian Pacific American New Yorkers, a group of social service providers created the Coalition for Asian American Children and Families (CACF). CACF realized early on the importance of building the political voice of Asian Americans and has since been working to create a pan-Asian movement, unifying and representing all the Asian ethnic communities in New York City. Today, CACF is the only organization of its kind in the nation to advocate for the rights of and for better policies to serve children and families of all Asian Pacific American backgrounds.

In its years of experience, CACF has seen the lack of voice and the exclusion of the Asian American community in their work: (1) with city, state, and federal government officials and administrators; (2) with fellow policy advocates and community organizations working on similar issues of economic and social justice, child welfare, education, and health care; and (3) with researchers in academia, government, policy think tanks. With each of these groups, CACF has encountered a general *disconnect* in understanding the Asian American community. Many are swayed by the ever-present myths of the model minority—that Asian American families are better off than average New Yorkers and that they therefore don't require the attention of policies or programs that could benefit them. Additionally, CACF observes a *pooling* effect where Asian Americans are often assumed to consistently exhibit similar levels of success and well-being as non-Hispanic whites, without knowledge of the reality of the communities' experiences.

Often, the disconnect with the Asian American community stems from a lack of awareness of the immense diversity within Asian Americans, not only by nationality/ethnicity, but by language, culture, migration experience, level of education, and socioeconomic status. In fact, all too often *Asian* has been wrongly and narrowly assumed to mean *Chinese*. Yet even upon learning about Asian American diversity, CACF has found that politicians, advocates, and researchers do not spend the time necessary to understand how to appropriately reach, study, and represent the community, a challenging but necessary task. In data collected on specific community demographics and issues, Asian Americans often fall into default data categories such as *Other* or *Unknown*. Currently, the New York City Department of Health and Mental Health (DOHMH) issues many reports on racial/ethnic health disparities without data on Asians, and with the racial/ethnic categories White, Black, Hispanic, and Other. As recent as 2002, CACF advocated successfully for the NYS Department of Social Services to change its ethnicity data category from the derogatory term *Oriental* to the acceptable term *Asian,* but the Department still does not provide disaggregated data about various Asian ethnic communities.

Data that are not disaggregated and that therefore do not represent the diversity between Asian ethnicities can serve to wash out the statistical differences between each Asian ethnic community. For example, the Bangladeshi and Pakistani communities in New York City both face elevated low-income rates of 63 percent and 54 percent, respectively, as compared with the average low-income rate for all Asians of 41 percent. Exclusion from and inaccuracy in statistics has made it difficult for Asian Americans to validate their communities' struggles and to enter the social welfare dialogue. It has also perpetuated the inability of the Asian American communities to create and promote a strong and unified pan-Asian political agenda inclusive of the multiple common needs of each Asian ethnic group, because communities are apprehensive about being washed out.

CACF's work in New York City has been groundbreaking, as they successfully implement a pan-Asian strategy to unify and mobilize the entire Asian American community in a fight to resist the exclusion of the community. CACF's is a fight for inclusion. Below is a diagram of CACF's theory of change, which can be found on its website at www.cacf.org.

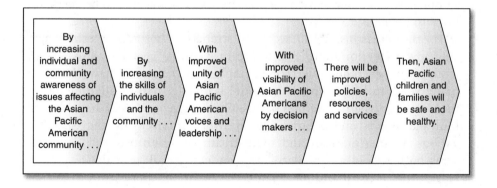

To create a pan-Asian movement, CACF employs a number of tactics, including the following: forming coalitions; producing reports and briefs compiling available data; conducting community-based research, breaking out information on the different Asian ethnic groups whenever possible to expose untapped issues; providing trainings/education about diversity, demographics, strengths, and challenges of the populations to public officials and government agency staff, as well as Asian American community organizations, members, and youth; and conducting public demonstrations, conferences, and campaigns.

To increase the strength of their advocacy efforts, CACF has realized the need to employ not only a pan-Asian strategy to unify and mobilize the entire Asian American community but also to employ a broader pan-immigrant and pan-minority community strategy. Each of the broader immigrant and minority groups CACF collaborates with shares common platforms of fighting for inappropriately served and oppressed communities. The tactics involved are similar but embody a larger constituency, thereby strengthening the power of the common arguments around equality and access and increasing the ability to resist the existing structures that perpetuate exclusion.

Employing each strategy poses interesting challenges to CACF in its work. With the pan-Asian strategy, CACF works to ensure that public policy, services, and funding keeps the growing Asian American community explicitly in mind. But defining and accurately representing the *pan-Asian* community, and subsequently getting the buy-in of various Asian ethnic communities to the concept has, at times, been difficult. As mentioned earlier, many individual Asian ethnic communities feel lost or overshadowed under the pan-Asian umbrella. They feel that their ethnic-specific agenda and needs would not be prioritized and would be washed out, which is something CACF has had to be very cautious to avoid.

For these reasons, CACF works to strengthen both Asian ethnic specific advocacy efforts and also to create common agendas across Asian groups whenever possible. For example, CACF has been working for many years to build a pan-Asian and a broader pan-immigrant movement to address child welfare issues. Over the years, CACF has released multiple reports and policy briefs, provided trainings on the issues to various Asian American and mainstream communities and organizations both locally and nationwide, conducted multiple advocacy campaigns, and created and participated in coalitions and committees that have impacted child welfare policy and practice to be more inclusive of broader issues around language and cultural competence. But realizing the more severe issues of poverty faced specifically by certain South Asian ethnic groups in New York City, including Bangladeshis and Pakistanis, and the extreme lack of resources and supports in those communities, CACF is partnering with New York's Administration for Children's Services and leading a South Asian specific child welfare Immigrant Community Partnership Initiative (ICPI). The South Asian ICPI addresses specific community resource issues through engendering partnerships between local South Asian community organizations and leaders, and the city's child welfare system to build cross-capacity and to share knowledge and resources.

The challenges that arise with CACF's pan-immigrant and pan-minority strategies are similar to those faced in employing a pan-Asian strategy. Creating broader coalitions makes representing specific Asian ethnic groups even more difficult. CACF is wary of the complications of organizing across race and ethnic groups under the pan-immigrant agenda. Race and immigrant status are not synonymous but are often used interchangeably by advocates in New York City. Allying with immigrant communities, although providing a framework within which to understand the complex Asian American community and increasing the communities' power and voice in particular platforms, also serves to maintain Asian Americans as outside of mainstream America. Most disaggregated data on Asian Americans are limited to issues related to the communities' foreign-born and limited English proficient subgroups and do not represent the breadth of the community. In advocating for immigrants, CACF cannot maintain focus on the nonimmigrant Asian populations. But overall, CACF has been able to represent the diversity and various needs of the Asian American community through the use of its multiple strategies and in joining forces with a number of partners.

⧅ THE PICTURE OF EXCLUSION: ASIAN AMERICAN WOMEN LIVING WITH DOMESTIC VIOLENCE

When broad sweeping policies are created with little attention to communities of families and individuals that they are likely to affect, the result for those families and individuals mirrors the larger policy story—it is a story of implicit regulation in the form of limited or lack of access to public programs and benefits intended to help struggling families. This nexus is best illustrated in the lives of Asian American women and children who struggle with poverty and violence, and for whom public supports and services are vital in achieving safety and in ensuring their families' safety and well-being.

For these families, access to services and public programs may be limited simply because of a lack of eligibility based on immigration status or lack thereof. Although the 1994 Violence Against Women Act contains specific provisions for some immigrant women to gain the immigration status necessary to be eligible for public benefits, many women continue to be excluded—left completely ineligible for benefits and public programs.

In other cases, limited access and exclusion are not caused by the lack of eligibility but rather the result of improper policy implementation. Often, the unique needs of Asian American families are not considered when policies and programs are conceived and implemented. Language access, cultural differences, lack of familiarity with services and programs as they are structured in America, and immigration status issues are some considerations that have not traditionally been addressed in program implementation. This leaves many Asian American families without services that they need and that they may be eligible to receive.

In New York City, it has become the burden of Asian community organizations to bridge the gap between eligible families in need and public programs that cannot reach or serve them, or that are unwilling or do not realize that they need to try. The case examples below exemplify the struggles created by a lack of or the improper implementation of social policy. They are based on the real stories of women survivors of domestic violence who received help from the New York Asian Women's Center (NYAWC), an agency that helps battered women overcome violence and govern their own lives, free of abuse.

NYAWC focuses on individual advocacy and counseling with each client served, rooted in a strong philosophy of empowerment, education, and support of individual choices. The individual advocacy is often intensive and focused on the various needs of families, including public benefits, housing, legal services, and ensuring their safety. Advocacy and education around these basic needs is made much more difficult given the lack of language and culturally appropriate information and services available. Therefore, NYAWC also raises awareness and encourages improved services through training government and community service agencies, law enforcement, legal and child welfare service providers, and other domestic violence agencies on cultural competence, language access, and other issues specific to domestic violence in the Asian American community. Following are two case examples of women that NYAWC has assisted. For the purposes of this chapter, the names of individuals and pieces of their stories are changed to maintain confidentiality.

Lynn married her husband in China in 2001. Lynn was in the middle of receiving a degree in nursing, but her husband, a U.S. citizen, promised her that he would provide a good life for their family in the United States, and she need not complete her degree. They arrived in the United States in 2002. They moved into a heavily Chinese neighborhood where Lynn felt comfortable and was able to shop and connect with friends in her native language. Lynn's husband sponsored her green card, and a few years later, she received it.

A few years into their marriage, Lynn and her husband had a child, but her husband began exhibiting tendencies to abuse alcohol. First, Lynn's husband was only inattentive when drunk, but after a while, he became belligerent. When he drank, he came home and began pushing Lynn around. She tried to address his behavior with him, especially because she wanted to protect her child, but things only escalated. Soon, Lynn's husband was coming home and hitting and choking her. After one incident, Lynn ran out of the house and found a police officer to take her to the hospital. From there, she called the New York Asian Women's Center (NYAWC) for assistance, and upon release from the hospital, Lynn and her young child moved in NYAWC's domestic violence shelter in 2006.

Lynn had no money and did not feel safe returning to her neighborhood friends, as she had heard that her husband had purchased a gun, and she knew he was very familiar with everyone she knew. She felt hopeless for herself and her child's future. NYAWC informed her of her and her child's eligibility for public benefits. At first Lynn was hesitant to take money from the government as she heard from others in her community that she may get deported if she asked for help from the government. After speaking with her NYAWC counselor, she learned that this was a myth and that temporary assistance could be helpful in the process of gaining independence and stability for herself and her child.

Lynn did not speak much English because she never had to, so a NYAWC case manager accompanied her to her first public assistance (PA) appointment. Lynn was taught to ask for an interpreter for her subsequent PA appointments, as interpretation by all NYC government

(Continued)

(Continued)

agencies is mandated by a Mayoral Executive Order. Lynn and her child soon began to receive benefits. In one subsequent PA appointment regarding child care, Lynn asked for interpretation services, and was told that they were not available. She tried to call a friend from the PA office to help interpret, and was able through her friend to speak with the worker about child care arrangements, or so she thought.

She then received notice that her benefits were being cut. She immediately brought the notice to the NYAWC counselor for assistance, and the counselor called the PA office on her behalf to advocate. In speaking with the PA worker, the NYAWC counselor learned that there had been a miscommunication during Lynn's previous appointment, and Lynn's friend had not accurately interpreted the information, being somewhat limited English proficient herself. The PA worker had made no further efforts to explain the case to Lynn. In fact, the NYAWC counselor found that the PA paperwork given to Lynn at the appointment was written in Spanish.

After speaking with two supervisors, the NYAWC worker was able to explain the situation, but it was too late as the process to end Lynn's benefits had begun, and her only option was to wait for notice of her benefits ending and then apply for a fair hearing to have them reinstated. As Lynn was left without cash assistance, she and her counselor discussed other options, and Lynn brought up her returning to her husband because he could provide for their child.

In this example, although Lynn was eligible to receive public assistance, she faced multiple barriers in the process of accessing what she was entitled to, some of which led to her exclusion from receiving benefits. The first was her lack of knowledge of the system of public benefits and her fears based on myths perpetuated in her community. These barriers, although they remain unaddressed, are likely some of the easiest for public systems to tackle by providing targeted and language appropriate outreach and education.

Another complicated barrier is the inability of the system to respond appropriately to Lynn's needs in the process of obtaining and maintaining her benefits. She was essentially excluded from receiving benefits because of a lack of professional interpretation, a lack of appropriately translated documentation, and the lack of training on the part of the PA worker to work with clients of limited English proficiency. In Lynn's case,

NYAWC provided intensive services, including information/education on rights and access, referrals, interpretation, counseling and support, and benefits advocacy. Lynn's benefits were eventually reinstated, and she and her child remained safe and away from her abuser. Without NYAWC, Lynn may have never gained (and regained) access to the valuable supports to keep her and her child safe.

Shenaz arrived in the United States from Nepal in 2007 to marry her fiancé, a U.S. citizen. She was eligible to come to the United States with a K-1 Fiancé(e) Visa. However, shortly after she moved into her fiancé's home, he became verbally, emotionally, psychologically, and financially abusive. He would often yell at her and put her down. He gave her little to no food or money. He was sometimes very controlling and held her in his house and did not let her go out. At times he would kick her out at night to fend for herself in a strange land. If he let her stay in the house at night, he would make her sleep on the floor.

Shenaz learned of the NYAWC through a sign at a neighborhood store and called the crisis hotline for help. She expressed her doubts to marry her fiancé, and her wishes to leave him. The NYAWC counselor offered her information on temporary emergency shelter and the police, but Shenaz was reluctant to go to the police even after the counselor assured her that the police in America can assist her. Shenaz's family had had very bad experiences with the police in Nepal.

Shenaz explored the shelter option and asked about help available to gain her independence without approaching the authorities. The counselor informed her that she was not eligible for public benefits such as housing, food or financial assistance at the time, but could be if she explored her legal options and filed a report with the police. The NYAWC counselor discussed other options with Shenaz, including vocational training and working, but the abusive and controlling situation with her fiancé made the possibility of her working very difficult. Shenaz also disclosed to the counselor that she is scared to return to her home country as she will be shunned by her community with no possibility for a job or to marry, and looked down upon by her relatives. In her culture, once a girl goes abroad and lives with a man without marriage, she is shunned from the community. The counselor offered to follow up with her and refer her case to legal services for more assistance. Shenaz thanked the counselor and said she would call back, but never did.

In this example, although there were mechanisms by which Shenaz could become eligible for services, they involved actions that she couldn't take. In many countries around the world, law enforcement has no community service function. Instead it is associated with abusive and often corrupt practices. By linking the process to establish eligibility for benefits to the police and law enforcement, we construct an almost tangible barrier to access. Despite information, referrals, and counseling offered by NYAWC, the lack of options outside of law enforcement effectively excludes Shenaz and many women like her from receiving the benefits that are vital to their safety.

These are only two of hundreds of stories of women struggling with abuse in the Asian American communities and facing a number of challenges accessing much needed temporary benefits and public programs. Like these women, many served by NYAWC face (1) a lack of familiarity and understanding about available services, with different preconceived notions based on cultural perspectives and different experiences and expectations in their home country; (2) limited English proficiency and the misunderstandings that result because of the substandard language accommodations in mainstream social services and public programs; and (3) a complete lack of eligibility, based on a lack of immigration status, to benefit programs that could provide temporary financial and food assistance, housing help, health insurance, and so on. The last is the most dire, and the most challenging for agencies such as NYAWC. "The silence of undocumented immigrants is the catastrophic silence of people taught by legislative harassment and relentless stereotyping to live mute and afraid" ("A Catastrophic Silence," 2008).

Efforts of the NYAWC are able to bridge the gap and reach and help hundreds of women and children every year who otherwise wouldn't have appropriate access to supports they need and are entitled to in order to stay safe and live healthy lives. Still, agencies such as NYAWC fight for families in the midst of systems and structures of support created by government policies that are intended to assist families but that too often aren't inclusive and fail to support them. In the end, many Asian American individuals and families in need often suffer not only with the multiple issues they face such as domestic violence, but they also suffer because of exclusion from supportive public programs.

∭ BRIDGING THE DIVIDE: THE FIGHT OF ASIAN AMERICAN SERVICE AGENCIES

Too often, programs structured to fit dominant cultures and languages are expected to be able to serve Asian American communities and fail to even reach let alone serve the community. Even more outrageous, the failure of mainstream programs to serve the Asian community has been misinterpreted as the communities' lack of needs and used to reinforce the model minority myth. In New York City, it is up to Asian American community organizations on the front lines to make up for the access inequalities and exclusion from public services faced by the individuals and families. NYAWC and other agencies like it are often challenged in their work. They struggle to balance their understanding of and abilities to respond to the unique needs of their communities with the reality of sustaining and fitting their services and programs within mainstream service and funding structures, practices, and ideologies.

NYAWC and other successful Asian American community organizations grew from within the community and therefore have an inherent knowledge of the community. Until the Asian American community has a voice and knowledge is shared, accepted, and integrated into mainstream policy and practice, community agencies will have to continue to find a way to maneuver in tight spaces—to work within existing models that are created for the mainstream and that don't fit with a fast-growing and increasingly challenging and diverse Asian American community.

The Asian American communities' lack of political voice and their systematic exclusion from the social welfare dialogue creates and perpetuates multiple complicated issues and needs, many that require further study and exploration to fully understand. In New York City, Asian Americans now number close to 1 million and comprise 12 percent of the entire population. Because of the efforts of advocacy and community organizations using strategies to educate, unify, and mobilize the community, Asian Americans have recently begun to gain voice and political presence. But there is still much work to be done.

Moving forward, there are many strategies that social workers can engage in to work toward ending the exclusion of Asian Americans from the social welfare dialogue. Advocacy efforts must be focused in a number of areas—policy, research, administration, and funding. Policy advocacy efforts can focus on changing existing policies that are not sufficient or appropriate and that may be harmful to or excluding of certain families/communities. These efforts can also aim to create new, more progressive and inclusive policies. Also important is increased advocacy and attention given to improving research about the various needs and strengths of the Asian American community. Targeted needs assessments of Asian American communities and data disaggregated by Asian ethnic community can promote understanding of the communities and of the challenges they face such as poverty, inadequate housing, and undereducation. Information and data gathered will be crucial to informing policies and programs.

Social workers must also focus energy on advocacy around the appropriate administration of policies and programs. Many times, a policy that intends to increase access to service is inappropriately executed by government administrations and service-providing agencies. For example, a person entitled to certain benefits may not be able to access them because of language barriers and inadequate in-language services. Advocacy in these cases is necessary to educate government officials and administrators as well as the service provider community about the Asian American communities' particular needs and to ensure that existing services and benefits appropriately reach the individuals in need. Advocacy must also focus on the evaluation of existing programs run through large agencies and government administrations, and their efficacy in reaching the Asian American community. At the same time, smaller successful community-based programs and practices that arise from within the community to meet the needs of marginalized populations must be promoted and used to inform mainstream service provision in the effort to make services more accessible to Asian American communities.

Finally, advocacy is necessary to fight for increased public and private funding to properly implement programs so they reach the Asian American community. Often, agencies implementing programs are limited by their financial resources. For example, translation and interpretation services are costly and must be specifically funded in order for them to be made available to the Asian American Community.

There continues to be an underlying current of anti-Asian, anti-immigrant, and Asian-as-outsider sentiment, creating obstacles such as overtly exclusionist and implicitly regulatory and racist policies. The model minority myth continues as a force that maintains a self-regulation of the community and weakens the community's political voice. Each new event—for example, 9/11 and the increase in global terrorism, the explosion of Asian countries into the business world, or the boom in Asian immigration to America—shapes and reshapes American mainstream's often misinformed views of Asian Americans.

Despite growing anti-immigrant and anti-Asian sentiments, community organizations and advocates are hopeful that one day, with an increasingly strong and unified Asian American voice, the community will be included in social welfare dialogues. They are hopeful that Asian Americans will fight back to gain enough political voice and power to be included and represented at all policy-making tables and to be considered appropriately in the planning, creation, and implementation of social policies and programs.

☰ REFERENCES

Bared, R., & Bobonis, G. L., (2006). Detention at Angel Island. *Social Science History, 30*(1), 103–136.

Barnes, J. S., & Bennett, C. E. (2002, February). *The Asian population: 2000. Census 2002 brief.* Washington, DC: U.S. Department of Commerce, U.S. Census Bureau.

Berman, Y., & Phillips, D. (2000). Indicators of social quality and social exclusion at national and community level. *Social Indicators Research, 50*(3). 329–350.

Byrne, D. (1999). *Social exclusion.* Buckingham, UK: Open U Press.

A catastrophic silence. (2008, November, 25). *The New York Times,* p. A32.

Chang, E. T. (1992). Building minority coalitions: A case study of Korean and African Americans. *Journal of Population and Development, 21*(1), 37–56

Diaz-Veizades, J. A. (1999). Social-psychological analysis of African American and Korean American relations in Los Angeles. In J. Diaz-Veizades (Ed.), *Collective violence* (pp. 3–34). Lanham, MD: Rowman & Littlefield.

Fisher, P., & Fisher, S. (2001). Congressional passage of the Chinese Exclusion Act of 1882. *Immigrants & Minorities, 20*(2), 58–74.

Fix, M., & Passel, J. (2002). *The scope and impact of welfare reform's immigrant provisions. Discussion papers. Assessing the new federalism: An Urban Institute program to assess changing social policies* (Report: UI-DP-02–03). Washington, DC: Urban Institute. (ERIC Document Reproduction Services No. ED462 496)

Forney, J. A. (1970). International migration of professionals. *Population Studies, 24*(2), 217–232.

Greene, J. P., & Forster, G. (2003). *Public high school graduation and college readiness rates in the United States* (Education Working Paper No. 3). New York: Manhattan Institute for Policy Research. (ERIC Document Reproduction Services No. ED 498138)

Gyory, A. (1998). *Closing the gate: Race, politics, and the Chinese Exclusion Act.* Chapel Hill: University of North Carolina Press.

Kennedy, E. M. (1966). The Immigration Act of 1965. *The Annals of the American Academy of Political and Social Science,* 367, 137–149.

Lee, E. (2002). Chinese exclusion example: Race, immigration, and American gatekeeping 1882–1924. *Journal of American Ethnic History, 21*(3), 36–62.

Luibheid, E. (1997). The 1965 Immigration and Nationality Act: An "End" to Exclusion? *Positions, 5*(2), 501–522.

Martin, P. L. (1991). Foreign-born workers in the USA: Past, present, and future. *Regional Development Dialogue, 12*(3), 162–176.

Mathur, S. (2006). Surviving the dragnet: 'Special Interest' detainees in the US after *9/11*. *Race and Class, 47*(3), 31–46.

Myers, M. (January 8, 2004). Social justice, social exclusion, and welfare policy. Paper presented at the annual meeting of the Southern Political Science Association, Inter-Continental Hotel, New Orleans, LA. Retrieved June 2, 2009, from http://www.allacademic.com/meta/p67689_index.html

New York City Center for Economic Opportunity. (2008). *The CEO poverty measure. A working paper by the New York City Center for Economic Opportunity.* New York: Author.

Ong, P. M., & Ishikawa, H. (2006). *A research agenda: Impacts of welfare reform on Asian Americans and Pacific Islanders (AAPIs).* Los Angeles: The Ralph and Goldy Lewis Center for Regional Policy Studies. Retrieved June 10, 2010, from http://repositories.cdlib.org/lewis/cp/03_Research_Symposium

Raveaud, G., & Salais, R. (2001). Fighting against social exclusion in a European knowledge-based society: What principles of action. In D. Mayes, J. Berghman, & R. Salais (Eds.), *Social exclusion and European policy* (pp. 47–71). Cheltham, UK: Edward Elgar.

Renteln, A. D. (1995). A psychohistorical analysis of the Japanese American internment. *Human Rights Quarterly, 17*(4), 618–648.

Rhoads, E. J. M. (2002). 'White Labor' vs. 'Coolie Labor': The 'Chinese Question' in Pennsylvania in the 1870s. *Journal of American Ethnic History, 21*(2), 3–32.

Simm, S. C. (2002). *An analysis of public funding provided to social service organizations serving the Asian American community in New York City.* The Harvard University John F. Kennedy School of Government Asian American Policy Review. Retrieved June 10, 2010, from http://www.hks.harvard.edu/aapr/volume_2002xi.html

Stoesz, D. (1999). Unraveling welfare reform. *Society, 36*(4), 53–61.

Takaki, R. (1989). *Strangers from a different shore: A history of Asian Americans.* Boston: Little, Brown.

U.S. Census Bureau. (2002). *State and county quickfacts. Data derived from Population Estimates, Census of Population and Housing.* Retrieved June 10, 2010, from http://quickfacts.census.gov/qfd/states/36/3651000.html

Vleminckx, K., & Berghman, J. (2001). Social exclusion and the welfare state: An overview of conceptual issues and policy implications. In D. Mayes, J. Berghman, & R. Salais (Eds.), *Social exclusion and European policy.* Cheltham, UK: Edward Elgar.

Wang, J. S. (2008). The double burdens of immigrant nationalism: The relationship between Chinese and Japanese in the American west, 1880s–1920s. *Journal of American Ethnic History, 27*(2), 28–58.

Wong, F., & Halgin, R. (2006). The "Model Minority": Bane or blessing for Asian Americans? *Journal of Multicultural Counseling and Development, 34*(1), 38–49.

Zia, H. (2000). *Asian American dreams: The emergence of an American people.* New York: Farrar, Straus and Giroux.

8

The Impact of Deportation on Chinese Americans

A Family's Pain, a Community's Struggle

Qingwen Xu

 INTRODUCTION

Daniel Kanstroom in his recent book *Deportation Nation* (2007) describes how the fear of deportation threatens every noncitizen in the United States. For millions of Chinese Americans working and living in this nation, the term *deportation* carries much of their pain from their struggles to survive. Today, approximately 2.9 million Chinese Americans live in this country (U.S. Census Bureau, 2000).[1] Among them are recent immigrants; about 1.8 million are foreign born (U.S. Census Bureau, 2000). Some have lived in the United States for decades and could be

---

[1]According to the Organization of Chinese Americans report in 2008, *A Portrait of Chinese Americans,* Chinese Americans today number approximately 3.5 million, an increase of 28.5 percent between 2000 and 2006; 7 in 10 (70.6 percent) Chinese Americans are foreign born (Organization of Chinese Americans, 2008).

decedents of the earliest Chinese immigrants who arrived during the 1840s' Gold Rush. Nevertheless, deportation for Chinese Americans has a more important meaning than immigration control or border control. Deportation implicates belonging, cleansing, and scapegoating; it facilitates tighter bonds of solidarity among groups, both the insiders and outsiders. The insiders, who are often racially bonded, share anger and indignation toward *foreigners*, whom they fear will take what is theirs. This in turn, tightens the bonds of the outsiders who share racial or ethnic heritages and creates a sense of alienation. This chapter describes the immigration (or *anti-immigrant*) policies and deportation practices since 1996 and traces the historical roots of immigration control and deportation practices back to the Chinese Exclusion Act of 1882, the law that fundamentally shaped Chinese Americans' experience throughout U.S. history. By emphasizing the psychosocial impact of the 1996 immigration policies and deportation practices on Chinese American families, this chapter explores the interactions between the U.S. immigration and social welfare systems and discusses the role of community organizing and resistance aimed to change immigration and welfare policies to create a more just, multicultural society. This chapter also explores the work of activist Chinese Americans whose persistence has strengthened today's Chinese American communities.

\\\\ IMMIGRATION POLICIEſ AND DEPORTATION PRACTICEſ ſINCE 1996

The United States began as a nation of immigrants and remains so in important ways that enhance our nation. However, this nation of immigrants has had a darker side; deportation is a major law enforcement mechanism that potentially affects millions of noncitizens who live, study, and work in this country. Nearly 33.5 million foreign-born persons now live in the United States; millions of them are unable to naturalize and thus subject to deportation (U.S. Census Bureau, 2004). The current undocumented population is estimated at approximately 12 million (Martin, 2005; Passel, 2006), and an estimated half million are from China (Huus, 2006). Since 1996, when stricter immigration regulations and deportation practices were implemented, millions of noncitizens—many undocumented but hundreds of thousands with legal immigration status—have been ordered to leave. From 1998 through 2007, approximately 2.2 million immigrants have been formally deported from the United States; among them, 8,900 deportees were from China (U.S. Department of Homeland Security, 2008). Although 222 nationalities are recorded formal removal proceedings, 10 countries account for some 80 percent of removals (U.S. Department of Justice, 2008). No European country is on the top-10 deportation country list; China is the only country that is not Spanish speaking (U.S. Department of Justice, 2008).

Two laws passed in 1996 ushered in stricter U.S. immigration regulations and deportation practices: the Antiterrorism and Effective Death Penalty Act of 1996 (Pub. L. No. 104–132, 110 Stat. 1214 [1996]) and the Illegal Immigration Reform and Immigrant Responsibility Act of 1996 (Pub. L. No. 104–208, Div. C, 110 Stat. 3009–546 [1996]). Passed in the aftermath of the Oklahoma City bombing, these laws radically changed many grounds of exclusion and deportation (Morawetz, 1998; Taylor, 1997), including (1) adding retroactive aggravated felony grounds and expanding criminal grounds for deportation (8 U.S.C. §1101(a)(43)); (2) eliminating some and limiting other discretionary waivers of deportability (8 U.S.C. §1229(b)); (3) creating mandatory detention for many classes of noncitizens (8 U.S.C. §1226), including authorization of the U.S. Attorney General to incarcerate and detain noncitizens if the government has "reasonable grounds to believe" that the individual may be a threat to national security (Pub. L. No. 107–56, 115 Stat. 272 [2001] §412); (4) expediting deportation procedures for certain types of cases (8 U.S.C. §1228 [1999]); (5) eliminating judicial review of certain types of deportation (removal) orders (8 U.S.C. §1252 [1999]); (6) authorizing increased state and local law enforcement involvement in deportation (8 U.S.C. §1103 (a)(8) [1999]); and (7) creating a new streamlined removal proceeding for noncitizens accused of "terrorist" activity (8 U.S.C. §§1531–1537 [1999]). Because of the two 1996 laws, in 2007 the number of immigrants deported reached an all-time record high in U.S. history. As shown in Figure 8.1, U.S. deportations rose steadily from 1925 to 2007 (U.S. Department of Homeland Security, 2008).

The 1996 immigration law reforms and associated aggressive deportation practices have demoralized and prevented millions of immigrants from remaining in U.S. society. Because of the expanded criminal grounds for deportation, criminal arrests are widely used today, and immigrants are consequently detained for various amounts of time without the right to see their family members. Deporting a permanent resident is usually based on the use of the most serious, and demoralizing, "aggravated felony" criminal charges (8 U.S.C. § 1101(a)(43) [2000]). However,

Figure 8.1 Immigrants Removed in the United States: 1892–2007

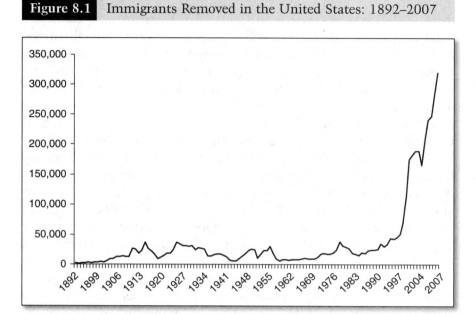

Source: U.S. Department of Homeland Security (2008).

"aggravated felony" could be two shoplifting convictions (8 U.S.C. § 1227(a)(2)(A)(ii)) or tax evasion charges that result in the loss of more than $10,000 (8 U.S.C. § 1227(a)(2)(A)(iii)). In these two examples, mandatory detention and deportation clearly outweigh the crimes that trigger it. In cases wherein government policies seem to ignore the basic notions of fairness and proportionality (Human Rights Watch, 2007; Morawetz, 2004), deportation becomes a harsh punishment to people whose only trait that sets them apart from mainstream society is their lack of citizenship. In essence, the punishment does not fit the crime.

Some argue that deportation of undocumented people is justified considering their *illegal* entry. In fact, following the 1996 immigration law reforms, U.S. Immigration and Customs Enforcement (ICE) significantly enhanced its efforts to seize unlawfully employed undocumented immigrants. As a result, workplace raids, administrative and criminal arrests of undocumented workers are increasing, to much public fanfare; and ICE practices are more harsh and callous. For example, in March 2007, ICE agents raided a leather goods factory in New Bedford, Massachusetts, arresting 361 immigrants charged with working there illegally. Before the workers could speak to lawyers or their families, they were transferred to detention centers on the Texas-Mexico border, thousands of miles from their homes (Sauter, 2009). The extraordinary speed and scale of the operation was unprecedented. However, the law enforcement heavily leaned to unlawfully employed undocumented workers, not the U.S. business employers who in fact hired these undocumented workers and initiated the unlawful working relationship. Figure 8.2 presents the arrests made by ICE from 2002 to 2008: Criminal arrests far exceeded administrative arrests, and the arrests in 2007 represented a tenfold increase from 5 years prior. As these arrests include both undocumented

Figure 8.2 Arrests Made in Work Site Enforcement, 2002–2008

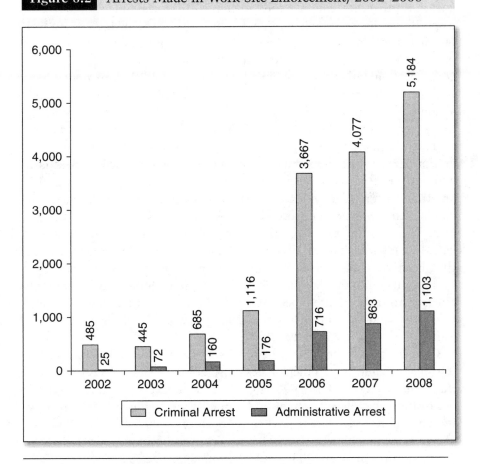

Source: U.S. Immigration and Customs Enforcement (2008).

workers and their employers, there appears to be little actual increase overall in employer sanctions (Schmall, 2008). It should be noted that undocumented immigrants have traditionally filled some of the country's least attractive jobs. The American labor market's foundation, past and present, has been dependent on undocumented immigrants to provide cheap labor (Lofstrom & Bean, 2002). Thus, deporting undocumented immigrants not only demoralizes this hard-working and exploited population and harshly punishes them, but fails to recognize the integral role they play in the U.S. society.

Immigration policies and deportation practices since 1996 have modeled a postentry social control system, in contrast to the immigration border control system (Kanstroom, 2007). Although U.S. immigration laws govern immigrants' conduct and/or behavior from the time they arrive for a specific period of time (e.g., they are barred from receiving certain welfare benefits for 5 years), current immigration policies and deportation practices punish immigrants' criminal behavior or regulate their political conduct often without a time limit (Kanstroom, 2007). Many noncitizens have been deported because of earlier criminal behavior. These legal provisions and administrative regulations go beyond the immigration system's realm of responsibility, which should directly connect to visa issuance, or admission or immigration processes. In addition, no immigration law or policy demands that noncitizens be informed of these laws and policies at entry. Indeed, these laws and policies may be changed at any time with retroactive effects, that is, a noncitizen may be deported for conduct that was not a deportable offense when it occurred. As such, the 1996 U.S. immigration laws and policies and deportation practices have been in fact a mechanism of social exclusion. Critics of the system assert that both the mass incarceration of criminally charged or prosecuted immigrants and the broader detention of undocumented immigrants emerge from racial prejudice, xenophobia, and economic stresses and insecurity and not on well-founded cause (Cole, 2002; Ismaili, 2007; Kanstroom, 2007; Miller, 2002).

Over the past two decades, the postentry social control deportation system has become more efficient, less discretionary, and much more rigid (Kanstroom, 2007). The 1996 laws have been severely criticized for the devastation they have wrought on families, their rigidity, their retroactivity, and more (e.g., American Bar Association, 2004; Schuck, 2000). A constitutional challenge to mandatory detention brought by a long-term permanent resident in 2003 failed (*Demore v. Kim*, 538 U.S. 510 [2003]). The Supreme Court upheld the mandatory detention statute, noting that,

Congress, justifiably concerned with evidence that deportable criminal aliens who are not detained continue to engage in crime and fail to appear for their removal hearings in large numbers, may require that persons such as respondent be detained for the brief period necessary for their removal proceedings. In the exercise of its broad power over naturalization and immigration, Congress regularly makes rules that would be unacceptable if applied to citizens. (*Demore v. Kim*, 538 U.S. at 521)

〰 HISTORICAL ROOTS OF DEPORTATION AND CHINESE AMERICANS' EXPERIENCE

The current immigration and deportation systems can best understood within a broad historical perspective, such as that of the Chinese Americans who began immigrating to the United States in the early 1800s. Discriminatory immigration and deportation practices against the Chinese began in the late 19th century with the Alien Enemies Act and Alien Friends Act of 1798, which empowered the president to expel any noncitizen that he deemed dangerous. These acts were followed by the Chinese Exclusion Act of 1882, which enabled the removal of Chinese laborers. Although large numbers of Chinese came to the United States in response to the need for low-cost, low-paid labor, especially for construction of the transcontinental railroad, the Chinese Exclusion Act came at a time when the United States was beginning to show alarm about immigrants (Choy, 1994). At that time, California in particular suffered several years of severe economic depression and unemployment, which bred resentment on the part of Caucasians about the Chinese who worked for low wages (Choy, 1994). A working class movement led by Dennis Kearney demanded that "[t]he Chinese must go peaceably if they will, forcibly if they must" and, surprisingly, people from all over the coast enthusiastically endorsed this sentiment ("Denis Kearney on the Chinese Veto," 1882). Congress responded with the Chinese Exclusion Act of 1882. It is clear the Chinese immigrants became the scapegoat during the financially unstable 1870s: they were strangers; the men wore queues (long braids); they lived in Chinatowns and socialized with each other only, and were very productive (Daniels, 1988). Cartoons and other propaganda reinforced the view that the Chinese "worked cheap and smelled bad" (Daniels, 1988).

The Chinese Exclusion Act of 1882 proved to be the first of many laws during the next 42 years that restricted opportunities for foreigners who wished to settle in this country (Vellos, 1997). This law marks the first time in American history that the United States barred an immigrant group based on race and nationality (Lee, 2003). The act also represents the first time that illegal immigration was defined as a criminal offense in the U.S. law and subjected violators to fines and imprisonment (section 2 of Chinese Exclusion Act of 1882) (Lee, 2005). The next significant exclusionary legislation was the Act to Prohibit the Coming of Chinese Persons into the United States of 1892 (the Geary Act of 1892), which required Chinese to register and secure a certificate to prove their right to live in the United States. Imprisonment and/or deportation were the penalties for those who failed to have the required papers or witnesses (section 4 of the Geary Act of 1892). The legal doctrines that permitted many of the tactics used against Chinese immigrants developed in the *Fong Yue Ting v. United States* case, 149 U.S. 698 (1893), where the plaintiff was a Chinese laborer deported because of his inability to find a "credible white witness" required by law to prove his right to live in the United States. The extreme judicial deference to such racist laws was formally grounded in a particularly blunt theory of sovereign authority over immigration-related matters. The majority of the Supreme Court declared that aliens remained subject to the power of Congress to expel them, or to be removed and deported in the broader interests of the U.S. public (*Fong Yue Ting v. United States,* 149 U.S. 698, p. 714). These earliest federal immigration/social control laws set forth that the millions of noncitizens legally living and working in the United States, even long-term lawful permanent residents, were subject to the government's whim and could be deported for any reason (Kanstroom, 2007). To enforce the 1882 Exclusion Act and the subsequent exclusion laws, an immigration station at Angel Island in the San Francisco Bay was built in 1910. For 30 years, Angel Island served as a detention and deportation center for thousands of Chinese immigrants, who were interrogated and held in a prisonlike environment for weeks, months, and, sometimes, even years.

In response to the exclusion laws and policies, Chinese immigrants took advantage of legal loopholes and cracks in the government's enforcement practices. They became the country's first illegal immigrants, both in technical and legal terms (Lee, 2002). Various factors drove the late-19th- and early-20th-century immigration from China to the United States, including deteriorating and repressive political and economic conditions in southern China, and the availability of jobs in the United

States as a result of the thriving economy flowing from the Industrial Revolution. These factors pushed thousands of Chinese people to illegally cross the Mexican and Canadian borders; it is estimated that at least 17,300 Chinese immigrants entered the United States through the back doors from 1882 to 1920 (Lee, 2002). Consequently, the U.S. Office of the Superintendent of Immigration[2] increased its border inspection to prevent the illegal entry of Chinese immigrants and, shortly afterwards, formulated the government body extending border enforcement into the interior cities and regions of the United States and instituted a vigorous policy of raids, arrests, and deportations of suspected illegal Chinese immigrants (U.S. Department of Commerce and Labor, 1906, 1909; U.S. National Archives & Records Administration, 2009). The first federal division aimed to prevent illegal immigration was called the Chinese Division; the first immigration officers, known as *Chinese catchers*, were assigned to arrest and deport Chinese unlawfully living in the country (Lee, 2002, 2003). By 1909, the system of immigration interior enforcement was in place (U.S. Department of Commerce and Labor, 1906, 1909; U.S. National Archives & Records Administration, 2009), which is the early version of today's immigration control system.

In addition to immigration regulating efforts specifically targeting Chinese, the public media and other propagandas portrayed undocumented Chinese crossing the border as "smugglers" and "imported" (Wu, 1982). Such labels compared smuggled goods such as liquor and drugs (which were forbidden in the United States in the early 1990s) and hardworking Chinese immigrants, thus rendering Chinese immigrants as contraband that did not belong in the United States and that tainted communities (Lee, 2002). Even though both Europeans and Asians were illegally crossing the borders into the United States in the early 1900s, Europeans were not seen or treated as a threat to America as were Chinese immigrants; public attitudes toward European immigrants remained welcoming and supportive, for the most part, and reflected the view that Europeans—even illegal European immigrants—were future American citizens (Lee, 2002). The racialization and dehumanization of Chinese immigrants as illegal had a long-term negative impact on the Chinese community. For a long period of time, Chinese Americans were labeled and were treated with undue harshness, disrespect, and mistrust.

---

[2]The first federal office regulating immigration issues in 1891. This office evolved into the Immigration and Naturalization Service (INS) in 1933, which later on was transferred to the Department of Homeland Security (DHS).

This contrast in how the Chinese and European immigrants were treated in the early 1900s attest the racist and exclusionary nature of U.S. immigration policies and deportation practices—aimed at social control and exclusion of a group of people based on race and nationality.

After 61 years, the Chinese Exclusion Act was repealed in 1943 when China and the United States became allies during World War II. As Angel Island no longer remained a detainment center for Chinese immigrants, however, many of the racial-exclusion immigration policies remained in place well into the early 20th century and impacted generations of Chinese Americans. Large-scale Chinese immigration did not occur until 1965 when the Immigration and Nationality Act of 1965 lifted national origin quotas. Today, the Chinese constitute the largest ethnic group of Asian Americans (U.S. Census Bureau, 2000). Each year, hundreds of thousands of ethnic Chinese people immigrate, legally, from the People's Republic of China, Taiwan, Hong Kong, and other Southeast Asian nations to work or be united with their families living in the United States. Meanwhile, the same forces of capitalistic exploitation, which were operating in the late mid-19th century to draw Chinese immigrants to America to work long and hard days for low wages, are still at work in the present-day United States, and unknown number of Chinese are still attracted to cross the border illegally and enter the United States for the same reasons their precedents have.

Chinese Americans are a highly diverse group in terms of their social and economic characteristics as well as their level of acculturation. Chinese Americans are overrepresented in the well-paid, educated, white-collar sector of the workforce on one hand and in the low-paying service jobs on the other, creating a bimodal distribution (OCA, 2008; Ong & Hee, 1994). According to the latest U.S. Census figures, 11.5 percent of Chinese American families lived under poverty line, and about 22 percent had an annual income greater than $100,000 (U.S. Census Bureau, 2000). A recent study also indicates that Chinese Americans are simultaneously one of the most highly educated and least educated groups in the United States; the Chinese American community is split nearly 50/50 between poorly educated recent immigrants from China and a more settled, acculturated, educated, and prosperous group of older immigrants and second-generation Americans (OCA, 2008).[3] Nevertheless, contrary to popular belief, Chinese Americans often face extra barriers to economic success, despite their educational achievements (OCA, 2008). Although this is a pattern expected after a wave of immigration, for Chinese Americans, this reflects how

---

[3]U.S. Census Bureau (2000) data report: 29.3 percent of Chinese Americans have no high school diploma while 22.9 percent have earned graduate degrees or professional degrees.

the long-term settled population has yet to achieve fully equal treatment in U.S. society. Beyond language barriers that some face, the difficulties Chinese Americans face stem from being seen as *outsiders, foreigners,* or *imported.*

⟨⟨⟨ IMPACT OF DEPORTATION ON CHINEJE FAMILIEJ

The tougher immigration and deportation rules initiated in 1996 have profoundly affected Chinese Americans, their families and their communities. Particularly since the tragedy of 9/11, the number of Chinese immigrants being deported has grown (see Figure 8.3). Even though the

Figure 8.3	Immigrants Removed by Criminal Status: China, People's Republic, 1998–2007

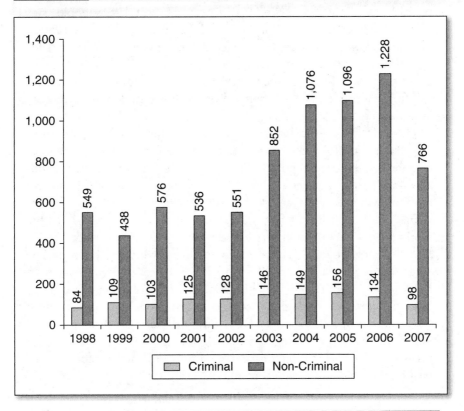

Source: U.S. Department of Homeland Security (2008).

actual number of deportations of Chinese Americans is relatively small (U.S. Department of Homeland Security, 2008), a large segment of Chinese Americans, like other immigrant groups such as those from Latin America, Africa, and Southeast Asia, both with legal status and without, live in the fear that they or their family members might be deported at any given moment, without warning or opportunity for appeal. Like all other immigrant groups, Chinese Americans' experience of deportation reveals the unfairness and in some instances, the absurdity of the 1996 immigration laws, policies, and deportation practices. Eddy Zheng and Lin Yan Ming's cases exemplify the experience of thousands of Chinese Americans.

CASE ONE

Eddy Zheng came to the United States with his family from China as a legal immigrant with a green card when he was 12 years old. He pled guilty to crimes associated with a 1986 robbery he participated in when he was 16. He was convicted and sentenced to 7 years to life. He ended up serving more than 19 years before being granted parole in March 2005, at the age of 35. In prison, Zheng taught himself English and earned his general equivalency diploma and a college degree.

He won his parole by demonstrating to the parole board and Governor Arnold Schwarzenegger that he was a model inmate and had been rehabilitated. The judge who sentenced Eddy, the Assistant District Attorney who prosecuted him, a former director of the California Department of Corrections, and 12 state legislators wrote letters of support for his parole. Since being freed, he has worked with at-risk youth, developed a curriculum for at-risk youth, and has had several job offers to implement his youth program. After finally winning his parole and ready to serve the community, he is facing deportation to China based on his convictions dating back 20 years (for which he served his sentence) all because the 1996 immigration law makes his felony a deportable ground. Eddy was unable to get his citizenship while incarcerated. His family members are all U.S. citizens and live here (for more information, visit http://www.eddyzheng.com).

CASE TWO

Lin Yan Ming, 35, a survivor of the Golden Venture, a rusty freighter crammed with 286 Chinese immigrants on the night of June 6, 1993, in New York, swam the last 300 yards to shore, and spent the next 3 years and 8 months in jail. When President Clinton ordered the release of the last 53 Golden Venture passengers still detained in February 1997, Mr. Ming was one of these detainees. However, like most of detainees, he was still in danger of deportation because the release had not given him legal status. Mr. Ming applied for asylum and failed. He went to work for take-out restaurants in a rough section of Brooklyn, New York, braving beatings and robberies, and saved enough to buy his own business. During this time, he married and had two sons now, both of whom are U.S. citizens. Then, 7 years after his release, he received a deportation letter. (Bernstein, 2006)

Although the 1996 immigration policies and deportation practices most directly affect the poorly educated, recent immigrants from China, the impact goes beyond this group. Most Chinese immigrants, with legal residence status or not, have family relations in America. What seems to be overlooked by the immigration policymakers is that when one member of a family is deported or detained, their entire family and the Chinese American community are affected. The experience of Mr. and Mrs. Chen highlights the tough deportation practices that overlook the broader effects of the policy along with family values and children's well-being.

CASE THREE

More than 10 years ago, Mr. Chen came to the United States via the assistance of a human smuggler. He married a Chinese American woman 3 years later; the Chens had two children, a daughter and a son. In 2001, the Chens finished paying off their debt and bought a take-out Chinese restaurant in Long Island; they also bought a duplex. Like many Chinese immigrants, in order to focus on earning a living,

(Continued)

(Continued)

the Chens sent their children to China to be cared for by their extended families. When their lives stabilized, the Chens sent for their son to return to the United States for school. The Chens were arrested by immigration agents at Kennedy International Airport when a paid in-flight nanny was flying with Chens' daughter back to the United States. The couple, after living in the United States for more than 10 years, was deported with their daughter even though she was born in the United States and is a U.S. citizen. The Chens had to leave their 11-year-old son in the United States with a family friend. (Jian, 2006)

As such, particularly for millions of children living in mixed-status families, deporting one immigrant can result in separation from their mothers, fathers, and their beloved family members—siblings, aunts, uncles, grandparents, and so on. And many U.S.-born children are forced to leave the United States with their deported parents and be uprooted from the community in which they have spent most if not all of their lives. Although Lin Yan Ming and the Chens represents the experiences of many early Chinese immigrants' route of migration and settlement in the era of anti-Chinese immigration—crossing the border illegally, working hard as cheap labor, and establishing a family and business, in the post-1996 United States, they are no longer able to complete the route to successful immigration. They now have to face the possibility of family separation and other resettlement problems such as prosecution and joblessness.

The effects of these wide-reaching immigration policies and deportation practices on immigrant children and families, however, are largely unknown. Specifically, few social science studies have examined and quantified the developmental and psychosocial effects of deportation policies and practices on immigrant children and their families. There is even less literature addressing the struggles of Chinese immigrants. We can only speculate about the effects of disrupted family relationships upon children's attachment and early development from the literature on children displaced by war and diasporas (Arditti, 2003; Farias, 1994; Wessells & Monteiro, 2006), children separated from their parents because of migration (Suarez-Orozco, Todorova, & Louie, 2002), and children of incarcerated parents (Clarke-Stewart, Vandell, McCartney, et al., 2000; Poehlmann, 2005).

The literature suggests a strong correlation between a sense of insecurity (i.e., intense ambivalence, disorganization, violence, or detachment) and prolonged separation from primary caregivers.

Deportation entails family separation, often permanently, and the process of family reunification is often impossible. In deportation cases parents are removed (often forcibly) and most of them are barred for reentering the United States for a lifetime. In many cases, their U.S. citizen children will either accompany them or stay behind (Thronson, 2006) as is exemplified in the Chens' case. That is, children have to either leave their familiar U.S. environment and live in a "foreign" country (and have to learn a new language and acculturate into a new culture), or cope with the traumatic loss involved in family disruption and separation. Under current policies, family reunification in the United States is nearly impossible. This situation is unlike that of children who have experienced parental separation because of divorce, as most of these children can maintain close contact with and receive emotional support from the noncustodial parent. In the case of parental incarceration, children similarly have a chance to visit and maintain contact with the parent and the prospect of the parent's release from jail fuels the child's hope for a return to family unity. Even refugee children, including those who travel to the United States as unaccompanied minors, are afforded special immigrant juvenile status under U.S. law (8 U.S.C. § 1101(a)(27)(J) [2000]) as well as access to a procedure affording family reunification; in fact, unaccompanied refugee children's best interests are protected by state family courts and state social service departments (Xu, 2005). Therefore, unlike other causes of family disruption and separation—caused by divorce, incarceration, immigration, and even war—deportation leaves the intact family and children's best interests in the hands of immigration adjudicators, and children left behind have little chance for reunification with their deported parents under the current legal system. A stressful family environment can negatively affect children's well-being and can lead to poor school performance.

In addition, separation from parents (i.e., in divorce or incarceration) has documented detrimental effects on children, including in the realms of academic achievement, self-esteem, and psychological adjustment. Findings in this body of research are quite consistent: Children who have experienced separation from their parents have more behavior problems (including delinquency), more social difficulties, and more psychological distress (i.e., Clarke-Stewart et al., 2000; Human Rights Watch, 2002; Parke & Clarke-Stewart, 2002; Videon, 2002). The impact of separation on children commonly lasts into adulthood. Adults who experienced separation during childhood, compared with those from continuously intact two-parent families, score lower on indicators of psychological, interpersonal, and socioeconomic well-being (i.e., Amato, 1994; Cherlin, Chase-Lansdale, & McRae, 1998; Hetherington, Bridges, & Insabella, 1998; Parke & Clarke-Stewart, 2002).

Because immigration and deportation systems likely affect poorly educated recent immigrants from China, the loss of a family member(s), and in particular, the breadwinner, can devastate family functioning and negatively affect children's development and well-being. Psychologically, while families with limited resources attempt to achieve the same basic conditions for their children as do most families with adequate incomes, research indicates that economic vulnerability affects family functioning negatively because adult caregivers experience a higher level of stress both about not being able to provide their children with the support, education, and basic needs that every child needs and deserves (Conger et al., 2002). A stressful family environment can eventually negatively affect children's well-being in the form of poor school performance, adjustment problems, and poor nutrition (Conger et al., 2002; Kwon, Reuter, & Lee, 2003; Mistry, Vandewater, Huston, & McLoyd, 2002).

Although we lack studies that systematically investigate the impacts of deportation on Chinese American families, available literature concerning the general population and theoretical models suggest deportation's destructive effects on children and families. Chinese American immigrant families have gone through numerous dynamic changes during their resettlement and acculturation process, such as changed gender role, intergenerational relationship, and family structure. Although much of the old structure and many of the traditional values of the Chinese family have been replaced by a new structure and new values of the modern Chinese American family, Chinese Americans continue to embrace the traditional values of loyalty, love, and respect for family, particularly family elders, to maintain close family links, to invest in their children's education, and to hold high expectations for their children's academic and professional achievement. In traditional Chinese families, there is a strong bond between parents and children and extended family members, who often live in close proximity. Therefore, although family values, familial relationships, and children are at the center of the Chinese cultural system, the impact of immigration policies and deportation practices on children and families are of concern for Chinese American community.

\\\\ A FAMILY'S PAIN, A COMMUNITY'S STRUGGLE

Stories of recent Chinese Americans' experiences with the country's immigration policies and deportation practices replicate stories from over a century ago beginning with the initial immigration of the Chinese who were demonized, expelled, and labeled as criminals and aliens. These early immigrant struggles represent those of the entire Chinese American community from the far past to the present day. Like other immigrant groups in America, the history of Chinese Americans is essentially a labor history of hard-working immigrants in America fighting for the promised justice and equality of democracy and the promise of economic opportunity. Throughout their history, Chinese American immigrants eagerly sought opportunities for collective action to improve their situations. As early as 1867, some 2,000 Chinese who were engaged in tunnel work in the high Sierra Mountains in California and Nevada went on strike to protest against the inhuman treatment and poor working conditions. As one spokesman put it, "Eight hours a day good for white men, all the same good for Chinamen" (Chinn, Lai, & Choy, 1969). They acted militantly and with determination, despite the hostility of other working-class Americans to their cause (Kwong, 1997). In the 1960s and 1970s, Chinese Americans have also organized successfully with other Asian American communities to combat anti-Asian violence and fight for a just social environment in the United States. The pan-ethnic Asian American association emerged during the human rights movement and addressed a common struggle against racism targeted at Asian Americans, who share the key historical and ideological connection across Japanese, Chinese, Filipino, Korean, and many other Asian American ethnic groups in the United States (Kurashige, 2000; Vo, 2004).

At present, the community struggles of Chinese Americans encompass issues broader than labor issues such as working conditions and wages. The Chinese American community's struggles embrace aspirations for justice and dignity of immigrant communities, promote justice and equality for Asian Americans, and are linked to broader movements for human rights. For example, the Chinese Staff and Workers Association, the first independent restaurant union in New York City's Chinatown, has aggressively challenged the tightly knit world of New York's restaurants to improve their horrific working conditions (Kwong, 1997). In 2004, the Chinese Staff and Workers Association organized to secure the first wage increase in 10 years for New York State's tipped employees; and more recently, it sparked a labor movement to secure these rights to control health, time and life (Chinese Staff and Workers Association, 2009).

Yet, in contrast to its strong and successful efforts in organizing around labor issues, the Chinese American community has faced challenges in organizing itself against unfair immigrations policies and particularly for deportees and detainees and their families. Various cultural and structural factors contributable to the Chinese immigrant community's lack of organizing efforts around these issues. One factor is the post-9/11 anti-immigrant sentiment against undocumented Arab and Muslim people—as well as Latinos—who bear the brunt of public attacks. In addition, the USA Patriot Act gives government agencies and officials the right to detain suspects under "reasonable suspicion" of terrorist activity. As such, the propaganda against certain types of immigrants is generally strong and constant in the mainstream corporate media. The Chinese American community has been greatly impacted by the propaganda, which serves as acceptance and tolerance for detaining and deporting Chinese immigrants and any ethnic minority.

Moreover, a primary reason for the Chinese American's lack of community organizing on the immigration issue is the very small number of Chinese American deportees. Although Chinese people account for a small share of those ordered deported, they are the largest group that the Department of Homeland Security (DHS) had difficulty in returning, as the central government of China refused to cooperate with the deportation process. In the fiscal year of 2006, the DHS was able to deport just 522 Chinese whose appeals had been exhausted. Even that was a drop from about 600 in each of the two previous years (Kronholz, 2006). Among the deportees, many are undocumented; and some are so-called criminals. Culturally, Chinese families perceive being an undocumented or a criminal as a norm violation, which causes them to lose face in the Chinese community. Because of the criminalization of deportees, many Chinese families and the extended Chinese community view deportation as a justifiable legal action against the individual's violation of U.S. law. Letting such an individual, a *criminal*, be deported is seen as a face-saving action that can prevent loss of face for family members. Shame is usually associated with an individual's detention or deportation, and the person's entire family feels this shame.

Both cultural and structural barriers make it critical for all Chinese immigrants and people of conscience to stand in firm solidarity with those whose rights are threatened, and whose families are shamed and torn apart. But this is not an easy task, even for an organization such as the Chinese Progressive Association, an organization with a history of educating, organizing, and empowering the low-income and working-class immigrant Chinese to build collective power and provide a progressive voice in the Chinese community (Mar, 2007). Despite hardships, the Chinese American community is organizing to support deportees and their families, to challenge the laws and procedures based on due process and equal protection, and to seek fundamental changes of American immigration and deportation law. In the case of Eddy Zheng and many others, the Chinese community organized activities to support people unjustly deported. Attorneys from private law firms, the Asian American Bar Association, and Asian Pacific Islander Legal Outreach worked together to help Eddy Zheng; more than 50 community leaders attended the deportation hearing to support him on March 16, 2005, and his case received wide media coverage in both the mainstream media and Chinese American newspapers, which have made his case a *cause célèbre* in the Chinese American community.

Today, Zheng is still fighting deportation—even after he was released in February 27, 2007—and he is still living under enormous uncertainty, as deportation still remains a possibility. Although community support and organizing efforts helped bring attention to Zheng's case and free him from detention, without change at a policy level, cases such as Zheng's will plague the Chinese community and the larger immigrant community across the United States for some time to come. Like other disenfranchised groups in the United States, the Chinese American community needs to build community capacity through coalition and increase community power that will go hand in hand with policy changes. Immigrants have the right and the responsibility to help shape the society in which they live.

》 IMPLICATIONS FOR PRACTICE AND POLICY

Building a broad, inclusive immigrant movement to change current immigration policies and deportation practices is a challenging task that requires sophisticated strategies, which can be drawn from the experience of the Chinese American community's past struggles. Learning from history, three strategies appear to be essential for success. First, the Chinese American community must strongly, vocally, and continuously advocate for the principle of family unity in deportation and detainment cases and in the larger realm of immigration law. Unjust immigration practices and procedures, including deportation and the threat of deportation, significantly affect the family unit, particularly the healthy development of children. Given the abundant evidence that separation from family members negatively affects children and the family, the Chinese American community should advocate for its rights based on this premise and highlight how the extended family unit is deeply rooted in Chinese culture. A conscientious response to Chinese American children's and families' struggles must strive to accompany the community. As Justice Field stated in *Fong Yue Ting* (149 U.S. 698) in 1892, "As to its cruelty, nothing can exceed a forcible deportation from a country of one's residence, and the breaking up of all the relations of friendship, family, and business" (p. 730).

Second, the Chinese American community has the personal experience and sensory awareness of internal and external events that occurred during the era of anti-Chinese immigration and thus has the obligation and responsibility to urge U.S. policymakers, politicians, and the American public not to repeat past mistakes, that discrimination and social exclusion based on race, class, and nationality should not and cannot be carried out in the name of patriotism and/or the public's interest. The Chinese community should raise its collective voice to show how criminalization of illegal immigrants can create problems not only for present but for future generations as well, a lesson well learned by the Chinese American experience. Turning hard-working, vulnerable undocumented immigrants with no criminal record, people who have struggled to make it to the United States in search of the American dream, into felons, serves no useful purpose except to feed racial prejudice and xenophobia. The U.S. immigration and deportation system should be a fair system based on rights and humane treatment.

Finally, the Chinese American community needs to form a collation with other ethnic immigrant groups based on their common ground—their fight for human rights and social justice. Human rights violations—family disruption, deportation and detention without due legal process, and lack of emotional and physical security—are common experiences of Chinese American families and all other ethnic immigrant families. These violations ignore norms of fairness, family unity, human rights, and human decency. U.S. immigration laws, policies, and practices, although making it easier for the federal government to arrest undocumented immigrants and to expedite deportation without due process, in fact seem to serve another social purpose, albeit a racist and xenophobic one, to exclude the people of certain ethnicities from becoming members of American society. They help the government to control certain groups of people in the name of antiterrorism, at the expense of civil liberties. Grassroots efforts should strengthen community relations and the social fabric that has been ruptured in the immigration and deportation process. Through these efforts, the Chinese American community and many other ethnic immigrant communities will be empowered by uniting and allying with each other in an effort to change power relationships in the discourse and redefining this country's immigration issues.

In addition to organizing immigrant communities, there have to be adequate discussions in academic literature and in the mainstream media concerning immigration deportation and social welfare system. It is important to emphasize the interplay between U.S. immigration and social welfare systems because the welfare system is conceptualized to structurally address issues such as individual, family, and community well-being, equality, human rights, and justice. Although the post-1996 immigration laws and policies and deportation practices label groups of immigrants as *criminals* thus marking them as *deportees*, likewise, the post-1996 welfare system, in denying immigrants' rights to access public welfare benefits, differentiates immigrants that are considered wanted (such as skilled labor, well-educated immigrants) and unwanted, (poor, unskilled workers), and it creates an *us-them* mentality (e.g., U.S. citizens vs. foreigners). Both the U.S. immigration and welfare systems are discriminatory and prejudiced from this perspective. However, immigration and welfare policies cannot counteract trends toward openness and inclusion of the "unwanted" immigrants; with a growing number of immigrants and increased diversity among populations, along with today's struggling economy, it is becoming difficult for people to identify a universal solution to such issues as undocumented immigrants, immigration control, and welfare eligibility for immigrants.

The U.N. Universal Declaration of Human Rights (UDHR) asserts that all human beings have the right to leave their country (Article 13), and the right to a standard of living adequate for health and well-being (Article 25). Following the UDHR principles, categorizing immigrants into wanted and the unwanted categories is discriminatory; refusing access to public welfare benefits violates human rights; a government's failure to help its residents secure an adequate standard of living is morally questionable; and deporting those unwanted immigrants without consideration of justice and fairness is against the founding values of the United States. In fact, deporting the unwanted could jeopardize the wanted, including U.S.-born children, U.S. citizens in general, and the fabric of American society. In fact, we all live under one roof (Fix & Zimmermann, 2001). Given the historical experience of Chinese Americans, today's immigration control and deportation practices will surely raise future social costs and fiscal budgets to address the impact of deportation on individuals, families, and communities.

Therefore, working together among immigrant communities and encouraging activism within communities to address the needs of deportees' children and their families are believed to promote policy changes of not only immigration system, but also social welfare and social service systems in the United States. A number of professions are involved in providing services and interventions to deportees, their children, and families, including lawyers who represent people facing deportation, psychologists who treat children and parents with trauma and chronic mental illness, and school social workers who help children to cope with the stress associated with family disruption and separation. However, fewer services target children and families who are affected by deportation, and social service professionals have yet to develop a fully structured, systematically organized approach to addressing this even larger population. Social welfare policies therefore have to respond to the plight, and the larger social service community needs to build interdisciplinary collaboration in addressing the needs of this population, which is extremely vulnerable to legal action. Such policy changes and interdisciplinary collaboration must be based on international human rights standards.

Chinese Americans' experience in the history and the impact of today's immigration policies and deportation practice on immigrant families and communities also need to reach a larger audience. A better public understanding of the effects of U.S. immigration and deportation policies on children and families will result in greater societal awareness of the issue, and will make it more likely that the public's attitude and concern for immigrants will change for the positive; combined, the enhanced understanding and changed attitudes can effect changes at the political and policy levels. As the immigrant rights movement is at a historical crossroads, immigrants and their allies have to be mobilized not only defending against bad policies that endanger immigrant families and communities, but also improving public understanding of what good polices should actually take place.

\\\ CONCLUJION: NOT AN END

The 1996 immigration law reforms and associated deportation practice threaten the unity and well-being of millions immigrant families in the United States. Noncitizens can be deported because of crimes they committed as minors, even though the conduct may not have been a deportable offense when it occurred. The immigrant law and policy have become mechanisms of social control that unfairly punish immigrants (often people of color with non-Western value systems and behavioral standards). Although an undocumented immigrant was deported because of his or her *illegal* entry, the immigrant law and policy ignored the important role played by the U.S. labor market and greedy employers and punished the victims. The impacts of 1996 immigration laws and deportation practice should not be underestimated; deporting one immigrant affects a family and the whole community. As the Chinese Exclusion Act of 1882 and enforcement practice in the 19th century established a precedent for the 1996 immigration reform, Chinese American's historical efforts in organizing and resistance also provide valuable experience to today's Chinese American community and other immigrant communities in order to change immigration and welfare policies and create a more just, multicultural society.

In April 14, 2009, Eddy Zheng, who was released from detention center and now faces deportation, wrote in his blog:

> Dragging my feet as I walked up the steps of the 38L (limited) *Muni* bus, I felt the winter-like wind penetrating my sweatshirt. The journey home after a long day at work was still an hour or so away. My head was down as I pulled out my Fast Pass and showed it to the bus driver. . . . "Hey, hey," the bus driver said, "I just want to shake your hand. I'd followed your story on TV. I know who you are. It's so good to finally meet you in person." . . . He then started talking rapidly about his feeling on my experience and transformation, as well as how he could relate to my story. What really hit me was when he told me [that] my story made him feel that life truly is meaningful. . . . Being recognized on the bus and on the streets is not a rare occurrence for me. Due to ethnic media support and [the] community's acceptance of my new role in life, I got to meet many wonderful folks who had kept me focused and [prevented me from going] astray. Thanks to Gordon [the bus driver], life has a renewed meaning to me. (Zheng, 2009)

Like millions of Chinese Americans living in the United States, Zheng and his community of supporters and activists are working to help millions of immigrants realize the American dream. Although the Chinese Exclusion Act changed generations of Chinese immigrants' lives and mindsets, the Chinese American community is still resilient and organizing itself now for their rights and a just society.

◈ REFERENCES

Amato, P. R. (1994). Life-span adjustment of children to their parents' divorce. *Future of Children, 4,* 143–164.

American Bar Association. (2004). *American justice through immigrants' eyes.* Washington, DC: American Bar Association.

Arditti, J. A., Lambert-Shute, J., & Joest, K. (2003). Saturday morning at the jail: Implications of incarceration for families and children. *Family Relations, 52*(3), 195–204.

Bernstein, N. (2006, April 9). Making it ashore, but still chasing U.S. dream. *New York Times.*

Cherlin, A. J., Chase-Lansdale, P. L., & McRae, C. (1998). Effects of parental divorce on mental health throughout the life course. *American Sociological Review, 63,* 239–249.

Chinese Staff and Workers Association. (2009). *A community-based workers' center model: An alternative to traditional trade unionism to build a new labor movement.* Retrieved July 26, 2010, from http://www.cswa.org/modx/index.php?id=5

Chinn, T. W., Lai, H. M., & Choy, P. P. (1969). *A history of Chinese in California.* San Francisco: Chinese Historical Society of America.

Choy, P., Dong, L., & Hom, M. (1994). *The coming man.* Seattle: University of Washington Press.

Clarke-Stewart, K. A., Vandell, D. L., McCartney, K., Owen, M. T., & Booth, C. (2000). Effects of parental separation and divorce on very young children. *Journal of Family Psychology, 14*(2), 304–326.

Cole, D. (2002). Enemy aliens. *Stanford Law Review, 54,* 953.

Conger, R. D., Wallace, L. E., Sun, Y., Simons, R. L., McLoyd, V. C., & Brody, G. H. (2002). Economic pressure in African American families: A replication and extension of the family stress model. *Developmental Psychology, 38*(2), 179–193.

Daniels, R. (1988). *Asian America.* Seattle: University of Washington Press.

Denis Kearney on the Chinese veto. (1882, April 15). *New York Times.* Retrieved June 21, 2010, from http://query.nytimes.com/gst/abstract.html?res=9902EFDC113EE433A 25756C1A9629C94639FD7CF

Farias, P. (1994). Central and South American refugees. In A. J. Marsella, T. Bornemann, S. Ekblad, & J. Orley (Eds.), *Amidst peril and pain: The mental health and well-being of the world's refugees.* Washington, DC: American Psychological Association.

Fix, M., & Zimmermann, W. (2001). All under one roof: Mixed-status families in an era of reform. *International Migration Review, 35*(2), 397–419.

Hetherington, E. M., Bridges, M., & Insabella, G. M. (1998). What matters? What does not? Five perspectives on the association between marital transitions and children's adjustment. *American Psychologist, 53,* 167–184.

Human Rights Watch. (2002). Collateral causalities: Children in incarcerated drug offenders in New York. *Human Right Watch, 14*(3(G)), 1–15.

Human Rights Watch. (2007). Forced apart: Families separated and immigrant harmed by United States deportation policy. *Human Right Watch, 19*(3(G)), 1–86.

Ismaili, K. (2007). *Creating crime and criminals: The social exclusion of non-citizens in Canada and the United States.* Paper presented at the annual meeting of the American Society of Criminology, Atlanta Marriott Marquis, Atlanta, GA.

Jian, C. (translated by Chien, E.) (2006, November 3). Chinese family deported after nanny held at airport. *World Journal.* Retrieved July 19, 2010, from http://news.newamericamedia.org/news/view_article.html?article_id=7ecb3f2fc44c26c4efb6de07539e416b

Kanstroom, D. (2007). *Deportation nation: Outsiders in American history.* Cambridge, MA: Harvard University Press.

Kronholz, J. (2006, August 4). In spat over asylum policy, Beijing refuses return of illegal entrants. *Wall Street Journal.*

Kurashige, S. (2000). Pan-ethnicity and community organizing: Asian Americans United's campaign against anti-Asian violence. *Journal of Asian American Studies, 3*(2), 163–190.

Kwon, H.-K., Rueter, M. A., & Lee M. (2003). Marital relationships following the Korean economic crisis: Applying the family stress model. *Journal of Marriage and Family, 65*(May), 316–325.

Kwong, P. (1997). *Forbidden workers: Illegal Chinese immigrants and American labor.* New York: New Press.

Lee, E. (2005). Echoes of the Chinese exclusion era in post-9/11 America. *Chinese America: History and Perspective, 19.*

Lee, E. (2003). *At America's gates: Chinese immigration during the exclusion era, 1882–1943.* Chapel Hill: University of North Carolina Press.

Lee, E. (2002). Enforcing the borers: Chinese exclusion along the U.S. borders with Canada and Mexico, 1882–1924. *The Journal of American History, 89*(1), 54–86.

Lofstrom, M., & Bean, F. D. (2002). Assessing immigrant policy options: Labor market conditions and post-reform declines in immigrants receipt of welfare. *Demography, 39*(4), 617–637.

Mar, G. (2007, May 3). *Organizing documented immigrants to fight for the rights of the undocumented. Migrant diaries.* Retrieved June 16, 2009, from http://migrantdiaries.blogspot.com/2007/05/organizing-documented-immigrants-to.html

Martin, D. A. (2005). *A closer examination of the unauthorized population.* Washington, DC: Migration Policy Institute.

Miller, T. A. (2002). The impact of mass incarceration on immigration policy. In M. Mauer & M. Chesney-Lind (Eds.), *Invisible punishment: The collateral consequences of mass imprisonment* (pp. 214–238). New York: The New Press.

Mistry, R. S., Vandewater, E. A., Huston, A. C., & McLoyd, V. C. (2002). Economic well-being and children's social adjustment: The role of family process in an ethnically diverse low-income sample. *Child Development, 73*(3), 935–951.

Morawetz, N. (1998). Rethinking retroactive deportation laws and the Due Process Clause. *New York University Law Review, 73,* 97.

Morawetz, N. (2004). Understanding the impact of the 1996 deportation laws and the limited scope of proposed reforms. *Harvard Law Review, 113,* 1936–1962.

Organization of Chinese Americans. (2008). *A portrait of Chinese Americans.* College Park: University of Maryland Asian American Studies Program.

Ong, P., & Hee, S. (1994). Economic diversity. In P. Ong (Ed.), *The State of Asian Pacific America: Economic diversity, issues, and policies* (pp. 31–56). Los Angeles: LEAP Asian Pacific American Public Policy Institute and University of California at Los Angeles Asian American Studies Center.

Parke, R., & Clarke-Stewart, K. A. (2002). *Effects of parental incarceration on young children.* Washington, DC: Urban Institute.

Passel, J. S. (2006). *The size and characteristics of the unauthorized migrant population in the U.S.: Estimates based on the March 2005 current population survey.* Washington, DC: Pew Hispanic Center.

Poehlmann, J. (2005). Representations of attachment relationships in children of incarcerated mothers. *Child Development, 76*(3), 679–696.

Sauter, G. G. (2009). Case study: *Aguilar v. ICE;* Litigating workplace immigration raids in the twenty-first century. *Bender's Immigration Bulletin, 14,* 389.

Schmall, L. (2008). *Worksite enforcement of U.S. immigration laws.* Dekalb: Northern Illinois University College of Law, The Professor's Column.

Schuck, P. H. (2000). *Citizens, strangers, and in-betweens: Essays on immigration and citizenship.* Boulder, CO: Westview Press.

Suarez-Orozco, C., Todorova, I., & Louie, J. (2002). Making up for lost time: The experience of separation and reunification among immigrant families. *Family Process, 41,* 625–643.

Suárez-Orozco, C., Todorova, I., & Qin, D. B. (2006). The well-being of immigrant adolescents: A Longitudinal perspective on risk and protective factors. In F. A. Villarrue & T. Luster (Eds.), *The crisis in youth mental health: Critical issues and effective programs* (Vol. 2, pp. 45–62). Westport, CT: Praeger.

Taylor, M. H. (1997). Promoting legal representation for detained aliens: Litigation and administrative reform. *Connecticut Law Review, 29,* 1647.

Thronson, D. B. (2006). Choiceless choices: Deportation and the parent–child relationship. *Nevada Law Journal, 6,* 1165–1214.

U.S. Census Bureau. (2000). *Census 2000 demographic profile highlights: Selected population group: Chinese alone or in any combination. Summary File 2 (SF 2) and Summary File 4 (SF 4).* Available at http://factfinder.census.gov

U.S. Census Bureau. (2004). *The foreign-born population in the United States: 2003.* Washington, DC: Author.

U.S. Department of Commerce and Labor. (1906). *Annual report of the Commissioner-General of Immigration to the Secretary of Commerce and Labor: For the fiscal year ended June 30, 1906.* Washington, DC: Author.

U.S. Department of Commerce and Labor. (1909). *Annual report of the Commissioner-General of Immigration to the Secretary of Commerce and Labor: For the fiscal year ended June 30, 1909.* Washington, DC: Author.

U.S. Department of Homeland Security. (2008). *Yearbook of immigration statistics: 2007.* Washington, DC: Author.

U.S. Department of Justice. (2008). *FY2007 statistical yearbook.* Washington, DC: U.S. Department of Justice, Office of Planning, Analysis & Technology.

U.S. Immigration and Customs Enforcement. (2008). *Worksite enforcement.* Washington, DC: Author. Retrieved June 21, 2010, from http://www.ice.gov/pi/news/factsheets/worksite.htm

U.S. National Archives & Records Administration. (2009). *Chinese immigration and the Chinese in the United States.* College Park, MD: Author. Retrieved June 21, 2010, from http://www.archives.gov/locations/finding-aids/chinese-immigration.html

Vellos, D. (1997). Immigrant Latino domestic workers and sexual harassment. *American University Journal of Gender, Social Policy and the Law, 5*(2), 407.

Videon, T. M. (2002). The effects of parent–adolescent relationships and parental separation on adolescent well-being. *Journal of Marriage and the Family, 64*(May), 489–503.

Vo, L. T. (2004). *Mobilizing an Asian American community.* Philadelphia: Temple University Press.

Wessells, M., & Monteiro, C. (2006). Psychosocial assistance for youth: Toward reconstruction for peace in Angola. *Journal of Social Issues, 62*(1), 121–139.

Wu, W. F. (1982). *The yellow peril, Chinese Americans in American fiction, 1850–1940.* Hamden, CT: Archon Books.

Xu, Q. (2005). In the "best interest" of immigrant and refugee children: Deliberating on their unique circumstances. *Child Welfare, 84*(5), 747–770.

Zheng, E. (2009). *Life has new meaning to me.* Retrieved June 21, 2010, from http://eddyzheng.blogspot.com

Part III

Regulation and Resistance Among Latino/Latina Americans

Latin@s in the Public Square

Understanding Hispanics Through the Prism of United States Immigration Policy

Gregory Acevedo

⁂ INTRODUCTION

In 2006, 44.3 million Hispanics lived in the United States and comprised 14.8 percent of the total population. Between 2000 and 2008, the Hispanic growth rate (31.7 percent) was more than four times the growth rate of the total population (7.8 percent) (U.S. Census Bureau, 2008a). Foreign-born Hispanics comprise a substantial proportion of the Latino population in the United States: 40 percent (in comparison to the overall 12.5 percent foreign-born among the total U.S. population). The pan-ethnic population represented under the labels *Hispanic* or *Latino* varies in terms of such important characteristics as immigration status, national origin, racial and ethnic identification, language use and proficiency, place of residence, and socioeconomic status. Common elements of Hispanic identity include the following: the preponderance of

Spanish-language use; similarity in sociohistorical and geopolitical influences; the psychosocial influence of family origins, socialization, and personal feelings; and the geospatial context of barrio life.

The term *Hispanic* was created by the U.S. Census Bureau in 1970. Latin@s[1] was constructed from the bottom up, in the everyday interpretative and linguistic practices of Hispanics in the United States. The term *Latino* came into official usage when it appeared on the census form for the first time in 2000. At the aggregate level, Latino is the more inclusive term. It is not limiting linguistically, nor is it an imposed bureaucratic category. The Hispanic rubric remains "under construction" (Torres-Saillant, 2002). This construction has been most influenced by the long-standing black–white dichotomized thinking of race in the United States (O'Brien, 2008). Ultimately, Hispanic self-ascription must interact with the realities of the "color line" in the United States and phenotypical characteristics (López, 2008).

Although more than half of the Latin@ population in the United States is native-born, the focus of public perceptions, debates, and policies center on Hispanic immigrants. This casts a shadow over all Latin@s, whatever their legal status or origin. A recent report by the Southern Poverty Law Center (2009) noted: "The assumption is that every Latino possibly is undocumented. So [discrimination] has spread over into the legal population" (p. 5). As the words of Samuel Huntington (2004) attest, the fear that these demographic realties have engendered are pronounced:

> The persistent flow of Hispanic immigrants threatens to divide the U.S. into two peoples, two cultures, and two languages. Unlike past immigrant groups . . . Latinos have not assimilated into mainstream U.S. culture, forming instead their own political and linguistic enclaves . . . and rejecting the Anglo-Protestant values that built the American dream. The U.S. ignores this challenge at its peril. (p. 1)

Hispanic immigrants and, by default, their native-born Latin@ counterparts in the United States are currently embroiled in a number of policy related debates. The issues that are the subject of these debates are quintessential illustrations of the practice of policy deployed to regulate

---

[1]The term *Latin@* simultaneously signifies the masculine and the feminine forms in the Spanish language and underscores the constructed nature of the term.

the lives of people of color. These include immigration and border control but also policies related to citizenship, bilingual education, welfare reform, and labor rights. As the quote by Huntington (2004) powerfully illustrates, Hispanics also find themselves at the center of a *culture war.*

Latin@s are an essential element in the sociocultural, political, and economic life of the nation. Latin@ immigrants are altering the demographic landscape of the United States. Hispanics immigrants are a large part of the *browning* of the nation; by 2050 more nonwhites than whites will inhabit the United States (U.S. Census Bureau, 2008b). Set against a brief historical overview of U.S. immigration and the ways in which policy has regulated the lives of Latin@s, this chapter's discussion and analysis will focus on the recent exclusionary turn in U.S. immigration policy and the resistance by Latinos and Latinas to these regulatory practices.

\\\\ HI*S*PANIC *S*OCIOECONOMIC WELL-BEING

An essential thread in the history of the Hispanic experience in the United States is social marginalization, poverty, and political disenfranchisement. Latin American immigrants have the least educational attainment, work in the least favorable labor market conditions (in terms of earnings and occupation), and have the highest rate of poverty among the foreign born (Larsen, 2004). Immigrants from Latin America have the lowest rates of citizenship among regional source areas for the U.S. foreign-born population (Schmidley, 2001). Among the foreign-born population in the United States, citizenship is highly correlated with increased economic and social mobility. In 2007, 16.5 of immigrants fell below the poverty line in the United States, but the poverty rate among naturalized citizens was only 9.5 compared with 21.3 for noncitizens (U.S. Census Bureau, 2008c).

This brief profile underscores many of the inequalities Latin@ immigrants are contending with in the United States. For many Hispanic immigrants, the problem of poverty as push factor is ameliorated or even resolved during their temporary, circular, or permanent residence in United States. In the aggregate, poverty is the typical condition in which immigrant groups experience upon arrival, while over time, each group rises out of poverty (again, in the aggregate), and experiences economic and social mobility. It is a typical way of describing immigrant group succession in the United States, as various national origin groups make their way up the ladder of socioeconomic mobility (it has also been dubbed the *last of the immigrants thesis*). However, for a good many others, poverty continues in the aggregate and at the individual, family/household, and community levels. In fact, it is often intergenerational.

Low levels of Hispanic educational attainment, weak standing in terms of occupational status, and poor earnings contribute to the high poverty among both immigrant and native-born Latin@s in the United States. Although the overall poverty rate in the United States for 2007 was 12.5 percent (8.2 percent for non-Hispanic whites), it was 21.5 percent among Hispanics, second only to non-Latino blacks (24.5 percent). Among the critical issues facing Hispanics in the United States today, one of the most troubling is economic vulnerability. Given their overall youthfulness, birthrate, and levels of immigration, the socioeconomic well-being of the Latin@ population has tremendous consequences for the entire U.S. population and the nation's economic future.

The overall portrait of Hispanic socioeconomic well-being in the United States is one of constraint. Latin@s have limited amounts of resources, both monetary and human, to invest in aggregate social and cultural capital development. Latin@s encounter significant barriers to the social and economic mobility, but there are several areas that loom large: schooling and civic and political inclusion. In addition to these factors, Latin@s are restricted in their access to social institutions because of cultural barriers, such as limited English language proficiency. Hispanics in the United States have struggled for decades to increase resources for bilingual/multilingual educational programming. Latin@s encounter similar barriers in health and social service systems, and political participation and policing. Through years of effort, the trend has been toward the development of cultural competent policies and practices in many of systems. These have enhanced opportunity for many Latin@s but still remain woefully inadequate.

For Hispanics, migration and immigration have been principle means of contending with socioeconomic vulnerability. Whether immigrant or native-born, Hispanics live a life of "mixed status"; many Latin@ family households and communities have members who are nonimmigrant and immigrant, some documented and others undocumented. Hispanic migration and immigration to the United States is a common legacy that binds Hispanic in the United States together.

$\%$ HIJPANIC IMMIGRATION
AND THE UNITED JTATEJ

Voluntary, indentured, and forced migratory movements have affected the cultural life and political economy of the United States from its roots as a colony. A number of trends have characterized migration patterns in U.S. history: colonization and slavery; the expansion into the Frontier and the displacement of indigenous populations; emigration from Europe; the Great Migration of African Americans away from the Jim Crow South throughout the Depression and post–World War II eras; large-scale Puerto Rican migration in the post–World War II period; and the new waves of immigration from Latin America, the Caribbean, Asia, and more recently Africa, in the post-1965 period. At various points in time and place, Hispanic immigration has been substantially affected by every one of these trends.

Immigration today, as it was in previous eras, is connected to the political, economic, and sociocultural forces inherent in global integration (Acevedo & Menon, 2009; Menon & Acevedo, 2008). Immigrant labor is an integral part of economic productivity in the United States: "In 2006, foreign-born workers accounted for 15 [percent] of the U.S. labor force, and over the last decade they have accounted for about half of the growth in the labor force" (U.S. Council of Economic Advisers, 2007, p. 1). On average, U.S. natives benefit from immigration in that immigrants tend to complement (not substitute for) natives, raising natives' productivity and income (U.S. Council of Economic Advisers, 2007). Immigration is an essential element in the U.S. economy, and it is a determinative component of its labor markets and wages and working conditions. Immigration is also a direct link between the U.S. and global economies.

A link also exists among the Hispanics, the U.S. economy, and poverty. For Latino immigrants, poverty is often the principle push factor that instigates migration, whether from rural to urban areas within their country of origin or from their nations of origin to nations with more expansive economic development. In search of higher wages and better working conditions, people living in Latin America and the Spanish-speaking Caribbean often *choose* migration. Even refugee movements are linked to poverty; the civil wars and Cold War struggles that have destabilized the region are associated with the violent confrontation between the competing political-economic frameworks of free market and socialism, which, at their core, are both models proposed as solutions to long-standing poverty in the region. U.S. foreign policy has been deeply entangled with its immigration policy toward Latin America and the Caribbean. U.S. relations with Mexico and Puerto Rico illustrate this well.

\\\\ U.S. NEOCOLONIAL FOREIGN POLICY IN LATIN AMERICA AND THE CARIBBEAN: PUERTO RICO AND MEXICO

The roots of Hispanic immigration lie in U.S. territorial expansion and intervention (Chomsky, 1999; Galeano, 1997). As Roberto Suro (1998) underscores:

> Mexican-Americans and Puerto Ricans account for most of the native-born Latino population. They are the U.S.-made vessel into which the new immigration flows. They have been Americans long enough to have histories, and these are sad histories of exploitation and segregation abetted by public authorities. (p. 9)

Mexico and Puerto Rico became two valuable assets as the U.S. expanded abroad during the mid- to late-1800s. Unlike, most other national origin groups that make up the foreign-born stock of the U.S. population, many Mexicans and all Puerto Ricans followed very peculiar paths to U.S. citizenship as *involuntary citizens*.

Puerto Rico was incorporated as a territory of the United States, but administratively and culturally, it is treated as a separate country (for histories of the Puerto Rico–U.S. relationship, see Ayala & Bernabe, 2007; Malvet, 2004). Large swaths of the Mexico were incorporated into the United States, and the Mexicans that remained in places such as Texas, California, New Mexico, Nevada, and Arizona would ultimately become citizens, while those south of the border became foreigners. Socioculturally and economically, this boundary has been highly permeable, and life along the border has been highly transnational.

For Puerto Ricans, U.S. citizenship has not been associated with the level of progress nor inclusion that might be expected: "The Puerto Rican case especially illustrates the contradiction that legal citizenship does not in itself confer or imply that people enjoy full and equal rights in the U.S." (Benmayor, Torruellas, & Juarbe, 1997, p. 201). Second-class citizenship of Puerto Ricans on the island is demonstrated among both the stateside and island populations in their long-standing and widespread poverty, unemployment and low-wage employment, and high rates of crime and delinquency. As a U.S. territory, the prospects for advancement on the island are dim. A recent World Bank (2008) report ranked Puerto Rico's economy toward the bottom of world's economies, among such troubled nations as Zimbabwe and Chad, and the territory of Palestine. Economic growth in Puerto Rico ranked 211th out of 215.

Like Puerto Rican citizenship, Mexican citizenship has been second class. Mexicans have experienced Jim Crow–style segregation and disenfranchisement in the United States. One horrifying example was the massive deportation of Mexicans from California and the Southwest in the 1930s. A good number of these deportees were actually citizens, but their status offered little protection.

The Mexican and Puerto Rican experiences in the United States demonstrate a few of the crucial dynamics of U.S. immigration policy: its links with neocolonial foreign policy and its association with ethnocultural and economic factors. A brief historical overview of U.S. immigration leading up to the present exclusionary period illustrates how these forces affected Hispanics.

\\\\ U.S. IMMIGRATION POLICY: 1880–1965

U.S. immigration policy was a way of regulating labor and was intentionally deployed to control its racial and ethnic demographic composition. It is, as Zolberg (2006) describes, "a nation by design," which actively devised policies and laws to effectively shape its population and overall makeup. Foner (2005) discusses how racial conceptualizations in the United States have been powerfully influenced by immigration patterns. She notes that race matters in the United States differed during its two great waves of immigration: 1880–1920 and the period since the 1960s to the present. U.S. public policies have regulated Hispanic migration, labor, citizenship, and their construction of racial and ethnic identity. Historically, this regulation was accomplished primarily through immigration, labor, and foreign policies.

Changes in immigration policy have been linked to economic development and U.S. neocolonial territorial expansion. Overall, there has been a pendulum shift between eras of fairly *open* immigration and exclusionary periods. From 1880 until 1921, immigration developed within an open door period that came to a close with the First Quota Law of 1921 and the creation of the national origins system. In 1965, a major shift toward inclusion occurred. The current era began in 1980s and has been marked by an increasingly exclusionary bent.

The architecture of the national origins system in U.S. immigration policy was created in the period from 1921 to 1929. The First Quota Law of 1921 limited immigration of each nationality to 3 percent of the number of foreign-born persons of that nationality living in the United States in 1910. It institutionalized a national origins system as the foundation for U.S. immigration policy and solidified a biased preference toward accepting European immigrants. This bias was reinforced through the National Origins Act of 1924, which limited immigration of each nationality to 2 percent of the number of persons of that nationality as determined by the 1890 census, and the National Quota Law of 1929, which set annual quotas apportioned according to each nationality's percentage in 1920 census.

After 1929, the dire economic circumstances of the Great Depression weighed particularly heavy on Mexicans: state governments passed legislation prohibiting the employment of *aliens* on public works projects; work in the private sector became scarce; public opinion tilted toward the view that immigrants supplanted American workers; and the Herbert Hoover administration targeted aliens with widespread pubic raids. Anti-Mexican sentiment adopted rhetoric of *repatriation*. This term was crafted "to mask the unconstitutional deportation of Mexicans, many who were legal residents and had lived in the United States for decades" (Valenciana, 2006, p. 2).

Compounding restrictive immigration, oppressive labor policies have placed a double burden on many Hispanics. One of the most marginalizing public policy decisions in the New Deal era was to exempt agricultural and domestic workers from the old-age insurance program of the Social Security Act of 1935. Although the Roosevelt administration's New Deal policies protected other workers in areas such as overtime and disability pay, days of rest and union organizing, in deference to Dixiecrat politicians and Jim Crow segregation, agricultural and domestic were excluded. As a result, African Americans and Mexicans, who comprised the majority in these sectors, were condemned to continued marginalization as low-wage workers. This legacy remains and falls hard on the backs of Hispanic immigrant workers: "The injustice they spawned has never been corrected. Poverty, brutal working conditions, and legally sanctioned discrimination persist for new generations of laborers, who are now mostly Latino immigrants" ("Farm Workers' Rights," 2009).

Labor policy had a net-effect on social welfare policy and the welfare state's provisioning to Hispanics in the United States. The Social Security Act of 1935 was the cornerstone piece of social policy legislation for the structuring the welfare state. Its tiered social programming ensured the availability of a low-wage labor force that favored market priorities by socializing the costs of production through federal government subsidy. The protections initiated by the Social Security Act of 1935 primarily benefitted non-Latino whites male workers employed in the manufacturing and professional and business occupations; a privileged cadre of workers well served by unionization, social insurance programs, including veterans' programs, and the expanding Cold War economy. Labor and social welfare policy impeded Hispanics socioeconomic development. It resulted in their overrepresentation in low-wage labor markets and overreliance on the meager and punitive public assistance programming of the welfare state.

The World War II era, with a prime ordinate need for labor to replace the native-born, white male workers in military service, made immigrant labor a valuable commodity. The era saw two significant changes in U.S. immigration policy. First, as a measure of national security, the Immigration Act of 1940 transferred Immigration and Naturalization Service (INS) from the Department of Labor to the Department of Justice.

The second major change in World War II–era U.S. immigration policy that deeply affected Mexicans was the *Bracero Program*, which operated between 1943 and 1964. The Bracero Program provided for the importation of a large number of *temporary agricultural laborers* from Mexico (as well as British Honduras, Barbados, and Jamaica) to the United States. It was initiated through the Department of Labor in 1942 but formalized by the Department of Justice in 1943. Current debates on immigration reform include the issue of guest worker programs. The experiences of the Bracero program (and the H-2 visa system for agricultural workers in general) should serve as a basis for this part of the debate.

The 1950s were relatively quiet with regard to changes in immigration policy that affected Hispanic immigrants. Overall, U.S. immigration policy in the 1950s was formulated within a context dominated by Cold War politics and concerns. The most significant development in Hispanic immigration in the 1950s came as the decade was ending with a massive Cuban refugee migration. Widespread Cuban migration to the United States was the by-product of neocolonial foreign policy as it operated in the Cold War period. After the Cuban Revolution in 1959, successive waves of out-migrating Cubans made their way to United States in the 1960s and 1970s. Although Cuban immigration to Florida was already an established pattern by the late 1950s, the actual total number of Cubans in the United States was small. In the aftermath of the Cuban Revolution, Cuban immigration to the United States shifted dramatically, and between 1959 and 1980, in a series of intermittent waves, entrants arrived primarily as refugees (Masud-Piloto, 1996).

The initial intent of U.S. policy was to manage escalating Cuban immigration in two ways: by encouraging resettlement to Latin America and Europe rather than exclusively to the United States and by relocating Cuban refugees throughout the country in order to prevent their concentration in any one locale; however, many Cubans who initially resettled abroad, or in other cities in the United States, eventually made their way to Miami-Dade County, Florida. Miami-Dade became the favored destination for Cuban immigrants in the United States. Almost two thirds of all Cubans in the United States now live in the South Florida region. By 1965, the United States organized its management of Cuban refugee migration with the Cuban Refugee Act, which authorized the adjusted the status of Cuban refugees to that of permanent resident aliens.

Historically, U.S. immigration policy toward Cuban immigrants was generally favorable, guided by an open-door stance for Cuban refugees. The treatment that Cubans in the United States received from the federal government was in sharp contrast to that extended to Mexicans and Puerto Ricans, easing their entrance through the Golden Doors. As Tienda and Liang (1992) underscored: "The Cuban exodus marked an important turning point in the posture of the federal government toward refugees in that admission was accompanied by resettlement assistance" and that "the legal distinction between economic migrants and refugees also implied distinct social contracts, one with and one without guarantees to state-administered social supports" (p. 12). As "welcomed exiles," to invoke the title of Masud-Piloto's (1996) book, Cubans benefited from this material and symbolic support in ways that Mexicans and Puerto Ricans could not as mere economic migrants.

In 1980, the Mariel boatlift brought another massive wave of Cubans to Florida. Unlike previous Cuban cohorts, this group was less educated and skilled and more likely to be of Afro-Cuban descent. In the context of a diverse Miami, with an increasingly competitive labor market, this distinct wave of Cuban immigrants had a destabilizing effect on the city and region, and the Mariel immigrants encountered a more difficult path toward socioeconomic mobility than their predecessors. The social problems that manifested themselves as a result recast public perceptions about Cuban refugees in a more negative light.

The dissolution of the Soviet bloc also powerfully altered the geopolitical position of Cuba, leaving it more isolated and vulnerable, and of lesser interest to U.S. policy formulation. Overall, since the 1990s, Cubans have experienced a restrictive trend in U.S. immigration policy (Masud-Piloto, 1996). Under these new circumstances the United States moved from a *wet-foot* policy that for the most part guaranteed entrance for Cubans intercepted at sea to a *dry-foot* policy in which Cubans refugees now had to make it on to U.S. soil for admission or more likely be excluded. In an interesting twist, there is an emerging stream of *dusty-foot* migrant Cubans who are migrating to the U.S. via Mexico (Potter, 2007). In general, the more than four-decades-long U.S. embargo against the island and lack of full diplomatic relations have mitigated against coming to a more humane resolution to the problems of Cuban immigration.

The Hispanic experience within the first great wave of U.S. immigration was substantial but overshadowed by the number and proportion of European-descended immigrants. Latin@s, however, have become the face of the new wave of U.S. immigration. The second great wave of immigration to the United States was the result of the momentous Immigration and Nationality Act Amendments of 1965. This was the key that finally unlocked the doors to the United States that had been closed to the developing world, especially Latin American and Asia, and to a lesser degree, Africa.

\\\\ U.S. IMMIGRATION POLICY: POST-1965

The Immigration and Nationality Act Amendments finally abolished the national origins system. This instigated a new wave of immigration that has been dominated by a Hispanic influx, most especially by those of Mexican origin. The act also created a visa system based on a seven-category preference system. This was the most significant shift in U.S. immigration policy since the 1920s, and it opened the U.S. to a flood of immigrants from Latin America and the Caribbean. It took more than four decades, 1921–1965, to undo the national origins system opening the doors to non-European immigrants. By 1985, a mere two decades later, the doors were beginning to close.

In the mid-1980s, concerns over escalating immigration rates would result in the passage of the Immigration Reform and Control Act (IRCA) of 1986. The law marked a clear shift to more punitive and restrictive immigration policies for both documented and undocumented Hispanic immigrants. IRCA imposed employer sanctions and reinforced border patrol but in a conciliatory gesture granted certain undocumented aliens permanent resident status, or amnesty. Several historical developments contributed to swinging of the pendulum towards exclusion. In terms of economy, in the 1970s concerns over economic instability, unemployment, and the shift to postindustrial economy were reconfiguring the national and global political economic framework. Immigration dynamics were increasingly seen in light of the international division of labor between the developed and developing nation states. Today these have culminated in national outcries against illegal immigration and also denouncements of practices such as off-shoring jobs.

In the 1990s, anti-immigrant sentiments dovetailed with a conservative ethos of welfare reform, leading to the passage of the Illegal Immigration Reform and Immigrant Responsibility Act (IIRIRA) of 1996. IIRIRA (1) restricted public services to immigrants, prohibiting future legal immigrants from receiving most federal benefits during their first 5 years in the United States (although most legal immigrants were already unable to receive food stamps and Supplemental Security Income; (2) increased binding income requirements for sponsors of legal immigrants; (3) expanded and border and criminal alien enforcement activities, including increased official policing of immigrant neighborhoods; and (4) changed the term *deportation* to *removal* and expanded the definition of *criminal aliens.*

By the end of the 20th century, Hispanic immigration had swelled and become a frequent subject of political and public debates, but with little to no changes to U.S. immigration policy other than those related to national security. The United States has continued to demonstrate a "persistent reluctance to pay the social, cultural, and human services costs of a rapidly expanding, increasingly permanent population of Latino immigrants and their dependents" (Cornelius, 2002, p. 182).

The trend toward the increasing emphasis on internal security and a more punitive criminalization of immigration violations reflects a dramatic shift from viewing immigrant as laborer, illegal or not, to the perception of immigrant as a threat. The PATRIOT (Uniting and Strengthening America by Providing Appropriate Tools Required to Intercept and Obstruct Terrorism) Act of 2001 dissolved INS and replaced it with the United States Citizen and Immigration Service (USCIS). It put a primacy on border protection in managing immigration to the United States. The Office of Homeland Security that the act created controls the operations of the new U.S. Immigration and Customs Enforcement (ICE) agency. In partnership with state and local law enforcement via 287(g) agreements, immigration policy has been substantially criminalized.

As result, federal detentions and immigration prosecutions have sky-rocketed since 2001 and have overloaded federal courts, deflecting their resources away from more serious criminal activity ("A Sense of Who We Are," 2009). According to a recent report:

> Sharp growth in illegal immigration and increased enforcement of immigration laws have dramatically altered the ethnic composition of offenders sentenced in federal courts. In 2007, Latinos accounted for 40 [percent] of all sentenced federal offenders—more than triple their share (13 [percent]) of the total U.S. adult population. The share of all sentenced offenders who were Latino in 2007 was up from 24 [percent] in 1991. (Lopez & Light, 2009, p. 1)

As of late, the punitive nature of anti-Hispanic immigration policy has taken a deadly turn. In November of 2008, an Ecuadorian immigrant was killed when group of seven high school students decided that they wanted "to beat up some Mexicans" (Eltman, 2008). Marcello Lucero was beaten, stabbed, and murdered in Long Island, New York. Advocates for Hispanic day laborers and Latino immigrants argued that this was a lethal escalation of previous incidents of violence that have included beatings and arson, and an overall pervasive anti-immigrant sentiment in various communities in Long Island, New York. Latin@s, immigrant and nonimmigrant, continue to struggle for full inclusion in U.S. society. Fortunately, today's Hispanics have a long tradition of resistance to draw upon.

⧵⧵ REJIJTING EXCLUJION

In large part, the social, political, and economic conditions that Latin@s in the United States currently grapple with today are the net result of the implementation of past immigration and social policies. These policies have been an important force among Hispanic populations, both native and foreign-born, in shaping institutionalized Latin@ narratives of colonialism and resistance, and the existence of an activist tradition with long traditions of community and labor organizing. The resistance activities of Latin@ immigrants in the United States have clustered around issues that are closely related to immigration: labor and foreign policy. Latin@ resistance efforts have tended to focus on expanding the civil and political inclusion and participation. These efforts have often been pursued within a larger framework of human rights. In the realm of social policy, Latin@ resistance has tended to focus on education and enhancing the benefits and protections afforded Hispanics by the U.S. social welfare system.

Across the United States, Latin@s, both immigrant and native-born, have played a major role in organizing for educational, political and civic participation, immigrant rights, and for human rights in general. Hispanics in the United States have long traditions of community and labor organizing. This is partly explained by institutionalized narratives of colonialism and resistance (Grosfoguel, Maldonado-Torres, & Saldivar, 2006) and an activist tradition *imported* from Latin America and the Caribbean and *locally grown* in Latin@ communities throughout the United States. These cultural resources are activated by the threat of anti-immigrant legislation and the push for immigrant and labor rights.

For both Mexicans and Puerto Ricans, the seeds and early roots of current Latin@ resistance activities were sown in the era of the 1950s civil rights movement. A watershed moment in their progress toward equal rights was the case of *Hernandez v. Texas* in 1954. Mexicans in Texas had consistently faced all white, non-Hispanic/non-Mexican "juries of their peers." According to the state of Texas, Mexicans were "white," therefore, there was no disenfranchisement. The U.S. Supreme Court ruled that this was not the case: in effect, Mexicans were deemed "not white." The lead plaintiff in the *Hernandez v. Texas* case was the League of United Latin American Citizens (LULAC), a political advocacy organization founded in 1929 in Corpus Christi, Texas. LULAC remains active today, maintaining a focus on civil rights in addition to economic advancement, educational attainment, and health.

Resistance struggles began to come of age in the 1960s. Cesar Chavez, Dolores Huerta, and others who had been educated and trained in these earlier community organizing efforts and civil rights struggles coalesced around the farm worker movement. At first, they formed the National Farm Workers Association (1962) and later merged with the Agricultural Workers Organizing Committee to form the United Farm Workers. Their resistance simultaneously spoke to issues related to labor, migration, and immigration, and civil and political inclusion.

In 1968, the Southwest Council of La Raza (SWCLR) was formed in Phoenix, Arizona. La Raza Unida brought a transnational focus to the plight of Mexicans as *La Raza,* a hemispheric people, or *race.* In 1973, the SWCLR expanded from a regional organization to a national platform and changed its name to the National Council of La Raza (NCLR). Also, in 1968, the Mexican American Legal Defense and Education Fund (MALDEF) was formed. It was cofounded by James DeAnda, the attorney who took on the *Hernandez v. Texas* case in 1954.

Puerto Ricans, also known as *Boricuas* in homage to the indigenous name for the island, crafted a resistance tradition that reflected its unique status in U.S. neocolonial foreign policy. The Puerto Rican Independence Movement tended to dominate the political and economic focus of Puerto Rican resistance. Although never a majority, the independence movement was the lighting rod around which three contesting forces structured themselves. Opponents of the independence advocates fell into two camps, mirroring and allied to the stateside Republican and Democratic parties, the statehood and commonwealth (favorable to a status quo arrangement) supporters, respectively.

In the 1930s, Pedro Albizu Campos and the Nationalist Party were the most strident militants in the independence movement on the island. From the 1930s to the 1950s, an increasingly violent struggle took place between members of the independence movement and U.S. federal authorities. The conflict continued throughout the 1960s and 1970s, and both the armed and nonviolent currents of the independence movement on the island, and now stateside as well, were a major focus of the Federal Bureau of Investigation and its Counter Intelligence Program (Bosque-Pérez, 2006). The conflict spiked again in the 1980s, ebbed in the 1990s, but continues today.

A significant engagement occurred in September 2005 when independence leader Filiberto Ojeda Ríos was killed by federal agents on the island. More recently, on July 26, 2010, Carlos Alberto Torres was released from prison after 30 years. Viewed as a political prisoner by many in the independence movement but considered a terrorist by his detractors, his release was controversial (Coto, 2010). Others in the independence movement, such as Oscar López Rivera, a decorated Vietnam War veteran, still remain in prison even after decades. On August 1, 2010, a forerunner and icon to later generations of Puerto Rican nationalists, Lolita Lebron, died. Her violent attack on the U.S. Capitol in 1954 led to her decades-long imprisonment, but upon her release and until the time of her death, she remained an advocate for independence. The question of the island's status has attracted renewed interest and instigated legislative action. In June 2009, the United Nations (U.N.) Special Committee on Decolonization approved a draft resolution calling upon the U.S. government "to expedite a process that would allow the Puerto Rican people to exercise fully their inalienable right to self-determination and independence" (U.N. General Assembly, 2009). Currently, there is a bill in the U.S. Congress (H.R. 2499, the Puerto Rico Democracy Act of 2010) that may lead to a plebiscite vote on the island. These developments are taking place at time when the island is at a boiling point of crisis. Amid a fiscal implosion and austerity-measure budget cuts, there has been a wave of labor unrest and protest as well as a student strike that shutdown the island's public university system for almost 2 months. Several of the confrontations between protesters and police have been marked by violence and accusations of the use of excessive force by authorities, instigating Puerto Rico's civil rights commission to launch a probe of the police response (Graves, 2010).

Stateside Puerto Ricans, although not dismissive or unaware of island politics, focus their resistance activities on different goals, including social service provisioning and education. In 1958, the Puerto Rican Forum met in New York City to begin to strategize and coordinate activist efforts. Spearheaded by community-based service agencies, especially the Puerto Rican Association for Community Affairs, which formed in 1953, the Forum inspired a number of social workers to link their direct practice to community organizing and advocacy around issues related to child welfare, education, and civil and political participation. One of these pioneering activists was Dr. Antonia Pantoja, who in 1954 acquired her Master of Social Work degree from Hunter College, City University of New York. In 1961, she founded Aspira, a grassroots organization dedicated to enhancing educational success, civic participation, and leadership among Puerto Rican youth.

Historically, the Puerto Rican Legal Defense and Education Fund (PRLDEF) has been closely allied with Aspira's efforts. Founded in 1972 by attorneys Jorge Batista, Victor Marrero, and Cesar A. Perales, it was established to provide Puerto Ricans with the legal resources to fight for civic and political inclusion. On behalf of Aspira, PRLDEF fielded its first lawsuit, *Aspira v. New York City Board of Education*, which resulted in the groundbreaking Aspira Consent Decree of 1974. The decree forced New York City's public school system to implement bilingual education as way of enhancing educational outcomes for Puerto Rican youth. The decree also facilitated the entrance of Latin@ educators into the teaching ranks of New York City's public school system.

Another major form of resistance and activism among stateside Puerto Ricans was embodied in the Young Lords, founded in 1968 in Chicago, Illinois. Styled along the lines of the Black Panther Party, the Young Lords combined militancy and activism. Among its founding members, a number had lived a *street life* existence of crime and delinquency. They focused their efforts on opposing oppressive forces in society, such as racism, and advocating in support of self-determination and community control of institutions. They also supported independence for Puerto Rico and socialist political economy. In addition to their protest activities, the Young Lords took to providing free breakfast, clothing, health and day care programs, as well as focusing on cultural and educational activities such as Puerto Rican history classes. Several founding members went to become well-respected leaders, for example Juan Gonzalez, the *New York Daily News* columnist, and Felipe Luciano, a TV news reporter, poet, and radio personality.

By the mid-1970s, Mexicans and Puerto Ricans were coordinating their efforts through national organizations such as the National Association of Latino Elected Officials formed by politicians in 1975, and the Congressional Hispanic Caucus formed a year later by Democratic members of the House of Representatives from Texas, California, and New York as well as the resident commissioner of Puerto Rico. However, disputes in the caucus have been all too frequent between Cuban and non-Cuban legislators over Cuba, foreign policy, and party politics. Groups such as LULAC, MALDEF, and PRLDEF have generalized to a wider focus on Latin@s as a pan-ethnicity, attempting to integrate the concerns and efforts of emerging Hispanic national origin groups, and expanding their focus both regionally and nationally. Despite the tensions within the Hispanic rubric, there is voice of resistance.

The merging of resistance activities under the larger tent of Hispanicity reflects an *Americanness* that is Latin@ in character. In 1891, the Cuban intellectual and revolutionary Jose Marti captured his sentiment and vision for a mutual respect and recognition of the American hemisphere as a familial partnership of North and South in his poem "Our America" (Sacerio-Garí, 1994). This dream has been held in abeyance, and even mutual cooperation among Hispanics has been difficult. However, when Domínguez (2000) commented that "Latin@s are a problematique of Americanness" (cited in Torres-Saillant, 2002, p. 449) he underscored the fact that the term *America* has a contested meaning. For many, the term has one-to-one correspondence with *United States*. In Latin America, however, the term is hemispheric in nature. Typically, the use of the term

American conflates it with U.S. citizenship and residence; the U.S. nation-state is equated with Americanness. The contestation over the meaning of American is part of a broader struggle for Latin@s; a narrative of colonialism and resistance generated in Latin America as a response to globalization and migration. Colonialism and neocolonialism were crucial formative stages of globalization (Acevedo, 2005, p. 138). Globalization has had a displacing effect in the developing world as capital penetration disrupted traditional social and economic relations.

Migration, both within and between nation-states, is one of the principle components of globalization. In this sense, Latin America (and the Caribbean) can be seen as the net result of the colonial and neocolonial eras of globalization in the West. Latin Americans (and those in the Caribbean) are very much a hybrid and transnational people. As Grosfoguel, Maldonado-Torres, and Saldivar (2006) argue, Latin@s pose and important challenge to contemporary debates about political transformations in the United States and around the world. Latin@s are racially diverse, come from various nation-states and are multiethnic, practice many religions, often times syncretically, and are of varied legal status (immigrants, citizens, and undocumented immigrants.) In the 21st century, this hybridity has the potential to fully decolonize the hemisphere.

\\\ CONCLUSION: LATIN@S, HUMAN RIGHTS, AND STRUGGLE IN THE PUBLIC SQUARE

The ongoing battle for civic and political inclusion has had to meet the challenge of a rekindled nativism and its backlash against Hispanic resistance efforts that were successful in the 1970s, such as bilingual education. This includes the English-only movement and antiaffirmative action campaigns. In addition, the newer voices of resistance from the Latin@s living in America has taken up causes that are central to the overall struggle for human rights: labor rights and immigrant rights.

In terms of labor rights, perhaps it's not hyperbole to suggest that the future of the labor movement in the United States rests very much on the backs of Latino labor, when "one out of six new workers in the U.S. is Latino" (Trumpbour & Bernard, 2002, p. 126). Unionization of low-wage workers, among whose ranks Latin@s, both immigrant and native-born, are highly represented, is one of the targeted priorities of union organizers today. Unions such as Service Employees International Union (SEIU) have benefited with increasing membership from these ranks. For Latin@s, the benefits of unionization are clear: "Latin@s who are unionized received a remarkable 54.3 percent higher wage than Latin@s who lack union representation" (Trumpbour & Bernard, p. 128). In many, cities, states, regions, and sectors of the labor market, Latin@s are reinvigorating the labor movement.

Much of this activism is supported by cultural resources: "Latino sojourners managed to combine the experience of work and labor organizing with family and community" (Trumpbour & Bernard, 2002, p. 129). Latino workers have also drawn on the cultural resources of faith-based institutions and "have taken the lead in promoting the combination of labor and communities of faith as a powerful moral and political force committed to the dignity of labor" (p. 129). Latin@s have crafted a form of "social unionism," organizing around a broader set of issues, including immigrant rights (Trumpbour & Bernard, 2002). This distinguishes it from the labor "activism" of formal unions. Latin@s are also transforming the labor movement in the United States through their overt internationalism and *North-South* solidarity (Trumpbour & Bernard, 2002). Although traditional, formal unions may have gone global, they have done so through a fairly top-down model, which has been deployed more for strategic reasons than internationalist vision.

In light of the political, economic, sociocultural history of Latin America and the Spanish-speaking Caribbean, Latino North-South internationalism and solidarity make sense. It is an expression of resistance to the by-products of a colonial and neocolonial history and geography. An important part of the narrative of colonialism and resistance that has been cultivated throughout much of Latin America is the solidarity between labor rights and other social movements. The history of labor and activism in Latin America is long and rich, for example, the Chilean Workers' Movement dates back to the early 1900s. Whether resisting the latifundia/plantation economy of colonialism and neocolonialism or more recently struggling against the apparatus of neoliberalism (such as the North American Free Trade Agreement), laborers in Latin America have long resisted the master narrative of globalization. Importantly, this resistance has consistently involved bottom-up coalitions of workers, students, intellectuals, artists, among others, and has tended to be enveloped under, or aligned with, a larger array of social concerns and social movements.

Hispanics are also fighting the human rights struggle, perhaps the most important of all, on the immigrant rights front. In recent years there have been a number of immigrant rights demonstrations in several U.S. cities. The immigrant rights marches were triggered by proposed restrictive legislation such as HR 4437, the Border Protection, Anti-terrorism, and Illegal Immigration Control Act of 2005, commonly known as the Sensenbrenner Bill, which tried to make it a felony to be undocumented in the United States and would have applied criminal sanctions to anyone who helped undocumented aliens to enter and/or remain in the United States (Díaz & Rodriguez, 2007, p. 98).

The rallies were organized through the efforts of various social movements and community-based organizations in pursuit of economic and social justice, and labor, immigrant, and human rights. Mexicans, both immigrant and native-born, played a major role in organizing and participating in the demonstrations (Díaz & Rodriguez, 2007). The largest took place in Los Angeles, Chicago, and New York cities with a substantial population of Mexicans, and long traditions of community and labor organizing (Trumpbour & Bernard, 2002).

Grassroot organizations have received support from Latino radio stations disc jockeys around the country, and they have been pivotal for the immigrant rights movement to flourish (Díaz & Rodriguez, 2007, p. 99). Mexican soccer clubs have also been central for the mobilization of immigrants. Soccer clubs have historically served as bridges between Mexicans in the United States and those in Mexico. More traditional political organizations, including the Democratic party, several labor unions, among them the SEIU and UFW, and groups such as the NCLR, LULAC, MALDEF, and the Catholic church have also been instrumental in the immigrant rights movement (Díaz & Rodríguez, 2007, p. 99).

The struggle for full social, political, and economic inclusion of Latin@ immigrants will continue to fall short if its resistance strategies and tactics do not ultimately supersede the parochial limitations of nation-state's self-interests. This effort should include staunch resistance to the neoliberal tendencies typical of most nation-states' political economies. The internationalist principles inherent in a human rights framework are one of some of the most powerful sources of moral authority and solidarity. With respect to immigration policy, this has important implications. Above all else, native or foreign-born, citizen or not, from whichever nation of origin, it is our humanity that is prime ordinate. The Mexican hip-hop group Control Machete crafted a song for their album *Mucho Barato* (1997) titled "Humanos Mexicanos" with lyrics that speak to this: "Somos humanos y nos llaman Mexicanos" [We're human beings, but they call us Mexicans].

⧓ REFERENCE*J*

Acevedo, G. (2005). Caribbean transnationalism and social policy formation. *The Caribbean Journal of Social Work, 4*, 137–151.

Acevedo, G., & Menon, N. (2009). A breakwater in the waves: Social work and the history of immigration to the United States. *The International Journal of Interdisciplinary Social Sciences, 4*, 123–137.

A sense of who we are. (2009, January 13). *New York Times*, editorial page.

Ayala, C. J., & Bernabe, R. (2007). *Puerto Rico in the American century: A history since 1898*. Chapel Hill: University of North Carolina Press.

Bosque-Pérez, R. (2006). *The FBI and Puerto Rico: Notes on a conflictive history*. Invited testimony before a Congressional Briefing held by the Judiciary Committee Democratic Office at the U.S. House of Representatives, March 28, 2006.

Chomsky, N. (1999). *Latin America: From colonization to globalization*. Hoboken, NJ: Ocean Press.

Cornelius, W. A. (2002). Ambivalent reception: Mass public responses to the "New" Latino immigration to the United States. In M. M. Suárez-Orozco & M. M. Páez (Eds.), *Latinos remaking America* (pp. 165–189). Berkeley: University of California Press.

Coto, D. (2010, July 28). Violent nationalist group leader welcomed in PR. *Associated Press News*. Retrieved from http://hosted2.ap.org/vastr/APWorld/Article_2010-07-28-CB-Puerto-Rico-Independence-Leader/id-4142ecff35a945dbb73add80e181bf21

Díaz, J., & Rodriguez, J. (2007). Undocumented in America. *New Left Review, 47*, 93–106.

Eltman, F. (2008, November 10). Police: Slaying of NY immigrant was a hate crime. *USA Today*. Retrieved August 4, 2010, from http://www.usatoday.com/news/nation/2008-11-10-2775952356_x.htm

Farm workers' rights, 70 years overdue. (2009, April 5). *New York Times*, editorial page.

Foner, N. (2005). *In a new land: A comparative view of immigration*. New York: New York University Press.

Galeano, E. (1997). *The open veins of Latin America: Five centuries of the pillage of a continent*. New York: Monthly Review Press.

Graves, L. (2010, July 6). Puerto Rico protests: Government probe to investigate civil rights abuses. *The Huffington Post*. Retrieved August 4, 2010, from http://www.huffingtonpost.com/2010/07/06/puerto-rico-protests-gove_n_636379.html

Grosfoguel, R., Maldonado-Torres, N., & Saldivar, J. D. (Eds.) (2006). *Latin@s in the world-system: Decolonization struggles in the twenty-first century U.S. empire*. Boulder, CO: Paradigm Publishers.

Huntington, S. P. (2004, March/April). The Hispanic challenge. *Foreign Policy*, pp. 30–46.

Larsen, L. J. (2004). *The foreign-born population in the United States: 2003* (Current Population Reports, P20-551). Washington, DC: U.S. Census Bureau.

López, I. (2008). Puerto Rican phenotype: Understanding its historical underpinnings and psychological associations. *Hispanic Journal of Behavioral Sciences, 30*, 161–180.

Lopez, M. H., & Light, M. T. (2009). *A rising share: Hispanics and federal crime*. Washington, DC: Pew Hispanic Center.

Malvet, P. A. (2004). *America's colony: The political and cultural conflict between the United States and Puerto Rico*. New York: New York University Press.

Masud-Piloto, F. R. (1996). *From welcomed exiles to illegal immigrants: Cuban migration to the U.S., 1959–1995.* Latham, MD: Rowman & Littlefield.

Menon, N., & Acevedo, G. (2008). "Hidden transcripts" of globalization: The role of social work in the development of social welfare in the United States. *The Global Studies Journal, 1,* 39–48.

O'Brien, E. (2008). *The racial middle: Latinos and Asian Americans living beyond the racial divide.* New York: New York University Press.

Potter, M. (2007, October 1). More Cubans entering U.S. through Mexico. *MSNBC.* Retrieved August 4, 2010, from http://www.msnbc.msn.com/id/21087459

Sacerio-Garí, E. (1994). *Heath anthology of American literature* (2nd ed., Vol. 2, pp. 819–829). Lexington, MA: D.C. Heath and Company.

Schmidley, A. D. (2001). *U.S. Census Bureau, Current Population Reports, Series P23–206, Profile of the foreign-born population in the United States: 2000.* Washington, DC: U.S. Government Printing Office.

Southern Poverty Law Center. (2009). *Under siege: Life for low-income Latinos in the South.* Montgomery, AL: Author.

Suro, R. (1998). *Strangers among us: Latino lives in a changing America.* New York: Vintage.

Tienda, M., & Liang, Z. (1992). *Horatio Alger fails: Poverty and immigration in policy perspective.* Paper presented at the Institute for Research on Poverty conference, University of Wisconsin-Madison, Madison, WI.

Torres-Saillant, S. (2002). Problematic paradigms: Racial diversity and corporate identity in the Latino community. In M. M. Suárez-Orozco & M. M. Páez (Eds.), *Latinos remaking America* (pp. 435–455). Berkeley: University of California Press.

Trumpbour, J., & Bernard E. (2002). Unions and Latinos: Mutual transformation. In M. M. Suárez-Orozco & M. M. Páez (Eds.), *Latinos remaking America* (pp. 126–145). Berkeley: University of California Press.

U.N. General Assembly, Special Committee on Decolonization. (2009). *Special committee on decolonization approves text calling on United States to expedite self-determination process for Puerto Rico* [Press Release]. Retrieved August 4, 2010, from http://www.un.org/News/Press/docs/2009/gacol3193.doc.htm

U.S. Census Bureau. (2008a). *Hispanics in the United States.* Retrieved August 4, 2010, from http://www.hacu.net/images/hacu/conf/2010CapForum/RobertoRamirezHispanicsInUS2008.pdf

U.S. Census Bureau. (2008b). *An older and more diverse nation by midcentury.* Retrieved August 4, 2010, from http://www.census.gov/PressRelease/www/releases/archives/population/012496.html

U.S. Census Bureau. (2008c). *Population estimates July 1, 2000 to July 1, 2006, Hispanic population: 2000 to 2006.* Washington, DC: U.S. Government Printing Office.

U.S. Council of Economic Advisers. (2007). *Immigration's economic impact.* Retrieved August 4, 2010, from http://www.whitehouse.gov/cea/cea_immigration_062007.html

Valenciana, C. (2006). Unconstitutional deportation of Mexican Americans during the 1930s: A family history & oral history. *Multicultural Education, 13,* 4–9.

World Bank. (2008). *World development indicators 2008.* Washington, DC: World Bank Publications.

Zolberg, A. (2006). *A nation by design: Immigration policy in the fashioning of America.* Cambridge, MA: Harvard University Press.

10

Immigration, Dehumanization, and Resistance to U.S. Immigration Policies

Pushing Against the Boundary

Ana L. León and Debora M. Ortega

 ## INTRODUCTION

Immigration and the politics of immigration are as old as humanity itself. Many historians still do not agree on the specific factors related to the first immigrants who settled in the geographic area now identified as the United States. Although the historical debate continues, one fact remains clear: the reason that a majority of people immigrate is for a better life. Yet, there has been tension between those *seekers* of a better life and those *living* the better life. This tension frequently resulted (and results) in behaviors and policies that create the dehumanization of and danger for new immigrants (not all indigenous people welcomed the pilgrims with open arms, contrary to what our elementary history books would have us believe). Additionally, resistances to actions or policies that restrict the settlement of new arrivals have also occurred since immigration began on this continent. This chapter describes the United States' ambiguous relationship between its *nation of immigrants* as seen through contemporary immigration policy and the resistance to these policies by Latino immigrants and their allies.

☒ HISTORICAL ANTECEDENTS

The first time U.S. citizenship laws and policies applied to Latinos was in 1842 after the Treaty of Guadalupe Hidalgo. This treaty extended citizenship to as many as 80,000 Mexicans. However, many of the 80,000 to 100,000 people who were entitled to citizenship did not receive it (Spickard, 2007). "For all the Treaty of Guadalupe Hidalgo had supposedly conferred on Mexican Americans the full citizenship of White people . . . Anglos insisted on seeing them as un-American and non-White, legally, socially and culturally" (p. 217). The controversy about the rights of Mexicans living in U.S. territories after the Treaty of Guadalupe Hidalgo ended in an 1897 Texas Federal court decision upholding the U.S. citizenship of people who were Mexican citizens prior to the war. This initial immigration skirmish would set the tone regarding policies and perceptions about Latino immigrants. The word *Latino* (or Hispanic) coupled with immigration would conjure up visions of all Latino immigrants being Mexican and only Mexican.

For many years, U.S. immigration policies toward Latin Americans were different than policies governing the rest of the world. Although other immigrants were restricted by quotas or other policies, immigration from the western hemisphere was not restricted. The border between the United States and Mexico was not clearly defined, and people would cross back and forth. Slowly, the United States restricted immigration from Latin America, specifically from Mexico. Henceforth, U.S. immigration policies governing Mexicans followed a predictable historically established pattern that continued until the onset of the Great Depression. As the economy worsened during the Great Depression, "Mexican immigrants became convenient scapegoats for widespread joblessness and budget shortfalls" (Massey, Durand, & Malone, 2002, p. 33). Policymakers knew that immigrants were not the root cause of the depression; however, as a symbolic decision, the U.S. government conducted a massive roundup and deportation of Mexican immigrants. As a result, the Mexican population in the United States was reduced by 41 percent (Massey et al., 2002).

As World War II became imminent, U.S. farms experienced a labor shortage. The response to this shortage was the Bracero Program that brought 168,000 workers from Mexico. Despite this increased workforce, agricultural growers were still in need of more workers. Agricultural growers solicited undocumented workers through other braceros on their farms. In the best cases, growers would facilitate the legalization of their Mexican workers after the fact; however, all too often in the other cases, growers ignored U.S. laws and continued to exploit Mexican labor without support for changing their legal status (Massey et al., 2002). In addition, growers pressured congress to provide more workers, and Congress responded by providing more than 100,000 bracero visas. However, this was still not sufficient, and the growers continued recruiting undocumented workers; the number of those workers grew drastically from 69,000 in 1945 to 883,000 in 1950 (Massey et al., 2002).

As the demand for laborers continued, undocumented Mexicans and braceros continued crossing the border. U.S. citizens became worried about the number of unlawful and legal immigrants, which led to stricter immigration policies. Immigration again became a heated issue after the Korean War and the recession that followed. Congress was in a difficult place, the citizens demanded control of the borders, while the agricultural growers demanded more workers. To appease both sides, Congress enacted Operation Wetback in 1954. Local and federal authorities worked together to detain and deport more than 1 million Mexican immigrants, which appeased U.S. citizens who believed that immigration was being controlled. However, at the same time as the deportations, Congress was granting more visas. "At one point, the INS [Immigration and Naturalization Services] was raiding agricultural fields in the Southwestern United States, arresting undocumented workers, transporting them into the waiting arms of the United States department of labor, who promptly processed them as braceros and transported them back to the very place they had been arrested in the first place!" (Massey et al., 2002, p. 37). It appeared that the borders were under control and growers had access to cheap labor.

In the 1960s with the Civil Rights movement in full force, many U.S. citizens questioned the contradiction in immigration policy. "In an era of expanding civil rights, immigration policies that systematically blocked the entry of Asians, Africans Eastern and Southern Europeans came to be seen as intolerably racist" (Massey et al., 2002, p. 39). In 1965, the Immigration and Nationality Act that was approved was intended to be more neutral. The 1965 Immigration and Nationality Act finally extirpated overt racism from immigration and it put, for the first time, limitations on immigration from the Western hemisphere. Also, the 1965 the civil rights coalitions succeeded in killing the Bracero Program. The growers, realizing that the end of the Bracero Program would mean a shortage of labor, continued recruiting undocumented immigrants. They also sought visas for former braceros (Hutchinson, 1981).

In the 1970s, once again the economic situation put more pressure on restricting immigration. The government tightened the border, which made it more difficult to cross. The immigrants that were more likely to migrate were the young, strong workers. This system benefited the elite employers who had access to a readily cheap male labor force who did not intend to stay in the United States. The demand of cheap labor in the United States coupled with the economic and political crises in Latin America increased the number of Latin Americans migrating to the United States, making them more visible.

In the 1980s, anxiety about the so-called problem of immigration increased, and many bills were introduced to Congress to address the problem. Ronald Reagan led the way to immigration reform by framing the border control problem as one of national security. This was partly a result of the paranoia of the communist regimes in Latin America. He "exacerbated the Cold War hysteria by linking border control not only to national security but to the threat of terrorism" (Massey et al., 2002, p. 86). In 1986, the Immigration and Reform act was passed; it legalized more than 3.1 million immigrants, and more money was invested to try to control the border (Massey et al., 2002).

From 1986 to 1996, immigration became a national security issue as illegal immigration was portrayed as a vehicle for military invasion. In 1994, California passed proposition 187, which prohibited providing public education, welfare, and health services to undocumented immigrants. It was later declared unconstitutional (Hutchinson, 1981). However, it was a fueled attack on immigrants and their rights.

\\\ CURRENT IMMIGRATION POLICIES AND THE EFFECTS ON THE WELFARE OF LATINOS

In 1996, the Illegal Immigration and Responsibility Act of 1996 and the Antiterrorism and Effective Death Penalty Act were passed. The intent was to strengthen border enforcement, make it more difficult to gain asylum, establish income requirements for sponsors of legal immigrants, streamline deportation procedures, remove procedural legal protections for migrants who lacked documents, and raise penalties for people who aid or employ people who lack documents (Spickard, 2007). The Oklahoma bombings and the attacks on the World Trade Center strengthened the view that immigration was an issue of national security.

Changes in 1996 made the U.S. deportation policies more drastic. Although most people think only undocumented immigrants get deported, in reality immigration policies apply to long-term lawful permanent residents as well (Human Rights Watch, 2007). Since 1996, deportation laws have become more punitive, and immigrants have fewer ways to appeal. Historically, even for immigrants who may have committed misdemeanors, judges would consider their family ties to the United States through a hearing process. Not only was this practice eliminated, but the laws were retroactive, which affected long-term residents that might have had one offense many years prior to the 1996 change.

In 1996, President Clinton signed a welfare reform act, the Personal Responsibility and Work Opportunity Reconciliation Act of 1996. This was President Clinton's solution to *end welfare as we know it* (Carcasson, 2006). The Welfare Reform Act had serious repercussions for immigrants. It denied unauthorized immigrants all but emergency services and made citizenship a condition of eligibility for most public benefits (this was actually a part of California's proposition 187) (Spickard, 2007).

The current immigration policies continue to be oppressive to minorities and to fuel the dehumanization of nonwhite foreigners. The new policies follow a long history of exclusion and oppression towards ethnic and racial minority groups, especially nonwhite immigrants who are predominantly Latino.

⚡ EXPLOITATION OF LABOR

Several patterns are related to the escalation of anti-immigration sentiment. First, nativism and nationalism surge in reaction to a perception of an increase in migration or an economic downturn. Second, the labor force is such that at times of war or rapid industrialization, there is a shortage of labor, which prompts policies that encourage foreign labor. The popular feeling that immigration has increased inevitably leads to pressure on politicians to enact and support strict immigration restrictions. Such restrictions are followed by the capture and deportation of immigrant workers by redefining and implementing *legal* means of detention and deportation (Salazar et al., 2008).

The acceleration of immigration enforcement has resulted in increased deportation and exploitation, humiliation, and death for many Latino workers. According to the United Nations Declaration of Human Rights, safety in the workplace is a basic human right. However, the state of fear created by these "convenient economic deportations" has left undocumented workers without the protection of this basic human right. A 2004 report by the Associated Press revealed that 80 percent of Mexicans were more likely to die on the job than were U.S. citizens (Pritchard, 2004). Illegal immigrants are too afraid to report unsafe working condition. Even when they find the courage to report injustices to the U.S. Department of Labor, they find a legal system that is ill equipped to deal with labor law violations (Southern Poverty Law Center, 2009). Furthermore, the lack of efforts from the U.S. Department of Labor sends the message that the safety and lives of Latino immigrants are not valuable. Hence, employers take advantage of the immigration policies and enforcement tactics to maximize their profits at the expense immigrants.

In addition to unsafe working conditions and constant discrimination, undocumented women face more challenges than men in the workplace. In a recent survey by the Southern Poverty Law Center (2009), undocumented female workers reported that they are forced to perform sexual favors for their supervisors with the threat of being fired or being deported.

Although undocumented immigrants contribute to the United States by paying taxes and Social Security, they are often denied social services such as preventative health care and the use of Social Security benefits upon retirement. It is estimated that immigrants earn approximately $240 billion a year, pay about $90 billion in taxes, and only use approximately $5 billion in public benefits (Salazar et al., 2008). Thus, although undocumented immigrants continue to contribute to Social Security and taxes, they are denied the public services that are funded with their contributions.

⫸ REGULATION OF INDIVIDUAL AND GROUP LIBERTY

One of the tools used to regulate the liberty of Latinos has been racial profiling. In the last several decades, most people targeted for deportation have been Latinos—specifically Mexicans. Custom and border patrol officers harassed those suspected of being undocumented based on the perception that they were Mexican, even though many of them were U.S. citizens.

Racial profiling is fueled by one of the most serious threats to the liberties of Latinos, the allowance of local police authorities to enforce federal immigration laws (Southern Poverty Law Center, 2009). Essentially, local law enforcement authorities detain Latino people for supposedly minor violations for the purpose of asking them about their legal status. They engage in this tactic by looking for excuses such as stopping people for alleged traffic violations and blatantly ignoring federal laws that prohibit racial profiling. Highlighting this abuse of power and violation of human rights is Sheriff Arpaio in Maricopa County, Arizona. Sheriff Arpaio has been using racial profiling and fear tactics to disproportionately arrest Latinos for minor traffic offenses to enforce immigration laws (Gonzalez, 2009). Furthermore, law enforcers across the country increasingly use racial profiling to detain those who appear illegal. This tactic has led many both legal and undocumented workers to feel imprisoned in their own homes, communities, and job sites (Southern Poverty Law Center, 2009).

Prison is a powerful social control to restrict liberties and freedoms. The United States has increased its incarceration capacity as a way to control the freedoms and liberties of noncitizens. Before the laws of 1996, Mexicans apprehended trying to cross the border illegally were placed in custody and then quickly returned to their country. However, as the number of border patrol officers grew, so did the number of illegal immigrants who were placed in prisons. Essentially, the criminalization of being present in the United States without papers has resulted in the significant increase of the number of noncitizens in prison. This has led to the rapid growth of local, state, and federal prisons (Bosworth, 2007). The use of imprisonment to control noncitizens has increased so dramatically that the government has resorted to the use of for-profit corporations to keep up with the ever-increasing number of noncitizens being jailed. These corporations profit from illegal immigrants in part by not providing adequate health care, mental health, or even adequate living facilities (Rosa, 2009). Simultaneously, the average length of time in jail for someone accused of immigration offenses has increased from 4 to 21 months (Bosworth, 2007). This has led many critics to question whether this increased length of incarceration is a result of the financial incentive of the for-profit jail industry.

\\\ EXCLUSION

These shifts in policies and laws combined with increased hostility toward immigrants fueled by mass media have effectively excluded noncitizens from society and its protections. According to the Federal Bureau of Investigation, Hispanics are the number-one target of hate crimes because of ethnicity (Navarrette, 2008). What is even more troubling is that these statistics do not represent all the crimes against Latinos. When immigrants report hate crimes that occurred in the United States to the police in their native countries, they are left unreported, uninvestigated, and unprosecuted (Southern Poverty Law Center, 2009). The exclusion from society by implementing harsh immigration policies makes Hispanics a target for crimes and denies them the right to justice. The poisonous debate about immigration has stripped undocumented immigrants of their humanity, resulting in a tolerance for crimes against Latinos. For example, in 2009 an all-white jury acquitted the killers of an undocumented immigrant in Pennsylvania and charged them with the lesser degree of assault (Rokus, 2009). Public opinion about this issue focused on the fact that the victim was in the United States illegally, and if he had only stayed where he belonged, then he would not have been killed. The victim's documentation status appeared to be more of an issue than the relatively light sentence of the attackers. Another consequence of these policies, laws, and anti-immigrant sentiment is the creation of fear in women and children who are sexually or physically abused. Despite a law that was enacted in 2000 to protect victims by demanding that police not ask questions regarding the victim's documentation status, the protection of victims is not guaranteed. A 13-year-old in Georgia was raped, and when the family wanted to press charges, the District Attorney threatened them by telling them that if he found out the girl was undocumented, he would have to report her to immigration services. The family was too afraid of deportation to press charges against the rapist (Southern Poverty Law Center, 2009). Many Latinos report that they will not call the police when they are victims of crimes to avoid having to disclose their documentation status. Innocent victims suffer in silence and criminals walk away free, which decreases the safety and security of everyone in the community.

〰 DEJTABILIZINC AND THREATJ TO FAMILIEJ

Three million U.S.-born children have at least one parent who is an unlawful immigrant. One in 10 families in the United States has mixed immigrant status, having at least one member of the family who is an undocumented immigrant (Rhor, 2007). The drastic increase of immigration raids in homes and workplaces has resulted in the separation of thousands of family members, including parents from children and disabled U.S. citizens from their financial and physical support system. Parents are arrested and deported without consideration for the health and safety of the rest of the family, especially their children.

There are many reports of children who are left stranded in day care centers, at school, and at home waiting for parents who, for all intents and purposes, are missing. Parents are without the right or ability to arrange for the care of their children during the detention and deportation process (Capps, Castaneda, Chaudry, & Santos, 2007). In the best-case scenarios, children are left to stay with friends or relatives. Even in these cases, the unexpected caretaker may be unprepared, ill equipped, of financially unable to take care of these children. In the worst-case scenarios, children are left to be cared for by the public child welfare system, a system that is widely criticized for the lack of adequate care and culturally responsive services. Regardless of the nature of the child's placement, these children find themselves unexpectedly dealing with the unanticipated trauma of family separation. The National Council of La Raza and the Urban Institute report that children of parents who have been detained by immigration experience symptoms congruent with severe trauma and depression. "They may even fail classes, mutilate themselves, and have suicidal thoughts. . . . For these children, physical separation often feels like death" (Salazar et al., 2008, p. 68). Mental health clinics, schools, and social services agencies do not have adequate resources, or in some cases, training, to deal with the emotional trauma of these torn apart families.

Among the most concerning threats to the family unit is the effect of domestic child welfare policies in combination with often contradictory immigration policies. The resulting consequence of these policies is that mothers and fathers lose all legal rights to their children, not because of poor parental care but because of the timelines required by the Adult and Safe Families Act of 1996, lack of linguistically appropriate child welfare assessments and services, lack of coordination with international child welfare agencies, and the number of days required for the detention and deportation process.

Prior to the immigration policy changes prompted by the 9/11 attacks, many child welfare experts expressed concern about the manner in which Latino children were being served by the United States public child welfare system. These concerns included shifting financial resources from family preservation to adoption services, shortening timelines to determine the permanent plan for the child (i.e., quicker termination of parental rights and a move toward adoption in shorter timeframes), and the lack services in Spanish (many of which are court-ordered and a condition of reunification of families) (Suleiman, n.d.). The recent changes in immigration policy have increased the number of people detained, which has led to a longer detention process. Essentially, while parents are waiting processing in detention, the possibility of their children being adopted by a (white) family increases because of federal child welfare policies and timelines.

In the event that a parent is deported, rather than just detained, and the child is in out-of-home care, the risk that a child will not be returned to their family increases. Currently, there are no standards of child welfare practice or policies that are systematically adhered to that coordinate assessments and services across nations. Consequently, children cannot return to their families because the U.S. child welfare system is unable or unwilling to accept international assessments and measures of safety (i.e., Mexican home studies for kinship care and psychological assessments). Again, the original circumstances that created the conditions that required that the child be placed in foster care are unrelated to the child safety concerns associated with the care of the child.

⫻ RESISTANCE: STORIES OF IMMIGRANT AND CITIZEN PARTNERSHIP RESISTANCE ACTIONS

Resistance to unjust immigration policies occurs at the macro, mezzo, and micro levels. Most acts of resistance occur in collaboration with citizen allies. The partnership and presence of citizen allies are key to immigration resistance acts, because the presence of citizens creates some safety for immigrants who are continually at risk for deportation, unequal treatment, and physical harm.

Immigrants' rights marches in large and small cities alike riveted the attention of the populace because of the number of participants and the degree of organization required for the marches' success. State policies have been enacted to ensure immigrants' rights or to provide a safer environment free from immigration practices that endanger their health and safety. Community and nonprofit organizations have resisted repressive immigration policies through fundraising for services that are directed specifically at people excluded from access social services. Families provide ongoing social and financial support for family members who suffer the consequences of immigration policies that destroy and endanger their family members. The following section will highlight a few of activities of resistance that occur at each of these levels.

Large-Scale Political Action as Resistance

In response to the oppression fostered by immigration policies, workplace and home raids, deportations, human rights' violations, Mexican bashing, and hate speech toward immigrants continue to rise. In March 2006, between 500,000 and 1.3 million documented and undocumented immigrants, hand-in-hand with Latino and non-Latino U.S. citizens, marched in American streets demanding immigrants' rights. The marches quickly spread across the nation, and on April 10, 2006, approximately 1 million people marched in Washington, D.C.; New York, New York; Phoenix, Arizona; Houston, Texas; Lincoln, Nebraska; Tyler, Texas; Garden City, Kansas; Jonesborough, Tennessee; and Pensacola, Florida. Then again, on May 1, 2006, more than 1 million people marched in favor of immigrants' rights across the United States in Los Angeles, California; Chicago, Illinois; Houston, Texas; San Francisco, California; Las Vegas, Nevada; Salem, Oregon; Detroit, Michigan; and Orlando, Florida. "The demonstrators were not defying the law or other Americans. They were calling America to be its better self" (Spickard, 2007, p. 448).

The sheer amount of people who participated in the march was stunning, and in many communities immigrants themselves organized the marches (Narro, Wong, & Shadduck-Hernandez, 2007). In some cases, immigrants' rights organizers found themselves without sound systems equipped enough to reach the ears of the masses because the number of marchers far exceeded their expectations (J. Garcia, personal communication, May 5, 2009). Likewise, the tools for coordination used by community organizers involved in the immigrants' rights marches included a combination of new and old technology. The new technology was peer-to-peer networks such as MySpace and text messaging, and the old technology included radio. The use of peer-to-peer networks mobilized many young immigrant and citizens who were familiar with cell phone and computer technology. Spanish radio programs accessed those people who might not have as much access or whose networks might not use texting. Sociologist and organizers studying the immigrants' rights marches attribute the pairing of radio and texting as one of the most important vehicles for creating the large number of marchers.

State and Local Policies of Resistance

At the state level, there are limited actions of resistance to the immigration policies especially when comparing them with local communities. However, Hawaii, Utah, Maryland, New Mexico, and Washington continue to issue licenses without requiring proof of legal status in the United States (National Immigration Law Center, 2008).This allows undocumented immigrants to purchase car insurance, transport themselves to jobs, take their children to work, save money to build assets, and to use a recognized identification to open bank accounts or cash checks. It also provides fewer opportunities for law enforcement agencies to engage in practices of immigration enforcement.

At the community level, immigrants and supporters of immigrants have also resisted immigration policies that they deem harmful to Latino immigrants. For example, despite the requirement of the 1996 Illegal Immigration Reform and Immigrant Responsibility Act that requires local governments to cooperate with Homeland Security's Immigration and Custom Enforcement (ICE), many cities such as New York and Chicago have adopted sanctuary policies. Sanctuary policies are formal or informal ways that cities prohibit the use of funds or resources for the enactment of federal immigration regulations. In sanctuary cities, employees are instructed not to alert the federal government of the presence of illegal aliens in their communities.

Some cities that have not been able to maintain themselves as sanctuaries still have sanctuary policies. In these cities, sanctuary policies allow for immigrants to access basic services and to cooperate with local enforcement without fear of being questioned about their residency status, arrested, or deported.

Community Organization and Nonprofit Resistance

At the national level, several national organizations such as the National Council of La Raza, National Association of Latino Elected and Appointed Officials (NALEO), AFL-CIO, American Friends Service Committee, American Civil Liberties Union (ACLU), Catholic Legal Immigration Network, and the Southern Poverty Law Center have worked to protect undocumented immigrants. Furthermore, several other organizations such as ACLU, the American Immigration Law Foundation, the National Center for Lesbian Rights, and the Catholic Legal Immigration Network provide legal support and litigation to undocumented immigrants to help with expedited deportations, labor disputes, asylum, and wage theft among other things. The work by these organizations ensures fair treatment under the law and upholds the diminishing rights of immigrants since the 1996 immigration reform and the later PATRIOT Act.

At the local level, nonprofit organizations have played an important role resisting the oppressive immigration policies harmful to Latinos. For example, many nonprofit organizations raise funds from foundations, corporations, and individuals for the express purpose of providing services to undocumented immigrants who pay into state and federal systems but cannot access federal funds. Nonprofit and advocacy organizations have also formed coalitions to help defend immigrants' rights. The tools of these collaborations include Listserves and the use of text messaging to inform, organize, and engage in the resistance of policies and actions that injure immigrant people and their families.

Churches have also been important community participants in the fight for the rights of immigrants. The most publicized religious figure calling his churches to resist immigration is Los Angeles Diocese Cardinal Roger Mahony. Cardinal Mahony connected the protection of immigrants with the church's prolife agenda. He publicly announced that the diocese would provide charitable and religious ministry to unauthorized immigrants despite efforts to criminalize these activities. Soon after, religious leaders across the country stood up against anti-immigrant policies that promoted hate as a national policy.

Family and Individual Action as Resistance

The current immigration policies at the core violate the basic human right to happiness. Therefore, it is not a surprise that family members will use the limited resources they have at their disposal to resist policies that seek to tear their families apart. When a family is deported, for example, family members will support those left behind. At the same time, family members will provide financial assistance so that families can be reunited.

Successful Resistance

Despite the implementation and enforcement of the new immigration policies, thousands of immigrants continue to cross the border illegally. "An estimated 850,000 people enter the U.S. illegally each year—more than double the number in the 1980s and early 1990" (Spickard, 2007, p. 445). Consequently, the ultimate individual act of resistance to immigration policy is the crossing of the border without U.S. authorization or the choice to remain beyond the time limit of a visa, to have children who will be citizens based on the geographical location of their birth, or to subvert a higher education system that cripples the opportunities of children and youth brought to the United States by economically desperate parents.

Although advocates of immigrants' rights have been pushing for a comprehensive immigration reform to eliminate the abuses toward illegal immigrants, many still wait for this reform. However, the wait has not been in silence, and acts of resistance have produced some positive outcomes for undocumented immigrants. One of the most important contributions made by proimmigrant organizations is to illuminate the numerous violations of human rights by ICE during deportation raids and in detention centers. ICE has responded by establishing more humane policies (providing alternatives to detention and family separation for immigrant mothers who are breastfeeding their citizen children) and investigating some of the alleged abuses (Watanabe, 2007). In addition, these organizations have provided educational and outreach material to undocumented immigrants, naturalized citizens, and those who may have the same phenotype as profiled immigrants so that they are aware of their rights if they are stopped by police, arrested, or incarcerated in detention centers.

Legal advocacy groups also had some success in courts fighting for immigrants' rights. The Southern Poverty Law Center has been at the forefront of defending immigrants rights with some successes. For example, in 2008 the Southern Poverty Law Center won a lawsuit against a corporation who stole wages from immigrants recruited to rebuild New Orleans (Southern Poverty Law Center, 2009). There have been several other lawsuits won on behalf of immigrants rights. Although triumphs for immigrants' rights have been few and far between, at the bare minimum it sends the message that violations of human rights are monitored and will not *always* be tolerated.

〰 IMPLICATION FOR FURTHER RESEARCH

The immigration rights movement is one of the most dynamic areas of policy because of the changing landscape. This landscape is influenced by public opinion, international and national politics, labor availability, and economics. Research about organized resistance behaviors of Latino people is just beginning to emerge in part because of the 2006 immigration marches. This area of research is rich with lessons about the mobilization of people who fear not only for their personal safety but the dissolution of their families as a result of participation in resistance movements. In addition, research about the cross-cultural features of organizing could provide important evidenced-based practice information about cross-cultural community organizing for the purposes of policy change.

〰 CONCLUSION

The immigration policies of the United States have elicited acts of resistance at the macro, mezzo, and micro levels of social structures. For social workers, resistance against immigration policies provides lessons both in terms of the topic and the tools available to create and support movements against inhumane policies. The history of current immigration policies highlights the underlying exploitative nature that has governed the development of such policies. Modern practice related to the enforcement of these policies coupled with the media's role in framing the immigration debate provides ample evidence of a dehumanization process. Widespread resistance to inhumane immigration policies is an indication that people can and will subvert policies of injustice that endanger the lives and safety of an identified group of people. The tools of resistance learned from issues about immigration provide important reminders about using all available resources in our quest for equity and justice. These resources include familiar tools such as television and radio but also require us to use the most advanced technology such as peer-to-peer networks (current examples include Facebook, text messaging, and Twitter) to create social action for the purposes of social justice. Finally, the acts of resistance against immigration policy highlight the importance of partnerships that extend beyond those impacted by unjust policies. The presence and activism of citizens in immigration reform create the opportunities for the humanization of immigrants to occur while creating some protection for immigrants who could be silenced through (the actual experience or fear of) arrest, detention, and deportation.

\\\ REFERENCES

Bosworth, M. (2007). Identity, citizen and punishment. In M. Bosworth & J. Flavin (Eds.), *Race, gender, punishment: From colonialism to the war on terror* (pp. 134–148). New Brunswick, NJ: Rutgers University Press.

Capps, R., Castaneda, R. M., Chaudry, A., & Santos, R. (2007). *The impact of immigration raids on America's children.* Retrieved July 23, 2008, from the Urban Institute and the National Council of La Raza website: http://www.urban.org/publications/411566.html

Carcasson, M. (2006). Ending welfare as we know it: President Clinton and the rhetorical transformation of the anti-welfare culture. *Rhetoric & Public Affairs, 9*(4), 655–692.

Gonzalez, D. (2009, March 11). Arpaio to be investigated over alleged violations. *The Arizona Republic.* Retrieved May 2, 2009, from http://www.azcentral.com/arizonare public/news/articles/2009/03/11/20090311investigation0311.html

Human Rights Watch. (2007). *Forced apart: Families separated and immigrants harmed by United States deportation policy.* Retrieved July 18, 2008, from http://www.hrw.org/en/ reports/2007/07/16/forced-apart

Hutchinson, E. P. (1981). *Legislative history of American immigration 1789–1965.* Philadelphia: University of Pennsylvania Press.

Massey, D. S., Durand, J., & Malone, N. J., (2002). *Beyond smoke and mirrors: Mexican immigration in an era of economic integration.* New York: Russell Sage Foundation.

Narro, V., Wong, K., & Shadduck-Hernandez, J. (2007). The 2006 immigrant uprising: Origins and Future. *New Labor Forum 16*(1), 46–58.

Navarrette, R. (2009, November, 24). Commentary: No time for hate. *CNN.* Retrieved May 2, 2009, from http://www.cnn.com/2008/POLITICS/11/13/navarrette.killing/index .html?iref=newssearch

Pritchard, J. (2004). AP investigation: Mexican worker deaths rise sharply even as overall U.S. job safety improves. *Associated Press.* Retrieved April 18, 2009, from http://fmmac2 .mm.ap.org/polk_awards_dying_to_work_html/DyingtoWork.html

Rhor, M. (2007). Kids left behind in immigration raids. *The Associated Press.* Retrieved March 11, 2009, from http://www.sfgate.com/cgi-bin/article.cgi?f=/n/a/2007/03/11/ national/a125442D32.DTL

Rokus, B. (2009, May 2). No murder conviction in Mexican immigrant's beating death. *CNN.* Retrieved May 2, 2009, from http://www.cnn.com/2009/CRIME/05/01/pa.immigrant .beating

Rosa, E. (2009 March1). *GEO Group Inc.: Despite a crashing economy, private prison firm turns a handsome profit.* San Francisco: CorpWatch. Retrieved April 18, 2009, from http://www.corpwatch.org/article.php?id=15308

Salazar, M., Bornstein, M., Mercado, S., Martinez, L., Somoza, O., Ortega, D., & Leon, A. (2008). *The state of Latinos 2008: Defining and agenda for the future.* Denver, CO: University of Denver.

Spickard, P. (2007). *Almost all aliens: Immigration, race, colonialism in American history and identity.* New York: Routledge.

Southern Poverty Law Center. (2009). *Under siege: Life for low-income Latinos in the South.* Retrieved May 1, 2009, from http://www.splcenter.org/legal/undersiege/UnderSiege.pdf

Watanabe, T. (2007, November 24). Guidelines to humanize immigration. *Los Angeles Times.* Retrieved April 16, 2009, from http://www.latimes.com/news/local/la-me-immig24nov24,1,359850.story

11

Fear of Calling
the Police

Regulation and Resistance
Around Immigration
Enforcement Activities

Lisa Magaña

⧟ INTRODUCTION

Maricopa County, largely composed of the Phoenix metropolitan area, is the fastest growing Latino immigration destination in the United States. In recent years, Mexicans from other states, particularly from the central and southern regions of Mexico, have been more visible in Arizona. The 2000 Census count revealed that the population in Arizona grew more than three times as fast as the rest of the nation (U.S Census Bureau, 2001). During the 1990s, Arizona increased its population by 1.5 million, and its Latino population increased by 88 percent (from 688,000 in 1990 to more than 1.2 million in 2000). During this decade, the Latino population increased its proportion of the statewide population from 18.7 percent in 1990 to more than 25 percent in 2000 (U.S. Census Bureau, 2001).

The more visible and increased presence of Latin American origin immigrants in Arizona, as has been the case for the rest of the nation, has led to some hostile responses. These responses are intended to make life for unauthorized immigrants increasingly difficult. The heightened sense of concern about undocumented immigration has in part been the result of the downturn in the state's economy that occurred in the context of an increased influx of immigrants in what is now the busiest undocumented immigration corridor into the United States. Such responses include the creation of several vigilante organizations along the border, including the Minutemen Project in spring 2005, the organization that sought to stop immigrants from crossing the U.S. southern border, "doing the job Congress won't do" (http://www.minuteman project.com). These responses also have included the approval of a barrage of anti-immigrant policies that include Proposition 200, which requires proof of eligibility to receive social services, state and local workers to report immigration violations to federal authorities in writing, and voters to document their U.S. citizenship when registering to vote and when voting. Moreover, it prevents undocumented immigrants from collecting punitive damages in civil lawsuits, denies them release on bail for serious felonies, and prevents them from participating in state-subsidized adult education and child care programs (Migration News, 2007). Because of these new stringent laws, Latino immigrants in Maricopa County have been stopped and arrested for minor traffic violations and then subsequently deported. As a result, Latino families are being separated and are afraid of calling the police.

This chapter examines how recent Latino immigration to Arizona has brought about unfair immigration policies and practices that engender considerable fear among Latino/as, especially fear of law enforcement officials and agencies. This chapter focuses on the unfair policy practices of the Maricopa County Sheriff's Office (MCSO), which is under numerous investigations for racially profiling Latinos as well as ignoring federal stipulations. This chapter further demonstrates how in response to the actions of the MCSO, nontraditional political players, such as noncitizens, are mobilizing at the grassroots level to counter anti-immigrant legislation. In unprecedented numbers, these nontraditional activists, many of whom have never participated in grassroots organizing strategies, are protesting and demonstrating in numbers never witnessed before in the state of Arizona. This chapter will conclude with some implications and recommendations, illustrating the resistance activities that can be employed by social work policy practitioners.

\\\\ FRAMING THE STUDY

Studies have been conducted on the dual mission of police officers, enforcement and service. That is, they are responsible for enforcing laws and servicing citizens in the community. Although the enforcement activities generate a significant amount of attention, they are only one part of the overall mission of the agency. In the last decade, there have been a number of new policies assigned to police agencies around immigration. These increased responsibilities have meant new roles and procedures for the officers to pursue. These mandates have not coincided with sufficient time to formulate clear agency guidelines and, as a result, implementation performance has suffered (Magaña, 2003).

Other studies examine the environments from which policy actors operate, having much to do with the way policy decisions are made. Theorists find that environments inculcate systems of rewards and values in the minds of policy actors. For example, local policy actors who work within federal agencies such as the Immigration Customs and Enforcement (ICE) have overwhelming and complex duties to perform. The expectations placed on them by their agencies are ambiguous, vague, and often conflicting. Furthermore, because agencies are often large, actors can only see problems narrowly and independently of their connections to other issues (Magaña, 2003).

Others explain that bureaucracies have the most pervasive influence on the implementation of policies. Factors that influence implementation within bureaucracies are the reorganization of staff and programs, resources, and the relationships with important other agencies' clients (Ripley, 1986, p. 59). A recent study illustrated the police agency's inability to carry out immigration policies effectively because of the lack of accountability and poor supervision (Government Accountability Office [GAO], 2009). Police officers, particularly those who work at the local level, have the most influence over policy decisions (Lipsky, 1980; Romzek & Johnston, 1999).

\\\\ LATINO REGULATION AND PROVISION 287(G)

Maricopa County, which includes Phoenix, has a population of nearly 4 million and the highest proportion of unauthorized immigrants in

Arizona. Joe Arpaio, the Maricopa County Sheriff, calls himself the "Toughest Sheriff in America." He is known for his publicity-seeking activities. He has been a frequent guest and subject of interest on national and international news outlets. Some of his most notable tactics were jailing inmates in outside tents in blistering Arizona heat and reducing the number of meals a day to only two in order to save the state money. One of his most famous practices was making jail inmates wear pink underwear and flip-flop shoes to humiliate them. He is a hero to some conservatives and populists and receives public support from racist organizations (Finnegan, 2009). He and the MCSO have been sued more than 2,300 times for various reasons, including cruel treatment to inmates, racial profiling, and illegally carrying out immigration policy. There have also been several lawsuits that have been won by families whose loved ones have died while in jail.

In 1996, the Illegal Immigration and Reform and Responsibility Act (IIRA) was passed, and a small provision of the Act, 287(g), allows local police officers to work with ICE. According to the Department of Homeland Security (DHS), it authorizes the secretary of DHS to work with local law enforcement agencies, allowing specially trained officers to implement immigration policies. However, officers must receive some training from ICE instructors. According to DHS, this coordination between ICE and local police officers allows officers necessary resources and latitude to pursue investigations relating to violent crimes, human smuggling, gang/organized crime activity, sexual-related offenses, narcotics smuggling, and money laundering (ICE, 2009).

Police agencies that participate in the training receive more funding in order to subsidize immigration enforcement activities. To carry out 287(g), you must be a U.S. citizen, pass a background investigation, have a minimum of 2 years of experience, and have no disciplinary actions pending. ICE provides 4 weeks of training at the Federal Law Enforcement Training Center (FLETC) ICE Academy (ICEA) in Charleston, South Carolina. According to the HMS, since January 2006, the 287(g) program is credited with identifying more than 100,000 potentially removable aliens. More than 950 officers have been trained and certified through the program, and there are 66 police programs that implement 287(g) (ICE, 2009).

The MCSO has the most deputies trained through 287(g), approximately 170. As noted, the policy is intended to pursue investigations relating to violent crimes, human smuggling, gang/organized crime activity, sexual-related offenses, narcotics smuggling, and money laundering—not immigration enforcement. In Phoenix, Sheriff Arpaio has implemented highly controversial and contentious programs under the 287(g), what he calls "crime suppression sweeps" in Latino communities. Latino immigrants have been arrested for minor traffic violations and then subsequently deported. As stipulated in 287(g), individuals are not to be targeted for minor offenses. The MCSO is under investigation for the practice of crime suppression sweeps. Police officers enforcing immigration policies have destroyed positive relations between police and Latinos. Immigrants that may have called the police for help may not, for fear they may be deported.

A recent report by the National Employment Law Project and Others (2009) illustrates the impact that crime suppression sweeps have on Latinos. They found that in 97 percent of the car stops made by MCSO in 2006 and 2007, supposedly for suspected smuggling, deputies made no arrests and wrote no tickets. Instead, cars were stopped because of broken windshields or taillights, unsafe lane changes, or outdated license plates. In 2008, the authors found that when crime suppression sweeps were conducted in white neighborhoods, Latinos were still more likely to be arrested.

In October 2008, a Maricopa County Sheriff arrested Alma Chacon. The officer offered no reason for the arrest and told her she had an expired license tag. Ms. Chacon began having labor pains that evening and was sent to the hospital from the jail. "The sheriff's deputy insisted that she remain chained to the bed by one hand and one foot, and it was in that position that she gave birth to a baby girl. Ms. Chacon is fighting deportation" (National Employment Law Project & Others, 2009). Maria Martinez was holding a garage sale in front of her home when she was arrested for "identity theft." Ms. Martinez had shown an expired California driver's license and a Mexican consular card. In June 2008, 30 Maricopa County Sheriff's deputies arrested janitors at the City of Mesa library and city hall. In August of 2008, 12 Latino corn vendors were arrested because they could not provide documentation. U.S. citizens who are Latino who refuse to answer questions regarding their citizenship status are also arrested. A landscaper named Pedro Marquina was arrested because he could not prove his U.S. citizenship. He was later released when proof of his citizenship was provided (National Employment Law Project & Others, 2009).

Mary Rose Wilcox, a Latina and the only Democrat on the Maricopa County board of supervisors, runs a youth program in Phoenix. "It's for fifth-grade kids who live near the ballpark but would never be able to afford to go to a Diamondbacks game," she said. "They all do community-service work, about a thousand of them, and then they get to go to a game. Sheriff's deputies always helped me with the program till two years ago. But I had to ask them to stop. The kids are just too afraid of those brown shirts. That's what their teachers told me. And I hate to say it but the Sheriff is responsible for all this fear. It's like a big joke to him," she said. "He has no idea the harm he's doing to children, families, and communities" (Finnegan, 2009).

Guadalupe is a small town in Maricopa County and has a contract with the MCSO for policing activities. The town is composed of Latinos, legal and undocumented, as well as Native Americans. The MCSO stopped and asked for the identification of citizens and anyone that looked foreign for identification. If the individual failed to provide documentation, they were arrested. This even generated significant national attention. The MCSO stated that it was asked by the town leaders to perform a crime suppression sweep. However, at no time could proof of such a request be provided.

In 2009, GAO released a report to Homeland Security on the impact of 287(g). They found that "immigration officials have failed to develop key internal controls over a controversial program that trains state and local police to identify illegal immigrants involved in crime, so some departments are focusing on minor violations rather than on serious offenses, according to federal investigators" (Aizenman, 2009). The report also showed that the program has expanded rapidly in recent years, "receiving $60 million between 2006 and 2008, training 951 state and local law enforcement officers in 67 agencies and resulting in the arrests of at least 43,000 immigrants, almost 28,000 of whom ultimately were ordered out of the country" (Aizenman, 2009). In the report, the GAO said that four local law enforcement agencies were arresting immigrants for minor violations such as speeding, contrary to the objective of the program (Aizenman, 2009).

The GAO report noted that although some local authorities said the program made their communities safer, the authors found that ICE failed to provide clearly defined objectives for the program or to create a consistent system for supervision. The authors warned that confusion over the purpose of 287(g) could result in referrals of an "unmanageable number" of low-priority illegal immigrants to ICE as well as "misuse of authority" by local officials. According to the report, one sheriff said that his understanding of his authority was that "287(g)-trained officers [can] go to people's homes and question individuals regarding their immigration status even if the individual is not suspected of criminal activity.

Although it does not appear that any officers used the authority in this manner," the report continued, "it is illustrative of the lack of clarity regarding program objectives and the use of 287(g) authority by participating agencies" (Aizenman, 2009).

In another study conducted by the Goldwater Institute, researchers found that the policy is highly ineffective and deters officers from pursuing more important law enforcement activities (Goldwater Institute, 2008). Researchers found that before 287(g), MCSO targeted more smugglers or coyotes—those individuals that illegally bring people into the country. In 2006 and 2007, the MCSO arrested only low-level operatives, such as drivers and drop-house guards. The researchers noted that out of the eight saturation patrol sweeps that had taken place in six communities in Phoenix, not one smuggler boss had been arrested.

More importantly, 287(g) has diverted substantial resources away from other law-enforcement activities. Arpaio maintains that the MCSO is quickly becoming an anti- immigration agency. The sweeps have involved a substantial number of deputies that were not trained to implement this policy. Furthermore, the response time to 911 calls has increased. In 2005, MCSO had a response of 5 minutes; in 2007, its median response time was more than 7 minutes, and its average response time was nearly 11 minutes. The Phoenix Police Department reports an average response time of 4 minutes (Goldwater Institute, 2008).

※ REJIJTANCE AND GRAJJROOTJ MOBILIZATION

On February 6, 2009, more than 70 immigrant, labor, and civil rights organizations convened in Phoenix to protest the Sheriff's most recent stunt, a forced march of shackled immigrants to a segregated area in his notorious *Tent City*. The organizations condemned the actions of the Sheriff. They also prepared a series of teach-ins throughout the county to "increase awareness, raise funds, and energize those who wish to restore decency to the immigration reform debate" (Somos America, 2009) Another conference was held in Phoenix on February 27, 2009, as well as a Peaceful Dignity Walk and Demonstration. Their message: Stop the raids and revoke all 287(g) agreements. Héctor Yturralde, president of Somos America, said, "We're closing Guantanamo Bay in Cuba. Now we must stop human rights abuses here on American soil. President Obama and Secretary of Homeland Security Janet Napolitano have the power and the moral obligation to do that now by halting immigration raids and revoking all 287(g) agreements" (Somos America, 2009). Lydia Guzman, vice president of Somos America, added, "Jailing landscapers, maids and dishwashers does not make us safer. But it does tear apart families. The small children who suddenly find themselves without parents cannot wait for Congress to pass comprehensive reform. The communities being terrorized by people like Sheriff Arpaio cannot wait" (Somos America, 2009)

Of note, Phoenix Mayor Phil Gordon has condemned the actions of Sheriff Arpaio. He asked Attorney General Eric Holder to investigate these activities. The Mayor Gordon stated at a Cesar Chavez luncheon, "Sheriff Joe Arpaio is locking up brown people for having broken tail lights." He also says that illegal immigration is a race issue, and it is a shame that this long after Cesar Chavez we are still battling with this "race issue." Mayor Gordon has also criticized Sheriff Arpaio for his public relationship and admiration for neo-Nazis. Arpaio said that it is an honor to be called KKK and has posed for photos with high-profile neo-Nazis (Lemons, 2009b).

Sherriff Arpaio has also attracted the attention of activists, singers, and celebrities. Zack de la Rocha of Rage Against the Machine stated, "Parading human beings shackled in chain gang stripes is a misguided effort to collectively humiliate and to terrorize an entire population; he reopened the wounds from which we all still suffer, by invoking the painful memories of slavery and segregation . . . by doing so, he has not only brought shame upon the state of Arizona, but is bringing shame upon the entire nation. If Janet Napolitano seeks to perform her mission as head of the so-called Homeland Security Department, she must realize the dangerous threshold that the 287(g) agreements have crossed. She must deal directly and quickly with the real threat to peace and security here in Arizona, by terminating the 287(g) agreement with Sheriff Arpaio's office and joining the courageous members of congress who have begun an investigation into his criminal behavior" (Mala, 2009).

In Los Angeles, immigrant advocates held a press conference outside the taping of the television show *Real Time With Bill Maher.* Protestors urged Mr. Maher to question DHS Secretary Janet Napolitano as to why she had not ended the 287(g) contract with Sheriff Arpaio. Ironically, the Secretary was the previous governor of Arizona and Sheriff Arpaio supported her election. She is a Democrat and he is a Republican.

Roberto Reveles was one of the more prominent and vocal leaders in Phoenix. Interestingly, the former mining executive was retired and virtually unheard of in the Latino community until the demonstrations. His activities as a political player somewhat peaked in the 1980s. He was an organizer during the United Farm Workers boycotts as well as a strong advocate for Latino veterans. In the later 1970s, he worked for Congressman Mo Udall and then he himself unsuccessfully ran for Congress. Perhaps one of his greatest achievements was unifying a multitude of Latino interest groups and organizations, including unions, churches, immigrant advocates such as Immigrants Without Borders, and students, calling them Unidos en Arizona.

His organizing strategies exceeded the expectations of many leaders from the Latino community. One observer contends that he was significantly responsible for mobilizing at least 20,000 Latinos in Phoenix. Later, Mr. Reveles was chosen as president of We Are America, or Somos America, and led the organizational efforts for the April 10, 2006, demonstration. Mr. Reveles maintains that his coalition has now shifted its direction to that of electoral or ballot politics. "These people are coming across the border for the simple act of providing food and shelter for their families" (Gonzalez, 2006b). He later called for a boycott of businesses, generating greater attention from more established leaders and lawmakers nationally.

The Catholic Bishops Conference, among others, has been speaking on behalf of the immigrants and lobbying for more just immigration policy (MacDonald, 2006). There have been coalitions of churches and ecumenical efforts to protect immigrants' rights and to provide different forms of assistance to immigrants. Los Angeles's Cardinal Roger Mahony urged Catholics and Christians to oppose laws that were anti-immigrant. Advocating immigrant support, he stated, "I would say to all priests, deacons and members of the church that we are not going to observe this law" (MacDonald, 2006). Much of the support for immigrants is based on the biblical texts of Deuteronomy 10:19. "You, too, must befriend the alien, for you were once aliens yourselves in the land of Egypt" (Vara & Karkabi, 2006). In Atlanta, another Catholic group carried standards bearing images of the patron of Mexico, the Virgin of Guadalupe, recalling the 19th-century Mexican priest, Miguel Hidalgo, who rallied peasants behind a similar flag during the country's war of independence from Spain (Borden, 2006). In Arizona alone, there are several similar examples, contemporary and historical (e.g., the Sanctuary Movement). Thus, the involvement of religious groups, particularly the mainline protestant churches and the Catholic Church, in mobilizing on behalf of the immigrants is not new and continues to play an important role as catalyst of protest.

Importantly, however, in Phoenix, it was not only the traditional religious organizations that were involved in the mobilization. Other vocal participants in the demonstrations included Latino evangelicals, traditionally perceived as apolitical. Pastors in churches and on Spanish gospel radio urged participation in the demonstrations. One report maintained that in Phoenix Latino evangelical pastors played the major role in recruiting the more than 100,000 demonstrators (Gonzalez & Wingett, 2006). Gonzalez (2006) notes that there are about 300 evangelical Latino churches in the Valley. About 75 percent of the approximately 15,000 members of these churches are estimated to be undocumented immigrants, and many have seen family members deported or die crossing the border. For the members of these churches, as well as for the pastors, the immediacy of debates about immigration policy cannot be overstated. But unlike the larger churches, the organizational structure and approach to serving the needs to the flock in these evangelical (mostly Pentecostal) churches differ, as they are smaller and members are usually personally connected with the pastors. Thus, it might not come as a surprise to see that some of these churches, particularly the smaller congregations with membership of fewer than 200 members, sent entire congregations to the demonstrations. For example, Jose Gonzalez, pastor of Iglesia Bautista Nuevo Nacimiento, a Latino evangelical church in west Phoenix, maintained that he knows of more than 40 evangelical Latino pastors working with the cause. "At first, churches saw this as a political movement, but then we could see our people needed our support. It was a community need. It was beyond politics" (Gonzalez & Wingett, 2006). Other churches made sure that fliers were passed out after Sunday services. The demonstrations were also promoted on Spanish-language Christian radio stations, such as Radio Manantial (91.1 FM) and KASA-AM (1540). Because of the small size of these churches, personal contact with members makes it possible for pastors to engage their churches and mobilize them in ways that often the larger congregations cannot.

And Latino evangelicals are a growing constituency in Phoenix, just as in the rest of the Spanish-speaking world, including Latin America itself (Stoll, 1990). Although characterized as politically conservative, they define themselves as advocates of fair immigration reform. Immigrants Without Borders, a prominent Latino immigrant advocacy group in Arizona, was able to work with evangelical churches as well as organize many of the participants in the demonstrations. Indeed, organizers of the demonstrations maintain that Latino evangelical pastors, who are sometimes undocumented immigrants themselves, played a major role in politically mobilizing the community.

Before the demonstrations, members of evangelical churches, mostly Latino, disseminated information in the community. Many pastors offered rides to members of their congregation who had no transportation. Magdalena Schwartz, a pastor at Iglesia Palabra de Vida in Mesa, said many evangelical Latino pastors wanted to get involved because not only would it make immigrants criminals, it would also make them very vulnerable to prosecution (Gonzales & Wingett, 2006).

Not all evangelicals have taken what might be called a progressive position on immigration, however. Reverend Samuel Rodriguez, president of the National Hispanic Christian Leadership Conference, which serves 10,700 Hispanic evangelical churches with 15 million members, noted: "This is the watershed movement—it's the moment where either we really forge relationships with the white evangelical church that will last for decades, or there is a possibility of a definitive schism here . . . there will be church ramifications to this, and there will be political ramifications" (Cooperman, 2006). Rodriguez went on to add the following statement, "So down the road, when the white evangelical community calls us and says, 'We want to partner with you on marriage, we want to partner on family issues,' my first question will be: 'Where were you when 12 million of our brothers and sisters were about to be deported and 12 million families disenfranchised?'"

More recently, evangelical leaders launched an ecumenical national grassroots and ad campaign advocating comprehensive immigration reform. The Christians for Comprehensive Immigration Reform (CCIR) plans to engage in a massive mobilization campaign to put pressure on Congress for an immigration bill that strengthens the border but also provides a legalization road for the millions of undocumented immigrants in the United States (Vu, 2007). The National Hispanic Christian Leadership Conference, which claims 15 million evangelical Latinos, endorses the CCIR plan (http://www.nhclc.org).

In July 2009, DHS Secretary Janet Napolitano announced the expansion of 287(g). Programs previously signed up would remain, and 11 new enforcement agencies would soon begin the controversial program. The newly revised 287(g) program has been criticized for not making any significant changes. Although Napolitano maintains that the program would make apprehension of criminal immigrants its priority, the kinder gentler 287(g) has no provisions for ensuring that these abuses by police officers are under real scrutiny.

The American Civil Liberties Union (ACLU) maintained that the revised program does very little to correct the racial profiling and civil rights abuses targeted toward Latinos and "in some respects the new MOA is actually worse than the original from the Bush administration" (Lemons, 2009a). The ACLU finds that the new agreement actually expands the powers of 287(g) officers and lessens the amount of experience needed to carry out the policy (Lemons, 2009a).

Some maintain that the newly revised program will have no impact on the MCSO policing activities. "There's not need of a 287(g) to make our community safe. The police can choose to do their job, which is prioritizing dangerous criminals and violent acts," said Linda Brown, president of the Arizona Advocacy Network, a nonprofit agency that defends civil rights (Fernandez, 2009). Time will tell what impact these changes will have on the MCSO.

\\\\ IMPLICATIONf FOR REfIfTANCE PRACTICE AND REfEARCH

The Phoenix metropolitan area is an extremely dynamic area that provides important national implications for immigration politics. Based on recent demographic, economic, and census forecasts, immigration to Arizona will continue. Anti-immigrant policies will continue to be enacted by elected officials to appease their constituents. Policy players, such as social workers and police, will continue to carry out poorly articulated objectives, destroying positive relations with the Latino and Latino-immigrant community. Because of the large proportion of foreign-born and noncitizen voters, greater political mobilization in the Latino community is expected to not only continue but also flourish.

Although enforcement activities generate a significant amount of attention, they are only one part of the overall mission of a police agency. In the last decade, numerous new policies have been assigned to police agencies around immigration. It is clear that police agencies that are assigned immigration directives will continue to destroy positive relations with the Latino community and, in some cases, instill fear. Those who may want to call the police for help may not for fear that they will be deported. These increased responsibilities have also meant new roles and procedures for the officers to pursue with insufficient time to formulate clear agency guidelines. Police officers, particularly those who work at the local level, have the most influence over policy decisions.

In general, the Phoenix case illustrates the multifaceted forms of nontraditional politics, such as coalitions with unions, churches, and community organizers, that came together to oppose vitriolic responses to perceived threats of undocumented migration. As political clout grows, coalition building becomes increasingly important. Organizers feel that coalitions should be based on common interests and not exclusively around racial considerations.

Notably, as was the case in other instances of protests around the country, religious groups were also important organizers. However, Latinos are no longer exclusively Catholic. The Protestant and more Pentecostal denominations are making inroads into the Latino immigrant community. These smaller denominations provide social networks and support for newly arrived immigrants and may provide other avenues for political mobilization.

Mobilizing Latinos at the local level also has proved successful. Creating agendas that are relevant and meaningful has gotten first-time players involved in politics. Furthermore, grassroots organizing is also no longer limited to issues within one's country. As communities outside the United States continue to be connected, international influence at the local level will continue to be important.

Finally, more research is needed to identify the specific methods that are most effective to mobilize Latinos for collective resistance. The mass protest approach that has occurred recently appears to show some effectiveness, but there continues to be the need to focus more on specific ways that this approach, along with others, either helps or hinders the elimination of unjust social policies. At the center of this research should be the value that immigration policies should seek to affirm cultural diversity and the strength this has for the future development of the nation.

⑅ CONCLUSION

Using Phoenix, Arizona, as its focus, this chapter has examined how unfair immigration policies and practices harm Latino/a communities and how these communities have and can be mobilized to engage in resistance activities. As this nation increasingly becomes populated by immigrants of color, it will have to be more willing to fairly grapple with a more diverse sociocultural landscape. Latino and Latina immigrants have the constitutional as well as human right to make America their home, and social policy development and practice needs to seriously affirm this belief. Latino and Latina immigrants contribute much to this society and very much want the opportunity to realize their vast potential for future contributions in a nation that unfortunately continues to be reluctant to abandon its cultural and political hegemonic proclivities. Social policy development and practice should seek to eliminate this domination so that this nation can truly fulfill its oftentimes elusive values of freedom, justice, and equality for all.

☒ REFERENCES

Aizenman, N. (2009, March, 4). Report cites problems in ICE training program. *The Washington Post*. Retrieved June 30, 2010, from http://www.washingtonpost.com/wp-dyn/content/article/2009/03/03/AR2009030304231.html

Cooperman, A. (2006, April 5). Letter on immigration deepens split among Evangelicals. *The Washington Post*. Retrieved July 30, 2010, from http://www.washingtonpost.com/wp-dyn/content/article/2006/04/04/AR2006040401606.html

Finnegan, W. (2009, July 20). Sheriff Joe: Sheriff Joe is tough on prisoners and undocumented immigrants. What about crime? *The New Yorker*, p. 42.

Goldwater Institute. (2008). *Mission unaccomplished: The misplaced priorities of the Maricopa County sheriff's office*. Phoenix, AZ: Author.

González, D. (2006b, September 4). Latino Leader came to forefront from shadows. *Arizona Republic*. Retrieved from http://www.azcentral.com

González, D., & Wingett, Y. (2006, March 29). Power of the pulpit inspired immigrants to protest. *Arizona Republic*. Retrieved from http://www.azcentral.com

González, D., Melendez, M., & Flannery, P. (2006, April 11). March of strength/Over 100, 000 rally in Phoenix for immigration reform—Massive crowds highlight economic, political might. *Arizona Republic*. Retrieved from http://www.azcentral.com

Government Accountability Office. (2009). *Immigration enforcement better controls over programs authorizing state and local enforcement of federal laws*. Washington, DC: Author. Retrieved June 30, 2010, from http://www.gao.gov/new.items/d09109.pdf

Immigration Customs and Enforcement. (2009). *Delegation of Immigration Authority Section 287(g) Immigration and Nationality Act: The ICE 287(g) Program: A law enforcement partnership*. Washington, DC: Author. Retrieved June 30, 2010, from http://www.ice.gov/pi/news/factsheets/section287_g.htm

Lemons, S. (2009). Neo-Nazis and extreme right-wingers love Joe Arpaio, and there's evidence that the MCSO keeps them close. *Phoenix New Times*. Retrieved June 30, 2010, from http://www.phoenixnewtimes.com/2009-05-14/news/neo-nazis-and-extreme-right-wingers-love-joe-arpaio-and-there-s-evidence-that-the-mcso-keeps-them-close

Lemons, S. (2009). DHS doublecross: ACLU denounces 287(g) changes as "cosmetic." *Phoenix New Times*. June 30, 2010, http://blogs.phoenixnewtimes.com/bastard/2009/07/snowed_by_ice_aclu_denounces_n.php

MacDonald, J. G. (2006, March 11). Conservative Christians mum on immigration bills. *The Seattle Times*. Retrieved July 30, 2010, from http://seattletimes.nwsource.com/html/faithvalues/2002857859_religionimmigration11.html

Magaña, L. (2003). *Straddling the border: The immigration policy process and its effect on the INS*. Austin: University of Texas Press.

Mala, M. (2009). *Thousands protest racist Sheriff Joe Arpaio in Arizona*. Retrieved June 30, 2010, from http://vivirlatino.com/2009/03/04/thousands-protest-racist-sheriff-joe-arpaio-in-arizona.php

Migration News. (2007, January). Elections, Voters, Arizona. *Migration News, 14*(1). Retrieved June 30, 2010, from http://migration.ucdavis.edu/mn/more.php?id=3244_0_2_0

National Employment Law Project & Others. (2009). *Reply to U.S. response to specific recommendations identified by CERD: The rise of racial profiling, discrimination and abuse in immigrant communities as a result of local enforcement of immigration laws*. Retrieved June 30, 2010, from http://nelp.3cdn.net/58e5286d88ea74d7c5_3im6bhosa.pdf

Ripley, R. B. (1986). *Policy implementation and bureaucracy*. Chicago: Chicago Dorsey Press.

Somos America. (2009). *National protest in Phoenix against Sheriff Joe Arpaio* [Press Release]. Retrieved June 30, 2010, from http://www.indybay.org/newsitems/2009/02/18/18571809.php

Stoll, D. (1990). *Is Latin America turning protestant? The politics of Evangelical growth*. Berkeley: University of California Press.

U.S. Census Bureau. (2001). *U.S. census of the population, 2000*. Washington, DC: Author.

Vara, R., & Karkabi, B. (2006, April 1). Catholics are urged to join debate as "the people of God"; House immigration bill also opposed by other denominations. *The Houston Chronicle*. Retrieved from http://www.chron.com

Vu, M. (2007, May 8). Evangelicals launch immigration reform campaign. *The Christian Post*. Retrieved July 30, 2010, from http://www.christianpost.com/article/20070508/evangelicals-launch-immigration-reform-campaign/index.html

12

Creating the Latino Agenda for Eliminating Health Disparities in Communities

A Call to Action

Catherine K. Medina

 INTRODUCTION

According to the Institute of Medicine's (2002) landmark report *Unequal Treatment*, there is a long-standing and well-documented pattern of health disparities in the United States. The report states that this pattern is apparent in health care outcomes and utilization of care, and is most evident in the disproportionate incidence of disease and death among specific racial and ethnic groups. Specifically, health disparities refer to those avoidable differences in health that result from cumulative social disadvantage. As the United States becomes more culturally diverse, the reality of a productive nation will increasingly rely not only on its ability to keep all its residents healthy, but also on eliminating health disparities, especially for racial and ethnic groups. The U.S. Census Bureau (2001) projects that by the middle of the 21st century, largely because of the growth of the

Latino population, the U.S.-based racial and ethnic minority population will exceed the white population. Historically, it is an established fact that racial and ethnic groups experience poorer health outcomes than their white counterparts, and that within communities of color, health disparities are both persistent and increasing. Although there have been numerous efforts to document and address racial and ethnic health disparities such as *Healthy People 2010* and the Hispanic Health Act of 2000, there continue to be "differences in the incidences, prevalence, mortality and burden of diseases and other adverse health conditions that exist among specific population groups in the United States" (LaVeist, 2005, p. 108; National Institutes of Health [NIH], 2000). Furthermore, although health care disparities for Latinos have been documented, efforts to ameliorate prevalence of illness by translating research into policy and practice have been limited (Aguilar-Gaxiola et al., 2002).

According to Davis and Iron Cloud-Two Dogs (2004), the effect of many American public policies has been to deny certain groups access to a livable share of the nation's wealth and resources, and policies also have limited these groups' political power to change their lives' circumstances. Over the last decade, the divide between the *haves* and the *have nots* has widened, whether it involves access to health care, education, food, housing, earning power, or technology. This lack of access and political power feels very real for the Latino population because of their growing numbers and the large percentage of young people affected by structural inequities that influence their well-being. The history of U.S. health policies has not seriously addressed inequities that lead to social conditions that contribute to health disparities in racial and ethnic groups.

This chapter describes the process of resistance by Latino leadership's refusal to accept the continuing invisibility of the poor health status of their Latino communities. The process of Latino resistance, within the political, public, and private sectors, emerges as a response by Latino leadership to change the social fabric of health care inequities in policy, research, and political decision making. The Latino resistance is influenced by linking research with political advocacy to affect health care policies that guide our national and state health care delivery systems. The chapter covers four areas of particular concern: the demographics of the Latino population; the current health status of Latinos; overview of contemporary U.S. health initiatives; and *Healthy People 2010* and Latino invisibility. The author proceeds with a look at regulating the nation's prevention and health promoting agenda in eliminating Latino health disparities through a structural inequity lens. The national Latino leadership public call for action in health policy emerges through the Hispanic Health Act of 2000 (H.R. 5595). This chapter concludes with an illustration of a translational research model used by the Hispanic Health Council (HHC), an organization in Connecticut. This agency has bold, visionary, and committed leadership whose goal is to eliminate health disparities in Latino communities. The translational research methods described can be adapted by other states and communities to redress Latino health care needs.

\\\\ DEMOGRAPHICS OF THE LATINO POPULATION

The U.S. Latino population, estimated at 15 percent, is the fastest growing, youngest, and largest ethnic group of color (U.S. Census Bureau, 2007). Often in Latino blogs, as a source of pride, this reference is followed by a statement that there has been a shift in the nation's center of gravity. Many refer to Latinos as the new *bebé boomers*, stronger in numbers, bilingual, bicultural, relatively young, with 36 percent of the population less than 18 years old and a median age of 27 (Latinos.us, 2004; U.S. Census Bureau, 2007). Latinos will drive growth in the U.S. population (3.5 percent a year in comparison with 0.8 percent for the rest of the population) as well as the U.S. workforce as far as statisticians can forecast. Over the past decade, Latinos have made up half of all new workers, with an annual spending power of more than $580 billion (Pew Hispanic Center, 2006). The purchasing power of Latinos continues to grow at triple the rate of the overall population. The children of today's Latino immigrants will be the largest contributing group within the U.S. population (Latinos.us, 2004). Therefore, the well-being of the various Latino subgroups is essential to the nation's present and future well-being as they continue to be the largest and fastest growing ethnic group.

\\\\ HEALTH STATUS OF LATINOS

As a matter of public policy, it is essential to identify those disparities in health status or access to health care that threaten the well-being of Latino groups. In relationship to health, many Latinos appear to be in good health not because of access to health care, but because of healthy lifestyles from their countries of origin (Pew Hispanic Center, 2002).

According to this Pew report, as soon as Latinos adopt the lifestyle of the mainstream, they acquire habits that lower their health status. Of all major racial and ethnic groups, Latinos have the lowest rate of health care coverage, while concurrently experiencing a lack of available data on various health issues to adequately describe health-status trends (Hispanic Health Council [HHC], 2006). Lack of health coverage contributes to the fact that Latinos are less likely to use health and mental-health services for preventive care, attributing to chronicity and comorbidity of diseases (Pew Hispanic Center, 2002). The lack of adequate health data poses unique challenges in analyzing the origin of health inequities, trends, and solutions to eliminating health disparities among Latino subgroups (HHC).

On the favorable side, Latinos tend to have lower mortality rates than people in other ethnic groups. According to a public health official, Dr. Hynes, because Latinos have a less-than-favorable socioeconomic profile (poverty, less educational attainment, less access to health care), one would be predisposed to think that they would have high mortality rates. On the contrary, Latinos in the United States have lower age-adjusted, all-cause mortality than do white non-Latinos (Abraido-Lanza et al., 1999). This phenomenon has been referred to as the Hispanic epidemiological paradox (Franzini, Ribble, & Keddie, 2002). For example, Latino males have lower mortality rates between the ages of 15 to 44 excluding HIV, alcohol-related liver disease, unintended injuries, and homicides. Latino males ages 55 and older have lower mortality rates than whites and lower rates of mortality for most of the major chronic illnesses such as heart disease, cancer, diabetes, and suicide (Hynes, Mueller, & Amadeo, 2004; LaVeist, 2005).

According to Hynes (personal communication, March 4, 2007), Latinas have significantly lower all-cause mortality compared with white females, and this phenomenon is consistent across all age groups with the exception of 40-year-olds to 44-year-olds. In this age category, Latinas have significantly greater all-cause mortality compared with white women. This difference can be explained by premature mortality caused by HIV and unintentional injuries (motor vehicle injuries, accidental poisonings, falls and fall-related injuries and suffocation). These causes account for 21 percent of all premature mortality rates in Latinas compared with 11 percent of white women.

A possible explanation of the Hispanic epidemiological paradox is that Latino death rates are affected by bias in underreporting of deaths and underestimation of the population (Smith & Bradshaw, 2006; Stratton, Hynes, & Nepaul, 2009). According to some scientific studies, the Hispanic epidemiological paradox is not real, but rather an artifact of undercounting resulting from inconsistencies in counts of Latino-origin decedents or data not collected at all (Franzini et al., 2004; LaVeist, 2005; Stratton, Hynes, & Nepaul, 2009). This type of data collection leads to misclassification and underestimation of deaths that occur among Latinos. This will be further discussed in the next section.

Although it appears that Latinos on average have a lower mortality rate, they suffer from many chronic conditions that affect their well-being. These conditions cannot be cured once acquired, and have a long duration (LaVeist, 2005). Chronic conditions are the major cause of death in the United States; the five leading causes of death for Latinos are heart disease, cancer, accidents and unintended injuries, strokes, and diabetes (LaVeist, 2005; National Center for Health Statistics, 2003). According to the U.S. Congressional Hispanic Caucus (CHC, 2008), diabetes affects 2 million Latinos (10.2 percent), and the risk of Latinos dying from diabetes is twice that of non-Hispanic whites.

When one looks at the 10 leading causes of death, suicide ranks 10th as a leading cause of death for whites; in contrast, it ranks eighth as the leading cause of death for Latinos. Latino adolescent girls are a major concern when it comes to suicide. According to HHC (2006), nationally twice as many Latina adolescents (21 percent) attempt suicide as African American (11 percent) or non-Latino white adolescents (10 percent). These mental health issues carry over into adulthood, with the same source of statistics indicating that twice as many Latinas report depression (11 percent) as African Americans (6 percent) or non-Hispanic white women (5 percent). Additionally, the health status of Latinos is affected by homicide and HIV as the sixth and ninth leading causes of death (LaVeist, 2005). When adjusted for age, AIDS is the fourth leading cause of death for Latinos/Latinas in their 40s. In 2006, Latinos accounted for 18 percent of all new HIV/AIDS cases in 33 states based on confidential HIV reporting (CDC, 2008).

〰 OVERVIEW OF CONTEMPORARY HEALTH INITIATIVES: *HEALTHY PEOPLE* 1979–2010

For four decades, the U.S. Department of Health and Human Services (HHS) established and monitored national health objectives through a "healthy people" framework. *Healthy People* regulates the focus and direction of national health policies. In 1979, *Healthy People* focused on the prevention of chronic disease and injury as health goals. *Healthy People 1990* set health objectives based on individual lifestyle factors and personal behavior change. However, it was not until 1986 that HHS launched the first large-scale effort toward understanding racial and ethnic health disparities through the *Secretary's Task Force Report on Black and Minority Health*. The objectives of the report were to study the health status of minority groups, health care access, factors contributing to disparities, and relevant research and services for minority populations. The findings influenced recommendations about redirecting federal resources and suggested strategies for the public and private sectors to improve minority health. The task force adopted a statistical technique of "excess deaths" to compare health between minority and nonminority populations. The task report concluded that 80 percent of differences in death rates between racial and ethnic groups and whites were accounted for by six health areas: cardiovascular disease; cancer; substance use; diabetes; homicide, suicide, and accidents; and infant mortality and low birth rates (Giles et al., 2002, 2004). In the 21st century, these areas and HIV/AIDS continue to have an adverse impact on the well-being of Latino communities.

Healthy People 1990 laid the groundwork for *Healthy People 2000* (HHS, 1998), which established three national goals: to reduce disease; to promote quality care for healthier, longer lives in the United States; and to achieve universal access to appropriate health services (M. Hynes, personal communication, March 4, 2007). Building on the last two decades' challenging goals, in 2000 HHS proposed the third decade national health agenda, *Healthy People 2010* for the 21st century. HHS advanced its national goals to introduce objectives with measurable targets for eliminating health disparities for all Americans within the next decade. For the first time, *Healthy People 2010* provided a platform that acknowledged the seriousness and persistence of health disparities for different racial and ethnic groups as a matter of public policy. Understanding the roles of community in healthy lives, *Healthy People 2010* emphasized individuals in healthy communities and embraced contextual factors that influence health status such as gender, race and ethnicity, income, geographic locations, and environmental toxins. Therefore, *Healthy People 2010* is a policy statement of national health goals and objectives designed to identify the most significant preventable health threats (Barr, 2008). This federal initiative focuses on eliminating health disparities, particularly for racial and ethnic groups. *Healthy People 2010* establishes 467 health-status objectives, organized into 28 prime areas of public health. These health-status goals, with measurable targets, frame the ways the nation conceptualizes, explores, and addresses health issues in terms of education, prevention and treatment (Stratton, Hynes, & Nepaul, 2009). *Healthy People 2010's* national objectives guide all federal, state, and local health planning and services.

An important but unstated goal of *Healthy People 2010* is economic: it is a response to the nation's rapidly increasing population diversity (including the increasing aging population), and the imminent increasing demands and cost to the health care system if current disparities are not addressed.

Healthy People 2010: Latino Invisibility

According to the HHC (2006), the importance of assuring adequate data on Latinos' health status is essential for eliminating health disparities. To standardize race and ethnicity categories across all federal agencies for reporting purposes, the Office of Management and Budget (OMB) required all producers of federal statistics to be compliant with OMB 1997 data collection and reporting standards by January 2003. Absent data and inconsistent data collection methods are the result of unreliable implementation of these standards across federal and state agencies, and influence Latino invisibility in assessing their health status. Comprehensive data collection, particularly for Latinos and their subgroups, is a challenge because of Latinos' relatively small numbers in the population and geographic dispersion.

In 2006, HHS released its midcourse review, the Executive Summary of *Healthy People 2010*. This report assessed national progress toward increasing quality and years of healthy life and eliminating health disparities (HHS, 2006). The Executive Summary reflects data that emphasize both promise and caution: the nation's overall health is improving, but health disparities for racial and ethnic minority groups remain virtually unchanged. *Healthy People 2010* was not able to regulate change and healthy outcomes for minority populations. Disparities compared among ethnic groups—measured in terms of relative difference from the best group rate—are not declining. According to *Healthy People 2010*, Latinos have the best group rate for 18 percent of the objectives and subobjectives related to injury and violence, nutrition, and tobacco use. However, Latinos have the least favorable rates (100 percent worse than other groups) when it comes to having health care insurance coverage among persons under 65 (that is, basically throughout the life span), having a source of ongoing care, having new HIV/AIDS-related deaths, and some objectives related to violence. Among Latinos, disparities also increased with exposure to new cases of tuberculosis, physical assault, and congenital syphilis. However, *Healthy People* reports a decrease in new AIDS cases, hepatitis A and B, syphilis, and nonfatal firearm-related injuries. Urban or metropolitan areas showed more disparities, especially regarding environmental issues such as air pollution (carbon monoxide and ozone).

However, *Healthy People 2010* reports no racial and ethnic data for about 15 percent of the population-based objectives among certain groups, Latinos being one of those groups (HHS, 2006). According to the National Alliance for Hispanic Health, 40 percent of *Healthy People 2010* population-based objectives do not include Latino baseline data, making it impossible to measure this ethnic group's progress toward objectives. An unintended consequence is that Latinos become invisible because of the absence of baseline data and a tracking system to measure this ethnic group's incidence, prevalence, proportion rates of disease, and health outcomes over multiple years. For example, no data were available for Latino hospitalizations resulting from pediatric asthma, uncontrollable diabetes, and preventable pneumonia for persons 65 years and older. For policymakers, researchers, health providers, and advocates, health-status invisibility limits understanding the prevalence of health issues disproportionately affecting Latinos. Who or what factors contribute to identifying members of an ethnic group are often changeable and dependent on social, political, and historical situations. Defining disparities has resource-allocation implications for funding disease prevention, treatment, and health promotion. Therefore, the Latino leadership questions the usefulness of *Healthy People 2010* as a national policy initiative to eliminate health disparities.

Another concern is that, according to the National Alliance for Hispanic Health, more than two thirds (86 percent) of the Latino community leadership recommendations were not incorporated under *Healthy People 2010*. Although the Latino leadership praised its inclusion of community and environmental factors, it did not meet Latino concerns about their health status (National Alliance for Hispanic Health, 2009). According to the Office of Minority Health and Health Disparities (2007), to make informed assessments of the extent of health problems affecting the Latino population, comprehensive data including data on subgroups are important. The health profile of each Latino subgroup is unique. For example, while Puerto Ricans suffer disproportionately from asthma,

HIV/AIDS, and infant mortality, Mexican Americans suffer disproportionately from diabetes (National Center for Chronic Disease Prevention and Health Promotion, 2002). Although Puerto Ricans have the highest infant mortality rates (8.2 per 1,000), exceeding the national rate, Cuban Americans have the lowest infant mortality rates (4.2 per 1,000). Available scientific evidence indicates that there is more genetic variation within racial and ethnic groups than between racial groups (American Anthropological Association, 1998; Williams, Lavizzo-Mourey, & Warren, 1994). Data limitation such as missing and inaccurate information, missing relevant ethnic variability, and underreporting fosters invisibility that creates challenges for education, prevention, and treatment to eliminate health disparities for Latinos. The Alliance advocated for identifying specific Latino subgroup (Puerto Rican, Cuban, Mexican, and South American) goals that are culturally and linguistically appropriate under each objective. For example, data should include the country of origin and generational status (i.e., first-generation U.S. born, second-generation U.S. born; language spoken) because there are intragroup differences among Latino subgroups and their birthplace (Arias, 2008).

In some areas, Latino leadership also questioned the low targeted objective rates to be achieved within the decade. For example, although Latinos have the lowest number of health care professionals, the targeted objective to raise racial/ethnic minority representation in health professions has been projected at a low percentage (6.4 percent). To create a viable and visible Latino workforce in health care, the target objective needs to be representative of the proportion of Latinos in the United States (15 percent) in the next 10 years (National Alliance for Hispanic Health, 2009). According to the nation's most influential Latino health leaders, *Healthy People's* commitment to monitoring, analyzing, and eliminating health disparities for the largest and fastest-growing ethnic minority group is questionable (MinorityNurse, 2002).

〰 REGULATING THE NATION'ſ PREVENTION AND HEALTH PROMOTION AGENDA: ELIMINATING HEALTH DIſPARITIEſ

In principle, *Healthy People 2010* embraces individuals and communities adapting individual lifestyle change, and it is the basis for regulating national health policy. Although reaching out to communities is an essential component in reaching successful health outcomes, multiple social factors influence public health within racial and ethnic populations (Stratton, Hynes, & Nepaul, 2009). In reality, *Healthy People 2010* does not change the root causes of health disparities such as poverty, lack of livable wage and health insurance, delayed diagnosis and treatment, perceived discrimination, racism, health care provider bias, and other structural factors affecting Latinos. Health disparities are evidence of inequalities in numerous social factors, and it is important to identify the multiple levels of inequities affecting Latino individuals and their well-being. This section focuses on the complex relationship among multiple social factors affecting Latinos' health such as inequities in health care and access, health literacy, cross-cultural and language barriers, poverty, and socioeconomic status (SES).

Inequities in Health Care and Access

Latinos experience inequities in health care through the life span that result in differences in outcomes or in quality of care. These differences in health are not only unnecessary and preventable, but, in addition, are indicative of injustice or unfairness within the health care delivery system (Anand, Diderichsen, Evans, Shkolnikov, & Wirth, 2001; Whitehead, 1992). This includes the behaviors of health care providers as contributing to health care disparities through stereotyping and biased attitudes. According to HHC (2006), health inequities experienced during critical stages of the life cycle dramatically reflect the failure of our public health and socioeconomic systems to protect the health of those most vulnerable. For example, widespread lack of health insurance is one of the most urgent problems within the Latino population that contributes to poor health outcomes and premature death (HHC, 2006, p. 2). More than 32 percent of Latinos lack health insurance—a higher percentage than that among any other racial or ethnic group (CHC, 2008). This same report indicates that nearly 25 percent of Latino children do not have health insurance, and more than 50 percent of Latino low-income, noncitizen children do not have any health insurance. An estimated 43 percent of Latinos nationwide have employer-sponsored health insurance, compared with 68 percent of Whites (Latino Policy Institute [LPI], 2008). CHC attributes the lack of insurance to lack of employer-sponsored insurance and Latinos' lack of opportunities for permanent employment. Uninsured Latinos are two to three times more likely to go without needed care, resulting in higher rates of preventable disease and premature death (Rios, 2001).

Latinos face other issues with regard to access to quality health care; for example, they get care late in the progression of illness and do not have continuity of care because they often do not have an established source of care. This results in more emergency room visits as a standard of care. Evidence points to less-complete health histories, fewer referrals to specialists, and lower quality of care (HHC, 2006). The data show that often after care is provided, patients incorrectly follow through on health instructions and referrals. Many health providers complain that the patient is nonadhering, but this lack of follow-through usually stems from misunderstanding related to health literacy (HHC, 2006).

Health Literacy

Latinos tend to underutilize health and mental health, social services, and other public delivery systems, and drop out early after treatment (Ortega, Feldman, Canino, Steinman, & Alegria, 1996; Sue, 2003; Vega & Alegria, 2001). Some of the difficulties with service utilization may stem from the actual helping process itself. For a patient to adhere to medical treatment, the process is dependent on the level of health literacy—" the degree to which individuals have the capacity to obtain, process, and understand basic health and service needed to make appropriate health decisions" (HHC, 2006). There is a growing interest in health literacy as a major factor contributing to medical adherence. Current research indicates that more than 90 million people (including English-speaking individuals) in the United States struggle to understand basic health information such as reading materials, prescription labels, filling out medical and insurance forms, and communicating with their providers (Institute of Medicine, 1999). The disproportionate low level of educational attainment among Latinos is a factor that influences their degree of health literacy to navigate the complex health care delivery system involving so many needed skills. Patients are often faced with complex information and treatment decisions that require skills such as evaluating information for credibility and quality, weighing risks and benefits, calculating dosages, understanding test results and implications for care, and locating health information. Particularly in a managed-care environment, where the patient is a consumer in a competitive market, a low health-literacy level is integrally linked to the many barriers to access and the utilization of services by many Latinos.

Cross-Cultural and Language Barriers

According to a bilingual survey cosponsored by the Pew Hispanic Center and the Robert Wood Johnson Foundation and representative s of 4,013 Latinos nationally, not only do more than 25 percent of Latino adults lack a consistent health care provider, but a similar proportion receive no health information from a medical professional when they visit a care source (Pew Hispanic Center, 2008). This report indicates that 80 percent receive health-related information from an alternative source such as television and radio. Significantly, half of the participants (50 percent) were high school graduates, 30 percent were U.S. born, and those who had health insurance (45 percent) had no usual place (provider or clinic) for medical treatment. When asked why they lacked a provider, 41 percent stated that they are seldom sick (perhaps a self-fulfilling prophesy of the Latino epidemiological paradox). This results in Latinos, on average, not getting preventive health information from a consistent provider, and being sicker when they do acquire health care.

According to Doty (2003), 44 percent of Latinos report that they have a difficult time speaking to or understanding a medical provider. They attribute the problem to language discordance and poor communication. Inability to communicate with a health care provider can result in serious injury or death. Mandated by federal legislation, Language Access to Services guarantees non-English-speaking patients the right to interpretation services. Medical interpretation is a necessity because it increases health literacy. With interpretation services, Latinos report a 70 percent increase in their ability to understand a doctor's instructions. Good provider–patient communication is essential to quality care. LaVeist and Nuru-Jeter (2002) demonstrated that patients from all racial and ethnic groups were more satisfied and had better health outcomes when doctors were from their same group. A structural inequity exists when only two percent of all physicians in the United States are Latinos (Carillo, Trevino, Betancourt, & Coustasse, 2001).

Poverty and Low Socioeconomic Status

An estimated 21.5 percent of Latinos nationwide live in poverty (Latino Policy Institute, 2008). Poverty and low SES are significant risk factors in health disparities. Latinos experience inequity in income and have the highest poverty and unemployment rates of any ethnic group in

Connecticut (HHC, 2006). Poverty is at the root of many health-related problems such as health care access, health status, and health behaviors. In addition, poverty and SES are linked with exposure to environmental issues, violence, crime, poor housing, incarceration, and homicides. These factors intersect with well-being and behavioral health. When considering risk behaviors and lifestyle changes for the poor, providers may forget that people living in the margins of society are subjected to the difficulty of weighing between competing priorities and health behaviors (hunger vs. nutrition, shelter vs. medications, caring for another vs. self-care, and stigma vs. public health concern).

Healthy People needs to address these inequities to regulate a successful national prevention and health promotion agenda. Opportunities for action to reduce Latino health disparities require full community participation and the public will to address the realities of structural inequities.

\\\\ LATINO COMMUNITIEſ AND HEALTH POLICY: A CALL TO ACTION

Health disparities are products of society's political and economic systems and the illness-generating social conditions that these systems create. Successfully eliminating health disparities requires political and public will to deal with the root causes of diseases affecting Latino communities over their life span. As previously discussed, health disparities are rooted in inequities, and the political leadership has not been silent about Latinos' well-being. They voiced their resistance through a call to action with the Hispanic Health Act of 2000. This legislation was introduced in the House of Representatives by Hon. Ciro D. Rodriquez, Chair of the Congressional Hispanic Caucus (CHC) Task Force on Health (*Congressional Record E1986*, 2000). Its aim was to address Latino disparities in access to health care, research, program funding, cultural competence, and representation of Latino health care professionals (*Congressional Record E1986*, 2000). The political will behind this legislation intended to draw national attention to the seriousness of Latino health disparities and to improve the health care delivery system by making it more responsive to Latinos. It advocated for programs in Latino communities to address diabetes, AIDS, depression, and substance abuse, and suicide rates and gun possession among adolescent girls. The Act was based on data and testimony from community leaders, health providers, and policymakers. Primary emphasis sought accurate data collection and research in minority communities to develop cures that take health disparities into account. The Hispanic Health Act requested an annual report from the Secretary of Human Services on the progress of Latino initiatives for the purpose of accountability and monitoring of actions taken. The act was a historic step and a call to action to reverse the trends of health disparities that threaten the well-being of Latinos. Public will saw the act go through various committees but never become law. However, the act created a strong political health care agenda for the CHC. The resistance to health disparities is voiced through Latino leadership taking action in incremental steps to advance national health policies affecting Latino communities.

In 2002, the CHC, along with the National Hispanic Medical Association (NHMA), sponsored the National Hispanic Health Summit, which brought together 175 experts in Latino health care. The purpose was to build consensus around strategies to improve national policies regarding Latino health care. The 2-day summit resulted in recommendations to Congress. CHC and NHMA continue their political advocacy role by educating political leaders, providers, and key stakeholders in Latino health policy. Emphases have been *Education and Training* to enhance cultural competence in provider communications, *Care and Access* through demonstration projects with diverse ethnic groups, *Research* in collaboration with the National Center for Minority Health and Health Disparities, *Data Collection* that is representative of the various Latino subgroups and oversampling, and a *Leadership, Collaboration and National Action Plan* in conjunction with the Office of Minority Health and Health Disparities to expand access, quality, awareness, and clinical trials (Rios, 2008).

░ AN AGENCY'S CALL TO ACTION

On a state level, agencies play a critical role in resisting health disparities through research, direct practice, and political advocacy. A model program in Connecticut, the HHC, envisions a time when all individuals live in social conditions that facilitate health, that they have the capacity to make informed health decisions, and that they can effectively utilize health services (DeJesus, Medina, & Werkmeister Rozas, 2007). With this vision in mind, HHC created the Latino Policy Institute (LPI) to promote health equity and healthy communities. The Institute works with Latino communities to define health care needs, to develop policy recommendations, and to advocate for policy and practice changes within health care delivery systems. One of the first steps of the LPI was to document the current research, findings, and recommendations about Latino health status and the inequities that are prevalent nationally and within the state. The report, *A Profile of Latino Health in Connecticut,* outlines the crisis and the urgency to resist policies and practices that perpetuate social conditions that generate Latino health inequities. The resistance is actualized in a call to action of Latino leadership within the public and private sectors and broad collaborative networks (including insurance companies) working together to voice issues and solutions to achieve the political and public will for change. Policy and practice must represent the Latino faces that will be the future of the nation's workforce, the majority of young people who will be tomorrow's leaders, and the elderly who support and promote family strength and resiliency. Health as a right needs to be guaranteed to the fastest growing and underserved population for societal well-being. The Latino Policy Institute's call for action addresses poverty. It advocates for an equitable, living wage; it seeks to eradicate health inequities by guaranteeing universal health care coverage; it promotes informed health decisions by improving health literacy; and it determines to eliminate cross-cultural barriers to health care by a cultural competency approach that includes class, gender, race, ethnicity, disabilities, sexual orientation, social class, literacy, language, age, and spirituality (HHC, 2006, p. 14). A core belief of the Institute is that language discordance impacts health literacy, service utilization, and prevention.

HHC uses a translational research framework—this is a process of applying ideas, insights, and discoveries generated through basic scientific inquiries to the treatment and prevention of diseases (Block, 1999). It is a multidimensional approach that stresses the importance of applicability and feedback between community populations and research communities. Translational research data become dynamic in nature because they involve many constituents (research scientists, clinicians, physicians, patients, and community members) in the processes of inquiry, findings, interventions, and dissemination of knowledge to the various communities. The translational model involves the community by listening to its members and reflecting their issues, solutions, and views for the future. HHC develops innovative models for eliminating health inequities and building healthy communities through *direct service, research,* and *policy advocacy.* Each component informs the other in a feedback loop.

This chapter focuses solely on policy advocacy, based on data and research, as a method of action to resist inequities that contribute to health disparities. The Institute has developed the Latino agenda to identify health priorities for the coming year by using the current research to guide discussions and decision making and to inform legislators. According to Hudgins and Allen-Meares (2000), conversations with congressional staff in Washington have voiced a need for research to guide the nation's policy decisions and to support legislative action.

Most recently, LPI resisted health inequities by holding a Latino Health Summit at the University of Connecticut School of Social Work involving leaders, providers, social work graduate students, community members, and state policymakers to prioritize Latino health issues. The summit's first event was a networking activity at the Legislative Office Building to foster collaboration and partnerships among the participants. According to LPI, the Latino Health Summit was the first step in creating a powerful network of cohesive Latino voices to change the system and improve the well-being of Latino people. The summit focused on six health-problem focus areas: asthma, cancer, depression, HIV/AIDS and sexually transmitted diseases, obesity, and, in general, access to care. At the end of the summit, two objectives were achieved: an action agenda for Latino health priorities and an action network of engaged and energized advocates ready to make change (LPI, 2008). Most participants signed a pledge to make a difference in the health status of Latinos by identifying opportunities for policy change. The social work students had their own focus group to plan and develop an agenda as future leaders to make a difference in social, health, and political arenas.

The vital leadership of the HHC promoted a healthier community via media coverage. Just days after the summit, the President and CEO, Jeannette DeJesus, M.P.A., M.S.W., announced that during a special session to address budget deficits, the legislature had restored full funding (4.7 million) to make medical interpretation a covered service under Medicaid. The state's Medicaid plan was amended to add interpreting as a covered service by June 30, 2009 (J. DeJesus, personal communication, December 4, 2008). The Connecticut Coalition for Medical Interpretation had coordinated a response to resist the cutbacks in this crucial area for health literacy and service utilization. The creation of a funding stream for medical interpretation serves as a catalyst for the establishment of a systematic and professional approach to the provision of interpretation services across the state, thereby helping to reduce language-based health disparities (Fact Sheet on Medicaid-Reimbursed Medical Interpretation, 2007).

◊ CONCLUJION AND IMPLICATIONJ FOR JOCIAL WORK

This chapter described the U.S. national initiative, *Healthy People 2010*, which regulates health policy to improve the well-being of all its citizens. A just society benefits from social conditions that influence all peoples' well-being. Yet disparities and structural inequities continue to challenge the well-being of many Latinos through their life span. By a call to action, Latino leadership, both in the national and state political arenas, resisted invisibility. Although *Healthy People 2010* was seen by many as a first step to a systemic approach to national health policy, many Latino leaders expressed concerns about Latino data collection, which influences monitoring and changes in health status over time. To assess the prevalence of health issues disproportionally affecting various Latino groups, current and adequate research data are needed. From birth, Latinos have a greater prevalence and burden of disease than others in this nation. They experience differences in infant mortality rates, death in adolescent girls as a result of higher rates of suicide and gun possession, and a higher rate of injuries and accidents among young Latino males. In addition, homicide rates, chronic illness, and infections adversely affect the health status of Latinos. The SES of Latinos creates barriers to healthy communities because of poor environmental and social conditions affecting their neighborhoods (poverty, toxic waste, violence, and lack of access to insurance coverage and resources). There must be a multidimensional approach to target health care equity for an underserved and vulnerable population. Social workers' political advocacy role is essential to the process of social justice. Political advocacy acts as a voice of resistance to regulation that adversely affects the well-being of a population. Jansson (2008) stresses the importance of knowledge of the issues and understanding the significance of problems through research and accurate data collection. Research by political advocates is guided by needs assessments of communities and populations, and an understanding of the social and cultural meanings of healthy communities. According to Jansson, social workers evaluate the severity of the problems, develop policy proposals with community involvement, and then develop strategies for change.

National leaders, agencies, and social workers have given voice to health inequities affecting Latino health status. They have used their power to influence policymakers by being part of the legislative decision-making process. Through public voice, they have given impetus to increase concern and awareness about structural inequities affecting Latino health. Social workers participate in resistance to inequities and the political will to create a just society. In this effort, as illustrated by the HHC, social workers give voice to vulnerable populations by participating in the creation of policy briefs, public testimony, coalition building, collaboration with other community-based organizations, summits, and the use of technology and media. The profession must be active in putting a human face on the policies that regulate everyday life. It is only with compassion grounded in theoretical principles, values, and research that social workers can advocate for policy change. The goal of eliminating disparities is to create a more just society for all people.

The Latino leadership in Connecticut responded to the health crisis through an agency's call to action in forming a collaborative network to resist the policies and forces that promote health inequities. According to the HHC (2006, p. 85), creating an agenda for change requires a cohesive voice among advocates that must be as pervasive as the problems. Recently, the Connecticut Department of Public health released their findings of health disparities in the state and concluded that although there is still some missing data for Latinos, the completeness of the data is generally good (Stratton, Hynes, & Nepaul, 2009, p. 30). As previously stated, on a national level, the CHC remains effective with its health agenda. Latinos do have a state and a national voice to resist inequities in health care policies. They no longer will remain invisible.

⬠ REFERENCEſ

Abraido-Lanza, A. F., Dohrenwen, B. P., Ng-Mak, D. S., & Turner, J. B. (1999). The Latino mortality paradox: A test of the "salmon bias" and health migrant hypotheses. *American Journal of Public Health, 89*(10), 1543–1548.

Aguilar-Gaxiola, S. A., Zeezny, L., Garcia, B., Edmondson, C., Alejo-Garcia, C., & Vega, W. (2002). Translating research into action: Reducing disparities in mental health care for Mexican Americans. *Psychiatric Services, 53*(12), 1563–1568.

American Anthropological Association. (1997). *American Anthropology response to OMB Directive 15. Race and ethnic standards for federal statistics and administrative reporting.* Retrieved April, 17, 2007, from http://www.aaanet.org/gvt/ombdraft.htm

Anand, S., Diderichsen, F., Evan, T., Shkolnikov, V. M., & Wirth, M. (2001). Measuring disparities in health: Methods and indicators. In T. Evans, M. Whitehead, & F. Diderichsen, et al. (Eds.), *Challenging inequities in health: From ethics to action* (pp. 49–67). Oxford: Oxford University Press for the Rockefeller Foundation.

Arias, E. (2008). The validity of race and Hispanic origin reporting death certificates in the United States: Data collection and methods research [National Center for Health Statistics]. *Vital Health Statistics, 2*(148).

Barr, M. (2008, April). *The patient-centered medical home.* Paper presented at the annual conference of Physician Workforce Research Conference, Crystal City, VA.

Block, A. J. (1999). Translational research is hurting. *Chest, 115*(2), 311.

Carillo, J. E., Trevino, F. M., Betancourt, J. R., & Coustasse, A. (2001). Latino access to health care: The role of insurance, managed care, and institutional barriers. In M. Aguirre-Molina, C. Molina, & R. E. Zambrana (Eds.), *Health issues in the Latino community* (pp. 55–74). San Francisco: Jossey-Bass.

Centers for Disease Control and Prevention. (2008). *Fact sheet: Estimates of new HIV infections in the United States.* Retrieved July 1, 2010, from http://www.cdc.gov/nchhstp/newsroom/docs/Fact-Sheet-on-HIV-Estimates.pdf

Congressional Hispanic Caucus. (2002 August). *Healthy Hispanic communities.* Summit conducted at the National Hispanic Health Leadership, San Antonio, TX. Retrieved January 22, 2009, from http://www.nhmamd.org/files/CHCISept2002HealthSessionSummary.pdf

Congressional Record E1986: Introduction of the Hispanic Health Act of 2000: Hearing before the House of Representatives, 106th Cong., Extension of Remarks (October 28, 2000) (testimony of Hon. Ciro D. Rodriguez).

Davis, K. E., & Iron Cloud-Two Dogs, E. (2004). The color of social policy: Oppression of indigenous tribal populations and Africans in America. In K. E. Davis & T. B. Bent-Goodley (Eds.), *The color of social policy* (pp. 3–19). Alexandria, VA: Council on Social Work Education.

DeJesus, J., Medina, C. K., & Werkmeister Rozas, L. (2007, October). *A call to action: A model for addressing Latino health disparities.* Paper presented at the 2007 Council on Social Work Education Annual Program Meeting, San Francisco, CA.

Doty, M. M. (2003). *Hispanic patients double burden: Lack of health insurance & limited English.* New York: The Commonwealth Fund.

Fact sheet on Medicaid-reimbursed medical interpretation. (2007). *Medical interpretation Fact Sheet, April 2007. From the Connecticut Coalition for Medication Interpretation, an initiative of the Latino Policy Institute.* Retrieved November 13, 2008, from http://www.healthlaw.org/library

Franzini, L., Ribble, J. C., & Keddie, A. M. (2002). Understanding the Hispanic paradox. In T. A. LaVeist (Ed.), *Race, ethnicity, and health: A public health reader* (pp. 280–310). San Francisco: Jossey-Bass.

Giles, W. H., Tucker, P., Brown, L., Crocker, C., Jack, N., Latimer, A., et al. (2004). Racial and Ethnic Approaches to Community Health (REACH 2010): An overview. *Ethnicity & Disease,* 14.

Hispanic Health Act of 2000, H.R. 5595, 106th Cong. (2000). Retrieved October 23, 2008, from http://thomas.loc.gov/cgi-bin/t2GPO/http://frwebgate.access.gpo.gov/cgi-bin/getdoc.cgi?dbname=106_cong_bills&docid=f:h5595ih.txt.pdf

Hispanic Health Council. (2006). *A profile on Latino health in Connecticut: The Case for change in policy & practice.* Retrieved July 1, 2010, from http://www.hartfordinfo.org/issues/wsd/health/Profile_Latino_Health.pdf

House, J. S., & Williams, D. (2000). Understanding and reducing socioeconomic and racial/ethnic disparities in health. In B. D. Smedley & S. L. Syme (Eds.), *Promoting health: intervention strategies from social and behavioral research* (p. 81). Washington, DC: National Academy Press.

Hudgins, C., & Allen-Meares, P. (2000). Translational research: A new solution to an old problem? *Journal of Social Work Education, 36*(1), 2–5.

Hynes, M. (2007, March). *Health people, healthy Connecticut.* Handout presented in class number SPTP 318, University of Connecticut.

Hynes, M. M., Mueller, L. M., Li, H., & Amadeo, F. (2004, November 6–10). *Connecticut Latinos: Lower age-adjusted death but higher premature mortality rates compared with white residents.* Paper presented at the 2004 American Public Heath Association annual conference on Public Health and The Environment, Washington, DC. Retrieved January 21, 2009, from http://apha.confex.com/apha/132am/techprogram/

Institute of Medicine. (1999). *To err is human: Building a safer health system.* Retrieved November 1, 1999, from http://www.iom.edu

Institute of Medicine. (2002). *Unequal treatment: Confronting racial and ethnic disparities of health care.* Washington, DC: National Academics Press.

Institute of Medicine. (2003). *Hidden costs, value lost: Uninsurance in America.* Washington, DC: National Academics Press.

Jansson, B. S. (2008). *Becoming an effective policy advocate.* (5th ed., Instructor's ed.). Belmont, CA: Thomson Brooks/Cole.

Latino Policy Institute. (2008). *About the LPI.* Retrieved January 1, 2009, from http://www .lpihispanichealth.org/about-the-lpi

Latinos.us. (2004). *Hispanic demographics.* Retrieved August, 8, 2007, from http://www .latinos.us/latinos/latinos/hispanic_demograchics/hispanic_demogr

LaVeist, T. (2005). *Minority populations and health: An Introduction to health disparities in the United States.* San Francisco: Jossey-Bass.

LaVeist, T. A., & Nuru-Jeter, A. (2002). Is doctor-patient race concordance associated with greater satisfaction with care among African American and White cardiac patients. *Medical Care Research and Review, 57*(Suppl. 1), 146–161.

Minority Nurse. (2002, Fall). *Is Healthy People 2010 ignoring Hispanics?* Retrieved June 16, 2009, from http://www.minoritynurse.com/vital-sign/healthy-people-2010-ignoring-hispanics

National Alliance for Hispanic Health. (2009). *Healthy People 2010: Hispanic concerns go unanswered.* Retrieved June 14, 2009, from http://www.hispanichealth.org/hp 2010.1asso

National Center for Chronic Disease Prevention and Health Promotion. (2002). *Diabetes disparities among racial and ethnic minorities.* Retrieved June 14, 2009, from http://www.ahrq.gov/research/diabdisp.htm

National Center for Health Statistics. (2003). *Health, United States, 2003.* Hyattsville, MD: Author; Centers for Disease Control and Prevention, United States Department of Health and Human Services.

National Hispanic Medical Association. (2002). National Hispanic Health Leadership Summit—cosponsored by NHMA and the Congressional Hispanic Caucus, August 2002. Retrieved from http://www.nhmamd.org/node/52

National Institutes of Health. (2000). *NIH strategic research plan to reduce and ultimately eliminate health disparities.* Retrieved June 14, 2009, from http://www.nih.gov/about/ hd/strategicplan.pdf

Office of Management and Budget. (1997). Revisions to the standards for the classification federal data on race and ethnicity. *Federal Register, 62*(210), 58781–58790.

Office of Minority Health and Health Disparities. (2006). *Hispanic or Latino populations.* Retrieved from http://www.cdc.gov/omhd/Populations/HL/HL.htm

Ortega, A. N., Feldman, J. M., Canino, G., Steinman, K., & Alegría, M. (2006). Co-occurrence of mental and physical illness in US Latinos. *Social Psychiatry and Psychiatric Epidemiology, 41*(12), 927–934.

Pew Hispanic Center. (2002). *National survey of Latinos.* Menlo Park, CA: The Henry J. Kaiser Family Foundation.

Pew Hispanic Center. (2006). *Health care coverage and access for Hispanics: How does it differ across America.* Menlo Park, CA: The Henry J. Kaiser Family Foundation.

Pew Hispanic Center. (2008). *Quarters of Latinos get no health information from medical professionals, new surveys finds.* Retrieved July 1, 2010, from the Robert Wood Johnson Foundation website: http://www.rwjf.org/pr/product.jsp?id=33631

Rios, E. (2001). Testimony. *Hearing on the Uninsured.* 107th Cong. (August 16, 2001).

Rios, E. (2008). *Hispanic and health disparity policy 2008.* Paper presented at the Latino Health Summit, November 21, 2008, University of Connecticut, West Hartford, CT.

Smith, D. W. E., & Bradshaw, B. S. (2006). Variation in life expectancy during the twentieth century in the United States. *Demography, 43*(4), 647–657.

Stratton, A., Hynes, M. M., & Nepaul, A. N. (2009). *The 2009 Connecticut Health Disparities Report.* Hartford: Connecticut Department of Public Health.

Sue, S. (2003, November). In defense of cultural competency in psychotherapy and treatment. *American Psychologist,* pp. 964–970.

U.S. Census Bureau. (2001, March). *Current population survey: Table H101. Health insurance coverage status and type of coverage by selected characteristics: 2001.* Retrieved January 21, 2009, from http://ferret.bls.census.gov/macro/032002/health/toc.htm

U.S. Census Bureau. (2007). *Fast facts for Congress. Population estimates: 2007.* Retrieved January 23, 2009, from http://fastfacts.census.gov/home/cws/main.htm

U.S. Congressional Hispanic Caucus. (n.d.). *Health and the environment task force priorities.* Retrieved October 23, 2008, from http://house.gov/baca/chc/tsk-health.shtml

U.S. Department of Health and Human Services. *Healthy people 1990.* Retrieved from http://www.healthypeople.gov

U.S. Department of Health and Human Services. (1998). *Healthy people 2000.* Retrieved from http://www.healthypeople.gov

U.S. Department of Health and Human Services. (2000). *Healthy people 2010: With understanding and improving health and objectives for improving health* (2nd ed.). Washington, DC: U.S. Government Printing Office. Retrieved July 1, 2010, from http://www.healthypeople.gov/default.htm

U.S. Department of Health and Human Services. (2006). *Healthy people 2010: Midcourse review executive summary.* Retrieved February 22, 2007, from http://www.healthy people.gov

Vega, W. A., & Alegria, M. (2001). Latino mental health and treatment in the U.S. In C. W. Molina & R. E. Zambrana (Eds.), *Health issues in the Latino community* (pp. 179–208). San Francisco: Jossey-Bass.

Whitehead, M. (1992). The concepts and principles of equity and health. *International Journal of Health Services, 22,* 429–445.

Williams, D. R., Lavizzo-Mourney, R., & Warren, R. C. (1994). The concept of race and health status in America. *Public Health Reports, 109*(1), 26–41.

Part IV

Regulation and Resistance
Among First Nation Americans

13

Indigenist Oppression and Resistance in Indian Child Welfare

Reclaiming Our Children

Tessa Evans-Campbell and Christopher Campbell

 **INTRODUCTION**

The chapters in this book explore the impact of oppressive policies on communities of color and the resistance strategies employed by these groups to counteract such policies. In this chapter we explore federal policies related to American Indian/Alaska Native (AIAN) child welfare, the long-term impact of these policies on AIAN communities, and several strategies of resistance that AIANs and their allies have employed against them. Although we focus on two policies in particular, one—the federally implemented Indian boarding school system—a policy of oppression and systematic social destruction, and the other—the federal Indian Child Welfare Act—a federal policy of resistance and local empowerment, our discussion is broader than these two topics. To understand these policies we must situate them in a more complex history and context of AIAN oppression and resistance, a history that continues, in good ways and bad, even today.

What we learn from this overview is that in the context of child welfare policy, AIAN oppression and resistance has occurred at multiple levels and in complex ways. Shifting forms of oppression were accompanied by evolving strategies of resistance. Some of these forms of oppression and resistance were overt and easily identified. But others were more subtle and not as easily labeled. Policies of oppression, for example, though frequently explicitly racist and brutally genocidal, were also at times—some quite recent—undertaken with the intention of *helping* people and communities that members of the dominant society viewed as needing aid. Although the motives of the oppressor in no way excuse or lessen the profoundly negative effects that their actions had on AIAN communities, they did—and do—complicate practices of resistance. For the practitioner working within AIAN communities, therefore, it is critical to have some understanding of the complex, nuanced, and shifting terrain of AIAN oppression and resistance, particularly as it relates to child welfare policy.

The remainder of this chapter is divided into three sections: In the first, we provide a brief historical overview of federal child welfare policy as it relates to Native families. As we will see, the manipulation of AIAN children through formal systems of education and state child protection services has been one of the most powerful and insidious tools of oppression, cultural destruction, and social disruption used against AIAN communities. Targeting children is, of course, an especially effective method of oppression precisely because it impacts multiple generations simultaneously. Families and communities are deeply damaged in the present as children are removed or isolated from the social unit, but future generations are also compromised as children lose their ability to reproduce cultural traditions, identities, and social structures and instead carry forward self-perpetuating legacies of loss and dislocation. In the second section of this chapter, we discuss some of the ways in which AIANs as individuals and communities have responded to these policies and practices of oppression. We focus in particular on three broad forms of resistance: micro acts of resistance; overt collective actions of resistance; and formal resistance policies. We argue that the Indian Child Welfare Act (ICWA) is an example of the latter form. Finally, in the third section of this chapter, we discuss some broader lessons for social work practice and research as well as additional theoretical potentials and implications of this work.

⦂ OPPRE**JJ**ION AND INDIAN
CHILD WELFARE POLICY

The history of colonization and oppression experienced by AIAN people is well documented and includes centuries of targeted attacks on indigenous sovereignty and well-being. Over successive generations, these attacks have included community massacres, pandemics from the introduction of new diseases, forced relocation, the prohibition of spiritual and cultural practices, and, of most interest to this chapter, the forced removal of children though Indian boarding school policies and adoption practices (Stannard, 1992). Directly or indirectly, these events were facilitated by federal policy created to eradicate or forcibly displace AIAN communities and AIAN society. Individually, each of these events was profoundly traumatic; taken together they constitute a policy history of sustained cultural and ethnic disruption and destruction directed at indigenous people (Evans-Campbell & Walters, 2006).

Part of this process of oppression also included systematic government-sponsored efforts to acculturate, assimilate, and Christianize AIANs. For example, in 1883, the U.S. government established the Court of Indian Offenses on reservations with the explicit task of abolishing indigenous religious practices and replacing them with *civilized* practices under the auspices of Christianity. By 1892, the Court of Indian Offenses order supported harsh punishment for AIAN people, including imprisonment and withholding food rations from families, who engaged in traditional cultural and spiritual practices.

Early Forms of Oppression:
Child Education and Assimilation

During the 19th century, governments around the world began to employ mass education initiatives as tools to acculturate immigrant and indigenous children. In the United States, with increasing numbers of immigrants arriving each year, public education was considered the great unifier, an effective way to impart shared cultural values and a national identity among people from many cultural and ethnic groups. With an eye toward mainstreaming children, public schools across the country began using standard curricula and educational methods that taught a narrowly defined range of subjects rooted in the values of established white America and designed largely to prepare workers for the burgeoning industrial and agrarian economies (Coleman, 2007). Though American public education did not initially include Native children, the federal government had long used western education as an acculturation tool. Indeed, as early as the 17th century, government representatives encouraged newly arrived European settlers to adopt or tutor Native children (e.g., Earle & Cross, 2001). By the 19th century, however, these initial small-scale efforts had dramatically expanded into government-supported educational institutions aimed solely at Native communities. These new institutions formalized the assimilationist strategies of the federal government and were able to impact tens of thousands of children from tribes across the country.

The expansion of Native-target education began in 1819 with the passage of the Indian Civilization Act, which appropriated $10,000 a year for Indian education. At first, funds for Indian education were granted to private organizations that in turn developed Indian boarding schools with the overt mission of assimilation (Adams, 1995). The schools claimed great success in their work and advertised their *accomplishments* in newspapers across the country to garner support. Though funding for the Indian Civilization Act ceased in 1873, Congress's commitment to Indian education continued to grow. By the latter part of the 19th century, $750,000 a year was being directed to Indian education, and by 1900 Indian education funds exceeded $3 million a year (Coleman, 2007). The results were quite dramatic. One hundred fifty-three Indian boarding schools operated across the country at this time, enrolling approximately 18,000 students a year (Adams, 1995). These numbers continued to grow until by 1930 nearly half of all AIAN children were enrolled in a boarding or industrial school (U.S. Department of Health and Human Services, 2001).

The Boarding School Era

The most active period of the boarding school movement, between 1880 and 1930, is often referred to as the *boarding school era*. It was also the time of the most aggressive assimilation practices. During this period, students were not simply enrolled in these schools; many in fact were forcibly removed from their homes and villages and sent to schools hundreds, and sometimes thousands, of miles away where they were allowed only limited contact with their families. Though some former boarding school attendees report good experiences in these institutions, many more hold negative memories. Children were separated from their families and communities, often for years at a time, and grew up in institutional settings with few adult role models, Native adults in particular (e.g., Adams, 1995). In Washington state, for example, schools had more than 100 children for each adult caretaker. At some schools, siblings were not allowed to speak to one another. As part of the assimilation policy, children were forbidden to practice any form of their traditional ways of life and, instead, were forced to learn Western mannerisms and speak English. The punishment for speaking in a native language or attempting to practice traditional spirituality was often harsh, and children quickly learned to keep their traditional practices secret. As documented in numerous texts, physical abuse and neglect were commonplace; high numbers of children were also sexually abused (e.g., Smith, 2003).

Given the profound and pervasive nature of these negative experiences, it is not surprising that the boarding school experience left an enormous legacy of pain and trauma in Native communities. Families were torn apart, and communities were stripped of their right to raise their own children. Children came back from their time in boarding school profoundly changed by their experiences of cultural isolation and abuse. Cut off from Native parenting practices, generations were left doubting their own parenting skills and unfamiliar with culturally specific parenting knowledge (Evans-Campbell, 2002). Indeed, this period in AIAN history was so destructive that it is today recognized as a defining historically traumatic event (Evans-Campbell & Walters, 2006; Yellow Horse Brave Heart & DeBruyn, 1998), one that continues to touch most AIAN people regardless of whether they attended boarding school or not.

Indigenous Child Welfare and Children in the 20th Century

In the 1920s, non-Native reformers became increasingly concerned about AIAN health and welfare policies and its detrimental impacts on AIAN communities, particularly with regard to education (Coleman, 2007). After a wave of reformist attacks, the Secretary of the Interior ordered a full evaluation of Indian policy. Eight hundred pages long, the resulting *Meriam Report* detailed at great length the problems with AIAN policy and the widespread poverty, poor health, and distress in tribal communities. The report gave a detailed overview of conditions in Indian boarding schools, noting, among other problems, the strict regimes, poor student health, and pervasive neglect (Coleman, 2007). Overall, the findings had a profound impact on the thinking around Indian education policy and supported a number of radical changes in education practice for Native children, including a shift to day schools located close to family and community for as many children as possible (Adams, 1995).

After the *Meriam Report,* the government began to close or reform many of the boarding schools, while agencies serving tribal communities shifted their efforts to humanitarian relief. During this time, Congress passed the Johnson-O'Malley Act authorizing the Secretary of the Interior to contract with states and private agencies to provide health, education, and social services to AIAN communities (Mannes, 1995). The intent was to support the growth of health AIAN economies, but the Act gave great authority for Indian child welfare to states and government agencies. In the 1950s and 1960s, the Bureau of Indian Affairs and other federal agencies began to provide child welfare services to tribal children, and by 1970, the state was overseeing the majority of child welfare cases (Mannes, 1995). Though not overtly assimilationist, many of these efforts, including child welfare services, were frequently still predicated on the assumption that assimilation was in the best interest of Native children (e.g., Cross, Earle, & Simmons, 2000). This assumption clearly underlies foster care and adoption policies directed at Native families during this period, including the now (in)famous Indian Adoption Project. A collaboration between the Bureau of Indian Affairs and the Child Welfare League of America, the Indian Adoption Project was initiated in 1958 and directed transracial adoptive placements for Native children whose families were deemed *unsuitable* to care for them (Mannes, 1995). At a time when the vast majority of adoptive placements involved placing children in families of the same race, the Indian Adoption Project placed hundreds of Native children from Western states in white homes in the East and Midwest. The message of the project was clear: Native children were better off in white homes.

The assumption that Indian children were better off with white families permeated child welfare policy and services at the time. Indeed, during the mid-20th century, thousands of Native children were removed from their homes each year and placed in foster care and adoptive homes—the vast majority of which were non-Native. By the 1960s, the crisis in Indian child welfare had reached epidemic proportions. Though tribal communities were well aware of their plight and advocated for change, non-Native leaders and policymakers were firmly entrenched in business as usual.

By the late 1960s, however, tribal leaders began to make progress toward change. As Mannes (1995) details, after decades of having their children taken away by social service agents, the Devil's Lake Sioux Tribe of North Dakota requested assistance from the Association on American Indian Affairs (AAIA), a national organization dedicated to advancing Native communities. In response, the AAIA conducted a large-scale study of child welfare conditions in Native communities. The results were staggering. Researchers found that in the states with the largest Native populations, between 25 percent and 35 percent of all Native children had been removed from their homes and placed in out-of-home care. To make matters worse, nearly all of these children (99 percent) had been removed from their homes based upon a finding of child neglect (a more subjective ruling with a lower threshold than child abuse). Moreover, most of these cases were determined by non-Native social workers and the majority— 85 percent—of the removed children were then placed in non-Native homes (Byler, 1977). In states with large Native populations, the rates were particularly sobering. The out-of-home placement rate for Native children in Minnesota was 16 times that of non-Native children, while Washington state's adoption rate for Native children was 19 times that of non-Native children (Brown, Limb, Munoz, & Clifford, 2001). The study results highlighted the enormity of the problem across Indian country and gave AIAN child welfare advocates solid data on the number of Native children in the child welfare system. The evidence led to a dramatic rethinking of federal Indian child welfare policy and practice. No longer could politicians and child welfare agencies ignore the complaints of Native leaders and communities and continue with business as usual. Further empowered by the vindicating numbers, tribal leaders demanded more control over the rights of their own children and began vigorously advocating for federal policy to support their mission. The result, in 1978, was the passage of ICWA, the landmark legislation that changed not only how federal and state agencies treat AIAN families and children, but also how AIANs interact with the agencies and governments that had, for so long, been responsible for their oppression.

Oppression Today

Child welfare continues to be one of the most pressing issues facing Native communities. Though ICWA has made major strides in improving public child welfare for tribal people, AIAN children continue to be overrepresented in the public child welfare system. Overrepresentation occurs at multiple levels with relatively high rates of reported child maltreatment for AIAN children in the United States (21.3 for every 1,000 AIAN children compared with 11.0 for every 1,000 white children; U.S. Department of Health and Human Services, 2005) as well as higher out-of-home placement rates. Indeed, AIAN children are three times as likely as white children to be placed in out-of-home care (Hill, 2007), and though AIAN children represent approximately 1 percent of the U.S. child population, they make up 2.1 percent of the children in out-of-home care (U.S. Department of Health and Human Services, 2005). Of the 405,000 AIAN children who live on or near reservations, about 6,500 are placed in substitute care each year (Cross, Earle, & Simmons, 2000), and though very few statistics are available on urban AIAN children, the existing data present an equally grim picture.

☒ RE/I/TANCE

Throughout this long history of oppression, AIANs responded to their conditions with a wide range of resistance strategies. Some are well known and documented. Through negotiations with newly arrived white settlers, for example, tribal leaders attempted to extract and guarantee Native political, economic, and social rights for future generations in exchange for land and other resources. Tribal military responses, which continued into the late 19th century before being quashed by overwhelming military force and the erosion of resistance through disease, starvation, and loss of resources, fought to stem the appropriation of Native lands and the destruction of Native communities by the dominant white culture and its government forces. More recently, in the mid-20th century, organized political action by grassroots, pan-Indian organizations such as the American Indian Movement fought—and continue to fight—for the reassertion of Native identity, sovereignty, and political power. For the most part, however, these strategies have been aimed at broader social and political goals rather than child welfare policies and practices specifically. There were some exceptions to this. When Indian schools were first developed, for instance, several large tribes either developed their own schools as a way to control the education of their children or became directly involved in the curriculum of the Western schools. After the boarding school movement grew, these tribal schools were taken over and closed or converted to the assimilationist agendas of the larger movement.

When we look more specifically at responses to oppressive child welfare policies, however, we see other forms of resistance that are not as well documented in the literature as resistance strategies per se. It is these forms of resistance, their recognition often obscured by the promotion of a history that mostly ignores AIAN struggles, that are particularly interesting to us. In the pages following, we focus on three of them: micro acts of resistance, emergent communal acts of resistance, and policies of resistance.

\\\\ MICRO ACTS OF RESISTANCE

As we use the term, micro acts of resistance are small acts intentionally carried out by individuals or small groups in response to what is experienced as overwhelming and persistent oppression and powerlessness. Acts of micro resistance can take many forms but are typically acts that in normal contexts might be ordinary or even unnoticed. In contexts of oppression, however, these simple acts take on new meanings that are both psychologically and symbolically powerful. In some conditions, a micro act of resistance may lead to formal penalties or retribution when it is explicitly banned or prohibited by a dominating force. In these cases, engaging in such an act can be understood as a form of explicit *defiance*, a conscious, if small and sometimes singular stand against the constricting rules of an oppressing society. Often, however, micro acts of resistance are better understood as forms of personal *resilience.* In such cases the intention is not to directly challenge the formal structures of oppression, but rather to resist them indirectly by demonstrating an ongoing unwillingness to be subsumed by them. As a form of individual resilience, the power of a micro act of resistance lies in its ability to display to oneself and to others an enduring commitment to an idea, practice, or people under siege. For an oppressor, multiple individual micro acts of resistance can collectively be experienced as a constant, sustained, low-level force resisting attempts to suppress, dominate, regulate, or otherwise control.

Though micro acts of resistance are found throughout the history of AIAN oppression and resistance, they were particularly prevalent during the boarding school era when attempts to assimilate children were at their strongest and other opportunities for resistance were unavailable to those trapped within their systems. For instance, within the schools themselves, students, who were among the most rigidly oppressed group of AIAN people, used a variety of subtle and sometimes covert resistance strategies in their everyday lives (see Adams, 1995, for a detailed discussion of these strategies). These included practicing in private what would in their Native communities be practiced openly and considered ordinary and normal. Engaging covertly in traditional ceremonies, for instance, or speaking tribal languages outside the earshot of white adults, were, according to accounts from the time, common forms of maintaining a sense of connection to home, family, and Native identity as well as ways of resisting the assimilation attempts of teachers and school administrators. Indeed, in some circumstances, these small acts of resilience were viewed by school officials as intentional acts of defiance and were consequently punished severely. Other micro acts of resistance were more overtly confrontational. Lying to and making fun of teachers, stealing food, and tricking white people into believing in false native practices were, in addition to being tools for *getting by* in very difficult living situations, also small ways of subverting and resisting the enforced white order and power structures that dominated the lives of Native children. At times, these micro acts of resistance became even more unambiguous. Burning school buildings (Adams, 1995), for instance, or running away from the school were attempts to eradicate or escape a system that Native children may have desperately wanted to avoid, but they were also acts that communicated an unambiguous message of rejection and refusal to the dominant powers.

Family members also practiced a range of micro acts of resistance. Though the mission of the schools was to forcibly assimilate children by isolating them from their families and communities, parents resisted by refusing to allow the bonds between them and their children to be broken. Some parents went to profound lengths to help their children. There is documentation, for instance, of parents traveling across the country to find children who had been sent to schools in the East. In the context of the time, this was an extraordinary undertaking that often required significant sacrifice, struggle, and tenacity. For other parents, especially in the early years of the boarding school era when few Native people had reading and writing skills, parents and tribal leaders would find ways to send letters to school officials inquiring about their children or requesting photos. Again, in the context of the time—a time that included forced migrations, warfare between tribes and the U.S. government, and other forms of overt oppression—these seemingly small acts carried great significance. Through the assimilation practices of Indian boarding schools, the U.S. government was in effect sending a strong message to AIAN parents and communities that their children would be better off without them. Writing letters, visiting the schools, advocating on behalf of their children, and hiding children from school authorities even at the risk of arrest and imprisonment[1] were reminders to the dominant white population that AIAN communities were not giving up so easily. In such circumstances, simply refusing to be compliant or invisible were forms of resistance and sent in reply to the government's message a countermessage declaring that they would not accept or internalize the white claim that as Native people they were not suitable parents for their own children.

⧼ IDENTITY AND COMMUNITY FORMATION AS RESISTANCE

Despite the explicit aim of Indian boarding schools to erase the Native identities of AIAN children and cut their ties to traditional communities and ways of life, one of the most consequential and pervasive forms of resistance to emerge from these experiences were in fact new Native identities and communities. Not only did the assimilationist intentions of the schools often fail, students sometimes ended up becoming more strongly tied to their tribal and Native identities as the direct result of their experiences in the institutions. As one former student attested: "I've found the more outside education I receive, the more I appreciate the true Hopi way" (Byler, 1977, p. 2). In this manner, the Indian boarding school experience inspired a deeper appreciation for the very ways they were meant to eradicate, while the display of and engagement in traditional Native practices became not only a source of strength, comfort, and pride for many individuals, but also a form of active resistance.

In addition to reviving and strengthening personal tribal identities, however, boarding schools also inspired a new collective identity among many of the students, one based less on tribal membership and more on

---

[1]An agent of the Mescalero Apache Reservation wrote: "Everything in the way of persuasion and argument having failed, it became necessary to visit the Indian camp with a detachment of police, and seize the children as were proper to take them away to school, willing or unwilling. Some hurried their children off to the mountains or hid them away in camp, and the police had to chase and capture them . . . the children almost out of their wits with fright."

pan-Indian affiliation. In *Education for Extinction,* Adams (1995) points out that the schools were places where children from many different tribes came into contact with one another, often for the first time. This tribal mixing exposed students to other indigenous people and practices and introduced them to tribal cultures and networks other than their own. Perhaps more importantly, even as historical and cultural differences between the tribes were tamped down within the strict assimilationist confines of the schools, new shared experiences of oppression, injustice, and racism rose up. These shared experiences eventually became the basis of an emergent, broader "pan-Indian consciousness" (Adams) and identity that today is rooted in an awareness of and commitment to tribally shared struggles, pan-Indian issues, and the importance of working collectively in resistance struggles.

Indeed, by the mid-20th century, collective action supported by a growing pan-Indian contentiousness and a common experience of oppression propelled the Indian child welfare movements that eventually produced the Indian Child Welfare Act. National organizations such as the Association on American Indian Affairs (AAIA), which became one of the first organizations of its kind to be led by Native peoples, took on broad agendas. As Alfonso Ortiz of the Pueblo of San Juan and president of AAIA from 1973 to 1988, remarked in 1973,

> The Association has set as its major and immediate goal the comprehensive implementation of Indian self-determination in all its aspects. . . . American Indian people today are at a crossroads in their destiny; the Association stands ready to help insure that Indian people themselves ultimately determine that future. (AAIA, n.d.)

Included prominently among these aspects of self-determination were Native health, education, and welfare.

Tribes too were also challenging child welfare policies in collective and dramatic ways. In the early 1970s, for example, the Standing Rock Sioux, Sisseton-Wahpeton Sioux, the three affiliated tribes of the Fort Berthold Reservation, and the Oglala Sioux Tribes passed a resolution demanding that the removal of children from Native families be stopped and, in particular, the placement of these children in transracial homes be ended (as cited in Mannes, 1995; Unger, 1978). Similarly, it was the collective action of the Devils Lake Sioux Tribe, which, after years of enduring child removal and high rates of out-of-home placement, requested the assistance from the AAIA that led to the landmark study that confirmed the shocking disproportionality in child welfare treat-ment suffered by AIAN children. With Indian child welfare emerging as a core national agenda and armed with the study's results, tribal gov-ernments and communities worked collectively to increase public aware-ness of their plight, to develop their own tribally based child welfare infrastructure, policies and codes, and to pressure the U.S. Department of Health, Education, and Welfare, the BIA, and the U.S. Congress into making sweeping changes to federal and local law regarding the educa-tion and welfare of Native children (Mannes, 1995).

\\\\ REJIJTANCE POLICY: THE INDIAN CHILD WELFARE ACT

The use of micro acts of resistance and the mobilization of emergent Native identities and communities are both forms of resistance that have a relatively long history within AIAN communities. As Native commu-nities gained political power and social capital from these earlier strate-gies, however, a new form of resistance and renewal became available to them in the form of federal policy. Though historically, federal policy had been used as the primary enabling tool of their oppression, by the 1970s Native communities had begun to effectively use these same mecha-nisms for their own ends. We call the products of these efforts *resistance policy*, which we define as a form of policy that meets two conditions: 1) It is intentionally designed to counteract, negate, repair or otherwise stand in opposition to current practices of oppression or social injustice; and 2) It is plays a constructive role in developing, supporting, or extend-ing the world view and formal power of the formally oppressed group. In this manner, resistance policy does not just rectify and protect; it also builds and strengthens new communities, identities, and voices in a manner that reflects or is sympathetic to the ethos and practices of the groups it is written to support.

The primary resistance policy to emerge in response to the genera-tions of destructive child welfare policy is ICWA. After many years of activism and advocacy, ICWA became law on November 8, 1978, and was implemented in May of 1979. The Act required strict requirements in Indian child welfare cases and deferred authority for Native children to the tribes. The Act is premised on the belief that protecting the cul-tural identity of Native children is fundamental to their well-being and to the cultural integrity of their communities (Weaver & White, 1999). Toward these ends, the Act outlines seven major provisions regarding Native children involved in the child welfare system: (1) tribes have exclusive jurisdiction over children who live on reservations except in cases where federal law already has designated jurisdiction to the state; (2) tribes can ask for jurisdiction at any point in a case, even when jurisdiction has already been granted to a state; (3) parents and their tribes have the right to intervene in state proceedings involving AIAN children; (4) there are higher standards of proof applied to Indian child welfare custody proceedings; (5) there is a preference for placement with family members, tribal members, or other AIAN families; (6) in placement or adoption proceedings, AIAN parents give informed consent and have an extended period of time to revoke such consent; (7) tribes and parents have access to state records regarding their cases (Blanchard & Barsh, 1980). In addition, agencies must provide culturally appropriate services to AIAN families before placement occurs.

ICWA has led to a number of positive changes, including an increase in tribal and other child welfare programs, more thorough training around child welfare work with Native children and families, and the formation of several new state-tribal agreements that support working toward the best care for Native children in the child welfare system. In addition, AIAN people have become more aware of child welfare issues. A recent study of urban American Indian parents in Los Angeles, for example, found that 89 percent of those interviewed were familiar with the basic tenets of ICWA (Evans-Campbell, 2002).

And yet, despite the many improvements that the Act has brought to Indian child welfare, findings from several surveys conducted to assess the impacts of ICWA indicate that there are also a number of serious challenges to its implementation that continue to result in problematic outcomes for Native children and families (e.g., Brown, Limb, Munoz, & Clifford, 2001; Earle & Cross, 2001; Mannes, 1995). These challenges include underfunding, limited education about the Act and its provisions among child welfare practitioners, and misidentification of Native children. Though greater numbers of placements of Native children are under the jurisdiction of tribal courts and Indian child welfare agencies, Native children are still placed in out-of-home care almost four times more often than non-Indian children (DSHS, 2006). Moreover, since the inception of the Act, there have been continuous attempts to reduce the scope of ICWA through proposed amendments that limit its applicability, particularly in regards to families living off-reservation (e.g., the "Existing

Family Exception"; Brown et al., 2001). These attempts by non-Natives to determine Native status are viewed by Native leaders as a serious threat to tribal sovereignty and AIAN family wellness.

Nonetheless, after enduring generations of destructive policies and practices aimed at their children, Indian child welfare remains one of the central issues uniting AIAN communities today. Though ICWA continues to weather attacks, resistance to historically oppressive Indian child welfare policies is unwavering, and Indian child welfare advocacy is a core element of indigenous policy work for virtually all tribes, tribal members, and intertribal organizations. For Native people, reclaiming and protecting their rights to their children is one of the greatest acts of resistance practiced today. These rights are about more than maintaining cohesive and healthy family structures. They are also a collective rebuttal to generations of oppression, racism, and genocidal social destruction, as well as a powerful reclamation of tribal self-determination and Native-defined futures.

〰️ INDIGENIST STRATEGIES FOR FUTURE RESEARCH AND PRACTICE

Our review of oppression and resistance in AIAN history has attempted to illustrate the depth and pervasiveness of oppressive practices perpetrated against Native communities and, especially, their children, as well as the multiplicity of approaches that AIAN people have mobilized in response. Of course in the space of a single chapter we have been able to only touch the surface of these two topics, and we urge any person who intends to work with Native communities, particularly in regards to education or child welfare, to investigate these histories further. Though many of the events discussed in this chapter are in the past, in affect and, sometimes, in practice, they very much live on today. To ignore this fact, or to fail to adequately educate oneself about this history, is an injustice in its own right.

What this means for the social services professionals, is that in terms of practice, work with AIAN populations must be contextualized within the experience of being indigenous survivors of colonization. Evans-Campbell and Walters (2006) outline a number of decolonization practice strategies for work with AIAN people, particularly those that have experienced colonizing events such as boarding school. They suggest that any mistrust encountered by practitioners be contextualized within the history of discrimination and colonization experienced by Native peoples. Relevant practice acknowledges the social, political, and historical context of AIAN lives today. In addition, documenting traumatic events in families and communities as well as responses to these events—including acts of resistance at multiple levels—will help practitioners uncover patterns of trauma and attempts to heal in family and community systems. It is also incumbent upon practitioners to support indigenous resistance to oppressive policies and practices, from micro acts of resistance to resistance policies. Perhaps most importantly, by working with clients in identifying familial and community histories of resilience, resistance, and survival strategies, practitioners can help connect AIANs to their ancestral strengths.

For researchers we recommend several practice strategies when working with tribal communities. Perhaps most importantly, future scholarship must directly investigate resilience, healing, and resistance around the history of Indian child welfare. Although much of the literature on AIAN communities has focused on negative outcomes, there is a small but growing literature exploring the strengths and resiliencies that result from survival, adaptation, and resistance. Indeed, engaging in acts of resistance is empowering for many people, and documenting these acts can engender community pride and healing. As we suggested in this chapter, in indigenous communities, a history of shared oppression has in some ways enhanced community ties and underscored the importance of retaining culture and tradition. How then can we build upon these strengths to begin collective healing and transforming communities after enduring generations of trauma? Research that explores the factors associated with resistance and resiliencies is critically important as practitioners and scholars search for pathways to heal the legacy of intergenerational trauma related to Indian child welfare.

Walters, Simoni, and Evans-Campbell (2002) also assert that those who collaborate with indigenous communities take on a profound responsibility. First, as Walters and colleagues point out, truly indigenous-centered research with AIAN communities involves, first and foremost, challenging racist or colonial policies and practices. When relevant, researchers must acknowledge their privileged status vis-à-vis community members, including educational and socioeconomic privilege as well as white privilege if applicable. In addition, collaborators have a responsibility to expand community knowledge and capacity to conduct resistance policy and advocacy work. Practitioners can do this by prioritizing hiring tribal youth and students in activities that provide them with training experience and engage them in thinking about these issues. Partners also have the responsibility of disseminating information about their research and the findings it produces in culturally relevant and meaningful ways. Additionally, work that fails to adequately consider the contextual factors and the history of colonization among indigenous communities may lead to reports that inaccurately blame the victim, switching the focus away from the need for policy changes that address structural inequities (Walters et al., 2002). Finally, researchers should work to promote indigenous-led projects, indigenous ways of advocating, and broader institutional policies that promote indigenous community work.

\\\\\\ CONCLUJION

The aim of this chapter was to outline the long history of oppressive federal policies and practices aimed at AIAN children and families, the continuing impact of this history on indigenous people and communities, and the multiple strategies of resistance that have developed in response. What we hope we have made clear is that even though many of these oppressive practices and policies took place in the past, their legacy continues to be an important part of contemporary AIAN experience, identity, collective action and policy debate. Indeed, although some of these oppressive federal policies were overturned many generations ago, others—such as decisions around child removal and adoption—were only recently modified and continue to carry forward in the form of dominant culture assumptions about indigenous families, indigenous patterns of communal behavior, AIAN distrust and disenfranchisement, and personal memories harbored by those who suffered directly under earlier oppressive policies and practices. Consequently, as we have argued throughout this chapter, AIAN family health and wellness issues cannot be decoupled from this history of federal oppression, and professionals, whether they are serving Native clients directly or working on other policy-related subjects, must take this context into account.

At the same time, however, we hope that we have also made it clear that AIAN populations and individuals have developed a variety of effective resistance strategies. In this chapter we focused on three types of resistance particular to child welfare—micro acts of resistance, emergent communal acts of resistance, and policies of resistance—that collectively constitute a continuum of strategies that are employed at different scales and in different forms throughout AIAN communities and among Native individuals and families. Like the oppressive histories that inspired them, these resistant strategies also cannot be ignored. For those working with Native peoples and communities, such indigenous resistance strategies must be integrated into individual, familial, and tribal or community-based assessments as well as into the design of interventions and policies. Indeed, given the wealth of resistance examples used by AIAN families and communities throughout history, we argue that a focus on a multilevel, strengths-based approach to tribal and pan-Native issues that builds on these survival strategies is a particularly appropriate and promising strategy. This is especially true when these efforts are tailored to the contemporary context of the tribal group, family, or individual given the varied histories with oppressive Indian child welfare policy, unique tribal and familial responses, and the particular resistance and resiliency strategies employed.

Finally, in this chapter we argued for, and reiterate here, the importance of continued research into the long-term affects of federal child welfare policies and practices on AIAN individuals, families, and tribal communities, as well as the resistance strategies that Native people and groups employ. To this end, we want to especially emphasize the importance of conducting research on new methods of assessment and intervention that build on these resistance strategies in the hope of developing new and more affective practices and policies that can better serve AIAN clients and communities.

☆ REFERENCES

Adams, D. W. (1995). *Education for extinction: American Indians and the boarding school experience.* Lawrence: University Press of Kansas.

Association on American Indian Affairs. (n.d.). *Association on American Indian affairs records, 1851–2008 (bulk 1922–1995).* Retrieved August 3, 2010, from http://diglib.prince ton.edu/ead/getEad?id=ark:/88435/z316q159f

Blanchard, E., & Barsh, R. (1980). What is best for tribal children: A response to Fischler. *Social Work, 25,* 350–357.

Brown, E. F., Limb, G. E., Munoz, R., & Clifford, C. A. (2001). *Title IV-B child and family services plans: An evaluation of specific measures taken by states to comply with the Indian Child Welfare Act.* Seattle, WA: Casey Family Programs.

Byler, W. (1977). *The destruction of the American Indian family.* New York: The Association of American Indian Affairs.

Coleman, M. C. (2007). *American Indians, the Irish, and government schooling: A comparative study*. Lincoln: University of Nebraska Press.

Cross, T. A., Earle, K. A., & Simmons, D. (2000). Child abuse and neglect in Indian country: Policy issues. *Families in Society: The Journal of Contemporary Human Services, 81*(1), 49–58.

Earle, K., & Cross, A. (2001). *Child abuse and neglect among American Indian/Alaska Native children: An analysis of existing data*. Seattle, WA: Casey Family Programs.

Evans-Campbell, T. (2002). Child welfare practice with urban American Indian families. In T. Wiko (Ed.), *No longer forgotten: Addressing the mental health needs of urban Indians*. New York: APA Books.

Evans-Campbell, T., & Walters, K. L. (2006). Indigenist practice competencies in child welfare practice: A decolonization framework to address family violence and substance abuse among First Nations peoples. In R. Fong, R. McRoy, & C. Ortiz Hendricks (Eds.), *Intersecting child welfare, substance abuse, and family violence: culturally competent approaches*. Washington, DC: CSWE Press.

Hill, R. (2007). *An analysis of racial/ethnic disproportionality and disparity at the national, state, and county levels*. Seattle, WA: Casey-CSSP Alliance for Racial Equity in Child Welfare.

Mannes, M. (1995). Factors and events leading to the passage of the Indian Child Welfare Act. *Child Welfare, 74*(1), 264–282.

Smith, A. (2003). Soul wound: the legacy of Native American schools. *Amnesty Now, Summer*, 14–17.

Stannard, D. (1992). *American holocaust*. Oxford: Oxford University Press.

U.S. Department of Health and Human Services. (2001). *Administration on children, youth and families. Child Maltreatment: 1999*. Washington, DC: U.S. Government Printing Office.

Unger, S. (Ed.). (1978). *The destruction of American Indian families*. New York: Association on American Indian Affairs.

Walters, K. L., Simoni, J. M., & Evans-Campbell, T. (2002). *Substance use among American Indians and Alaska Natives: Incorporating culture in an "Indigenist" stress-coping paradigm. Public Health Reports, 117*(suppl. 1), 104–117.

Weaver, H., & White, B. (1999). Protecting the future of indigenous children and nations: An examination of the Indian Child Welfare Act. *Journal of Health and Social Policy, 10*(4), 35–50.

Yellow Horse Brave Heart, M., & DeBruyn, L. M. (1998). The American Indian Holocaust: Healing historical unresolved grief. *American Indian and Alaska Native Mental Health Research, 8*, 56–78.

14

American Indian Child Welfare

The Impact of Federal Regulation and Tribal Resistance on Policies and Practice

Gordon E. Limb and Aaron Baxter

 **INTRODUCTION**

U.S. federal policy states that the purpose of child welfare services is to "improve the conditions of children and their families and to improve or provide substitutes for functions that parents have difficulty performing" (U.S. House of Representatives, 1998, p. 1).

Although the intent of this policy has been fairly consistent over the years, federal policy with its various practices impacting American Indians has had a strong influence in creating regulations that have given rise to the need for resistance in tribal communities. War, boarding schools, and cultural bias are only some of the debilitating institutional policies that have been implemented and given rise to a long history of social, economic, and cultural degeneration.

American Indians are unique among all the groups of color in the United States in that in addition to being a minority group, they also have a political status and relationship with the U.S. government unlike any other racial group. As a result, this chapter will examine American Indian child welfare within the context of two important federal regulations—Title IV-E and Title IV-B of the Social Security Act. Before one can understand the importance of these two regulations and their impacts on American Indians, it is imperative to have some understanding of the historical era relating to tribal sovereignty and Indian-white policy relations and their impacts on resistance. As such, the first section will examine tribal sovereignty. The next section will provide a brief synopsis of Indian-white policy relations and the need for child welfare protection and resistance leading up to the Indian Child Welfare Act. Next, Title IV-B and IV-E of the Social Security will be discussed as they relate to how resistance led to historic federal funding opportunities for American Indians. Finally, the current status and future prospects of these two laws are set forth as examples of advocacy activities designed to eliminate funding barriers.

\\\\ TRIBAL SOVEREIGNTY

There is much confusion about the legal standing of American Indians with respect to federal, state, and local laws. Throughout American history, American Indians have had a unique relationship with the U.S. government. Current federal policy involving American Indian tribes is based, in part, on a long-standing trust relationship between the federal government and Indian tribes as distinct and unique political communities (Utter, 1993). Although the legal definition of the trust relationship has caused great debate, "the relationship approximates that of trustee and beneficiary, with the trustee (the United States) subject in some degree to legally enforceable responsibilities" of the beneficiary [in this case American Indian tribal communities] (Canby, 1981, p. 32). In this trust relationship, the United States has taken upon itself the obligation to regulate services to American Indians and take other actions necessary to protect tribal self-government.

Although tribes can benefit from a relationship in which the federal government acts as a trustee, tribes are also recognized as sovereign entities with an inherent right or power to govern themselves (American Indian Policy Center, 2005; Kunesh, 1996). Tribal sovereignty therefore means that American Indian tribal powers originated from tribes managing their own affairs prior to white contact and reinforced through numerous treaties. Although federally recognized tribes are considered *nations within a nation*, case law has established that tribes reserve the rights they have never given away (American Indian Policy Center, 2005; Cross, Earle, & Simmons, 2000).

Canby (1981) summarizes the principal attributes of tribal sovereignty as follows: (1) Indian tribes possess inherent governmental power over all internal affairs, (2) states are precluded from interfering with tribal self-government (it is a federal relationship), and (3) Congress has plenary power to limit tribal sovereignty and thereby limit the first two attributes. *Self-determination* is an outgrowth of tribal sovereignty, covering a variety of concepts, including tribal restoration, self-government, cultural renewal, reservation resource development, self-sufficiency, control over education, and equal or controlling input into policies and programs arising from the Indian–federal government trust relationship (Waldman, 1985). Federal policy began to recognize tribal self-determination beginning in the 1930s, with a renewal in the 1970s, creating opportunities for tribes to retain a degree of sovereignty while overcoming some of the arbitrary restraints on sovereignty inflicted by regulation after regulation over the previous 150 years (Utter, 1993). Nevertheless, federal policy continues to be impacted by sovereignty and the ongoing debate as to what implications this has on Indian–white relations.

⧗ INDIAN–WHITE POLICY RELATIONS

Numerous books have been written on Indian–white relations, and although a detailed examination of this history is not possible here, it is important to note that child welfare service regulations in American Indian tribal communities today have been and continue to be heavily influenced by this relationship. From a Native perspective, resistance to these regulations is influenced by traditional indigenous approaches to child rearing. Historically, Native children were born into both a primary biological family as well as a kinship network. The kinship network or extended family, which includes the tribal clan or band, provides both protection, care, and discipline for the child (Cross et al., 2000). The raising of American Indian children falls into the hands of both the parents as well as the Indian community, and the cohesiveness of American Indian tribes was maintained through these kinship practices and communal connections (Kunesh, 1996). European American influence on traditional American Indian child-rearing practices made kinship and family systems less stable, and parent–child relationships were redefined under the influence of European American values and norms. Eventually, a number of regulations were passed that undermined many American Indian cultural values and traditional practices.

American Indian child-rearing practices and family systems have been greatly and negatively impacted by European conquest. The stated and unstated goals of this conquest were simple—disrupt American Indian families and assimilate them into the dominant culture. For example, as early as 1860 boarding schools were used by the Bureau of Indian Affairs (BIA) as a tool to *civilize* American Indian children by separating them from their families and tribal communities and forcing them to learn and speak English and to adopt European American practices and customs. Boarding schools, such as the Carlisle Indian School in Pennsylvania, went so far as to publicize the motto, "Kill the Indian and save the man." This systematic disruption brought about the "institutional manifestation of the government's determination to completely restructure the Indians' minds and personalities" (Adams, 1995, p. 97). Kunesh (1996) states that the close bonds of extended Indian families were seen as obstacles that had to be removed. If parents did not agree to send their children to boarding schools and assimilate to white society, the federal government took the children from their homes by force (Mannes, 1995).

One of the more prominent federal regulations designed to regulate and control American Indian families occurred in 1958, when the Indian Adoption Project was established by the BIA and the Child Welfare League of America. This project was implemented "to provide adoptive placements for American Indian children whose parents were deemed unable to provide a 'suitable' home for them" (Mannes, 1995, p. 267). States were often paid by the BIA to remove Indian children from their homes under the charge of neglect (Kunesh, 1996). Most of the children removed from their "unsuitable" environments were placed in non-Indian homes because of the cultural bias and lack of suitable American Indian families available to care for Indian children.

In an effort to resist the negative impacts of these regulations, between 1969 and 1974, the Association on American Indian Affairs (AAIA) conducted studies on the impact of these federal and state regulations toward American Indian children and families. They found that 25 percent to 35 percent of all Indian children were being removed from their homes. In some states, such as Minnesota, it was found that one in four Indian children under the age of 1 was being placed for adoption (George, 1997). Many in state and federal government positions saw these removal rates as demonstration of the regulations success. One county attorney stated,

> If you want to solve the Indian problem you can do it in one generation. You can take all of our children of school age and move them bodily out of the Indian country and transport them to some other part of the United States. Where there are civilized people . . . if you take those kids away and educate them to make their own lives, they wouldn't come back here. (cited in George, 1997, p. 169)

However, response to statements like this began prompting significant outrage in both Indians and non-Indians and initiated a nationwide public policy dialogue regarding the high rates of removals (Red Horse et al., 2000).

To address this alarming finding and the devastating impact this rate of removal was having on American Indian communities, the AAIA began pushing for federal change in the way American Indian child welfare was handled and administered (Mannes, 1995). Beginning in the mid-1970s, relentless political advocacy by national Indian and non-Indian organizations, Tribes, members of Congress, and journalists aided this effort. The AAIA prepared an Indian child welfare bill that was eventually passed after numerous hearings and amendments. On November 8, 1978, the Indian Child Welfare Act (ICWA) went into effect. President Carter approved ICWA over the objection of the Departments of the Interior, Health, Education and Welfare, Justice, and the Office of Management and Budget (Washington State Department of Social and Health Services, 2008).

ICWA gave tribal jurisdiction over child custody proceedings including foster care placement, termination of parental rights (TPR), preadoption placement, and adoption placement. This legislation was enacted with the intention that tribal jurisdiction would ensure the survival of tribal culture and tradition as well as supplement tribes' right to self-determination (MacEachron, Gustavsson, Cross, & Lewis, 1996). The legislation states:

> An alarmingly high percentage of Indian families are broken up by the removal, often unwarranted, of their children from them by non-tribal public and private agencies and an alarmingly high

percentage of such children are placed in non-Indian foster and adoptive homes and institutions. (Indian Child Welfare Act of 1978, Public Law 95–608, Sec. 2, Article 4)

ICWA called for tribal heritage protection and family preservation by mandating an end to the out-of-culture-placements of American Indian children. In commenting on the effects of this resistance in American Indian communities, Cross et al. (2000) state:

> ICWA was a huge step in the right direction. However, being given the right to provide a service does not mean that the funding, desire, or know-how will come together in a timely way. For Indian tribes, program development has been hampered by lack of funding, jurisdictional barriers, lack of trained personnel, lack of information about the extent of the problem, lack of culturally appropriate service models, and community denial. . . . The struggle is still new and while great strides have been made most of the work is yet to be done. (p. 53)

ICWA put in place requirements and standards that child welfare agencies must follow when placing Indian children. Included among these was providing culturally appropriate services for American Indian families prior to a child being placed and notifying tribes of the placement of Indian children (Cross et al., 2000). In addition to jurisdiction over child welfare proceedings on the reservation, ICWA also gave tribes the right to accept or reject jurisdiction over Indian children living off the reservation (Plantz, Hubbell, Barrett, & Dobree, 1989). American Indian tribes were given the opportunity to develop their own family and child welfare services. Further, ICWA supported "self-determination policies and decision making to ensure the collective right of tribal survival" (MacEachron et al., 1996, p. 452).

ICWA also established a small grant program, under Title II, to fund tribal development and operation of child welfare services. However, this funding provision was and continues to be insufficient for tribes to run their own foster care and adoption programs. The largest share of ongoing funding for all child welfare is administered by the Department of Health and Human Services under the provisions of the Social Security Act (Cross et al., 2000). This funding source for tribal foster care and adoption services is an integral aspect of the struggle to implement appropriate and effective child welfare services in tribal communities.

⟨⟨ FROM REIIITANCE TO REGULATION: TITLEI IV-B AND IV-E OF THE IOCIAL IECURITY ACT

In looking at ways that resistance activities have been effective for American Indians, developments of Title IV of the Social Security Act provides a good example. Title IV programs are one of the most important federal funding opportunities for American Indians. The largest of these programs is authorized under Title IV-B and Title IV-E of the Social Security Act and "are intended to operate in consort to help prevent the need for out-of-home placement of children, and in cases where such placement is necessary, to provide protections and permanent placement for the children involved" (U.S. House of Representatives, 1998, p. 2).

Title IV-B authorizes the Title IV-B Child Welfare Services Program and the Promoting Safe and Stable Families Program. It provides funding to states and tribes for family preservation and family support services. Title IV-E authorizes funding for foster care and adoption assistance. Although these programs continue to be important funding sources for American Indians, the complexity of funding opportunities continue to be problematic for tribes. Therefore, it is important to understand the intent of Title IV-B and IV-E and how these federal child welfare funds are utilized by American Indian tribes to overcome historical challenges.

Title IV-B of the Social Security Act

Title IV-B, Subpart 1 of the Social Security Act is a federally funded formula grant program that provides states and tribal governments with federal support for a wide variety of child welfare services. These child welfare services include preplacement preventive services to strengthen families and avoid placement of children, services to prevent abuse and neglect, and services related to the provision of foster care and adoption (45 C.F.R., Part 1357, 2000). Title IV-B also contains a second subpart, known as Subpart 2, which refers to the Promoting Safe and Stable Families program (formerly titled Family Preservation and Support Services). The aim of the Promoting Safe and Stable Families program is to promote services to prevent the removal of children from their homes, reunify children with their families when possible after removal, and provide services to support adoption when it is not possible for the child to return to his or her home (Cross et al., 2000).

One of the main goals of Title IV-B, Subpart 1, is to help state child welfare agencies, as well as American Indian tribes, improve their child welfare services in order to keep families intact (U.S. Department of Health and Human Services, 2000). Subpart 1 of Title IV-B provides opportunities for states to receive funding for public social services with the following objectives: (1) Protect and promote the welfare and safety of all children; (2) prevent, remedy, or assist in the solution of problems that may result in the neglect, abuse, exploitation, or delinquency of children; (3) prevent the unnecessary separation of children from their families; (4) restore to their families children who have been removed and may be safely returned; (5) assure adequate care of children away from their homes; and (6) place children in suitable adoptive homes, in cases where restoration to the biological family is not possible or appropriate (Social Security Act, 42 U.S.C. § 609 [a][1], 2001).

To qualify for funding under Title IV-B, Subpart 1, regulations require states and tribes to submit a 5-year Child and Family Services Plan (CFSP) for the administration of their child welfare programs. Specifically, Title IV-B, Subpart 1, requires that to become eligible for payment, states and tribes must develop plans that meet various requirements outlined within the statue for child welfare services in conjunction with the federal government. The purpose of CFSPs is to provide "an opportunity to lay the groundwork for a system of coordinated, integrated, culturally relevant family-focused services" (Administration for Children and Families, 1999, p. 5).

CFSPs detail how each state and tribe intends to allocate federal resources for the 5 years immediately following submission of the plans. Additionally, states and tribes are required to update their CFSPs each of the remaining years by submitting an Annual Program and Services Reviews (APSR) (U.S. Department of Health and Human Services, 2000). APSRs must contain information regarding progress made on each of the goals and objectives established in the CFSPs, changes made to those goals and objectives, and descriptions of each state's/tribe's child welfare services, including the Independent Living Program and the programs under the Child Abuse Prevention and Treatment Act.

Even though ICWA has been mandated in child welfare settings since 1978, states were originally not required to include ICWA-related content in their CFSPs. Therefore, a number of tribes and tribal organizations initiated efforts to resist this regulation by demanding that ICWA compliance be included as part of state's CFSP and APSR. This process began with relatives of Indian children who had been taken from their families submitting testimony to state and federal agencies. These families contended that they received inadequate notification and that the children were placed in non-Indian foster homes off the reservation and that extended family members, who could have provided appropriate homes, were never notified or deemed unqualified (e.g., State of South Dakota, 2004). Similar testimony was heard in many other states. The National Indian Child Welfare Association also presented testimony on a number of occasions to the Senate Committee on Indian Affairs, which brought to light many of these discrepancies in ICWA compliance.

Therefore, after much advocacy and lobbying, tribal groups and advocates were successful in bringing this issue up for public policy debate. Concerned in part with ensuring that states meet the important requirements of ICWA, Congress passed the Social Security Act Amendments of 1994 (Public Law 103–432). Since that time, states have been instructed to include the development of specific measures for compliance with ICWA within their CFSPs. These plans require a description, developed after consultation with tribes/tribal organizations, of the specific measures taken by the state to comply with ICWA. Therefore, for tribes, Title IV-B allowed access to funds to support their child welfare services. For states, Title IV-B became the only ongoing monitoring tool available to the federal government to examine state ICWA compliance. Other elements of the Social Security Act amendments are also important.

Title IV-E of the Social Security Act

The Title IV-E Foster Care Program and Adoption Assistance Program is a permanently authorized entitlement under which the federal government has a "binding obligation" to make payments to individuals or government entities that meet the eligibility criteria established by law (U.S. House of Representatives, 1998). The purpose of this regulation has been to provide federal matching funds for foster care and adoption services for economically disadvantaged children and children with special needs. Title IV-E provides funds for (1) monthly maintenance payments for eligible children in foster care, (2) monthly assistance payments for children with special needs in adoptive placements, (3) administration costs associated with placement of eligible children, and (4) training costs for personnel administering the programs and for foster and adoptive parents.

Under Title IV-E, federal matching funds are provided for foster care maintenance payments to eligible children and families, adoption assistance, program administration, and staff/caretaker training. When Title IV-E was authorized, American Indian children under tribal juris-diction were not eligible for these funds. Instead, tribes were required to work through state governments in order to participate in this program. For many tribes, this idea of *devolution*, where the federal government devolved or reallocated its power position to states, became problematic. Here, tribal sovereignty was jeopardized as the nature of the agreement was between tribe and state, and not tribe and federal government (Brown, Limb, Clifford, Munoz, & Whitaker, 2004). For many tribes, these intergovernmental agreements presented barriers to accessing Title IV-E funds because of differences in needs, values, and expectations among the different state and tribal entities (Brown et al., 2004). Instead of developing intergovernmental agreements with state governments to access Title IV-E funds, most tribes preferred a direct funding option.

Although tribal/state relationships can be problematic, it does present opportunities for tribes and states to work together to achieve mutual bene-fits for their citizens. Goodluck (1997) suggests that the purpose of these agreements includes clarifying specific roles, relationships, tasks, and con-tingencies to specify better understanding and agreement. Other benefits that can come from entering into agreements include providing a standard to evaluate the effectiveness of the implementation of the agreement and collaboration of the tribes and state, as well as providing a path by which conflicts may be resolved between the two entities. Because tribes and states will vary in their specifications and expectations, the specifics of each agree-ment may also vary and include considerations of the culture and history of the state and tribe, as well as past experience and future provisions. The remaining section will detail how resistance efforts have influenced the cur-rent and future prospects of these important funding sources.

⟋⟍⟍ FROM REGULATION AND RESISTANCE TO FUTURE PROSPECTS OF TITLES IV-B AND IV-E

Title IV-B funding remains a major resource to American Indian tribes for child welfare services. Currently IV-B funding is accessed through direct funding from the federal government under both subparts. Under Subpart 1, tribes are eligible for funding in an amount set by the Secretary of Interior. Under Subpart 2, tribes can receive a specific set-aside from the federal government (American Indian Policy Center, 2005). Under both subparts, tribes can receive financial assistance to provide services such as family preservation, family reunification, child abuse and neglect prevention, and adoptive services. At this point, it is unlikely that either the services or method for tribes to obtain IV-B money through direct funding will change in the near future.

Conversely, in 2008, changes related to Title IV-E funding began to take shape. In October of that year, new legislation titled "Fostering Connections to Success and Increasing Adoptions Act" (also known as P.L. 110–351) was implemented. This legislation provides tribal access to Title IV-E monies either directly from the federal government or through an intergovernmental agreement with states where money and services may be passed from the state to the tribes. This funding will initially be made available through start-up grants and technical assistance for a small group of tribes as a pilot program. After this initial step, direct funding should be made available to all interested tribes.

The options that tribes will have to receive direct funding for IV-E programs or to continue to participate in intergovernmental agreements with states can have great impact on child welfare programming in tribal communities throughout the United States. There are an estimated 91 tribes currently receiving IV-E money through intergovernmental agreements (L. Echohawk, Casey Family Programs, personal communication, January 26, 2009). With direct funding available to all federally recognized tribes, that number should increase, giving more tribes the capacity to strengthen child welfare services within their communities.

Tribes that choose to collaborate with states may also take advantage of a relationship that may provide training for child welfare workers, foster parent training, and other workers to provide appropriate services. This may provide another avenue for tribes to pursue as they effectively care for children within their child welfare systems.

With greater capacity to provide service to tribal children, it is likely that a greater number of children will be cared for within the tribal organizations rather than out-placing children into state foster care or adoptive services. This will accommodate tribal attitudes of passing on tribal heritage, traditions, language, and culture. Ultimately, these changes related to child welfare services within tribal communities will increase tribe's capacity to exercise sovereignty. As Canby (1981) pointed out, tribes should have an "inherent" right to govern *all* internal affairs. Such changes in funding opportunities increases this power and can ultimately contribute to strengthening American Indian tribal communities throughout the United States.

⟋⟍⟍ CONCLUﬁON

As a result of combined resistance and advocacy efforts among tribal groups and organizations, child welfare services are on the cusp of potentially great changes and opportunities within Native communities. These are unprecedented opportunities that can function to support tribal sovereignty as well as enhance the care for children within a tribal setting. Ultimately, it may serve to sustain tribal language, culture, and identity for these families. As these changes occur, it is imperative that social workers become competent in understanding tribal sovereignty, white–Indian relations, and current and past legislation that affect American Indian child welfare services.

Once competent in these and other key areas, social workers and other professionals can provide support to American Indian communities in development and maintenance of effective child welfare services. Some suggested areas of focus for assistance include continued advocacy for direct funding options and consultation for tribes pertaining to these policies, procedures, and training. As these changes are implemented, research to determine outcomes for child welfare services within an American Indian setting will be imperative for long-term effectiveness. Overall, federal regulation on Native communities continues to impact all aspects of American Indian life. But tribal resistance efforts are making a positive impact on American Indian child welfare policies and practice.

⟋⟍⟍ REFERENCEﬁ

Adams, D. W. (1995). *Education for extinction: American Indians and the boarding school experience.* Kansas City: University of Kansas.

Administration for Children and Families, United States Department of Health and Human Services. (1999). *Program instruction.* March 25, 1999. Log Number ACYF-CB-Pl-99-07. Retrieved May 10, 1999, from http://www.acf.hhs.gov/programs/cb/laws_policies/policy/pi/1999/pi9907.htm

American Indian Policy Center. (2005). *American Indian tribal sovereignty primer.* Retrieved June 17, 2009, from http://www.airpi.org/pubs/indinsov.html

Brown, E., Limb, G., Clifford, C., Munoz, R., & Whitaker, L. (2004). Using tribal/state Title IV-E intergovernmental agreements to help American Indian tribes access foster care and adoption funding. *Child Welfare, 83*(4), 293–316.

Canby, W. C., Jr. (1981). *American Indian law in a nutshell.* St. Paul, MN: West Publishing.

Cross, T. A., Earle, K. A., & Simmons, D. (2000). Child abuse and neglect in Indian country: Policy issues. *Families in Society: The Journal of Contemporary Human Services, 81,* 49–58.

George, L. (1997). Why the need for the Indian Child Welfare Act? *Journal of Multicultural Social Work, 5*(3/4), 165–175.

Goodluck, C. (1997). *Tribal-State Child Welfare Project.* Final Report. Prepared for the National Center on Child Abuse and Neglect. Englewood, CO: American Humane Association.

Indian Child Welfare Act of 1978. P.L. 95–608, 92 Stat. 3069.

Kunesh, P. (1996). Transcending frontiers: Indian child welfare in the United States. *Boston College Third World Law Journal, 16*(17), 17–34.

MacEachron, A. E., Gustavsson, N. S., Cross, S., & Lewis, A. (1996). The effectiveness of the Indian Child Welfare Act of 1978. *Social Service Review, 70*(3), 451–463.

Mannes, M. (1995). Factors and events leading to the passage of the Indian Child Welfare Act. *Child Welfare, 74*(1), 264–282.

Plantz, M. C., Hubbell, R., Barrett, B. J., & Dobrec, A. (1989). Indian child welfare: A status report. *Children Today, 18*(1), 24–29.

Red Horse, J. G., Martinez, C., Day, P., Day, D. D., Poupart, J., & Scharnberg, D. (2000). *Family preservation: Concepts in American Indian communities.* Portland, OR: NICWA.

Social Security Act, 42 U.S.C. § 603 (2001).

Social Security Act, 42 U.S.C. § 609 (a)(1) (2001).

State of South Dakota, Office of the Governor. (2004). *Indian Child Welfare Act: Commission report.* Retrieved May 11, 2010, from http://www.state.sd.us/oia/files/report.pdf

U.S. Department of Health and Human Services. (2000). *Child and family services review procedures manual.* Retrieved May 6, 2000, from http://childwelfare.net/cfsreview/manual/manual.htm

U.S. House of Representatives. (1998). *1998 green book: Background material and data on programs within the jurisdiction of the Committee on Ways and Means.* Retrieved July 26, 2010, from http://aspe.os.dhhs.gov/98gb/11cps.htm

U.S. House Report. (1978). No. 1386, 95th Congress, 2nd Session. *Establishing standards for the placement of Indian children in foster or adoptive homes, to prevent the breakup of Indian families,* July 24, 1978. Washington, DC: U.S. Government Printing Office.

Utter, J. (1993). *American Indians: Answers to today's questions.* Lake Ann, MI: National Woodlands Publishing.

Waldman, C. (1985). *Atlas of the North American Indian.* New York: Facts on File.

Washington State Department of Social and Health Services. (2008). *Indian child welfare manual.* Retrieved May 17, 2010, from http://www.dshs.wa.gov/ca/pubs/mnl_icw/chapter1.asp

15

Restrictions on Indigenous Spirituality in the Land of the Free

"A Cruel and Surreal Result"

Hilary N. Weaver

 **INTRODUCTION**

"A cruel and surreal result." These are the words of Justice Brennan who wrote the dissent in a 1988 Supreme Court case that allowed destruction of sites of spiritual significance to Native Americans. The Supreme Court's hostility toward protection of indigenous religious freedom is part of a long line of assaults ranging from prohibition of religious ceremonies, banning use of spiritual items such as peyote and eagle feathers, and failure to protect sacred sites. These acts all threaten indigenous spirituality and indeed indigenous cultures themselves since for many Native Americans spirituality is an intimate part of what it means to be indigenous. Although spiritual oppression comes from many directions, perhaps the most threatening of these forces is the judiciary since they are charged with interpreting the law. The Supreme Court has been particularly hostile toward indigenous issues, including matters of religious freedom.

The concepts of freedom and equality so cherished in American society have never been extended fully to Native people, either historically or in contemporary times. This is evident in the contemporary failure to fully protect the free exercise of indigenous religions (Linge, 2000). Conflicting worldviews and the imbalance of political and economic power in our society are at the heart of contemporary struggles between the United States and indigenous peoples over freedom of religion (LaDuke, 2005).

This chapter gives an overview of Native American spirituality and how it has been legally restricted. Laws and legal cases that challenge these restrictions and the social movements striving for freedom of religion are reviewed, along with a discussion of how resistance activities inform contemporary social work practice and implications for the future. In particular, this chapter highlights three significant policy initiatives: (1) the 1883 Indian Religious Crimes Code, (2) a cluster of judicial rulings that fail to protect sacred sites, and (3) the Supreme Court decision in the case of *Employment Division v. Smith* (1990).

\\\ NATIVE AMERICAN SPIRITUALITY

Indigenous religious practices are intimately tied to the land. This tie persists even when Native peoples are displaced from their lands, yet this immutable connection is often not fully understood by non-Natives (Hendry, 2003). Indeed, all land is sacred, but some places have particular meaning as dwellings of spirit beings, "places of inherent, profound holiness where higher powers have revealed themselves to humans" (Hendry, 2003, p. 5).

Indigenous understandings are quite different from Euro-American ways of thinking. In Western conceptual schemes, there is a dualistic framework that sets humans apart from nature. In turn, a higher value is placed on humans, often at the expense of nature. No such dualism exists in Native American traditions, thus the link between indigenous spirituality, nature, and land cannot be severed (Hendry, 2003). For example, there is a sacred bond between Hopi people and the land that sustains them. "For traditional Hopis corn is the central bond. Its essence, physically, spiritually, and symbolically, pervades their existence. For the people of the mesas corn is sustenance, ceremonial object, prayer offering, symbol, and sentient being" (Wall & Masayesva, 2004, p. 436). For other

Native Americans peyote, a hallucinogenic substance that comes from a cactus, holds spiritual significance. Although the Native American Church was not formally organized until 1918, the use of peyote goes back 10,000 years or more (Dayish as cited in Smith, 2006).

Indigenous ceremonies often must take place at specific sites of spiritual significance. For example, Mt. Shasta has been the site of the Wintu healing ceremony for more than 1,000 years. Hikers have found the sacred healing springs an appealing place to bathe naked. Traditional Wintu healer Florence Jones noted that if she went naked into a church she would be arrested for indecency, but her spiritual traditions receive no such reciprocity (McLeod, 1995). Today, even though this part of Mt. Shasta is protected as a historic district, it is still public land. This leaves it vulnerable to intrusion and degradation from those for whom it has no spiritual significance.

\\\ REGULATION OF SPIRITUALITY IN THE LAND OF THE FREE

Freedom of religion is a commonly cited doctrine in the United States, but this has never been a reality for indigenous people in this country (LaDuke, 2002). Early religious persecution was justified as part of conquest. Subsequently, it became a political act intended to force assimilation (Venables, 2004). John Collier, a former settlement house worker who would later lead the Bureau of Indian Affairs, summarized attacks on Native American religions and tied them to political goals: "The destruction of the native religions that yet lived was viewed by the Indian Bureau as a *political* necessity. The religions made the tribes strong, and made the individuals of the tribes immune to intimidation or corruption" (Collier as cited in Venebles, 2004, p. 289; emphasis in original). The constant losses in the fight for spiritual freedom reflect and solidify the fact that Native Americans have little political, economic, or social power with which to assert their own needs and right to existence.

To illustrate how policies have systematically regulated spirituality for Native Americans, three related areas will be reviewed. First, to give a historical perspective, the 1883 Indian Religious Crimes Code will be reviewed. This will be followed by a cluster of significant legal rulings related to sacred places. Finally, the Smith case, a Supreme Court ruling on the use of sacred objects, will be discussed.

⧄ THE 1883 INDIAN RELIGIONS CRIMES CODE

The suppression of indigenous spirituality has been consistent since 1492 but did not receive systematic codification until the 1883 Indian Religious Crimes Code. This Act explicitly prohibited many forms of indigenous spirituality such as the Sun Dance, a ceremony integral to the spirituality of the indigenous peoples of the Great Plains region.

Historically the United States has suppressed and persecuted Native American spiritual beliefs and practices out of the conviction that they hindered progress toward civilization. Native Americans were considered to be subhuman beings who should step aside in the face of Manifest Destiny, pagans to be civilized and assimilated, and wards to be protected. These societal attitudes shaped and continue to shape United States social policies for Native Americans.

Under the Indian Religious Crimes Code, participation in any traditional religious activity was punishable by imprisonment (Forbes-Boyte, 1999; O'Brien, 1991). Federal regulations required Indian males to cut their braids and outlawed the Sun Dance (O'Brien, 1991). "The proselytizing religions of the Old World have claimed religious superiority over the indigenous religions of the New World. The attitude was 'my religion is better than yours,' and this attitude led to the belief that native religions do not warrant human rights protection" (Echohawk as cited in Smith, 2006, p. 31). Although Native religious expression was outlawed, missionaries preaching Christianity were sent to reservations to convert and assimilate Native people. "For the United States, a leading democracy in the world, to completely ban the practice of tribal religion for generations is an unparalleled act. We have had very little legal protection for native religions in the United States" (Echohawk as cited in Smith, 2006, pp. 31–32).

Racial Regulation and This Law

As this law specifically criminalized Native American religious practices, it constitutes a clear form of racial regulation. Denying spiritual practices cuts at the heart of what it means to be indigenous. This law was designed to further the goals of assimilation and cultural genocide. Those who promulgated this law targeted it only to Native Americans. Therefore, it is a law based only on race and the cultural practices of a particular racial group.

Resistance to the Law

Indigenous peoples have resisted the suppression of their spirituality. In the 1880s when many ceremonies were banned, they continued to be practiced in secret. This type of surreptitious resistance led to the preservation of ancient ceremonies still practiced today.

Native Americans who persisted in practicing their spiritual traditions did so at great risk. In 1890, the U.S. military massacred 390 men, women, and children gathered for Ghost Dance ceremonies at Wounded Knee in present-day South Dakota. Congress subsequently awarded 30 medals of honor to those who conducted the massacre (LaDuke, 2005; O'Brien, 1991). Likewise, during this period hundreds of Native American spiritual leaders were sent to the Hiawatha Asylum for Insane Indians for their spiritual beliefs (LaDuke, 2005).

Resistance efforts led to crackdowns and assertions of federal power. In the early 1900s, Hopi families resisted sending their children to school since the schools enforced Christianity. The Hopi resistance was an attempt to retain their culture and spiritual practices. In 1906, in response to this resistance, U.S. military forces attacked Hopi men gathered for Buffalo Kachina Dance at Shungopavi on Second Mesa in Arizona. Some these men were later imprisoned or sent to Carlisle boarding school in Pennsylvania. All men sent to Carlisle were already married, thus forcing family disruption (Venables, 2004).

By the 1960s indigenous activism and meetings promoting intertribal solidarity became common (Treat, 2003). Some of the most visible examples of indigenous activism were the takeover of Alcatraz Island in 1969 and the armed standoff at Wounded Knee in 1973. These protests contained a spiritual foundation as well as political aspects. Indigenous spirituality centers people within the natural world along with land and all forms of life. Conflict will continue to exist between Native Americans and any group that does not care for the land in a respectful manner (Deloria, 1994).

\\\\ EVALUATING THE SUCCESS OF RESISTANCE EFFORTS

During the late 1800s and early 1900s, Native Americans had virtually no voice or influence in American society. Under these circumstances, it was difficult to mount activist efforts and activists efforts that did take place were of minimal effectiveness. In the face of the crushing power of the United States, secrecy was one of few options available to indigenous peoples.

Resistance efforts were successful at preserving some ceremonies but at a cost. Legal prohibitions forced spiritual traditions to go underground. Although some ceremonies were still practiced, the need to do so covertly resulted in the loss of substantial elements of indigenous cultures.

Restrictions against Native American religions continued until President Franklin D. Roosevelt appointed John Collier as Commissioner of Indian Affairs in 1932. During his tenure, Collier, who had studied Pueblo life and spirituality, ended official prohibitions against Native American religious practices (O'Brien, 1991).

When relief did come from the ban on indigenous spiritual practices, it resulted not primarily from a movement of resistance and advocacy but rather because of the efforts of one key person. As a person with some sensitivity toward Native American concerns (albeit it seen through his own lens and priorities) and some power in the Roosevelt administration, John Collier had both the will and the power to bring about change. Conversely, the legalization of indigenous ceremonies would have been meaningless had it not been for the secret resistance of indigenous spiritual leaders who were able to keep some cultural knowledge alive.

Subsequently, the renewed pride in Native American identity and the comparative safety of the 1960s led to resuming some ceremonies publicly. This spiritual renaissance went hand in hand with political resistance and a new pride in Native identity. Today traditional ceremonial life remains vibrant and is being passed to the next generation as a testament to the persistent and enduring attachment of Native Americans to their cultures and spiritual expressions (Tinker, 2004).

⋙ JUDICIAL RULINGS ON SACRED SITES

Today blanket prohibitions against indigenous ceremonies no longer threaten Native religions, but different threats persist. Judicial interpretations of laws that cover access to sacred sites have often left Native people without a substantive way to practice their spiritual belief systems, even though legally they are entitled to hold their traditional beliefs. This constricted interpretation is as much a threat to indigenous spiritualities as more blatant laws that prohibited ceremonies. Native American cultural survival depends on the survival of indigenous spirituality (Venebles, 2004).

Understanding the blatant conflict between the United States' stated value of freedom of religion and contemporary acts largely conducted under the auspices of the federal government is a challenging proposition. Put simply, religious freedom exists in the United States only when conceived of as a set of beliefs. In other words, Native people are allowed to maintain their belief systems. Native people are not, however, guaranteed the right to practice their beliefs. Protection of spiritual beliefs does not include setting aside sacred sites or land for religious purposes (Deloria, 1994).

Courts have considered Native claims to religious freedom in very limited terms. In its capacity as owner or manager of public lands, the federal government has routinely acted or permitted private actions that render indigenous sacred sites inaccessible and unusable. "In each case, however, a federal court held that such destructive government activity was not an improper burden on the Indians' freedom to exercise their religious beliefs within the guarantees of the First Amendment. This conclusion—that rendering the practice of religion impossible does not burden the free exercise of religion—seems plausible only if one distinguishes *free* exercise of religion from *full* exercise of religion" (Linge, 2000, p. 315).

In a landmark case, the Supreme Court ruled in *Lyng v. Northwest Indian Cemetery Association* (1988) that the American Indian Religious Freedom Act does not extend to protection of sacred sites on public lands. In this case, "Justice O'Connor raised the argument that any recognition of the 'sacredness of sites' would, in effect, allow Native Americans to define the use of public lands and, in many cases, require de facto beneficial ownership of some rather large parcels of public property. The precedent set by this landmark Supreme Court decision places Native Americans in a difficult and perplexing position. Sacred sites are central and essential to the practice of Native American religions and a particular ceremony cannot simply be moved to another site just as the salmon cannot be requested to give up their spirits at a different place in the river. As such, the American Indian Religious Freedom Act does little to protect the rights to practice native religions when it fails to protect the lands on which these religious practices must be performed" (Hendry, 2003, p. 7).

In the Lyng case, the Supreme Court did not dispute the sincerity of the Native people's religious claims nor the conclusion that the government's proposed action would have a severe, adverse, and perhaps even fatal, effect on Native Americans' ability to exercise their religion. In spite of this, the Supreme Court "held that destroying a sacred site essential to the exercise of religion does not burden the exercise of religion" (Linge, 2000, p. 331). Justice O'Connor for the majority argued that the crucial word was "prohibit"; thus because the government was not actually prohibiting or saying Native Americans could not practice their religion, the First Amendment did not apply. In their dissent in the Lyng case, Justices Marshall, Blackmun, and Brennan, "scoffed at the hypocrisy of a ruling which allows the Indians a 'freedom [that] amounts to nothing more than the right to believe that their religion will be destroyed,' and 'leaves native Americans with absolutely no constitutional protection against perhaps the gravest threat to their religious practices" (Linge, 2000, p. 307).

Public lands that contain both sacred sites and recreational opportunities have become places of significant controversy. At times, federal employees have attempted to support Native American religious freedom only to have their efforts thwarted. A notable example of this type of conflict centers around Devils Tower in Wyoming. This sacred site has become a major attraction for rock-climbing enthusiasts (Linge, 2000). The National Park Service has made sincere efforts to manage conflicting sacred and recreational interests. In 1995, the Park Service issued their "Final Climbing Management Plan," which placed some restrictions on rock climbing, including requesting that climbers voluntarily refrain from climbing in June because of ceremonies. Although technically a voluntary ban, the Park Service ensured compliance by not issuing climbing permits during this time. Other components of the plan such as provisions supporting raptor breeding or protecting areas of historical significance went unquestioned. The only component of the plan to garner controversy was the closure in June. This was challenged by a group of climbers and commercial guides on constitutional grounds. They argued that they had a right to climb on Devils Tower and that this right could not be interfered with in order to ensure the Native Americans' ability to exercise their religion freely. They concluded that the National Park Service policy of not issuing recreational climbing permits in June compromises the constitutional guarantee of freedom of religion (Linge, 2000). This resulted in an injunction and the Park Service reluctantly issuing commercial permits in the hopes that guides would comply with the voluntary restriction.

Another highly publicized site of contention is Mt. Graham in Arizona. Also known as Dzil Nchaa Sian, Mt. Graham is sacred to the Apache people. A consortium of astronomy organizations, including the University of Arizona and the Vatican, have built telescopes on this location and are completing another observatory. Ironically, the observatory is named after Christopher Columbus (Lopez as cited in Smith, 2006). The Vatican dismissed claims of sacredness of the mountain because they couldn't find physical evidence such as a church (Lopez as cited in Smith; Venables, 2004).

In 1998, an Apache man wanted to pray at Mt. Graham for his daughter's impending womanhood ceremony. He was arrested for trespassing (LaDuke, 2005). Today Native Americans seeking spiritual sustenance on Mt. Graham must seek a permit. "If you request a permit to pray, they will want to know the time and the duration of your visit to the summit. They will want to know where you are going. Then when you go, they follow you around with these Belgian police dogs. They will track you" (Lopez as cited in Smith, 2006, p. 158).

Racial Regulation and These Rulings

All the court rulings discussed above apply specifically to Native American sacred sites, thus restricting indigenous spirituality and adding an element of racial regulation to these court rulings. Although these judicial interpretations of laws do not specifically state that they apply only to Native Americans, the fact that it is Native Americans who hold these places sacred effectively renders restriction to these sites an act of racial regulation.

Resistance to These Rulings

As an act of resistance, as well as a cultural and spiritual necessity, many Native Americans continue to frequent sacred sites in spite of policies and regulations that restrict their access. Native Americans seeking to pray at Mt. Graham have faced harassment. In one example, a van of elders from the San Carlos senior center went there to pray. When they arrived at the gate and requested permission to enter. They were turned away but told to come back later. They returned to their camp where shortly they were surrounded by six police cars (Lopez as cited in Smith, 2006).

In 1967, traditional indigenous spiritual leaders and practitioners gathered at Bear Butte in South Dakota, thus generating a movement pushing for a law to support religious freedom. As time continued, meetings becoming more frequent and attendance grew. "Participants in these meetings were happy about achieving land returns, access agreements and protections for the use of feathers and other sacred objects. At the same time, each meeting was followed by the death of one participant. People joked about who the sacrifice person would be, but adhered ever more closely to traditional admonitions to greet and leave others as if it were the last chance to do so. Those meetings and that phenomenon would continue through the enactment of the repatriation and the peyote laws" (Harjo, 2003, p. 1).

Activism flourished in this era of self-determination and civil rights. In the mid-1970s indigenous spiritual leaders gathered in New Mexico to testify against the federal government's infringement on Native religions. Their complaints included prosecution for use of peyote and eagle feathers, preventing access to sacred lands, and dispossession of or destruction of sacred objects (O'Brien, 1991). The ultimate result of Native American and Hawaiian lobbying efforts for a bill to protect religious freedom was the American Indian Religious Freedom Act of 1978 (AIRFA).

AIRFA was originally comprehensive, recognized the inherent right of American citizens to religious freedom, and acknowledged that in the past the federal government had not protected the religious freedom of Native Americans. AIRFA articulated that religion was an indispensible, irreplaceable part of American life. The law charged government agencies with protecting and preserving Native Americans' inherent right of freedom to believe, express, and exercise their traditional religious practices, including access to sacred sites, the use of natural resources normally protected by conservation laws, and participation in traditional Indian ceremonies (AIRFA, 2008).

Although federal officials in the Nixon and Ford administrations opposed legislation protecting indigenous religious freedom, Jimmy Carter pledged his support for such legislation as a campaign promise to Native American leaders the week before his election as President. The measure moved quickly through legislative channels until it reached the floor of the House of Representatives, where lobbyists for the Forest Service succeeded in neutering AIRFA's ability to protect sacred sites (Harjo, 2003).

Today many activists have turned their attention to the issues of sacred sites. Current "Calls to Action" to protect sacred sites abound, particularly in the wake of the 2007 United Nations Declaration on the Rights of Indigenous Peoples. Article 12 of the Declaration states that

> 1. Indigenous peoples have the right to manifest, practise, develop and teach their spiritual and religious traditions, customs and

ceremonies; the right to maintain, protect, and have access in privacy to their religious and cultural sites; the right to the use and control of their ceremonial objects; and the right to the repatriation of their human remains. 2. States shall seek to enable the access and/or repatriation of ceremonial objects and human remains in their possession through fair, transparent and effective mechanisms developed in conjunction with indigenous peoples concerned. (United Nations, 2007)

In spring 2009, the Navajo Nation passed a resolution calling on newly elected U.S. President Barack Obama to protect sacred sites. It is likely that the protection of sacred sites will be an issue of concern and a focus point for advocacy and resistance efforts in years to come.

Evaluating the Success of Resistance Efforts

In spite of concerted efforts, little progress has been made on protecting scared sites. Although AIRFA was passed at a time of great concern over the wrongs done to indigenous peoples in the United States, the broad construction of the Act left it with "no teeth" as evidenced by subsequent court cases. Indeed AIRFA did nothing to prevent the building of a road through a forested land used for vision quests, disruptive tourist boats at Navajo sacred sites in Utah, construction of ski resorts on sacred Hopi sites in Arizona, or an astronomical observatory being built on an Apache sacred site in Arizona (AIRFA, 2008). A 1988 conference held to reflect on the impact of AIRFA 10 years after its passage determined that AIRFA contributed little to promoting or protecting religious freedom for Native peoples (Vecsey, 1991).

Later reflections still lamented AIRFA's limitations but also acknowledged progress in some types of religious protections. Twenty-five years after its passage, AIRFA had made a difference in some areas (Harjo, 2003). Repatriation is an important success emanating from AIRFA (Echohawk as cited in Smith, 2006). Ultimately, AIRFA laid the groundwork for the return of human remains and sacred objects housed in federal museums. These principles were codified in the repatriation laws of 1989 and 1990. Additionally, the 1993 amendment to AIRFA recognized ceremonial use of peyote, thus addressing a significant concern. Some sacred sites are now protected through comanagement agreements, but many others have been damaged or destroyed (Harjo, 2003).

Legal institutions and the U.S. laws that they interpret are grounded in Western ways of thinking. Legal concepts such as rights, property, and what is considered to be religion are anchored in Euro-American cultural expressions. Given the vast cultural gap between indigenous understandings and Western legal concepts, it comes as no surprise that Native American cases rarely win in court. "They have to make their cultures understandable to people from another culture, in a language that does not equate religion with spatiality. In short, the courts embrace Euro-American perceptions; to succeed in courts, American Indians must place their cultures in that framework, thereby isolating Indian beliefs from their cultural contexts" (Forbes-Boyte, 1999, p. 313).

Native American plaintiffs citing AIRFA protections for sacred sites have lost every suit that they have brought to court (Forbes-Boyte, 1999). In these cases, the court has failed to understand the significance of connections to place and their centrality in Native American spiritual traditions. Locales of particular spiritual significance must be available for ceremonies. The connection between spirituality and land is so strong that without these specific places, Native American religions will die (Forbes-Boyte, 1999).

President Bill Clinton's Executive Order 13007 (1996) attempted to protect Native religious practices on public lands by ordering federal agencies such as the Bureau of Land Management, the U.S. Forest Service, and the National Park Service to consult Native peoples on the management of sacred sites (AIRFA, 2008). Consultation with Native peoples is not likely to be a meaningful step toward protection of sacred sites when their input is routinely ignored or dismissed in the face of powerful special interest groups.

Resistance efforts have met with mixed success. On the one hand, they have led to the passage of key legislation such as AIRFA designed to enhance protection for indigenous spirituality and spiritual practices. On the other hand, such protections go against the current tide of political thought and primarily receive support in the abstract but not when spiritual practices conflict with other values such as recreational practices and federal control over lands in the public domain. Mixed success aside, indigenous activist groups such as Advocates for the Protection of Sacred Sites, Save the Peaks Coalition, Indigenous Environmental Network, International Indian Treaty Council, Seventh Generation Fund, Vallejo Inter-Tribal Council, and the Morning Star Institute continue to actively lobby the Senate Indian Affairs Committee to hold hearings and initiate legislation to protect sacred sites and spiritual practices. Regular updates on these efforts can be obtained through the First Peoples Human Rights Coalition at info@firstpeoplesrights.org.

Traditional and tribal leaders have made ongoing efforts to introduce appropriate federal legislation to protect sacred sites and practices, but political wrangling has made these efforts ineffectual and has led to compromises that exclude sacred sites of nonfederally recognized tribes and Native Hawaiians. Some of these efforts have also disenfranchised traditional spiritual leaders in favor of the oftentimes secular tribal governments (Harjo, 2003).

> The underlying problem is that the courts have pretty much abandoned their role as protectors of religion in the United States and relegated it to the political process, which makes it very difficult for Native American people. As minority groups, we are disadvantaged in the political process. If you are unpopular, it is hard to succeed in the cauldron of Washington's power politics. It's a very scary situation. (Echohawk as cited in Smith, 2006, p. 33)

◊ *EMPLOYMENT DIVISION V. SMITH* (1990)

The Smith case centered around a Klamath man who was a member of the Native American Church. One weekend he attended ceremonies where he ingested sacramental peyote. The following week at work he was subjected to drug testing, tested positive for a controlled substance, and was fired from his job. He contended that use of peyote was an integral part of his spiritual traditions. As a Native American he asserted his right to his spiritual practices.

The Supreme Court of the United States in the case of *Employment Division v. Smith* (1990) found that the First Amendment does not protect Native Americans who use peyote in religious ceremonies. This case received extensive attention and notoriety.

Racial Regulation and This Ruling

Federal laws systematically regulate items of spiritual significance to Native Americans such as eagle feathers and peyote. Peyote is a sacrament used in Native American Church ceremonies. Given that this sacrament is used specifically by Native Americans within the context of the Native American Church, federal prohibitions against peyote infringe on the spirituality of Native Americans and these laws constitute racial regulation. Non-Natives are not prohibited from using wine as a sacrament within the context of their church services, in spite of the fact that alcohol is a substance subject to legal regulation. Prohibiting a comparable recognition of peyote as a sacrament is tantamount to racial regulation.

Resistance to This Ruling

The *Smith* decision brought swift reactions from many parties seeking to bring about change. There were three different significant efforts aimed at decriminalizing the use of peyote in ceremonial contexts: one by Congress, another by a coalition with Native American leadership, and another by an interfaith alliance.

In 1993, Congress passed the Religious Freedom Restoration Act as a response to the unpopular Smith peyote decision. This legislation, however, was challenged and the Supreme Court struck down the Act in 1997 saying Congress has no authority to engage in judicial review (AIRFA, 2008). Subsequent advocacy led to a more successful result, and, in 1994, AIRFA was amended to provide for the traditional use of peyote by Native Americans for religious and other purposes (Public Law 103–344).

A resistance movement quickly developed in the wake of the Smith peyote decision. The Native American Religious Freedom Project, the Native American Church of North America, Native American Rights Fund, and the Association on American Indian Affairs worked in coalition to counteract this judgment. This activism and in particular the efforts of Reuben Snake, a Winnebago chief and peyote Road Man, led to the AIRFA amendments (Dayish as cited in Smith, 2006).

> Reuben was the person who put together the coalition and started the movement after the *Smith* decision came down. From that point many organizations started to come together to educate us on how to address Congress, how to address congressional members, and how to address congressional aides, so they could understand the issue we were confronting. . . . Several documentary films [were developed] to educate not only legislators and the American public but also

members of our church and the religious freedom coalition. . . . We met with experts such as non-Indian professors of law and of religion. . . . We had assistance from the National Council of Churches, The National Conference of American Rabbis, and many other religious and human rights organizations. (p. 106)

In part, resistance to the *Smith* decision took the form of an interfaith alliance. Many people from a broad range of spiritual traditions felt threatened and compelled to act when Native American religious freedom was challenged in the Smith case. The coalition that emerged included Jews, Quakers, Amish, and other Christian denominations. These spiritual traditions were right to feel that the Smith precedent had implications for their own faiths. Indeed, the Smith case was used as precedent in prosecuting Catholic priests and Jewish rabbis (Dayish as cited in Smith, 2006).

Evaluating the Success of Resistance Efforts

Although access to and use of some sacred items is still contentious, there has been notable improvement in this area in recent years. Probably the most successful resistance to policies suppressing indigenous spirituality can be found in the response to the Supreme Court decision in the *Smith* case. Negative reactions to the Smith peyote decision came from a variety of people. "It created a human rights crisis. It led to unrest, to fear of prosecution, for native people across the land. But this time we didn't take the decision lying down. The case prompted a native civil rights movement that began on the reservations and in Indian country and ultimately found its way all the way back to Washington, D.C." (Echohawk as cited in Smith, 2006, p. 32).

The largest interfaith coalition ever to come together in the United States asked the Supreme Court to reconsider its decision. When the Court refused, they took the issue directly to Congress, leading to the 1993 passage of the Religious Freedom Restoration Act (Dayish as cited in Smith, 2006). Ironically, the Native American Church was not allowed to join this religious coalition because they were deemed too controversial and the coalition too fragile. Ultimately, the law that was passed with the influence of interfaith coalition was struck down. As an alternative strategy, the Native American Church worked for an amendment to AIRFA, which not only passed but has survived legal scrutiny.

\\\\ IMPLICATIONS OF RESISTANCE ACTIVITIES FOR CONTEMPORARY SOCIAL WORK PRACTICE

An examination of Native American resistance to regulation of traditional spiritual practices provides prime illustrations of grassroots movements; both in terms of struggles and effectiveness. Although social workers have largely been outside these movements, the social work value of social justice, skills in advocacy, and knowledge of movements for social change make for a natural fit in the struggle for indigenous spiritual freedom.

Social workers can learn a lesson from the exclusion of the Native American Church from the interfaith coalition fighting to overturn the Smith peyote decision. Native American leaders and activists must be at the front of these struggles. Well-meaning outsiders cannot lead the charge. Social workers can play a meaningful role working in coalition with (rather than on behalf of) indigenous peoples.

Persistent indigenous struggles for spiritual freedom are a vibrant example of the social work values of empowerment and self-determination. In spite of more than 500 years of colonization and oppression, Native people continue to resist legal decisions that deny religious freedom. This is a clear illustration of the strengths perspective so often touted by social workers.

Social workers can learn from the success stories in protecting religious freedom; in particular the repatriation of sacred items and recognition of peyote as an integral part of some indigenous spiritual practices. We can also assess the environmental context and understand how American values and worldviews have contributed significantly toward failures in struggles for religious freedom. This assessment can lead to development of alternate strategies for pursuing the cause of indigenous religious freedom.

Ultimately, an examination of the pursuit of religious freedom for Native Americans informs our understanding of the implications of diverse worldviews. Indigenous and Western spiritual perspectives are fraught with inherent and fundamental differences. In a society where power is vested primarily in Western understandings and institutions, indigenous understandings have little support. If social workers can develop an understanding of these fundamentally different perspectives, it can serve to enhance their cross-cultural work at any level of practice, including clinical interactions.

⟩⟩⟩ IMPLICATIONS FOR FUTURE RESEARCH

Few social workers have a real, in-depth understanding of the multidimensional aspects of indigenous struggles for religious freedom. One of the best ways to increase our knowledge in this area is through first-person accounts. Interviews with indigenous activists and nonindigenous allies who have participated in these struggles are prime sources of information that have informed this chapter. See, for example, *A Seat at the Table* by Huston Smith (2006), a collection of interviews conducted with indigenous spiritual leaders gathered for the 1999 Parliament of World Religions in South Africa. Another example is *Around the Sacred Fire* by James Treat (2003) a book that reflects the history of Native religious activism as documented through the Indian Ecumenical Conference. Although not necessarily framed as *research*, this type of qualitative inquiry illuminates these complex issues. Likewise, when key individuals come together to reflect on the accomplishments (or failures) of policies such as AIRFA, it provides information similar to that gathered in focus groups as is evident in the conference to commemorate and examine the impact of AIRFA after 10 years (Vecsey, 1991).

These lines of inquiry provide a type of research that listens. Through this type of effort, social workers can enhance our understanding of the contemporary concerns of indigenous people, including current battles for religious freedom. Only after we have developed this fuller understanding can we begin to determine the most respectful and effective ways of helping.

⟩⟩⟩ CONCLUSION

Native American struggles for religious freedom have existed for hundreds of years and will continue into the foreseeable future. Often these struggles will take place far from public view as Native Americans perpetuate their ceremonies and spiritual practices away from public attention. Often these struggles will continue without public support. When Americans do see Native Americans trying to continue their spiritual practices, these are typically misunderstood and trivialized, viewed as in conflict with recreational practices and other land uses prioritized by mainstream Americans and governmental institutions.

As one Native American spiritual leader stated,

> I think that the survival of native people, and of their religions, is at stake in the United States. The only way that native worship is made possible is through a patchwork maze of administrative rules and regulations and some litigation, which has resulted in the government being involved in comprehensive regulation of native religious practices. For example, the government has limited our access to our own sacred sites and to our eagle feathers, has narrowed our ability to worship in prisons, and has regulated peyote, which is used in the Native American Church. Our important native religious practices are comprehensive and are often intrusively regulated by the United States. And this is the only way in which the United States has found to allow the worship of its own native people. (Echohawk as cited in Smith, 2006, p. 35)

The fundamentally different perceptions of religion held by traditional Native Americans and others in this country are a gulf that is hard to bridge. The lack of cultural understanding, coupled with the extreme power imbalance that exists between indigenous peoples and the dominant society is likely to perpetuate oppression of Native Americans and traditional spiritual practices.

Raising awareness of indigenous spiritual practices and how they have been systematically repressed is a step in moving toward positive change. Indeed, the activism of non-Native people as allies in the fight against indigenous spiritual repression is an essential ingredient in achieving true social change. Without a significant change in awareness and behaviors of the dominant society, resistance to indigenous spiritual oppression must remain surreptitious and largely extra-legal. As in the past, unjust laws and policies will be defied until such time as they can be changed.

⧉ REFERENCES

American Indian Religious Freedom Act. (n.d.). *U.S. history encyclopedia.* Retrieved May 28, 2008, from http:www.answers.com/topic/American-indian-religious-freedom-act

Deloria, V., Jr. (1994). *God is red: A native view of religion, the classic work updated.* Golden, CO: Fulcrum Publishing.

Forbes-Boyte, K. (1999). Fools Crow versus Gullett: A critical analysis of the American Indian Religious Freedom Act. *Antipode, 31*(3), 304–323.

Harjo, S. S. (2003, August 1). American Indian Religious Freedom Act at 25. *Indian Country Today*, p. 1.

Hendry, J. (2003). Mining the sacred mountain: The clash between the Western dualistic framework and Native American religions. *Multicultural Perspectives, 5*(1), 3–10.

LaDuke, W. (2002). The Salt Woman and the coal mine. *Sierra, 87*(6), 44–47, 73.

LaDuke, W. (2005). *Recovering the sacred: The power of naming and claiming.* Cambridge, MA: South End Press.

Linge, G. (2000). Ensuring the full freedom of religion on public lands: Devils Tower and the protection of Indian sacred sites. *Boston College Environmental Law Review, 27*(2), 307–339.

McLeod, C. (1995). Mount Shasta—A thousand years of ceremony. *Earth Island Journal, 10*(1), 8–9.

O'Brien, S. (1991). A legal analysis of the American Indian Religious Freedom Act. In C. Vecsey (Ed.), *Handbook of American Indian religious freedom* (pp. 27–43). New York: Crossroad.

Public Law 95–341 (1978). The American Indian Religious Freedom Act.

Public Law 103–344 (1994). American Indian Religious Freedom Act Amendments of 1994. Retrieved from http://www.lectlaw.com/files/drg25.htm

Smith, H. (2006). *A seat at the table.* Berkeley, CA: University of California Press.

Tinker, G. E. (2004). *Spirit and resistance: Political theology and American Indian liberation.* Minneapolis, MN: Fortress Press.

Treat, J. (2003). *Around the sacred fire: Native religious activism in the Red Power era.* New York: Palgrave Macmillan.

United Nations. (2007). *Declaration on the rights of indigenous peoples.* Retrieved from http://issuu.com/karinzylsaw/docs/un_declaration_rights_indigenous_peoples?mode=embed&layout=http%3A%2F%2Fskin.issuu.com%2Fv%2Fdark%2Flayout.xml&showFlipBtn=true

Vecsey, C. (1991). Prologue. In C. Vecsey (Ed.), *Handbook of American Indian religious freedom* (pp. 7–25). New York: Crossroad.

Venables, R. W. (2004). *American Indian history: Five centuries of conflict and coexistence.* Santa Fe, NM: Clear Light Publishing.

Wall, D., & Masayesva, V. (2004). People of the corn: Teachings in Hopi traditional agriculture, spirituality, and sustainability. *American Indian Quarterly, 28*(3/4), 435–453.

Conclusion

Jerome H. Schiele

Each chapter in this book has examined how social welfare policies have regulated the lives of people of color and how people of color have resisted the unjust and oppressive features of the policies. A common theme that cuts across each chapter is the continuity of social welfare policy injustice for people of color. Despite the group of color, social welfare policies in the United States both historically and contemporarily place people of color at risk of experiencing hardships disproportionately. These hardships manifest in sundry ways and engender similar consequences of political, economic, social, health, and cultural disempowerment. These policies unfortunately appear to have a racial component in their design and implementation by continuing to promote the diverse yet distinct interests of Americans of European descent. Whether the policies represented overt or concealed racism or a combination of both, their consequences produced significant racial inequalities between the material and symbolic lives of people of European descent and people of color. The policies essentially have presented obstacles to people of color's freedom and expression of positive potential.

However, these chapters also demonstrated an optimistic picture of how people of color resisted the oppressive consequences of these racially unjust policies. Throughout the book, it was shown that when faced with the adversities associated with specific social welfare policies and practices, people of color applied strength-based behaviors to sponsor micro- and macro-level protest activities or they established and supported alternative organizations that would provide services to offset the policies' deleterious consequences. Rather than accepting and accommodating to the injustice of these policies, these chapters demonstrated how people of color used their community resources, resiliencies, and strengths to sponsor resistance activities. At the heart of this resistance was the belief that all Americans have the inherent right of equality and fairness and the refutation of the grand narrative that casted people of color as morally and intellectually inferior.

⑉ TWO SCENARIOS

This book focused on the regulatory consequences of past and current social welfare policies, but a critical question for the future is how might social welfare policies continue to regulate the behavior and values of people of color? What are some factors that may influence future regulatory policy behavior and how might people of color respond? I offer two scenarios. First, one of the consistent observations among many contemporary scholars and commentators who study racial oppression is that this form of oppression has mutated and appears to manifest in more complex and diffused ways (Bonilla-Silva, 2003; Schiele, 2002). Although there continue to be overt expressions of racial oppression, new style racial oppression, as discussed in the introduction, relies more on subtle and insidious mechanisms of subjugation. These mechanisms increasingly imply that racism has either been eliminated or substantively diminished to the point that some today, especially after the election of President Barack Obama, argue that the United States has entered a postracism era.

A major component of this new form of racial oppression is to get people of color to increasingly believe that America is race-neutral in its political and economic institutions. The breaking down of the overt impediments to the freedom of people of color and offering more opportunities for them to participate in the main fabric of American society may place many people of color at risk of denying the continuation of racial injustice. The elimination of overt legal impediments to people of color freedom, beginning in the 1960s, has challenged the need for and emphasis on the value of in-group collectivity. With newfound freedoms and opportunities, the value of individualism was much more appealing, and, perhaps even appropriate, for people of color. This is because although relics of the racial caste system remained, the new civil rights laws of the 1960s gave individuals of color greater opportunities to demonstrate their personal skills and talents, which were increasingly, though not equally, being recognized and rewarded in newly integrated, workplace environments. Because these rewards were often provided by representatives of the racial power structure who had once barred people of color from entry into meaningful workplace participation, several people of color began to believe that with hard work and perseverance, progress was possible in white America (see, e.g., Connerly, 2000; McWhorter, 2003).

The personal opportunities afforded by the 1960s civil rights thrust coupled with the diminishing need for in-group collectivity has placed people of color in jeopardy of abandoning their collective critical consciousness. Gil (1998) conceives critical consciousness as awareness and reflection that challenges existing social patterns and ideas, especially those that create and sustain oppression. If people of color increasing abandon their critical consciousness, questions about the racial regulatory features of social welfare policies may be reduced. In this sense, the kind of critical lens needed to query about a policy's potential to foster racial regulation may be more difficult to obtain. Racial oppression's ability to continue through social welfare policies may gradually go undetected if greater numbers of people of color are seduced into affirming the narrative of American race-neutrality. Any racial characteristics or consequences of social welfare policies that appear to disadvantage people of color may be interpreted as unintentional and serendipitous. Moreover, these policies may be justified by people of color if the values of self-reliance and individualism increasingly define their worldview. Together, these trends would reduce the resistance efforts of people of color and solidify the achievements of the new era of racial oppression by incorporation.

A second scenario might depict the return to racial oppression by terror, that is, more overt and explicit forms of racism. In this scenario, domination by terror will be ushered in primarily by the dwindling birth and reproductive rates of white or European Americans. Low birth rates among European Americans and Europeans globally are currently reducing their population, and projections indicate that this trend will continue (Buchanan, 2002; U.S. Census Bureau, 2009). Simultaneously, the population of people of color has significantly increased. For example, in 2006, the U.S. Census Bureau (2007) reported that the people of color population exceeded 100 million and represented about a third of the overall U.S. population. This percentage represents an extraordinary increase since the early 1980s, when people of color only represented about 17 percent of the total U.S. population (U.S. Census Bureau, 1981).

A primary implication of the rising population of people of color is their increased social visibility. Increased social visibility of minority groups has been shown to create concerns and fears from majority group members (Bonilla-Silva, 2003; Hacker, 1992). This consternation is grounded in the belief that the increased population of people of color poses a threat to the maintenance of the cultural, political, and economic hegemony of European Americans. This demographic shift and its association with perceptions of dwindling European American power may bring about more drastic social welfare policy measures to protect and defend white hegemony.

Indeed, more drastic measures appear to occur in locations where people of color are now the majority or where their population has dramatically increased. For example, the new immigration law in Arizona may reflect this kind of consternation over the growing people of color populations, especially Latinos and Latinas. The law makes it legal for police officers in the state to stop and detain persons they believe may be in the state illegally. It also would make failure to carry immigration papers a crime (Archibold, 2010). Lisa Magaña's chapter discusses the antecedents to this law, and she suggests that the precipitous growth of the Mexican population is a primary motive. Moreover, throughout American history, some of the harshest policies against people of color have occurred in locations or regions where people of color have represented a large segment of the population, such as African Americans in the South. In the past, some of the most cruel segregation laws were in southern counties where African Americans either were in the majority or represented a large component. This situation in Georgia sparked segregationist Richard Russell Jr. to offer a proposal to disperse the African American population more evenly throughout the nation so that African Americans would not be concentrated in the south (Fite, 1991). In addition, the large numbers of African and Hispanic Americans in the central cities of the United States has prompted intense arrest and hyperincarceration rates of these persons and has prompted Alexander (2010) to conclude that this represents a new era of Jim Crow. If demographic projections suggesting that people of color will be the majority in the United States by mid-century are correct (see U.S. Census Bureau, 2009), more drastic and desperate social welfare policies that seek to sustain Eurocentric hegemony might become more apparent.

If social welfare policies become more overtly racist and terroristic, people of color may respond with more intense, and perhaps even violent, resistance activities. The frustration aggression school of psychology maintains that overt forms of injustice can lead to intense frustration that then can produce aggressive actions against self and others (Muller & Weede, 1994). Thus, more overtly racist forms of social welfare policy regulation might lead to greater feelings of alienation, despair, and frustration that spark resistance that is direct and confrontational.

⦚ PEOPLE OF COLOR AND POLICY PRACTITIONER ROLES

Whatever scenario occurs, social welfare policies will continue to play a major role in the lives of people of color, who continue to be disproportionately poor and politically vulnerable. Therefore, it is critical for social work policy practitioners to foster and facilitate resistance activities against policies that are unjust and oppressive. There are primarily three roles that social workers can assume in this effort: (1) community organizers, (2) policy formulators and analysts, and (3) cultural mediators. Community organizers are those who assist a community in identifying common experiences, problems, and solutions (Checkoway, 1997). They essentially assist a community in their positive growth or what is referred to as community development. Rubin and Rubin (1992) conceive community development as a process that involves indigenous efforts by people to "form their own organizations to provide a long-term capacity for problem-solving" (p. 3), while Biddle and Biddle (1965) view community development as a process through which people can come together to grapple with and "gain some control over . . . a frustrating and changing world" (p. 78). People of color often experience the brunt of the frustrations of a changing world, and social work community organizers can help communities of color to address these frustrations from within and without a community. These organizers work to advocate for the needs and goals of the community and to help solve everyday social problems that cripple a community's potential and power.

Social welfare policy formulation and analysis is a second role social work policy practitioners can use to help communities of color challenge and resist unjust policies. Policy formulation and analysis can be viewed as preventive mechanisms if they seek to undue existing oppressive policies and generate new, more egalitarian ones. Social welfare policy formulation involves the various activities used to convert ideas to remedy a social problem into formal rules and regulations. This can be done at the organizational, local, state, national, or international levels of sociopolitical relationships. Social work policy practitioners who engage in policy formulation serve in several roles, including lobbyists, elected officials, appointed officials, administrators, and community organizers. Policy formulators are skillful in the art of persuasion, political leveraging, and interpersonal relations. They use these skills to build support and coalitions for an idea that can benefit their constituencies and that can hopefully reduce or eliminate a social problem. They fundamentally engage in the process of transforming ideas into practical ways of implementation.

Social welfare policy analysis involves the application of oral and written communications to investigate and examine a policy's antecedents, philosophical assumptions, provisions, and intended and unintended consequences. This role requires the use of data collection procedures, scientific methods, and other information sources to create a conceptual and empirical narrative about the policy and its impact on communities. Questions about a policy's veracity, effectiveness, costs, and benefits are often used to guide the analyst's inquiry and information gathering process. Policy analysts are also advocates, too. Indeed, although their analysis may not be as personal and direct as others, social welfare policy analysts play a significant role in the policy formulation process. The proliferation of conservative think tanks in the 1970s and 1980s, for example, was critical in generating ideas that would undergird the social policy agenda of the Reagan–Bush Sr. years and the sweeping 1994 takeover of the House of Representatives by the Republicans (Stefancic & Delgado, 1996). Thus, the ideas and analysis of policy analysts are often used to advance political paradigms and agendas that undergird the product of social welfare policy. Social work policy practitioners who serve as policy analysts should employ their oral and written communication skills to advocate for the sociopolitical viewpoints and worldviews of people of color.

Finally, social work policy practitioners can also serve as cultural mediators. Cultural mediators are interpreters of divergent values and worldviews found in a society or that occur across societies (Al-Krenawi & Graham, 2001). For people of color in the United States, cultural mediators convey and explain the experiences, values, and interpretations of people of color to the larger society. As has been demonstrated and discussed in this book, the experiences, values, and interpretations of people of color often are marginalized and misunderstood. The marginalization process involves efforts to disregard and delegitimize the worldviews of people of color whereas the process of misunderstanding reflects sincere efforts to know their worldviews but an unwillingness to abandon hegemonic interpretive frameworks. In an increasingly diversified society, there will be an immense need to communicate and interpret the values and experiences of others. Cultural issues and differences are important from a social welfare policy standpoint because values, experiences, and interpretations play a major role in shaping social welfare policies (Day, 2006; Popple & Leighninger, 2008). Social welfare policies are fundamentally cultural products that reflect a group's values and priorities.

Social work policy practitioners who assume the cultural mediation role need to be extremely familiar with the historic and contemporary lives of people of color. They are required to obtain information about a group's culture through extensive reading and studying, through frequent and substantive personal experience, or both. The bottom line is that cultural mediators use their knowledge and experience to both explain and advance the unique, yet diverse, interpretative frameworks of a specific group. In this regard, cultural mediators can focus on explaining and interpreting the diversity within a group or the diversity between and among groups. Whichever method they select, cultural mediators have the critical task of suspending or subordinating their own cultural framework to understand and appropriately communicate the worldviews of others, unless they happen to be members of the group in question.

🕮 FINAL THOUGHTS

The themes and activities of social welfare policy regulation and resistance will be around for some time, and their applicability to people of color will become more pronounced in the future. How these themes manifest themselves will depend on the form of oppression dominant in the future. Whether this form is terroristic or seductive, there will be a need for social work policy practitioners who value the resistance activities of people of color and who care deeply about creating new realities that affirm the humanity of all. The efforts of these practitioners in collaboration with those of indigenous community leaders hopefully will help repair the dehumanizing consequences of America's appalling past.

☒ REFERENCES

Alexander, M. (2010). *The new Jim Crow: Mass incarceration in the age of colorblindness.* New York: The New Press.

Al-Krenawi, A., & Graham, J. R. (2001). The cultural mediator: Bridging the gap between a non-western community and professional social work practice. *British Journal of Social Work, 31,* 665–685.

Archibold, R. C. (2010, April 23). Arizona enacts stringent law on immigration. *The New York Times.* Retrieved July 5, 2010, from http://www.nytimes.com/2010/04/24/us/politics/24immig.html

Biddle, W. W., & Biddle, L. J. (1965). *The community development process: The rediscovery of local initiative.* New York: Holt, Rinehart, & Winston.

Bonilla-Silva, E. (2003). *Racism without racists: Color-blind racism and the persistence of racial inequality in the United States.* Lanham, MD: Rowman and Littlefield.

Buchanan, P. J. (2002). *The death of the west: How dying populations and immigrant invasions imperil our country and civilization.* New York: St. Martin's Press.

Checkoway, B. (1997). Core concepts for community change. *Journal of Community Practice, 4*(1), 11–29.

Connerly, W. (2000). *Creating equal: My fight against race preferences.* San Francisco: Encounter Books.

Day, P. J. (2006). *A new history of social welfare* (5th ed.). Boston: Allyn & Bacon.

Fite, G. C. (1991). *Richard B. Russell, Jr., senator from Georgia.* Chapel Hill: University of North Carolina Press.

Gil, D. G. (1998). *Confronting injustice and oppression: Concepts and strategies for social workers.* New York: Columbia University Press.

Hacker, A. (1992). *Two nations: Black and white, separate, hostile, unequal.* New York: Charles Scribner's Sons.

McWhorter, J. (2003). *Authentically black: Essays for the black silent majority.* New York: Gotham Books.

Muller, E. N., & Weede, E. (1994). Theories of rebellion: Relative deprivation and power contention. *Rationality and Society, 6,* 40–57.

Popple, P. R., & Leighninger, L. (2008). *The policy-based profession: An introduction to social welfare policy analysis for social workers.* Boston: Allyn & Bacon.

Rubin, H. J., & Rubin, I. S. (1992). *Community organizing and development* (2nd ed.). New York: Macmillan.

Schiele, J. H. (2002). Mutations of Eurocentric domination and their implications for African American resistance. *Journal of Black Studies, 32*(4), 439–463.

Stefancic, J., & Delgado, R. (1996). *No mercy: How conservative think tanks and foundations changed America's social agenda.* Philadelphia: Temple University Press.

U.S. Census Bureau. (1981). *Statistical abstract of the United States: 1981.* Washington, DC: Author.

U.S. Census Bureau. (2007). *Population estimates of the United States: 2006.* Washington, DC: Author.

U.S. Census Bureau. (2009). *Population projections of the United States: 2008.* Washington, DC: Author.

Index

Abramovitz, M., 2
Acevedo, Gregory, 18, 215–234
Action for Mental Health, 65
Adams, D. W., 306
Adoption and Safe Families Act
    (ASFA), 31
Adoption Assistance and Child
    Welfare Act of 1980, 31
Adult and Safe Families
    Act of 1996, 245–246
Advocates for the Protection of Sacred
    Sites, 340
African Americans, 16
  child welfare policies and, 31–32,
    38–39
  children, racial regulation of, 25–39
  children in child welfare system,
    29–30
  children in foster care, 16, 25–39
  children in out-of-home care,
    25–26, 29, 37
  club women's resistance to
    oppressive public policy, 43–60
  conflict with other minorities,
    116, 124, 170
  criminality, regulating, 98–99
  discriminatory laws enacted against,
    6–7, 26, 222
  deinstitutionalization, 68, 84
  education, 50, 53–55, 101–102
  employment, discrimination
    in, 32–33
  families, augmented, 95–96
  families, challenges to, 30–35
  families, preserving, 37–39
  female-headed households, 32–34
  HIV/AIDS and, 29–30, 38
  indolence and, 96–98
  involuntary psychiatric
    commitment of, 16–17, 63–87
  kinship care, 16, 25–39
  mutual aid organizations, 15–16
  passive resistance, 26–27
  poverty and, 29–30, 91–92, 68
  prison and, 34–35
  racial regulation, 16–17, 91–107
  regulating cultural values and
    norms of, 94–99
  religious congregations, 15
  resistance strategies, 25–39
  resistance strategies,
    history of, 27–29
  sexual licentiousness, regulating,
    98–99
  slavery, 15, 92–93
  stereotypes, 16, 30, 46–47,
    72, 96–99
  substance abuse, 29–32
  violence against, 45–49
  voting, 52–53
African American women's club
    movement, 16, 48–49
  group survival, 51–52
  institutional transformation,
    51–52
  resistance to oppressive public
    policy, 43–60
  voting rights and, 52–53

357

immigration policy in
regards to, 225–227
kinship care, 246
labor unions, 234
Legal Defense and Education Fund
(MALDEF), 229, 231, 234
resistance activities, 228
soccer clubs, 234
state and local policies of
resistance, 248
undocumented, 234, 238–240, 243
U.S. neocolonial policy in, 5–6,
220–221
Middleman minority theory,
117–120, 130
Mikulski, Barbara, 59
Minami, Dale, 156
Mineta, Norman, 156
Ming, Lin Yan, 196–198
Minuteman Project, 256
Mitchell, Lee Arthur, 116–117
Model minority, 166, 169
Morning Star Institute, 340
Morris, A. D., 7
Moss, Tom, 46
Mt. Graham, 336–337
Mt. Shasta, 331
Mt. Zion African Methodist
Episcopal Church, 58
Moynihan, D. P., 96
Muller, Eric, 144–145, 151
Murray, Alice Yang, 144–145
Myer, Dillon, 149–150, 152

Nakao, Annie, 156
Napolitano, Janet, 262, 265
National Alliance for the
Mentally Ill, 83
National American Service &
Education Consortium
(NAKASEC), 126–127
National Association for the
Advancement of Colored
Peoples (NAACP), 55, 101
National Association Notes, 57
National Association of Colored
Graduate Nurses (NACGN),
48, 55

National Association of Colored
Women's Clubs (NACW), 48
National Association of Community
Behavioral Health, 83
National Association of Latino
Elected and Appointed Officials
(NALEO), 231, 249
National Center for
Lesbian Rights, 249
National Council of La Raza (NCLR),
229, 234, 245, 249
National Employment Law Project
and Others, 259
National Farm Workers
Association, 228
National Hispanic Christian
Leadership Conference, 265
National Hispanic Health
Summit, 284
National Hispanic Medical
Association (NHMA), 284
National Indian Child Welfare
Association, 323
National Institutes of
Health (NIH), 272
Nationalist Party, 229
National Japanese American
Memorial Foundation
(NJAMF), 153–156
National Leadership
Council (NLC), 83
National Origins Act of 1924,
115, 194, 222
National Park Service, 158, 336, 340
National Quota Law of 1929, 222
National Telegram Campaign to
Restore Immigrant Benefits, 125
National Training School for Women
and Girls, 52
National Welfare Rights
Organization, 100
Native American Church,
341–344, 346
Native American Religious Freedom
Project, 342
Native American Rights Fund, 342
Navajo Nation, 339, 339
Negro Fellowship League, 54, 57

About the Editor

Jerome H. Schiele is a Professor and Associate Dean in the School of Social Work at the University of Georgia. He is a native of Hampton, Virginia, and received his bachelor's degree in sociology from Hampton University in 1983. He attained both his master's and doctoral degrees in social work from Howard University. Before arriving at the University of Georgia, he was Professor and Director of the Ph.D. programs in social work at Morgan State University in Baltimore, Maryland, and Norfolk State University in Norfolk, Virginia. Before that, he was an Associate Professor of Social Work at Clark Atlanta University in Atlanta, Georgia, and he also directed its Ph.D. program in social work for 4 years. His first teaching position was as an Assistant Professor of Social Welfare at the State University of New York at Stony Brook, where he directed the M.S.W. program for 2 years. Dr. Schiele's scholarly work focuses on social work practice theory, social welfare policy analysis, and racial oppression. He has published numerous scholarly articles, essays, and book chapters, many of which appear in major academic periodicals and publications. Dr. Schiele also is the author of the book *Human Services and the Afrocentric Paradigm* (2000). Dr. Schiele, along with Phyllis Day, is the coauthor of *A New History of Social Welfare* (7th ed., 2012). Dr. Schiele's primary teaching areas are social welfare history, social work practice theory, and social welfare policy analysis, and he is a member of several professional organizations.

About the Contributors

Gregory Acevedo, Ph.D., is an Assistant Professor of Social Work in the Fordham University Graduate School of Social Service. Much of Dr. Acevedo's scholarly work has focused on the political, economic, and sociocultural circumstances of Puerto Ricans and other Latino groups in the United States, and how these circumstances relate to public and social policies. His current work tackles a broad array of issues related to immigration and globalization, and examines how these issues affect social and economic well-being, especially among marginalized communities. He holds a B.A. in psychology and an M.S. in education from the University of Pennsylvania and a Ph.D. in social work from Bryn Mawr College Graduate School of Social Work and Research. Dr. Acevedo completed his externship training in family therapy at the Philadelphia Child Guidance Clinic (1987–1988). He has professional practice experience in various children and family, and mental health agencies.

Aaron Baxter, M.S.W., is currently a therapist for teens and children at the Utah State Hospital. He received his master's degree in social work from Brigham Young University. He has worked as a research assistant focusing on Tribal/State IV-E agreements and completed a master's research project on the current status of Tribal/State IV-E agreements.

Tricia B. Bent-Goodley, Ph.D., is a Professor of Social Work and Chair of the Community, Administration and Policy Practice Sequence at Howard University School of Social Work. Dr. Bent-Goodley's research has focused on violence against women and girls, HIV prevention, and healthy relationship education. She has developed community- and faith-based interventions in domestic violence and relationship education, with a focus on strengthening the black family. Dr. Bent-Goodley has a passion for building solutions to improve the safety and viability of black families, with a particular focus on the development of culturally competent interventions that build on the strengths of the community. She is the author/coauthor of three books in the area of social policy and people of color, is a consulting editor for several scholarly journals, and serves distinctly in a number of local, state, and national elected and appointed leadership positions. Dr. Bent-Goodley is an HIV Intervention Science Training Fellow, Chair of the Family Violence Coordinating Council of the D.C. Mayor's Advisory Committee on Child Abuse and Neglect, a member of the Prince Georges County Domestic Violence Fatality Review, Commissioner with the Council on Social Work Education Council on Leadership Development, and member of the National Association of Social Workers Committee on the Role of Women in the Profession. She is a former Hartman Child & Family Scholar, former Chair and Chief Instructor of the NABSW National Academy for African-Centered Social Work, and the National Public Policy Institute. Prior to coming to Howard University, she served as an administrator and clinical practitioner in Harlem and Queens County, New York. Dr. Bent-Goodley received her Ph.D. in social policy, planning, and analysis from Columbia University and her master's degree in social work from the University of Pennsylvania. Dr. Bent-Goodley finds greatest joy in being a wife and a mother of two boys.

Christopher Campbell, Ph.D., is a faculty member at the University of Washington where he directs the Community, Environment, and Planning program. Dr. Campbell holds a Ph.D. in cultural sociology from UCLA and is interested in place making and identity, community development processes, and the social contexts of wellness. In addition to his work on historical trauma, Dr Campbell has written on the social construction of place in urban settings and has conducted nationally funded research on the impacts of urban environments on Native health and healthcare access. Dr. Campbell teaches courses on community planning practice, institutional and social change, and social theory. He is also an administrator in the division of Undergraduate Academic Affairs, where he leads or supports several campus-wide program development and instructional innovation initiatives.

Tessa Evans-Campbell, Ph.D., is an Associate Professor at the University of Washington School of Social Work, Associate Director of the Indigenous Wellness Research Institute, and Director of the Center for Indigenous Child Welfare Research. She is an enrolled member of the Snohomish Tribe of Indians and served on her Tribal Council for 2 years. She has served on numerous advisory boards and committees related in indigenous health, including the Indian Child Welfare Advisory Committee in King County, the National Indian Education Association, and the Los Angeles Native American Indian Commission. Dr. Evans-Campbell's research interests include historical trauma, resistance, and healing; cultural buffers of trauma; Indian child welfare; and indigenous family wellness.

Iris B. Carlton-LaNey, Ph.D., is a Professor in the School of Social Work at the University of North Carolina at Chapel Hill. She received her Ph.D. from the University of Maryland at Baltimore, her M.A. from the University of Chicago School of Service Administration, and her bachelor's degree in social work from North Carolina A&T State University. Her research interests include aging in rural communities and African American social welfare history. She has recently completed service as the chair of the Book Committee for the National Association of Social Work (NASW) Press. She has also served as guest editor for special issues of the *Journal of Sociology and Social Welfare*, the *Journal of Community Practice* (along with Dr. N. Y. Burwell), and *Arête* (along with Dr. Tanya Brice). She has served on the editorial boards of several journals and has published articles in *Affilia, Arête, Generations*, the *Journal of Community Practice*, the *Journal of Sociology & Social Welfare*, the *Social Service Review*, and *Social Work*. Dr. Carlton-LaNey has coedited two books, *African American Community Practice Models Historical and Contemporary Responses* (with Dr. N. Y. Burwell) and *Preserving and Strengthening Small Towns and Rural Communities* (with Drs. R. L. Edwards and P. N. Reid). In 2001, the NASW Press published *African American Leadership: An Empowerment Tradition in Social Welfare History*. Dr. Carlton-LaNey has lectured on African American social welfare history and African Americans aging in the rural South at several schools of social work across the country. She also has published a book titled *African Americans Aging in the Rural South: Stories of Faith, Family and Community* (2005).

Hyunkag Cho, Ph.D., is as an Assistant Professor in the School of Social Work at Michigan State University. He received his Ph.D. in social work from Florida State University. His current research interests are at the intersection of domestic violence, criminal justice systems, and immigrants. He has conducted secondary data analyses of National Crime Victimization Survey and Collaborative Psychiatric Epidemiological Surveys, examining factors affecting intimate partner violence, mental health and service use, and relations between race/ethnicity and intimate partner violence. Cross-national comparisons of policy and multicultural competence are also included in his research agenda. He teaches the human behavior and the social environment, social work macro practice with groups, organizations, and communities, and the research and statistics courses.

King Davis, Ph.D., holds the Robert Lee Sutherland Chair in Mental Health and Social Policy at the University of Texas at Austin, School of Social Work. From 2003 to 2009, he was executive director of the Hogg

Foundation for Mental Health Services, Research, Policy and Education. He was a professor of Public Mental Health Policy and Planning at the Virginia Commonwealth University, Richmond, Virginia, from 1984 to 2000, retiring in 1999. As the Galt Scholar, he held full professorships at each of Virginia's medical schools from 1985 to 1988. From 1998 to 1999, he was the holder of the William and Camille Cosby Chair at Howard University, Washington, D.C. Also in 1998, he was appointed to the Libra Chair in the School of Business and Public Policy at the University of Maine. He taught at Norfolk State University School of Social Work from 1974 to 1984. Davis was awarded the Ph.D. from the Florence G. Heller School for Social Policy and Management at Brandeis University in 1971. He holds the master's and bachelor's degrees in social work (concentration in mental health) from California State University in Fresno California. Davis is a former Commissioner of the Virginia Department of Mental Health, Mental Retardation and Substance Abuse Services, serving from 1990 to 1994. He is coauthor of *The Color of Social Policy*, published in March 2004 by CSWE Press. His most recent article was published in the *American Psychologist* in 2007.

Ellarwee Gadsden, Ph.D., has a bachelor's degree in philosophy from Howard University, a master's degree in social work from Columbia University, and a Ph.D. in social work from Boston's Simmons College. Director of Women, Inc., one of the country's first substance abuse treatment programs housing African American women and their children. She moved to Baltimore to teach at Morgan State University. Her dissertation, *Searching for the Factors Contributing to the Continued AIDS Risk of Minority Women in Substance Abuse Treatment*, was nominated for dissertation of the year award in 2004 by the Society for Social Work Research. That research experience was chronicled in her article *I've Got Them in My Blood: Reflections on Countertransference in the Research Process*, which was published in 2008 in the journal *Reflections*. She has presented her research in this area at many juried conferences, both nationally and internationally. Assistant Professor and Chair of the Social Welfare Policy sequence, Dr. Gadsden teaches in that area and also in substance abuse.

Anita Gundanna, M.S.W., is the Deputy Director at the Fund for Social Change (FSC). She has worked for the past 10 years to prevent and address violence against women and children and to promote healthy families. Her work at FSC includes creating and coordinating a number of collaborations to affect positive change in the child welfare system. Prior to joining FSC, she served as Director of Client Services at the New York Asian Women's Center and managed all of the agency's residential and community-based services assisting women and child victims of domestic violence. In 2005, she cofounded Project Free, a New York City–based initiative to address human trafficking. Gundanna is also an adjunct faculty member at Columbia University's School of Social Work. Gundanna has a strong background in child welfare reform and worked for several years as an advocate for New York City's Asian American and immigrant families at the Coalition for Asian American Children and Families. Gundanna received a B.S. and elementary school teaching certification from Duke University, and she received a master's degree in social work from Columbia University.

Ana L. León, M.A., is currently a doctoral student of political science at the University of Colorado in Boulder. She received her M.A. degree in public policy studies from the University of Denver and a B.S. degree in science, technology, and international affairs from Georgetown University. Her main research is focused on Latino issues relating to immigration and education at the local and national levels. Most recently, she was part of a team that developed a policy white paper titled *The Agenda Latina*. This report was released to key U.S. decisionmakers, including the full U.S. Congress. León has a track record of demonstrated leadership and community involvement. She spent a major part of her career working in the nonprofit world, focusing on social issues facing Latino families and communities, and continues to do so.

Allen N. Lewis Jr., Ph.D., CRC, is an Associate Professor and the Chair of the Virginia Commonwealth University (VCU) Department of Rehabilitation Counseling in the School of Allied Health Professions. Dr. Lewis has conducted more than 50 refereed and invited presentations and workshops regionally, nationally, and internationally over the past 5 years on topics related to his research interests: 1) the intersection of disability and culture and 2) evaluating the effectiveness of rehabilitation services. He has written more than 30 publications (refereed journal articles, book chapters, abstracts, and technical reports). Dr. Lewis is principle investigator on more than $2.5 million dollars in grant funding. Dr. Lewis serves on the editorial board for the *Journal of Vocational Rehabilitation* and is an ad hoc reviewer for the *Journals of Black Psychology, Adolescent and Family Health,* and *Spinal Cord Medicine*. Dr. Lewis has had a long-standing commitment to working in the health and disability arena for more than 25 years, 10 years at VCU as an applied social sciences researcher, professor, and administrator and more than 15 years of experience prior to coming to VCU as a services practitioner, program administrator, program evaluator, and services researcher.

Gordon E. Limb, Ph.D., is the Director of the School of Social Work. He received his Ph.D. in social welfare from the University of California at Berkeley. Prior to joining the faculty at Brigham Young University, he had previously served as Assistant Professor of Social Work at Arizona State University and as Assistant Director of the Kathryn M. Buder Center for American Indian Studies at the George Warren Brown School of Social Work, Washington University in St. Louis. Dr. Limb concentrates his research activities around Native American families and children, with much of the focus on American Indian child welfare issues. Specifically, Dr. Limb's research focuses on the Indian Child Welfare Act, American Indian service utilization and adequacy of services received, child welfare outcome predictors, and cultural identification. His current research includes examining clinical applications of American Indian and Latter-day Saints spirituality, tribal/state Title IV-E intergovernmental agreements, and factors that impact American Indian fragile families. Dr. Limb's practice experience includes working with adolescents in a wilderness survival program, as a clinical social worker at a social service agency, and as a counselor at a community college. He has articles published in a wide range of top social work journals.

Lisa Magaña, Ph.D., is an Associate Professor in the Department of Transborder Studies at Arizona State University. She has published in the area of immigration and Latino public policy issues, such as in the *Harvard Hispanic Policy Journal*, the *Journal of Policy Studies*, and the *Journal of Social Psychology*. She is the author of the books *Straddling the Border* (University of Texas Press) and *The Politics of Diversity* (University of Arizona Press). Dr. Magaña has been a research associate at the Tomas Rivera Policy Institute and visiting lecturer and Assistant Professor at Pitzer College, University of California, Los Angeles, and Williams College. She received her doctorate from the Center for Politics and Economics at Claremont Graduate University.

Catherine K. Medina, Ph.D., L.C.S.W., is an Assistant Professor, School of Social Work, Puerto Rican/Latino Studies Project, University of Connecticut. Since 1993, her research, publishing, and teaching covers HIV, health disparities, policy practice, and the influence of media in creating social change in racial/ethnic communities.

Debora M. Ortega, M.S.W., Ph.D., is the Founding Director of the University of Denver Latino Center for Community Engagement and Scholarship. She also is an Associate Professor at the University of Denver Graduate School of Social Work. She received her undergraduate degree from the University of San Diego in religious studies, M.S.W. from Portland State University, and her Ph.D. in social welfare from the University of Washington. Dr. Ortega has taught in the areas of multicultural social work practice, family relationships, family therapy, clinical practice, and social work theory. Her research area focuses on the experience of historically marginalized people, with an emphasis on Latino people and their inter-secting identities. Her publications include several scholarly articles and book chapters addressing culturally responsive practice in child welfare, maternal depression, policies affecting Latinos and Latinas, immigration, and youth aging out of foster care. She is currently a member of the Council on Social Work Education Commission for Diversity and Social and Economic Justice, the national advisory board for the National Center for Lesbian Rights, and the Mayor's Commission for Early Childhood Education.

Rita Takahashi, Ph.D., is San Francisco State University's (SFSU) School of Social Work Director. For more than 30 years, she has been a social work educator, teaching and researching in areas of multicultural diversity, social policy, and social welfare history, human service administration, program development, chance strategies, professional values, and research. In addition, she has been a social service supervisor, a child wel-fare service provider, and a civil rights lobbyist in Washington, D.C. She received her Ph.D. in social work and a master of public and international affairs from the University of Pittsburgh; M.S.W. degree from the University of Michigan; and B.A. degrees in psychology and sociology from the University of Hawaii. Since she joined the SFSU faculty in 1989, she coordinated the M.S.W. program, B.A.S.W. program, Administration and Planning Emphasis, Social Action and Change Emphasis, and directed the Institute for Multicultural Research and Social Work Practice.

Albert Thompkins, M.S.W., is a doctoral student at the University of Texas at Austin School of Social Work and is a Council on Social Work Education Minority Fellow. He is in his fourth year in the Doctorate of Philosophy in Social Work program, with research interests in the eco-nomic cost of mental illness, mental health research, and mental health policy. Mr. Thompkins earned a bachelor of business administra-tion in economics and finance from Tennessee State University in 1996 and a master of science in social work from the University of Tennessee in 2004. He is also a member of Phi Alpha National Honor Society.

Hilary N. Weaver, D.S.W. (Lakota), is a Professor in the School of Social Work, University at Buffalo (State University of New York). Her teaching, research, and service focus on cultural issues in the helping process with a particular focus on indigenous populations. She currently serves as President of the American Indian Alaska Native Social Work Educators Association and Vice President of the Board of Directors of Native American Community Services of Erie and Niagara Counties. Dr. Weaver has presented her work regionally, nationally, and internationally, includ-ing presenting at the Permanent Forum on Indigenous Issues at the United Nations in 2005, 2006, 2007, and 2008. She has numerous publications, including the recent text, *Explorations in Cultural Competence: Journeys to the Four Directions* (2005). Dr. Weaver has received funding from the National Cancer Institute to develop and test a culturally grounded wellness curriculum for urban Native American youth, the Healthy Living in Two Worlds program.

Qingwen Xu, Ph.D., is the Assistant Professor of Boston College Graduate School of Social Work. His major research focuses on laws and social policies and their impacts on the well-being of populations in transition. Dr. Xu's projects include the following: legal vulnerability and the psycho-social well-being of immigrant children and families, immigrant children and families involved in the public child welfare system, and community-based interventions and immigrant community organizing.

Marianne R. Yoshioka, Ph.D., M.S.W., is an Associate Professor at the Columbia University School of Social Work and the Senior Assistant Dean of Academic Affairs. She teaches in the areas of clinical practice, advanced research methods, the developmental life course, and practice with battered women. Her professional and research interests include domestic violence among immigrant populations, HIV prevention, and the design of culturally appropriate intervention. She has received funding from the National Institute of Mental Health and private foundations to conduct research in these areas. She has worked as a social worker in the area of addictions and marriage and family therapy.

Ning Jackie Zhang, M.D., Ph.D., is an Assistant Professor of the Doctoral Program in Public Affairs and the Department of Health Management and Informatics, College of Health and Public Affairs, University of Central Florida, Orlando, Florida. He obtained his Ph.D. degree of health services research from the Department of Health Administration, Medical College of Virginia, Virginia Commonwealth University, Richmond, Virginia. His research interests focus on clinical outcomes research, policy analysis, long-term care, analytical modeling, and health informatics.